MW00574863

# SELINA
## COUNTESS OF HUNTINGDON

August 15·16, 2008

Love,
Women's Ministry
Providence Church
Phil 1: 27-30

# Selina
## Countess of Huntingdon

Faith Cook

THE BANNER OF TRUTH TRUST

THE BANNER OF TRUTH TRUST
3 Murrayfield Road, Edinburgh EH12 6EL, UK
P.O. Box 621, Carlisle, PA 17013, USA

\*

© Banner of Truth Trust 2001

ISBN 0 85151 812 5

\*

Typeset in 12/14 pt Bulmer MT at the
Banner of Truth Trust, Edinburgh
Printed and bound in Great Britain
at the Bath Press, Bath

TO
MY DAUGHTER,
ESTHER

# CONTENTS

# ILLUSTRATIONS

## ACKNOWLEDGEMENTS

We are indebted to the following for illustrations which they have kindly allowed us to use for this volume:

The Cheshunt Foundation, Westminster College, Cambridge, for the portrait by P. Soldi used on the cover, as well as the portrait of the Countess by J. Russell used as the frontispiece.

Coleg Trefeca, Aberhonddu/Brecon, Powys, for the photograph of the pulpit used at Trevecca anniversary services.

The Countess of Huntingdon's Connexion for the pictures of Trevecca College and Spa Fields Chapel.

# PREFACE
## AND ACKNOWLEDGEMENTS

MANY READERS WHO MAY HAVE A CONSIDERABLE KNOWLEDGE of the great revival of the eighteenth century find they have little more than a hazy idea of the part played in it by Selina Countess of Huntingdon. Yet one of her contemporaries, a man by no means given to over-statement, could describe the Countess as 'a star of the first magnitude in the firmament of the church.'[1] Why then do we know so little of her today? In part the responsibility must rest with the Countess herself. In her will she stipulated that no biography should be written of her and that no use be made of her many letters. In the same spirit, she asked to be buried in an unmarked grave. No funeral service commemorated the end of her influential life, and only three men attended her coffin to its last resting-place. And such was the respect for her wishes that no biography was attempted until almost fifty years after her death.

Then in 1839 Aaron Seymour published anonymously his two volumes on *The Life and Times of Selina Countess of Huntingdon.* This work is crammed with astonishing detail on all aspects of the eighteenth century revival and is therefore a mine of information. Running to more than a thousand pages, it has reigned supreme on its subject for over a hundred and fifty years,

---

[1] *Letters of Henry Venn*, (Edinburgh: Banner of Truth, 1993), p. 159.

with subsequent biographers largely dependent on it for their source material.[1] However, the discovery of many little-known family letters and other manuscripts, and the important work of the late Dr Edwin Welch in classifying and documenting them, have brought to light a number of new facts concerning the Countess. So, braving Selina's displeasure, this is an attempt to provide an up-to-date record of the life of one who was undoubtedly God's gift to his Church, raised up by him and uniquely qualified for her significant role in the evangelical revival.

I am indebted to Lady Catherwood for encouraging me to attempt such a work as this. My initial reluctance was gradually overcome by her own contagious enthusiasm for the Countess, expressed both in the public lectures she has given and in private conversation. But the work entailed in such a biography has been far more exacting than I had anticipated because the source material is so widely scattered. An additional obstacle, with which any would-be biographer must contend, is Selina's own 'miserable scrawl' – her almost illegible handwriting – coupled with a virtual lack of any formal punctuation or consistency of spelling.[2]

In any work of this nature the number of people to whom a researcher is indebted is legion. In mentioning a few I must also add my real gratitude to the many who have passed on information, provided photocopies of material, and helped me in countless other ways. I am most grateful to the Rev. Iain H. Murray of the Banner of Truth Trust who has encouraged me along the way, checked up on my accuracy and indicated further sources of information. To the Rev. Geoffrey Thomas of Aberystwyth, and the Rev. Matthew Hill, I am indebted for the generous loan of books, while I also owe my thanks to the staff at the Evangelical Library and Dr Williams's Library for the

[1] For a fuller discussion on this work and other biographies, see Appendix 2.
[2] Spellings have largely been regularized and updated.

prompt supply of the many books I have needed. Mrs Margaret Thompson of Westminster College, Cambridge, carried heavy tomes of manuscript letters up and down the long corridors without a word of complaint during my periods of study in the Westminster College library. I am grateful to the Cheshunt Foundation for permission to quote from this archive material. The John Rylands University Library of Manchester holds a unique collection of letters from the Countess to Charles Wesley and others. Excerpts from these are reproduced by courtesy of the Director and University Librarian. The Record Office for Leicestershire, Leicester and Rutland also houses a treasure trove of her early family correspondence, and I am also most grateful for the access I have been given to these manuscripts and for permission to quote from them. I am appreciative too of the help I received from Ms Wanda Willard Smith of Bridwell Library, Dallas. Not only did she arrange the supply of many of the Countess's letters on microfilm, but also established an encouraging e-mail friendship. I would also acknowledge the help I had from Dr Mary Robertson of the Huntington Library, San Marino, California, and from Mr Dale Patterson of Drew University, Madison, New Jersey. Both wrote most helpfully and supplied me with microfilm and photocopies from archive material that has been important for this work. Then I must mention the kindness of Mrs Margaret Staplehurst, the archivist of the Countess of Huntingdon's Connexion, Cottenham, Cambridge, who welcomed me into her home and did all possible to help me.

I could add many other names to my list, but Mrs Elspeth Raynar and her late husband John, who gave my husband Paul and me generous hospitality while I studied in Cambridge, must certainly not be omitted. Nor should I fail to mention the help I received from Dr Geoffrey Nuttall, whose letters were crammed with wisdom and advice. Mr Peter Conlan holds four original letters from the Countess and he kindly supplied photocopies of these, while Mr John Aaron of Swansea took much trouble in supplying me with accurate information about the chapel that the Countess had erected there. Lastly, to my husband, Paul, I owe most of all. His unstinted admiration for the Countess has motivated me to stay the course, and his self-sacrificing patience in reading and rereading my work, insisting always on the highest standards, has, needless to say, been invaluable.

'O that I may be more and more useful to the souls of my fellow creatures. I want to be every moment all life, all zeal, all activity for God, and ever on the stretch for closer communion with him', wrote the Countess of Huntingdon after more than twenty years of labour for the spiritual needs of her generation. If through this account of her life we too may catch something of that same fervour and devotion to the service of God, then I am sure she will excuse this biography, however much against her expressed wishes.

Faith Cook
Breaston
Derby
April 2001

# FOREWORD

GEORGE III IS REPUTED TO HAVE SAID to Charles Wesley's son, 'It is my judgement, Mr Wesley, that your uncle and your father and George Whitefield and the Countess of Huntingdon have done more to promote true religion in this country than all the dignified clergy put together, who are so apt to despise their labours.' Others have made similar comments. Bishop J. C. Ryle said that the Countess of Huntingdon was 'the mainspring of the revival', but in the English-speaking evangelical world, while the Wesleys and Whitefield are well known, the same has not been true of the Countess.

There are various reasons for this, one of which I discovered when I was asked to give the Evangelical Library Lecture on the Countess in London in 1991 – the bicentenary of her death. The problem is that since her death, since, in fact, the monumental and hagiographical life of her written by Aaron Seymour (1839), no full-blooded biography has been written that is detailed, balanced and thorough and, at the same time, fully shares the Countess's profound, evangelical and Calvinistic faith. Slighter memoirs have appeared, and also some interesting theses on particular aspects of her life; while, more recently, one or two accounts have been written in terms which range from pleasant objectivity to downright hostility.

So it became clear to me that a new biography was long over-due, and, having read with pleasure the books on Samuel Rutherford and William Grimshaw written by Faith Cook, I began to persuade, encourage and even, some would say, to bully her[!] into undertaking this project. To my delight – and relief – she accepted the task and so, thanks to her and to the Banner of Truth Trust, this book is now before us.

It is an excellent biography. Mrs Cook's research has been wide-ranging and meticulous, as her notes and bibliography show. She has battled with the Countess's terrible handwriting and has uncovered some interesting facts. The most encouraging of these, as far as I am concerned, is the probability that the critical comment on the atonement, said to have been made by Selina's husband, was, in fact, made by her openly unbelieving son. Furthermore, unlike Aaron Seymour's *Life and Times*, this biography is a well-balanced account of the Countess which recognizes her weaknesses as well as her great strengths.

Mrs Cook also gives us a broad sweep, both secular and spiritual, of the eighteenth century, with its tragedy of disagreements amongst the Christian leaders and yet with the triumphs of the gospel. As the Countess herself said, 'I am connected with many', and they all appear, 'warts and all', in these pages. It is my hope that very many will read this book and discover what God can achieve through a godly woman such as the Countess whose expressed heart's desire was that, 'that dear Lamb of God, my best, my eternal, my only Friend should have all dedicated to his service and glory'.

ELIZABETH CATHERWOOD
Cambridge
April 2001

# 1

# TROUBLED CHILDHOOD

NOT FAR FROM BRACKLEY IN NORTHAMPTONSHIRE an isolated tower breaks the rural skyline. Gaunt and grey it stands, guarding well the secrets of its historic past. Apart from the tower, in reality an impressive gatehouse stationed like a sentinel before the entrance of a one-time stately home, little else remains of the original manor house. Known as Astwell Castle, it is at present a working farm. But almost three hundred years ago within the walls of Astwell Manor House, as it was then called, a girl was born whose life was to prove of outstanding significance in the purposes of God. Yet not so much as an entry in some parish register or any documentation in an ancient family record can be found to mark her birth. A possible reason lies in the fact that Selina Shirley was born into a seriously divided family, a family wracked with bickering, ill-feeling and misunderstandings – a circumstance which would have life-long implications for the child.

The Shirley family, one of England's oldest and most aristocratic, could trace its lineage back to Saxon times. Edward the Confessor, the king whose death in 1066 had precipitated the Norman invasion, was among its forebears. Further links with royalty were established in 1615 when Sir Henry Shirley married Dorothy Devereux, a daughter of Robert Devereux, the unfortunate Earl of Essex, Queen Elizabeth I's erstwhile favourite, who was beheaded in 1601. The Earl of Essex's family boasted a direct line of descent from Edward III and his grandson Edward

IV, Plantagenet kings whose reigns spanned the fourteenth and fifteenth centuries.

Understandably, the Shirleys were staunchly loyal to the Crown during the troubled days of the seventeenth-century Civil War. Although the family had previously been predominantly Roman Catholic, Sir Robert Shirley, the infant Selina's great-grandfather, son of Sir Henry and Dorothy Devereux, had been brought up in the Protestant tradition by his mother. Four years after the execution of Charles I in 1649, he had built a chapel at Staunton Harold, one of his Leicestershire estates, and engraved a singularly self-congratulatory inscription over the door which reflected his views on the Cromwellian regime:

> In the yeare 1653 when all things sacred were throughout ye nation either demollisht or profaned, Sir Robert Shirley Baronet founded this church, whose singular praise it is to have done ye best things in ye worst times. And hoped them in the most calamitous. The righteous shall be had in everlasting remembrance.

Suspected of complicity with the banished Stuarts, Sir Robert languished in prison in the Tower of London during the early part of the Commonwealth period. His death in 1656, according to the chronicler of the Shirley fortunes, was 'not without suspicion of poison'.[1] His son, born shortly before his father was imprisoned and also named Robert, was Selina's grandfather. Not unexpectedly, this second Sir Robert had become a loyal supporter of Charles II after the Restoration of 1660 – a loyalty that brought its own recompense – for in 1677 the king restored the baronetcy of Ferrers to the family. But Sir Robert was unhappy with the Catholic beliefs of James II, brother of Charles II,

[1] E. P. Shirley, *Stemmata Shirleiana* (published privately, 1841), p. 116. This writer of the history of the Shirley family published his work the year after Aaron C. H. Seymour had published his two volumes on *The Life and Times of Selina Countess of Huntingdon* (London, 1839). Seymour claimed to be a member of the Shirley family but E. P. Shirley denied the claim.

and when James was driven from the throne in 1688, he quietly transferred his allegiance to the ex-king's daughter, Princess Anne. He therefore became a favourite at court when she finally ascended the throne in 1702. After naming his last daughter Stuarta, as a mark of respect to the House of Stuart, he asked the Queen to act as the child's godmother. Reward followed swiftly and only months later Queen Anne honoured him with the title of First Earl of Ferrers and Viscount Tamworth.

The wealth of the Shirley family lay in their estates. These included a mansion in Staunton Harold in Leicestershire and another at Chartley in Staffordshire, together with other properties in the surrounding areas. Property once owned by the Earl of Essex in Co. Monaghan in Ireland also passed to them. Among the family possessions were homes in Warwickshire, Derbyshire, Wiltshire and, of course, Astwell Manor House in Northamptonshire. But despite all their prosperity and prestige, the Shirleys were a disunited and unhappy family.

The problems appear to have stemmed from Selina's grandfather, Sir Robert. He had married fifteen-year-old Elizabeth Washington in 1671 when he was only twenty years of age. Elizabeth, an heiress in her own right, came from another old and respected family which could claim kin with the Washingtons who had emigrated from Northamptonshire in 1657 and later produced George Washington, first president of the United States. At least five sons and even more daughters were born in quick succession to Sir Robert and his wife, but Elizabeth died at the age of thirty-seven not long after her youngest son Lawrence was born.[1] Her second son, named Washington after her family name, and later to become father of Selina, was only sixteen when his mother died.

[1] G. E. Cokayne, *The Complete Peerage of England, Scotland, Ireland, etc.* (London, 1910), vol. 5, p. 331, states that in addition to seventeen children said to have been born to Elizabeth, and the ten to his second wife, a large number of illegitimate children were also born to Sir Robert Shirley, but he quotes no authority for the statement.

By the time Sir Robert remarried six years later, it appears that he had quarrelled with most of the children of his first marriage. His second wife, Selina Finch, only nineteen when she married and more than thirty years younger than her husband, bore him a further ten children. Relationships with his first wife's family deteriorated yet further when Sir Robert attempted to disinherit Elizabeth's children and leave as much property as possible to his second wife and her children. After the death of Elizabeth's eldest son, Washington would naturally have anticipated that the family title and estates would devolve upon him as the next in line of succession. But he was mistaken. Shortly before Sir Robert died in 1717 Washington discovered that his father had so worded his will as to leave little to him apart from the title of Second Earl of Ferrers. Washington was to be deprived of the majority of the family property and assets.

The main cause of the disruption in relationships between Washington Shirley and his father appears to have been Washington's marriage to Mary Levinge. Mary was the daughter of Sir Richard Levinge, a lawyer whose family property in Derbyshire bordered on some of the Shirley property. Perhaps this was the root of the trouble, we do not know. After their marriage, probably in 1702, it would appear that Washington and Mary moved to Ireland where, as we have noted, the Shirley family owned further property. For some time Washington served as a low ranking officer or ensign in the Coldstream Guards. Mary's first child, probably born in 1704, was named Elizabeth, doubtless after Washington's own mother. With no settled family home, her birth, like that of her younger sister, was not recorded on any parish register. But she too may have been born at Astwell Manor House for at the time this property, left to Washington's children by an earlier trust, was occupied by one of his nephews[1] and was therefore free from Sir Robert's disapproving presence.

[1] Hastings Family Correspondence, Huntington Library, San Marino, California. This source is hereafter designated 'HL'.

Soon after Elizabeth's birth, Washington resigned from his position in the Coldstream Guards, hoping instead for a promotion to a more senior rank in a newly formed Irish regiment. This he attained in 1706, but life in an army garrison in Ireland was rough and poorly paid, so when Mary became pregnant with their second child it is likely that she decided to go to Astwell in Northamptonshire for the birth. That summer, a few weeks prior to the confinement, Washington Shirley made a significant attempt to effect a reconciliation with his father, writing to him on 5 July 1707. More than this, he even chose his stepmother's name, Selina, for the infant, suggesting a wish to placate his father. But all his efforts were of no avail. The family rancour continued unabated.

Local tradition, backed up by early Northamptonshire histories[1] and the *Complete Peerage*, is explicit in claiming that Astwell Manor House was indeed the birthplace of Washington and Mary's second daughter, Selina. Originally built towards the end of the fifteenth century, Astwell had come into the possession of the Shirley family in 1586. Sir George Shirley, described as 'a gallant gentleman', demolished the old manor house, apart from its imposing gatehouse, and rebuilt it in 1606. Behind this forbidding entrance he erected a large and beautiful mansion. With forty rooms, including a great hall, a chapel, a picture gallery, a great and little parlour, it formed a splendid edifice. Elaborately furnished, it contained curtains and cushions of velvet, four-poster beds and a long oak table, reputed to be thirty feet long, three feet wide and made from a single tree. The new manor house did justice to Sir George's expensive lifestyle and needed a small retinue of servants to care for his cuisine, coaches, horses

[1] G. Baker, *The History and Antiquities of Northamptonshire* (London, 1822),p. 40; and *History, Gazetteer and Directory of Northamptonshire*, compiled by William Wheelan & Co.(London: Whittaker and Co., 1849), p. 646.

and gardens.[1] Little more than a century later this attractive home, set amidst gentle undulating grassy meadows, was to become the birthplace of one whose significance was to outlast by many generations all Sir George's finery. For there, on 24 August 1707,[2] Selina Shirley, later to become the Countess of Huntingdon, was born.

Those early years of the eighteenth century marked the birth of a number of children who would one day be of key importance in God's plans for his church, not only in Britain but also in America. When Selina was a mere four months old, Susanna Wesley's third son, Charles, was born. William Grimshaw, much used by God in Yorkshire and beyond, was born the following September. John Wesley had been born four years earlier in 1703, the same year as Jonathan Edwards of New England. George Whitefield, Benjamin Ingham, William Romaine, Daniel Rowland and Howell Harris were all born in the early part of the following decade, with John Cennick not many years later.

How long the baby Selina, her parents and sister remained at Astwell Manor House we are not in a position to say. Strong local tradition insists that Selina was christened at the attractive old parish church of Wappenham. Astwell was then included in the Wappenham parish and the church was little more than a mile from Astwell Manor. With a part of the church, still described as 'Astwell Aisle', an area that the residents of Astwell were supposed to keep in good repair, there were many links between Astwell and Wappenham parish church. This makes it likely that

[1] Details of the Old Manor House may be found in a pamphlet on the history of Astwell by J. Wake (1959), which quotes a description by an eighteenth century historian, John Bridges, *History of Northamptonshire* (1719), vol. 1, p. 214.

[2] Her date of birth, established by her own celebration of it and by the records of the Northamptonshire historian, is sometimes designated according to the Julian calendar as 13 August, and stated as that in *Complete Peerage*, but with the formal recognition of the Gregorian calendar in 1752 Selina celebrated her birthday on 24 August.

Selina was indeed christened there. In all probability the family would have returned to Ireland soon afterwards, for Washington Shirley's limited income depended on the duties he had to discharge in connection with his regiment.

As the Shirleys owned property at Carrickmacross in County Monaghan, it is likely that the family was based there for the next ten years. Certainly the sight of Washington Shirley, his wife and two girls was familiar to residents of Carrickmacross. When questioned about them more than twenty-five years later, locals could clearly recollect the presence of the family in the neighbourhood.[1] Life cannot have been easy for them; and despite the Shirley wealth, Washington's own income was, at best, modest during these years. A tutor would have been engaged to give the girls a basic education but Selina's lifelong problems with written English suggest that her early instruction must have been far from adequate. Though she maintained a prolific correspondence throughout her life in letters that revealed breadth of knowledge and thought, her handwriting, the bane of any would-be biographer, remained almost illegible, while she made little or no attempt to punctuate her letters either into sentences or paragraphs. Orthography, before the days of Samuel Johnson's dictionary,[2] was only partially standardized and Selina's spelling remained erratic throughout her life.

In 1712, five years after Selina's birth, a third daughter, Mary, was born in Dublin. Perhaps Mary's birth added to the financial strains under which the family was living. Certainly it was soon after this date that the saddest event of Selina's troubled childhood took place. When she was little more than six years of age her parents split up. It would appear from later correspondence that disputes over money probably contributed to the breakdown

[1] This information was noted by Edwin Welch from documents in the Public Records Office of Northern Ireland. For further information see his *Spiritual Pilgrim* (Cardiff: University of Wales Press, 1995), p. 11.
[2] First published 1755.

in relationships. More seriously there are suggestions in some family correspondence, dated nearly fifty years later, that constant marital unfaithfulness on Washington's part was the major cause of offence. In the event Selina's mother took her youngest daughter Mary and left Britain, living the rest of her life mainly in France and Spain. Meanwhile Elizabeth and Selina remained with Washington. A close bond of affection grew up between Selina and her father. He would often address her as 'Linny' and his letters would end with a loving greeting such as 'My dear, your most loving father, Ferrers'.[1] Selina's correspondence with her mother always remained formal.

In days when the unhappiness of children from broken homes is sadly a commonplace, it is not hard to imagine the effect of this tragedy on a child as sensitive as Selina Shirley. She rarely, if ever, spoke of her childhood in later life. Thomas Haweis, who was later to work closely with her, preserved the only information we have. In his *Impartial and Succinct History of the Church of Christ*, a work that was to run to three volumes, he includes a chapter which gives a brief account of her life work. In it he records several anecdotes of her childhood that must have come from Selina herself. The picture that emerges is of a serious-minded child who often thought about the eternal world. As a young child she would frequently find some isolated corner where no one could see her and there she would pour out her troubles to God in secret. Considering how many troubles the child must have known, we are not surprised to learn that she found consolation in this way. The other anecdote that Haweis noted tells of the day when the young Selina Shirley as a child of nine saw a funeral litter passing by carrying a child of about her own age to be buried. So distressed was she by the sight that she

[1] The Record Office for Leicestershire, Leicester and Rutland holds a large number of letters relating to the Shirley and Hastings families, and includes many of the personal letters from the Countess. This source is hereafter designated 'LRO'.

followed the coffin to the cemetery and watched the ceremony. Often afterwards she used to visit the grave of this unknown child and pray earnestly that whenever she herself came to die God would deliver her from her fears and grant her a 'happy departure.'[1]

In 1717 circumstances were to change radically for Washington Shirley and his daughters. When Selina was ten years of age her grandfather, Sir Robert, died. A month before his death he had finalized his will with details of arrangements for his funeral. An impressive affair it was to be, with fifty named mourners, though in the event it does not appear that any of his children were present for the occasion. A derisory sum of £20 'and no more' was allowed to Washington Shirley 'for mourning' but little else of the extensive Shirley properties was earmarked for his eldest son apart from the Northamptonshire estates. Anticipating that there might be trouble at his death, Sir Robert had stipulated that if any of his arrangements were overturned by the children of his first marriage, his executors were to pay his widow £1000 a year until any lawsuits were settled.

Washington acted swiftly and dramatically as soon as he learnt of his father's death. Proceeding on the principle that 'possession is nine-tenths of the law', he seized all the family properties and assets apart from the Wiltshire estates which he left for his stepmother and her family. His father-in-law helped him to secure the Irish estates. This turnabout would leave Sir Robert Shirley's executors encumbered with the legal responsibility of seeking redress for the second family and untangling the maze of claims and counter-claims that would necessarily follow such an action. The beautiful Staunton Harold estate in Leicestershire was now

---

[1] Thomas Haweis, *An Impartial and Succinct History of the Church of Christ* (London, 1800), vol. 3, p. 240. Corroborating evidence for this anecdote is found in a sermon preached to mark the funeral of the Countess of Huntingdon by J. H. Meyer entitled *The Saint's Triumph in the Approach of Death* (London, 1791). Meyer notes that as a child 'she was uncommonly desirous of attending funeral solemnities, particularly those of children.'

in the possession of Washington Shirley, but due to his Irish commitments the family did not live there on a regular basis for some time to come.

Washington allowed his father to be buried at Staunton Harold in accordance with his wishes, but did not erect any monument to his memory on the estate – an instruction Sir Robert had also stipulated in his will. Later one of Washington's half-brothers was to erect a monument at Lower Ettington, four miles from Stratford-upon-Avon in Warwickshire, adding the explanation in the inscription that Washington Shirley was responsible for it not being placed in Staunton Harold.[1]

Selina's father justified his highhanded actions not only by appealing to his position as the eldest remaining son of the first marriage, but also by basing his claims on certain documents authenticating his rights which he maintained had mysteriously disappeared. While his intervention secured for the family its due inheritance and lifted it from the struggle against comparative poverty, it also initiated those wearing and expensive lawsuits and inter-family controversies, which were to follow Selina Shirley for most of her life. By 1726 the majority of the estates had been settled but with only partial satisfaction, so that in 1729, three years after Washington's own death, further wrangling and legal battles would ensue.[2]

Far from an idyllic childhood sheltered from the realities of life, young Selina Shirley had early to face troubles which were to be etched forever on her mind and character. But through all these things we may trace a divine hand preparing this child for future usefulness.

---

[1] The ruins of this monument may still be seen in the old graveyard, but the inscription has been removed.

[2] According to E. P. Shirley in *Stemmata Shirleiana* the Chancery suits were not finally concluded until 1776.

# 2

# THE YOUNG COUNTESS

IN 1724 THE NINTH EARL OF HUNTINGDON, Theophilus Hastings, was enjoying life to the full. Now twenty-eight years of age, he had inherited his title from his half-brother George when he was only eight and, as a privileged peer of the realm, he was presently in the midst of his Grand Tour. A prerogative of the sons of the rich, the Grand Tour acted as a sort of finishing school for the nobility. With costs amounting to as much as £5,000, and that in days when a poor man's wage could sometimes be as low as £10 a year,[1] these wealthy young men would travel the Continent for three years or more. Sometimes they would search out rare art treasures or other antiquities and bring them home to adorn the walls and drawing rooms of their stately homes. France and Italy were the most popular venues for such tourists and in the heady days following the Duke of Marlborough's sweeping conquests on the battlefields of Europe, the English travelled as though they owned the world. Theophilus's Grand Tour was more extensive than that enjoyed by most young men and included a period in Spain, considered uncommon at the time.

Theophilus Hastings' father, the seventh Earl of Huntingdon, had married twice, as Selina Shirley's grandfather had done. Two years after the death of his first wife he had remarried, and Frances, herself already a widow, bore him a further two sons and four daughters, with Theophilus, born in 1696, being her eldest.

[1] Daniel Rowland's stipend amounted to only £10 a year.

There were other marked similarities between the Shirleys and the Hastings: both were wealthy and influential; both could trace their lineage back to one of the royal houses, in the case of the Hastings family to Edward IV of the House of York. But, in contrast to the Shirleys, the Hastings family was a united one with bonds of affection between George and Betty, children of the first marriage, and the six children of the second. The Hastings also owned extensive property in Leicestershire, with Ashby-de-la-Zouch and most of the surrounding area belonging to them. The first Lord Hastings had built the castle at Ashby – destroyed by Cromwell's soldiers in the Civil War and now no more than a ruin. Castle Donington and nearby Donington Hall, not far from Ashby, together with most of Loughborough, were numbered among their possessions. Their other properties included Ledston Hall, near Leeds, in Yorkshire, and estates in Cambridge and in Huntingdon.

When Theophilus's father had died in 1701 the earldom passed automatically to George, only surviving son of the first marriage. For a further three years Lady Frances cared for her six young children, all under the age of eight, until she remarried once more. Her third husband was a French prisoner-of-war, and in marrying him she surrendered custody of her children to Lady Betty Hastings, their half-sister. Fourteen years older than Theophilus, Lady Betty dutifully cared for the family, making a home for them on the Yorkshire family estate at Ledston Hall. When George himself died three years later, in 1704, at only twenty-eight years of age, he made generous provision for his sister Betty, leaving her Ledston Hall with its annual yield of £3000. But the earldom passed to his half-brother, Theophilus, though he was still only a child. Theophilus, Ferdinando, Frances, Catherine, Anne and Margaret appear to have stayed in Yorkshire for much of their childhood, with Lady Betty making arrangements for the boys' education. Theophilus, gentle by disposition, was sent to Christ Church College in Oxford at the age of fourteen where he developed a marked love for learning and classical literature. Martin Benson, later to become Bishop of Gloucester and a personal friend, was his tutor. Lack of any further reference to Ferdinando, the younger son, suggests he may have died in childhood.

In days when arranged marriages were still a frequent custom amongst the nobility, Lady Betty was concerned to find acceptable partners for Theophilus and his sisters. Catherine, the first to marry, had moved to Kent with her husband Granville Wheler. For the young Earl of Huntingdon, Lady Betty was anxious to discover a woman from the correct social echelon, one of sufficient wealth and with family connections acceptable enough to be worthy of him. This was no easy task. But in 1724, while the Earl was still abroad enjoying the Grand Tour, Lady Betty received a letter from Frances who, with her sister Anne, was then living at Donington Hall. One item of news she thought well worth passing on to the Earl: 'I had a letter the other day from Lady Frances, both she and Lady Anne are well and meet with the civility and regard they deserve from everyone. Lord Ferrers' daughters are now come into the neighbourhood.'[1]

In that simple sentence Selina Shirley, future Countess of Huntingdon and second daughter of Washington, Earl of Ferrers, first enters the pages of historical record. Clearly by the year 1724 Washington Shirley was sufficiently confident of the outcome of his family disputes to take possession of Staunton Harold, not far from Donington Hall. Little is known of Selina's teenage years or even where she was living for most of the time. With costly lawsuits in progress it is likely that the family would spend time in London where Washington owned a house and might be on hand for more contact with his lawyers as his case was argued in Chancery – the court which at that time had sole administration of cases of equity.

[1] HL.

At last after much wrangling and dispute Chancery pronounced that the charges brought against Washington Shirley were indeed well-founded and that he had, in fact, acted illegally in flouting his father's will and taking possession of much of the family property. Nothing daunted, and despite heavy legal costs, Washington took his case to the House of Lords and there in 1725 a compromise settlement was hammered out, but it was a settlement that only partially satisfied the interested parties. All this family conflict must unquestionably have had its repercussions on Selina and her sister Elizabeth, and we can well imagine the relief with which they contemplated life amid the beauty and peacefulness of the Staunton Harold estate with its rolling parkland and secluded lake.

Selina was now eighteen and her older sister twenty-one. Elizabeth was shortly to marry Joseph Gascoigne Nightingale and doubtless Selina's own thoughts were turning to the subject of marriage. Again it is to Thomas Haweis that we owe the information that at this time Selina used to pray that she might marry into a serious family – a prayer God was pleased to answer.[1] Perhaps Selina was already beginning to feel a sense of dissatisfaction with the emptiness and decadence that often characterized the social life of the nobility.

With Donington Hall[2] lying little more than five miles from Staunton Harold Hall there would inevitably be contacts between the two families. In all likelihood Selina's marriage was only 'arranged' in the sense that Lady Betty may have made initial suggestions to the Earl. In the years that followed Selina would have had a number of opportunities to meet Theophilus Hastings. She knew and corresponded with his four sisters before her marriage and ample evidence has survived to demonstrate the affection and compatibility the couple enjoyed. The dowry money of £15,000 – a breathtaking sum if transcribed into today's values – was so

[1] Haweis, *Church History*, vol. 3, p. 240.
[2] Rebuilt in 1793 and now the headquarters of British Midland Airways Ltd.

high that Washington found great difficulty in raising it. But at last a date was fixed for the wedding.

On 3 June 1728, Selina Shirley, soon to be twenty-one, was married to Theophilus Hastings, then aged thirty-two. The four Hastings sisters, Anne, Frances, Catherine and Margaret were happy to welcome Selina into the family. The Shirley family, too, was well pleased over the marriage.[1] Selina's mother wrote to the bridegroom from Paris congratulating him but she was highly displeased that she had received no notification of the impending marriage from her husband, Washington Shirley. Nor did she attend the ceremony, which took place in the church at Staunton Harold. Washington Shirley, meanwhile, relieved and pleased at the success of his negotiations, sent a wedding gift to Theophilus of seventy-two bottles of the best port.[2] The Earl and his bride made Donington Hall their first home and early portraits of the young Countess show an attractive and intelligent looking woman: her high cheekbones and small determined mouth convey the impression of a resolute and strong-minded personality; and yet there is a tenderness and warmth in the face. She was tall for the day at about five feet and six inches.[3]

In 1728, the year of Selina's marriage, court life was buzzing with excitement and swarming with covert place-seekers. George I had died the previous year and few English tears were shed on the occasion. A conscientious king, he had nevertheless failed to gain the hearts of his English subjects. His predominant loyalty to Hanover, his inability to master English, coupled with his intense animosity towards his son, Prince George, had made him far from popular. So great had become the tension between the father and son that Prince George had set up his own court, a court to which

[1] Lawrence Shirley, Selina's uncle, wrote to Theophilus saying that he was 'Sensible of the honour the family has received by so noble an alliance.' Leics. R.O.

[2] LRO.

[3] Her height has been calculated from three of her dresses which are sometimes on display at the Museum of Costume in Bath.

many of the younger nobility had flocked, including Theophilus and Selina. In 1727, as George II, he had ascended the throne at the age of forty-three, and to Theophilus Hastings had fallen the honour of carrying the Sword of State at the new king's coronation.

As a peer of the realm the Earl of Huntingdon and his wife were among the privileged families who held unquestioned influence in the England of the eighteenth century. Together with the other great landowners they provided subsistence for a considerable proportion of the population who cultivated farms and businesses on their lands. Under them in the social hierarchy came baronets, squires and knights whose lesser holdings still gave them an income in rents that made their way of life vastly different from that of the common people. The 'yeomen of England' or the smaller freeholders came next in the social scale – these were the farmers who owned and worked their own land, together with merchants and tradesmen; then came the tenant farmers, already mentioned, whose rents formed the bulk of the income of the landed gentry; coupled with them were the cottagers many of whom used their homes as mini-factories for spinning, weaving and carding wool. And at the bottom came the labourers, the large majority of the population. These consisted of manual workers of one sort or another, who toiled on the farms or in small industries, together with the small shopkeepers. And, of course, below them would fall that sorry class of people, the disabled, sick and unemployable whose lot in life could be pitiable in the extreme.

Criticisms have often been made for the expressions of veneration and deference used by the ordinary people when addressing members of the nobility such as the Countess of Huntingdon. But given this social structure and the virtual impossibility for the average person to rise out of the rank into which he was born, such terminology, though we may regret it from our egalitarian standpoint, is eminently understandable. At this time Theophilus and Selina Hastings were often to be found at court mingling both with royalty and others whose names are now enshrined in the history books for their literary, political or military achievements or their privileged status.

Among this social group was Selina's aunt, Lady Fanny Shirley, one of the acknowledged beauties of the Georgian court. Born the same year as the Countess, Lady Fanny was a daughter of Sir Robert Shirley's second marriage. A vivacious personality, she lived at Twickenham and was a near neighbour of the renowned poet, Alexander Pope.[1] Theophilus and Selina Hastings were often among her guests, and here also she entertained some of the outstanding literary figures of the day, including Pope himself. Lady Fanny's beauty had attracted Lord Chesterfield,[2] atheistic statesman and courtier, and she was reputed to be his mistress. Chesterfield himself, despite his unbelieving views and dissolute lifestyle, maintained a friendly relationship with the Countess and her family throughout his life. Lady Mary Wortley Montagu, poet, letter-writer and satirist noted for her acerbic wit, flamboyant and immoral lifestyle, was also a member of the same elite.[3] We may also mention the celebrated Sarah, Duchess of Marlborough, now elderly but no less vocal for that.[4]

Far from the milieu of frivolous and ruthless court life, a very different scene could be found in Oxford University where a

---

[1] Alexander Pope (1688–1744). Sensitivity over his deformed figure led him to quarrel with other leading literary figures. Best known for his satirical verse, especially *The Rape of the Lock*, published 1712.

[2] Lord Chesterfield (1694–1773), Philip Stanhope, was recognized leader of the Opposition in the House of Lords. He is best remembered today for his *Letters of Philip Dormer Stanhope, Earl of Chesterfield*, first published in 1774.

[3] Lady Mary Wortley Montagu (1689–1762).

[4] Sarah Churchill (1660–1744), wife of John Churchill, first Duke of Marlborough. She had gained total supremacy over Princess Anne after her father James II fled the country. Her power waned, however, after Anne ascended the throne in 1702, and the Duchess was finally dismissed from her service in 1710 because of her imperious attitude towards the Queen.

SELINA COUNTESS OF HUNTINGDON

young student named Charles Wesley and two friends, William Morgan and Robert Kirkham, had become seriously concerned about their spiritual state. Joining together to help each other to progress in a way of life that they hoped would be well pleasing to God, they were soon joined by a fourth in November 1729, an Oxford don named John Wesley, older brother of Charles. Here was the beginning of the Holy Club – that nursery of spiritual desire which would at length produce a handful of men, alive to God, whose preaching would shape the history of the eighteenth century and subsequent generations of the Christian church.

In that movement the young Countess of Huntingdon, too, was destined to play an important part in the purposes of God, although for the present, in her elegant Leicestershire home, Selina knew nothing of these things. With many new responsibilities her ability as an organizer soon became evident as she undertook the charge of a household of domestic servants, and the oversight of her husband's estates. Letters have survived in which she discusses the problems arising from the various estates, showing her personal involvement in many a detail, even to structural alterations of the properties, employing workmen and deciding where various works of art were to be hung.[1] At the same time she took upon herself the welfare, both moral and social, of those living on the Huntingdon estates. Less enviable was the task that also fell to her of collecting the rents, often seriously in arrears, from their tenant farmers.

Unquestionably her older sister-in-law, Betty Hastings, who had accepted Selina warmly into the family, became her role model. Renowned for her charitable works, Lady Betty was a conscientious member of the Church of England but still lacked a full understanding of the gospel of Christ. She subscribed to a number of educational causes, including one which provided exhibitions for poor Oxford students who wished to enter the ministry of the church. One who early benefitted from her

[1] HL.

largesse was a young student from Gloucester by the name of George Whitefield – a worthy enough young man in Lady Betty's eyes until he began to preach in the fields when her views of him changed markedly.[1]

Lady Betty was old enough to be Selina's mother. Having known so little of her own mother's affection, Selina developed a warm and loving relationship with her husband's half-sister, and a volume of correspondence passed between Ledston Hall and Donington Hall. Like Lady Betty, Selina also strove to support good causes: we discover that only months after her marriage she was buying Bibles and Prayer Books for distribution on the estate. But in spite of these things she remained a stranger to true heart religion. A loyal church attender, she could only hope that her good works might be sufficient to please the God to whom she had often prayed even from her childhood days.

The early years of Selina's married life were, however, far from easy. On 13 March 1729, less than ten months after her marriage, her first child, Francis, was born. Her father, now a lonely and sick man had hoped to attend his grandson's christening, but was too unwell to travel. He wrote to his daughter on 12 April 1729, addressing her as 'Dear Child', to explain why he could not be present: 'It is a concern to me I cannot come down to the Cristinging [sic], but I am not only in a very ill state of health but I have an affair to settle with your mother that prevents me.' 'I hope I am now out of all manner of danger,'[2] continued the sick man, who had been subjected to the usual eighteenth century treatment of 'being bled'. Two days later, at the age of fifty-two, he was dead.

This letter suggests further trouble in the family, which was indeed the case. Whilst their father lived, Selina and her sister Elizabeth were largely protected from the family wrangling, but as soon as he died the full weight of it fell on them and particularly

[1] *George Whitefield's Journals* (London: Banner of Truth, 1960), p. 78.
[2] LRO.

on Selina who seems to have taken the initiative. First their own mother filed a lawsuit against her daughters to obtain maintenance from the Shirley estates. Selina wrote her mother a letter reflecting her distress that she should act in this way: 'Your Ladyship, I am informed, has made a firm resolution of a bill in Chancery against us, which I reflect on with great concern that your children must defend any cause against you and that too without knowing for what.'[1] But the divisions had gone too deep to be healed, and not receiving financial satisfaction from her daughters, Selina's mother sent a message disowning them. Other family members also, far from satisfied at the financial arrangements, took the opportunity of Washington Shirley's death to re-open the disputes and set up further lawsuits in the hope of retrieving more of the Shirley property from his daughters. These legal proceedings were to rumble on far into the future.

Hard enough to bear under any circumstances, these things were in progress while Selina was pregnant again, this time with her second son, George, born on 29 March 1730, almost exactly a year after Francis. The following March their first daughter, Elizabeth, was born and just ten months later, on 23 January 1732, a third son, Ferdinando. After only three and a half years of marriage, the couple now had four young children, all under the age of three.

Childbirth was always attended by considerable risk in the eighteenth century, but should complications occur, the remedies to which unfortunate mothers were subjected rarely brought relief. The usual expedient for the nobility suffering from a wide range of complaints was to repair to Bath to 'take the waters'. Discovered by the Romans, the waters flowing from these natural hot springs were supposed to have medicinal properties. After remaining virtually unused for many centuries, the anecdotal value of the waters came to prominence once more after Charles

[1] LRO.

II and his court paid a visit to the city. Many gallons of hot water flowed each day from these springs and great faith was placed in their healing qualities both by those who drank and bathed and, not least, by those who profited from the business. In a journey undertaken in 1762 a German Count, Frederick Kielmansegge, describes his visit to Bath and the Bath waters:

> As is usual when you drink the waters which comes out of such springs, the taste differs little from that of bad warm water and you do not perceive any mineral flavour. Although the water is very strong it must not be drunk by persons who have a consumption ... it is of great use in all diseases which originate in the stomach.[1]

The way in which the rich and ill would bathe in the waters, is portrayed in a graphic eighteenth-century letter:

> They began by bathing at an early hour, between six and nine in the morning. The baths were sometimes taken at the doctor's orders, but more often as a diversion ... Men and women bathed together, keeping more or less apart, the men in drawers and jackets, the women in brown linen costumes and chip hats [to which handkerchiefs were fixed to wipe the perspiration and water from the face]. The ladies were carried from their lodgings to the baths in this costume in sedan chairs ... They were provided with a little wooden tray that floated on the water in front of them, and held handkerchiefs and snuff boxes and thus they walked about in the water.[2]

So it was that shortly after Ferdinando's birth in 1732 his mother made her first visit to Bath. By no means all visitors to the city were there for medical reasons, for Bath had become a playground for the indolent and wealthy. Clearly unwell and homesick Selina Hastings was not at all impressed, describing the city in a letter to her husband as 'the most stupid place I ever yet

[1] *Diary of a Journey to England in 1761-1762* (Longmans, 1902), p. 118.
[2] A. Barbeau, *Life and Letters at Bath in the Eighteenth Century* (London: Heinemann, 1904), p. 53.

saw.' Dominated by the influence of Richard Nash,[1] nicknamed *Beau Nash*, who had been elected Master of Ceremonies, city life was given over to entertainment and social amusements. Gambling, the social curse of the period, had free course among the idle rich of Bath, with some physicians even recommending it to their ailing customers as a form of social distraction.

The young Countess had to spend many months in Bath away from her four small children. Unlike other fashionable visitors, Selina was deeply unhappy during this period of separation. She took advantage of every post to write to Theophilus. He was not a natural letter writer, but when he did write Selina's joy knew no bounds: "'Tis with utmost joy I read my dear, dear jewel's. There is no wish of his heart towards me that is not restored to him from mine an hundredfold.'[2] These letters speak eloquently of the deep affection they shared for each other. Writing a week later her warm and intense personality shines out as she describes Theophilus as one 'whom my very life and soul dotes on and is the object of my words whenever it is in my power to talk of him.' 'I envy every creature that is near you', she continued.[3] Throughout these frequent absences from home the Countess continued to manage her estates by correspondence but always she longed to be back in Leicestershire. She missed her children, and would often think wistfully of them. On one occasion she sent them a box of toys, saying, 'My dear little ones will I fear quite have forgot me.'[4]

Dr George Cheyne, a Scottish-born medical practitioner, lived and worked in Bath. To him Selina was referred and for the next six years or more he took charge of her case. Described as the fattest man in the kingdom, Dr Cheyne, with his thirty-two stone bulk and philosophical turn of mind, must have been intimidat-

---

[1] A renowned gambler who had established the Bath Assembly Rooms soon after his arrival in the city in 1705.
[2] HL, 17 April 1734.
[3] LRO.          [4] *Ibid.*, 13 March 1732.

ing to his patients. Despite his own bulk, most of Cheyne's remedies involved diet. A vegetable and milk diet was a cure-all in his estimation and this he strongly recommended to Selina Hastings. Naturally anxious to retain the custom of so wealthy a patient, Cheyne encouraged the Countess to visit Bath as often as possible and during the next few years she was obliged to spend long months there following his regime of purgings and vomitings in addition to the severely restricted diet.

Naturally the Countess spent much of her time in the society of other members of the nobility also staying in Bath and in picking up the latest social gossip which she passed on in letters to her husband. But all this did not satisfy Selina Hastings. Often in her letters she would complain of the emptiness of the social round that seemed to gratify others. She longed for the comforting presence of Theophilus and often expressed her yearning to see him. 'My tenderest blessings are with my children, and rest assured, no creature under heaven is half so happy as your old Goody [a nickname sometimes used of a wife] at the thought of seeing my best of loves.'[1]

When she could endure the absence no longer she contravened her physician's advice and ordered a chaise to take her home. Writing to Theophilus she sent instructions that instead of coming himself he should dispatch one of the household to meet his 'old Goody' and added that she earnestly hoped 'that no condition of life shall ever force me from you again.'[2] Unable to prevent her departure, Cheyne continued to advise her by letter with the suggestion that she tried the waters at Scarborough to complete her recovery. Though Selina Hastings was back in Bath the following spring, 1733, she was apparently considerably improved and did not stay long. Dr Cheyne wrote to her husband on 29 August 1733, reporting the progress of his patient. Fulsome in his praise of Lady Selina, he spoke of her 'solid understanding, her sweet temper and honest heart', and

[1] HL.
[2] LRO.

continued by advising the Earl that 'she be suffered to go on in the method of diet and medicines I have put her, [and] in time she will be as healthy, cheerful and active as any lady in England and had she not been put in this method and regimen she must have died miserably of a cancer in her bowels.'[1]

Other concerns were now occupying the Earl of Huntingdon and his wife. In 1734 they decided to obtain the lease on two London properties for the family, in addition to the Leicestershire homes. One was to be in fashionable Savile Row in town and the other at Enfield Chase (then pleasant countryside ten miles due north of London), where part of the summer months could be spent. All arrangements for the two homes and the necessary alterations to the properties fell to Selina.

With a characteristic intensity and zeal for any project that she undertook, Selina showed a degree of impatience with the workmen employed on the project at Enfield Chase, which she proposed to convert into a small farm. Progress was slow and in a comment which reveals both the imperious streak in her personality and an ability to be objective, she writes: 'I have been in the most violent spirits ever since I came here and hurried the workmen to such a degree that I believe they wished my absence almost as much as I do myself.'[2] Clearly the temperament which had engendered strife in the Shirley family had been inherited by the Countess and a number of contemporary records refer to her quick temper. Reporting again on the situation at 'The Grove' in Enfield Chase, she admits, 'I thought my being there might hasten the workmen and it did . . . I thought the incessant knocking would drive me wild.'[3] But there were extenuating circumstances. The young Countess was pregnant once more and confessed to being low in spirits and missing her husband. 'My dearest jewel

[1] LRO.

[2] Historical Manuscript Commission, *Hastings Family Papers,* ed. F. Buckley (London: HMSO, 1934), vol. 3, p. 19. [Hereafter HMC, *Hastings Collection.*]

[3] Undated MS letter in Drew University, Madison, New Jersey.

will not fail to let me hear again next post,' she wrote, 'one line each day will make my life supportable.'[1]

These arrangements meant that the family spent more time in London than formerly and Selina's name begins to appear in letters from the nobility chronicling the gossip of the day. The Earl bought a racing horse that he stabled at Newmarket, and he and Selina enjoyed attending the races at Nottingham. They both dressed in a style suitable to their position in society; one of Selina's dresses being made from nineteen metres of exquisite multicoloured silk imported from France. Yet increasingly the Countess was not happy with her way of life. The loss of an infant daughter, their fifth child, also named Selina, shortly after her birth in June 1735 would have added to her sense of the meaninglessness of her way of life. With her own erratic health, the death of her baby, and being disowned by her mother, it is little wonder she was disconsolate.

Throughout this period a work of God was slowly yet certainly coming to fruition. In Oxford University four or five young men, each being prepared by God, would soon be called to play his part in an unforeseen work of grace that would ultimately have repercussions that would change the course of history. John Wesley and his brother Charles together with Benjamin Ingham were on the eve of sailing to Georgia in the New World with the brave hope of converting the heathen – a venture which was to reveal their own spiritual need. George Whitefield was in an agony of uncertainty over his own condition before God. Emaciated by his constant fasting, incessant in his prayers and good works, he was striving by every means in his power to make himself acceptable in God's sight. Meanwhile Howell Harris was beginning to preach – although he called it 'exhorting' – with unusual passion and persuasiveness. Soon all these disparate strands were to be woven together into a tapestry of grace that would bring honour to God and untold blessings to many people on both sides of the Atlantic.

[1] HL.

# 3

# ALL THINGS NEW

LEDSTON HALL, HOME OF LADY BETTY HASTINGS, with its massive multi-winged frontage, stood hidden among trees some ten miles from Benjamin Ingham's home town of Ossett. He would know, at least by hearsay, of Lady Betty's generosity to good causes and particularly to students, and of the comings and goings of the sisters. He had probably heard of the marriage of Theophilus Hastings to Washington Shirley's daughter shortly before he left home for Oxford in 1730 to begin his studies at Queen's College.

To appreciate the important role that Ingham was to play in the life of the Countess of Huntingdon, we must turn aside and follow his progress during his Oxford days and beyond. Seriously-minded since childhood, Ingham was uneasy at the profligate lifestyle he discovered amongst his Oxford contemporaries. Hearing of the scorn heaped on a group of men, known derisively as the 'Holy Club', young Ingham defended them vigorously against the verbal abuse of other students. With an increasing desire to know more about their way of life and perhaps even to join them, he at last sought out John Wesley and in 1733 became one with them. Like the other members of the Holy Club he strove by stringent religious endeavour to earn God's favour and would record his activities in a secret journal.[1]

Although constant in devotion and impeccable in outward conduct, Benjamin Ingham, like both John and Charles Wesley, still

---

[1] Recently decoded by R. P. Heitzenrater and published as *Diary of an Oxford Methodist* (Durham, N.C.: Duke University Press, 1985).

had no personal assurance of salvation. In 1735, following his ordination, he resolved in an apparently last-moment decision, to join his friends in their mission to Georgia. At the invitation of General Oglethorpe, they hoped to establish a Christian witness amongst the Indian peoples of the New World. Sailing with them on the *Simmonds* was a group of twenty-five Moravians whose influence on each of the three young men was to be far reaching. Of Benjamin Ingham we read:

> The Spirit of the Lord began to convince him of his sin in the ship as they were going over to Georgia but he laboured hard to estab-lish his own righteousness and underwent some conflict of soul. At length [after several months in Georgia] having used all means and finding them ineffectual and in deep distress he looked unto Jesus, called upon him for mercy and instantly obtained it.[1]

After little more than a year in Georgia, Ingham was back on English soil again, supposedly to recruit new volunteers for the American endeavour. A meeting with George Whitefield was soon arranged, for he knew that his old friend was anxious and willing to devote his life to that same cause, in response to appeals by letter from both John Wesley and himself. They met in London and we may well imagine with what surprise Ingham would have learnt of all that had been happening in his absence. Whitefield would have told him of the way God had delivered him from his increasingly desperate attempts to earn his salvation by his good works and had enabled him to 'lay hold of his dear Son by a living faith.'[2] He would have recounted his first nervous attempts to preach and the unexpected response that followed as the people clamoured for more. He learnt that whether in Bristol

[1] William Batty, *Church History, Collected from the Memoirs and Journals of the Revd. Mr Ingham and the labourers in connection with him. 1779*, tran-scribed by the Rev. M. Rattenbury, Hull, p. 2. MS in John Rylands University Library of Manchester.
[2] *George Whitefield's Journals*, p. 58.

or in Bath, in London or in Gloucester the desire to hear the young preacher was overwhelming. Clearly a door of opportunity for the gospel of Christ lay wide open.

Whitefield in turn noticed the change in Ingham and thought he had 'remarkably grown in grace' and hoped to 'catch some of that holy fire with which his soul was fired.'[1] Together the two men, Whitefield, now aged twenty-three years and Ingham twenty-five, sought in prayer to know God's will for their future ministry. For Whitefield, despite all the potential for usefulness in his home country, the call of God seemed unequivocal. To Georgia he must go. Ingham, however, returned to his home town of Ossett where the opportunities in his own county of Yorkshire soon engaged all his time and strength.

John Wesley, last of the three to return to England,[2] arrived early in February 1738. He too had learnt by frustration and failure the impossibility of profiting the people he had gone to serve without having a certain persuasion of his personal acceptance with God. Declaring as he disembarked, 'The faith I want is a sure trust and confidence in God that through the merits of Christ my sins are forgiven and I am reconciled to the favour of God,'[3] John Wesley was nearing the end of his long spiritual quest.

The year 1738 was to prove full of significance for the gospel of Jesus Christ. Although the actual date of John Wesley's conversion may be open to debate,[4] during this year both the Wesley brothers experienced an inner work of God in which they were given an assurance by the Holy Spirit of their acceptance with God. For Charles Wesley it was on Whitsunday, 1738, and for

[1] *Ibid.*, p. 85.

[2] Charles Wesley had returned in late 1736, ill and depressed.

[3] *The Journal of John Wesley*, ed. Nehemiah Curnock (London: Kelly, 1909–16), vol. 1, p. 424. Herafter Wesley, *Journal.*

[4] See Paul E. G. Cook, 'A Heart Strangely Warmed' (*Westminster Conference Papers*, 1978), for a fuller discussion of this issue.

John a few days later on 24 May. On that night in the Moravian society room in Fetter Lane, as John was later to express it, his heart was 'strangely warmed' and he knew at last that he 'did trust Christ, Christ alone for salvation; and an assurance was given me that he had taken away my sins, even mine, and saved me from the law of sin and death.'[1]

As he was nearing Ossett on his way home, Benjamin Ingham had also received an added inner assurance from the Spirit of God of his commission to preach the gospel.[2] Soon from every pulpit in the neighbourhood had sounded the arresting message that God was ready and willing to forgive the sins of the penitent, not on the grounds of their righteous deeds, but through the merits of Jesus Christ. This was a message that had rarely been heard before in the area, and we read that 'numbers were astonished and affected and crowds flocked to hear.'[3] News of these things must have filtered through to Ledston Hall, where an initial casual interest would soon lead on to profound spiritual changes in the lives of the Hastings sisters. And in touching them God also had his purposes for their wealthy but dissatisfied sister-in-law, the Countess of Huntingdon.

On 3 December 1737 another child had been born to Selina and Theophilus. Seeing in their newborn daughter a consolation for the infant whom they had lost two years earlier, they named the baby Selina once more. Francis, their eldest son, now eight years of age, was soon to start his education at Westminster School in London; Elizabeth, Ferdinando and George were all at home, aged seven, six and five respectively. With her own family so young the Countess was quickly moved to sympathy when she

---

[1] Wesley, *Journal*, vol. 2, p. 476.

[2] William Batty gives these details: 'On Woolley Moor, a hill about six miles from Ossett he sat down having a prospect of the country [before him] ... The Spirit of the Lord was poured upon him in a particular manner, and there and then he was ordained and commissioned to be a preacher of the gospel and was anointed by the Holy Ghost for the work.' *Church History*, p. 3.    [3] *Ibid.*

received a letter from a certain Thomas Coram asking for her support for a hospital he hoped to open in London specifically to care for dying, illegitimate and unwanted infants of the very poor. Known as the Foundling Hospital, it was a cause that Selina was happy to support financially.

During 1738 the Hastings family learnt with sadness that Lady Betty, to whom they all looked with deference, had breast cancer and would need surgery. This was a harrowing experience in days when medical knowledge was limited and anaesthetics unknown, and her progress was followed by the whole family, even the children. Francis, almost ten years old by this time, wrote from Westminster School about his aunt's illness, 'I am very sorry to hear my aunt continues so ill, and wish I could flatter myself with the hopes of hearing better accounts of her health.'[1]

In addition to the care of her family, Selina continued to help Theophilus in the oversight of the affairs of their estates throughout 1738. Like others of her social class, she and her husband travelled constantly between their various homes. Yet despite every diversion Selina was conscious of the meaninglessness of her way of life. She could confess to Lady Betty, in a letter written on 27 December 1738, that 'consideration must shew us the emptiness of all sublunary things without using this life as the way and means to lead us to a better', and could admit that 'she had lived a life so disagreeable to herself.'[2]

Just a month before the Countess wrote the above words, the youthful George Whitefield had returned to England after his first visit to Georgia. Church doors were steadily closing against the Wesleys, and Whitefield met with similar opposition. Yet this did not deter the crowds who flocked to hear these preachers, either in the pulpit or on the rough meadowland on the outskirts of London. Theophilus and Selina were in town at this very time and could not have missed the gossip, both the slurs and the

[1] 27 October 1738, LRO.
[2] LRO.

adulation, that buzzed around the capital concerning Whitefield and also the Wesleys. Although it is uncertain whether they actually heard the popular preacher for themselves, they would definitely have known of his message and there is some evidence to suggest that Selina was unhappy with it. Whitefield's emphasis on the inability of the sinner to satisfy God by an upright and respectable way of life and his need of the grace of God would have cut at the heart of all her previous religious concepts.

For Whitefield himself, the first purpose for his return from America was to gain ordination as priest from Martin Benson, Bishop of Gloucester, who had ordained him as deacon in 1736. Benson, who was Theophilus Hastings' old tutor from his Oxford days and a close family friend, would know of Selina's disquiet over Whitefield's preaching. He wrote somewhat apprehensively to the Earl to inform him of his intention to ordain the preacher:

> I hope that [it] will give some satisfaction to my lady and that she will not have occasion to find fault with your lordship's old tutor. Though mistaken on some points I think him [Whitefield] a very pious, well-meaning young man, with good abilities and great zeal ... I pray God grant him great success in all his undertakings for the good of mankind and a revival of true religion and holiness among us in these degenerate days; in which prayer I am sure your lordship and my kind good Lady Huntingdon will most heartily join.[1]

On 14 January 1739 Whitefield was duly ordained in Oxford. That same month, while the Earl and Countess were still in London, the young Prince of Wales celebrated his twenty-third birthday. Sometimes called 'Poor Fred' because of the harsh treatment meted out to him by his parents,[2] Prince Frederick held a

---

[1] A. C. H. Seymour, *The Life and Times of the Countess of Huntingdon*, vol. 1, p. 196. The dating of these events indicates that the Huntingdons were not yet in sympathy with Whitefield and the Wesleys.

[2] George II treated his own son in exactly the same way as his father had treated him.

banquet to mark the occasion. The lady guests would attempt to dazzle each other by the extravagance and elegance of their attire. Selina's appearance caused quite a stir:

> Her petticoat was black velvet embroidered with chenille [a soft silk or velvet thread], the pattern a large stone vase filled with ramping flowers that spread almost over a breadth of petticoat from the top to the bottom; beneath each vase of flowers was a pattern of gold shells, and foliage embossed and most heavily rich; the gown was white satin embroidered also with chenille mixed with gold ornaments, no vases on the sleeves but two or three on the tail; it was a most laboured piece of finery, the pattern much properer for a stucco staircase than the apparel of a lady – a mere shadow that tottered under every step she took under the load.[1]

Another glimpse of Selina presents a different picture – an amusing scene which demonstrated the young Countess's political affiliations. In March 1739, six weeks after the birthday celebrations, feelings were running high in the country against any appeasement with Spain, which was claiming sole shipping rights in all waters around her coasts. Spanish vessels would capture English ships and seamen at will whenever the opportunity presented itself and English sailors had allegedly been seriously maltreated. The incident of 'Jenkins ear', severed by some aggressive Spaniard, or so it was claimed, had inflamed English tempers and would soon become an excuse for outright war.

The matter was to be discussed in the House of Lords on 1 March 1739, but owing to the volatile nature of the case, the visitors' gallery was closed to all visitors. Lady Mary Wortley Montagu who was present has recorded a colourful description of the commotion, which followed. Evidently a contingent of about a dozen ladies, all but two of whom were titled, was determined to show that they were not to be barred from attending the debate

---

[1] *The Autobiography and Correspondence of Mary Granville, Mrs Delaney* (London, 1861), vol. 2, p. 28.

without significant protest. These ladies, including Selina
Hastings, presented themselves at the entrance to the House of
Lords at nine o'clock on the morning of the debate. Being politely
informed that the Lord Chancellor had ruled against their admittance, the ladies, led by the Duchess of Queensbury, promptly
pushed past the unfortunate man and stationed themselves outside the door of the gallery. Here they remained knocking on the
locked door, shouting, banging all day.

Members of the House of Lords, trying to conduct their debate
against the background racket, decided that hunger would eventually end the protest, if they could only keep the womenfolk at
bay for long enough. But it did not. By five o'clock in the evening,
however, one of the ladies had another idea: they would remain
totally quiet until their lordships thought they had given up. Half
an hour of total silence followed. When the doors were cautiously
unbarred from within all these noble ladies rushed in with shouts
of triumph and enlivened the rest of the debate, which lasted
until eleven at night, 'by noisy laughs and apparent contempts'.[1]

Throughout this period Benjamin Ingham was continuing to
preach wherever he could gain a hearing. William Grimshaw,
soon to be taken up by God and powerfully used in the same
movement of the Spirit, later reported on the results of such
preaching: 'The churches were soon crowded, and a great stirring up of the people to seek salvation by faith alone, in the
merits of the crucified Saviour quickly appeared.'[2] As the numbers of converts multiplied, Ingham gathered them together
into small societies in different towns in order to instruct them
and so that they might meet for prayer and mutual encouragement. At last he received an invitation to preach at Lady Betty's
private chapel.

[1] Seymour, *Countess*, vol. 1, p. 24.
[2] Grimshaw in a letter to Dr John Gillies, 19 July 1754, Appendix to
*Historical Collections of Accounts of Revival* (Edinburgh: Banner of Truth,
1981), p. 506.

The Hastings sisters now had an opportunity to make their own appraisal of Ingham and his message. Curiosity soon turned to heart concern, especially for Lady Margaret, as she weighed up the implications of Ingham's forthright message that good works alone could never merit God's favour – a lesson he himself had found so hard to learn. Ingham spoke to the sisters personally and would have told them of the remarkable Moravian Christians whom he had met on his voyage to Georgia: they were 'true Christians if there be any such upon earth.'[1] He introduced the sisters to the hymns the Moravians composed and sang. Words such as these were typical of their emphasis:

> What are our works but sin and death,
> Till thou thy quickening Spirit breathe?
> Thou giv'st the power, thy grace to move;
> O wondrous grace! O boundless love!

Before long, first Lady Margaret, and then later both Lady Anne and Lady Frances embraced the faith presented to them by the preacher from Ossett. Lady Catherine had already left Yorkshire.

Not many weeks passed before Margaret was writing enthusiastically to her sister-in-law, Selina, at Donington Hall to tell her about her new-found spiritual joys. The Countess, now pregnant once more, was filled with longing as she read the letters from Ledston Hall. How much she would give to know a similar happiness! Her formal religion and philanthropy had left her empty-hearted still. Writing to a friend of Lady Betty's earlier in the year Selina had said: 'I would undergo everything to come to the true knowledge of my Saviour.'[2]

In May or June 1739 Selina and her husband came to Yorkshire on a visit to the sisters at Ledston Hall. Undoubtedly they both met Benjamin Ingham for themselves, for he had become a

[1] LRO.
[2] *Ibid.*

frequent visitor there by this time. The transformation in
Margaret, now thirty-eight years of age, was immediately evident.
'Since I have known and believed in the Lord Jesus Christ for
salvation, I have been as happy as an angel,' she declared. Her un-
disguised joy affected Selina deeply. Upright and sincere though
she undoubtedly was, this was a dimension of spiritual life to
which she was a stranger, and she knew it.

More than this, the Countess was becoming increasingly aware
of the inadequacy of her own good works to satisfy either herself
or God. A small incident was used by God to reinforce her sense
of failure. To one of her housekeepers she had promised some gift
as a token of gratitude, but had entirely forgotten about it. By the
time she did recollect her pledge, the woman had left her service
and Selina did not know where she was. Now she had no means
of honouring her commitment. This circumstance 'made a
wound in her conscience and conviction of sin increased'. But as
the days passed her fears grew yet more acute as she now 'saw and
felt herself nothing but sin'. She began to realize that without an
inward and spiritual change of heart 'her destruction was inevitable'.[1] But what could she do? She knew no answers to her
spiritual predicament. Whenever she was entertaining nobility or
any of the clergy Selina would pose searching questions from the
Scriptures, urgently hoping for answers that would pacify her
troubled conscience. And as her questions were brushed aside or
inadequately answered, she grew yet more concerned. At length
her despair rose to such a pitch that her friends decided that
Selina must have lost her reason and advised the Earl to have her
put away.

Not surprisingly we learn that the Countess now became
seriously ill. Facing the all-too-real possibility of death, she would
have thought of her husband, of her five young children with
Francis, the eldest, only ten years of age, and of her unborn child.

[1] Sermon preached by William Aldridge at Jewry Street Chapel, 3 July 1791
(London, 1791), p. 16–17.

But mostly she thought of her spiritual condition. In her anxiety she wondered to whom she could turn for help. Perhaps Theophilus's old tutor, Bishop Martin Benson, who had previously been a domestic chaplain at Donington Hall, could help her. But, as she pondered sending for him, Lady Margaret's words flashed vividly upon her mind once again: 'Since I have known the Lord Jesus Christ for salvation I have been as happy as an angel.' Thomas Haweis describes what happened next:

> She felt an earnest desire, renouncing every other hope, to cast herself wholly upon Christ for life and salvation. She instantly from her bed lifted up her heart to Jesus the Saviour with this importunate prayer; and immediately all her distress and fears were removed.

So it was that this religious, even God-fearing woman was brought to cast herself as a helpless sinner on the same Saviour in whom her sisters-in-law, Margaret, Anne and Frances had also trusted. Like both Wesley and Ingham she had been saved not so much from a life of degradation as from her own self-righteousness. Describing the change in Selina, her first biographer, Aaron Seymour, hints at a possible reason for her earlier dislike of Whitefield's preaching:

> Her understanding was renewed in knowledge ... All offence at the gospel plan of salvation died away ... and from that moment she learnt to count all things but loss for the excellency of the knowledge of Christ Jesus her Lord.[2]

At peace in her heart, the Countess's physical condition began to improve. As soon as she was able, she wrote to her relatives at Ledston Hall to share with them the joy she now experienced in knowing her sins forgiven and in having an assurance of her acceptance with God. This letter of 26 July 1739 marks the date of her conversion and the beginning of a long life in the service of

[1] Thomas Haweis, *History of Church of Christ*, vol. 3, p. 242.
[2] Seymour, *Countess*, vol. 1, p. 15.

the kingdom of God.[1] Replying immediately to Selina's letter, Margaret's delight at the news is evident:

> I received my dear sister's letter . . . just as I was sitting down to supper [and] tho' it was at that time, my heart was so raised with gratitude to the ever blessed Jesus for the good work he had wrought in your Ladyship that it was pain to me not to repeat the 5th verse of the 103 Psalm, 'Praise the Lord, O my soul!'

The exhilaration amongst all three sisters at Ledston Hall on receiving the news can still be felt in these further words from Lady Margaret's letter:

> I had not read near half of my dear Lady Huntingdon's last letter before my sisters snatched it from me thinking it more than I could bear. Indeed I was quite overpowered with joy and thankfulness to infinite wisdom and goodness for manifesting himself in so extraordinary a manner to my dear brother and sister . . . What a reviving cordial it is to my spirits to read the account you give. The vigorous start you have made promises great things.[2]

Without a moment's delay Margaret wrote to Benjamin Ingham to share the news from Donington, sending the letter by a personal courier, for she knew how he would rejoice with her.

Both Selina and her husband now began to study the Scriptures seriously and as they did so their perspectives and joys began to alter: 'I feel every day there is no delight and pleasure in this world equal to the convictions of pious souls. It raises the heart so much above all earthly things.' So Selina confessed as she wrote to Lady Betty on 29 July 1739, three days after her letter to her other sisters-in-law. The effect on the Earl too was profound

---

[1] A confirmation of 1739 as the year of her conversion comes in a letter to Charles Wesley in 1766 where the Countess speaks of a prayer she has offered 'these seven and twenty years' that, if the Lord should find her placing her soul's trust in anything else, he would 'remove my wretched being from this earth.' Rylands MSS., Letter 103.     [2] LRO.

for, she continued, 'the Scriptures are become his whole study and I do think he has a humble heart and I am fully persuaded he does not think himself possessed of a least bit of merit.'[1]

News of the change in Selina and her husband spread rapidly. Court gossips were not slow to pass the information round. 'The Methodists have had the honour to convert my Lord and Lady Huntingdon both to their doctrines and practices',[2] reported the Countess of Hertford. Lady Betty Hastings, older half-sister to Theophilus, Anne, Frances and Margaret, had also been uneasy at the religious developments in her immediate family circle. It appeared that Selina was following her sisters-in-law and had been affected by this new religious movement which was gradually gaining adherents in different parts of the land. She therefore recommended to the Countess that she seek the spiritual advice of a friend of hers, Thomas Barnard. Selina had recently sent her second son, George, to Leeds Grammar School to be under Barnard's tuition, and had little option but to entertain his counsels. Three letters from Barnard are extant written between July and October 1739. In each he repeatedly urges on her restraint in religious matters. 'Observe moderation in all things, nor be hurried on with too much eagerness in spiritual combat,' he advised. Above all she must not in any way seek to change her way of life. 'Do not pray too much'; 'Do not take on spiritual burdens and commitments.' 'Keep the same manner in all things as formerly',[3] are phrases picked out at random from his closely written letters and could summarize his advice. Well-intentioned he might have been but he had little understanding of Selina Hastings. It is not surprising therefore to learn that towards the end of 1739 Thomas Barnard noticed that his 'correspondence with your Ladyship seems to be in a declining state'.[4]

---

[1] LRO.
[2] Seymour, *Countess*, vol. 1, p. 35.   [3] *Ibid.*
[4] Thomas Barnard wrote the *Life of Lady Elizabeth Hastings* (Leeds, 1742). In the preface he roundly attacked Methodists.

Lady Margaret, however, knew the sort of help her newly-converted sister-in-law would be needing. Writing to Ingham, therefore, she urged him to go to Leicestershire immediately and to spend time teaching both the Earl and Lady Selina. Describing him to Selina in her letter of 28 July 1739 as 'that humble and good man' from whom she herself had 'reaped great advantage', she assured her sister-in-law that 'from his conversation and expounding of the Scriptures, I doubt not but you will receive great comfort'.[1] Ingham, who had already been praying that the grace of God so evidently at work in the Hastings sisters might touch the lives of the Earl and Countess, stayed in Leicestershire throughout the month of August, 1739. Not only did he spend time with Theophilus and Selina Hastings, but also preached in the area, gathering the converts into societies as he had done in Yorkshire.[2]

Lady Betty was not the only one to express disquiet at events in the family circle. Mary, the Countess's youngest sister, had now returned from the Continent and had married a Viscount Kilmorey. Writing to Selina, Mary expressed her views:

> My compliments to Lady Margaret and am much obliged to her for remembering me, but am sorry to find she is turned Methodist as this sect is so generally exploded that it's become a joke of all companies, and indeed I can go nowhere but I hear of the uncommon piety of the Donington family. I find it the general talk of every place. I'm concerned to think that my dear sister who is so reasonable in everything else should encourage such a canting set of people who place all their religion for the external show of it and

[1] LRO.

[2] Seymour, following the account by Thomas Haweis, records that the Countess sent a message to the Wesley brothers 'who were then preaching in the neighbourhood' (vol. 1, p. 17). A careful study of their journals shows that the brothers did not visit Leicestershire at this time, nor for a further two years. She may have written to them expressing her support for their work, as Seymour suggests she did, but no letter has survived.

pass uncharitable censures on them who are not in the same way of thinking. But I hope God almighty who once endued you with a very good understanding will disperse the mist that now hangs before you and restore you to your former right way of judging.[1]

Worse was to follow. For one in the Countess's social position to make a profession of faith and to align herself with such despised Methodists as Benjamin Ingham could not but cause a stir. Her aunt, Lady Fanny, at Twickenham and the entire literary circle surrounding her would doubtless have felt embarrassed and apologetic over Selina's new religious bent. Not only had she brought disgrace on her family, but also in their view her support for the Methodists would appear a betrayal of her class, her lineage and the Church of England in which she had been reared. Perhaps the Earl, perceived to be more balanced than his wife, could moderate her enthusiasm. In response to a suggestion from other members of the nobility, Theophilus asked Selina if she would speak to their friend, Martin Benson, Bishop of Gloucester.

The interview that took place on 5 December 1739, just one week before Selina's confinement, and recorded by Thomas Haweis, left the Bishop at a considerable disadvantage in the verbal fray. Displaying an unusual mental sharpness, coupled with an extensive knowledge of the Church of England's Articles and Homilies, the Countess chose to use arguments that Benson could not well contravene. Much of the conversation, as Haweis recorded it, centred round the rights and wrongs of the activities of men such as the Wesley brothers, Ingham and Whitefield. As we have seen, Benson himself had ordained Whitefield on 14 January that year and had expressed a high opinion of him in his letter to the Earl. But Whitefield's determination to continue preaching outside stated parish boundaries had altered the prelate's view. Benson wrote a warning letter to the young preacher, but a reply from Whitefield dated 9 July 1739 had

[1] HL, Lady Kilmorey to the Countess, 9 June 1740.

clearly nettled Benson. In it Whitefield exposed the weakness of
the bishop's arguments, noting that he too preached out of his
own diocese and added, 'I hope your lordship will inspect the
lives of your other clergy, and censure them for being *over-remiss*
as much as you censure me for being *over-righteous*.'[1]

Selina took Whitefield's arguments even further, turning the
interview into a counterattack on the spiritual duties of men in
Benson's position. 'She plainly and faithfully urged upon him the
awful responsibility of his station under the great Head of the
church, Jesus Christ.' This was more than the Bishop could
stand. Jumping up he hurried to make his departure. But before
he left her room he said that he deeply regretted the day he had
ever ordained George Whitefield: he recognized that the change
in the Countess was directly due to the new preaching associated
with the young preacher's name. But Selina had the last word.
'My Lord,' she said, 'mark my words, when you come upon your
dying bed, that will be one of the few ordinations you will reflect
upon with complacence.'[2] Such a spirited defence gives us a
choice glimpse into Selina's verve and determination. It also
demonstrates the profound change that her conversion had
brought to her life. All things had indeed become new for the
Countess of Huntingdon.

[1] *George Whitefield's Letters, 1734–42: A Facsimile of Whitefield's Works,
Vol. 1, 1771* (Edinburgh: Banner of Truth Trust, 1976), p. 500.
[2] This prediction came true, for when he was dying Bishop Benson sent ten
guineas to Whitefield as a token of his favour, and begged to be remembered
in his prayers. Thomas Haweis, *Church History*, vol. 3, p. 243.

# 4

## SETTING THE SCENE

ON SUNDAY 17 JUNE 1739, while the Countess of Huntingdon was
still troubled and fearful concerning her spiritual state, John Wesley
was in London. That evening he wrote in his journal:

> I preached at seven [in the morning] in Upper Moorfields to (I
> believe) six or seven thousand people on 'Ho everyone that
> thirsteth, come ye to the waters.' . . . At five I preached on
> Kennington Common to about fifteen thousand people on these
> words, 'Look unto me, and be ye saved, all ye ends of the earth.'[1]

Charles Wesley, who had accompanied his brother in the
morning, estimated that the crowd that gathered was nearer ten
thousand. Later that day he himself preached twice in one of the
prisons, seeking to bring words of mercy and forgiveness from
God to offenders, many of whom awaited the death penalty.
Meanwhile George Whitefield, soon to leave English shores once
again, was preaching to a congregation of three hundred in the
morning, but was on Blackheath Common in the evening where
he noted in his journal that he preached to a throng of humanity
which he guessed could well number above twenty thousand
people.

These were extraordinary days, and Whitefield rejoiced in
them. At the close of that Sunday he was able to write: 'I retired
to bed much pleased to think that religion, which had long been
skulking in the corners, and was almost laughed out of the world,

[1] Wesley, *Journal*, vol. 2, p. 223.

should now begin to appear abroad, and openly shew herself at noonday.'[1]

Events such as these stood out sharply against the backcloth of the general religious scene in the 1730s. Since the last decades of the previous century there had been a growing acceptance of the tenets of Deism, with its elevation of human reason and its consequent rejection of the supernatural, and eventually of revelation itself. Such opinions inevitably led to the loss of vital Christian experience and consequently, church attendance, though theoretically still a legal obligation, was at a low ebb. Remunerative livings were much sought after by clergy who would often hold a string of smaller livings as well. These would be served intermittently by hard-pressed 'starveling curates', whom they would 'pay to do duty in their absence,'[2] leaving the people with little spiritual guidance.

Due to such loss of faith, a widespread materialism characterized the opening decades of the century. Commerce and trade became the national preoccupation, while money, and the making of more money, gripped the minds of merchant and smallholder alike. The 'Gin Age' was approaching its height. With the government ban on imported alcohol in 1689, cheap liquor was being brewed in private homes. By 1733 there were between four and five thousand gin shops in London alone. Spirits distilled in England in the eight years between 1734 and 1742 increased from 4,947,000 gallons a year to 7,160,000 gallons. These were the days, depicted in William Hogarth's conscience-stirring caricature *Gin Lane*, when it was possible to be 'drunk for a penny, dead drunk for twopence'. Alcohol abuse was prevalent throughout society, devastating homes and family life, with employers sometimes paying their men in gin rather than money. Even

---

[1] *George Whitefield's Journals*, p. 289.

[2] See description in Henry D. Rack, *Reasonable Enthusiast, John Wesley and the Rise of Methodism, Life and Influence of John Wesley* (London: Epworth Press, 1989), p. 11.

[43]

statesmen were not exempt. On various occasions parliament had to be adjourned early because the honourable members were too drunk to conduct the business of state. Funerals, particularly in the north of the country, could turn into drunken brawls, as mourners drank themselves silly.

Living conditions among working people were often appalling, with entire families crowded into a single room, and only straw as bedding. Disease was rife, with typhus, dysentery and smallpox exacting their toll on the lives of the under-privileged. Narrow streets became refuse tips, not only for household refuse but also for butchers' offal and even human wastes. Infant mortality was high: on average only one child in four attained to adult life. Crime had reached alarming proportions, with the death penalty imposed for over one hundred and fifty different offences. Picking pockets, vandalizing young trees, snaring rabbits, and even snatching fruit from barrows were all offences punishable by death. This in turn led to more crime, for if a man could be hung for some minor offence, he might as well commit a greater in order to cover his tracks. No greater penalty could be imposed upon him. Prisons, where insanitary conditions led to frequent deaths from typhus fever, were largely reserved for debtors, many of whom owed only trivial sums of money. Other 'justice', summarily inflicted, took the form of whipping, branding, and even transportation.

With so little to make life endurable, sports tended to be cruel and often bawdy. Bear and bull baiting, cock-fighting, badger-baiting and even goose-riding[1] were popular, while executions became public entertainment, with the rich paying for the best seats. Criminals passed through the streets in carts dressed in their best clothes bound for Tyburn or some other public gallows. Those who showed no fear at their approaching death, or even treated their fate as a joke, were said to 'die like gentlemen'.

[1] Swinging on the greased neck of a goose until the bird's neck was broken.

Such was the society into which the Wesleys, George Whitefield, Benjamin Ingham, Howell Harris and other pioneer preachers ventured with a message of hope and mercy through the gospel of Christ. Selina's childhood days in rural Ireland would probably have given her more understanding of such conditions than was commonly possessed by other members of the nobility. With her conversion came a deepening concern for the welfare of the men and women on her estates and a zeal for the salvation of her servants, her acquaintances, her family and the nobility amongst whom she mingled – a zeal that was to become the master passion of her life.

On 12 December 1739, when she was thirty-two years of age, Selina's seventh child, Henry, was born. Only days after the birth Theophilus and Selina learnt of the death of Lady Betty at Ledston Hall on 22 December. For thirty years or more Lady Betty had been the figurehead of the Hastings family and the one to whom they all looked. She had been distinctly troubled at what she considered to be the excessive religious zeal displayed by Theophilus's wife, and had a strong distaste for anything she regarded as a departure from the norms of the Established Church. Regardless of the fulsome comments in obituaries recording her life and her generosity to good causes, we may detect observations that suggest that hers was indeed a genuine faith.

Selina, who had known so little family affection, felt her loss keenly and carefully copied down different expressions of esteem into a small commonplace book which may still be seen in the Huntington Library in San Marino, California. The *Daily Advertiser* carried a particularly warm tribute, describing Lady Betty as 'a great pattern of purity and holiness, of resignation to God, of gratitude for and under all his dispensations towards her.' It further described her 'unwearied zeal for promoting true spiritual Christianity'; and quoted some lines of Isaac Watts that were often on her lips as she was dying:

A guilty weak and helpless wretch
    On thy kind arms I fall.
Be thou my strength and righteousness,
    My Jesus and my all.

It came, however, as a shock to both the Earl and the Countess, and a source of gossip at many an aristocratic fireside, to discover that Lady Betty had left the bulk of her estate, not to her family as might have been expected, but to educational and other charitable causes. As her nearest male relative the Earl had anticipated receiving a major part of all the Hastings properties that Lady Betty had inherited from her own brother, George. Instead Ledston Hall was bequeathed to his eldest son, ten-year-old Francis, to be managed by the family until the boy came of age. No money was left for its upkeep. This may be the reason why Theophilus decided to relinquish his lease on the property he rented in Savile Row at this time.

Not many weeks after Lady Betty's death came news from Paris of the death of Selina's mother, Lady Ferrers. Alone and embittered she had died without sufficient means even to finance the few minor legacies she made in her will. Only her favourite daughter, Mary, received a small number of mementos from her mother including a diamond-studded cross. Despite the fact that her mother had disowned her ten years previously, Selina made arrangements for an interment in Bath Abbey, in accordance with her mother's request. More than this she arranged for the legacies to be paid. Acknowledging her sister's initiative in these things, Mary wrote quaintly, though gratefully, to Selina on 22 March 1740:

> Your generous and filial regard for my poor mother's remains in fulfilling her dying requests is an act of such piety and goodness that it can never be enough admired and esteemed by all [and] renders you infinitely more dear to me.[1]

[1] LRO.

In addition Mary sent the diamond cross to Selina, acknowledging that her 'conduct on this occasion has so justly deserved it'.[1] As soon as she was well enough after Henry's birth Selina travelled to Yorkshire to oversee the upkeep of Ledston Hall. A splendid place, it had nevertheless fallen into a measure of disrepair and would need to be put in order and leased out until her son Francis came of age. With her flair for organization, Selina added the burden of Ledston to the cares for the Earl's estates that she already shouldered. She spent time there during most summers and her long and detailed correspondence with her agent, who had oversight of the property, can still be read. Ledston Hall was finally leased to a tenant in 1745.

An immediate priority for Selina was to suggest alternative accommodation for the three sisters who had lived at Ledston for much of their lives. All three agreed to move down to Ashby Place in Ashby, and Selina anticipated the joy of having her like-minded sisters-in-law living less than ten miles from Donington Hall. Lady Margaret, who had enjoyed a special place in the Countess's affections, showed an initial enthusiasm for the arrangements but suddenly and unaccountably appeared unwilling to move away from Yorkshire. She preferred instead to buy a house at Aberford, five miles further north. Not until then did the sisters appreciate a situation that had been growing increasingly obvious in recent months. Lady Margaret's attachment to Benjamin Ingham was stronger than mere gratitude for all the benefits she had received from his ministry.

The growing affection between them alarmed her high-born relatives. Ingham, though well-educated and from a comparatively wealthy family background, would not be considered a suitable life-partner for one in Lady Margaret's position. He was twelve years younger than she, and his itinerant preaching would inevitably lead to an unsettled lifestyle. News of an impending engagement had already leaked out to the court gossips

[1] Elizabeth, the eldest of the three sisters, had died in 1734.

by February 1740, so that Lady Mary Wortley Montagu could remark cynically that she had heard that Lady Margaret 'had disposed of herself to a poor wandering Methodist'. Meanwhile the Countess of Hertford noted, 'The town now says that Lady Margaret is certain to marry one of their teachers whose name is Ingham.'[1]

Throughout 1740, the year following her conversion, Selina was preoccupied with the weight of affairs that Lady Betty's will had forced upon her. It meant periods of separation from Theophilus, for, while she was in Yorkshire, he was attempting, though unsuccessfully, to sell Enfield Chase, north of London, with its adjoining farm. Not wishing to be without a London base, the Earl decided to rent a house in Downing Street, thought to be number 11, now the traditional residence of the Chancellor of the Exchequer. Here they would be closer to Westminster School, for by this time George[2] had joined his brothers there.

The school, where many an aspiring father wished to have his boy educated, currently had about 350 pupils of whom at least sixty were sons of the nobility. All the pupils received their lessons in the Great Hall, once the dormitory of the monks who served Westminster Abbey. Prominent in the Hall stood the seventeenth century table known as Rod Table with its two menacing birches visible, obtruding from half-open drawers during school hours. The headmaster's chair, donated by Charles II, was placed at the front of the Hall and occupied at the time by a Dr Nicholls, whose educational regime was of a benign nature. The boys were taught in large classes with mathematics and Latin dominating the curriculum. Most of the pupils were boarded out

[1] Seymour, *Countess*, vol. 1, p. 35. The Countess of Hertford, later to remarry and become the Countess of Somerset, was sympathetic to the Methodist cause and a friend of Isaac Watts.

[2] While George had attended Barnard's school he had often stayed with his aunts at Ledston Hall. Lady Margaret wrote to his mother on 7 July 1739 with a glowing description of the nine-year-old's character as 'sweetly good' and obedient.

and their health and personal needs cared for by 'dames' who ran the boarding houses.[1]

Because much of their time was still spent in Leicestershire, the Earl and Countess, like other parents, received letters from their boys, particularly when they were in need of anything. In the stilted and wordy style of the day, they wrote home making their requests and sometimes sending specimens of their work for their admiring parents to see. So, towards the end of 1739, ten-year-old Francis sent a letter in his copybook handwriting:

Brother Ferdy [Ferdinando] was very happy that you was pleased with his and will write again next week. I return you many thanks for the half crown you was so good as to order me. Enclosed I send an exercise which I can assure you I did myself and it has not been looked over by anybody. I hope it will not be long before you will be able to come to town for I long to see you, Papa and sisters . . . Brother Ferdy and I are both very well.[2]

And again, as older brother, Francis wrote home on behalf of eight-year-old Ferdinando in September 1740:

I pray you when you see my aunts give my duty to them. My brother Ferdy has worn out his black clothes so bad that he cannot wear them so that he is obliged to wear his grey every day, which are in a fine pickle. He joins me in sending duty to my dear Papa and Mama and love to sisters. Your most dutiful son, Hastings.[3]

Despite his protestations about his good work, Francis was not receiving very complimentary reports from the school. So after George's arrival at Westminster his parents thought it would be best to move Francis to Winchester College. Possibly this was because the boys were so close in age, but it does not appear to have been a successful arrangement and Francis was back at Westminster two years later. For the three younger children, the

[1] The poet William Cowper and Martin Madan, later to be associated with the Countess, were both pupils at Westminster School while the Hastings boys were there.    [2] LRO.    [3] *Ibid.*

Earl employed a tutor recommended by Dr Cheyne. He received £15 a year, in addition to his accommodation at Donington Hall. His responsibility had been to teach the boys before they went to London, and now to tutor Elizabeth and later still Selina and Henry. Described as competent in Latin, Hebrew, Greek, Italian and French, he added to his accomplishments the ability to 'cast accounts'. The Hastings children were therefore all well provided for educationally.

In addition to her own family, Selina had a further responsibility at this time. Lady Catherine, the fourth of the Hastings sisters who had married Granville Wheler in 1724, died in 1740 – the third death in the family in quick succession. Three years earlier Granville Wheler had been ordained; he and Catherine had moved from Kent to West Leake, south of Nottingham, where Theophilus Hastings had arranged for his brother-in-law to become rector of the joint benefices of East and West Leake. Following their mother's death, Catherine and Granville's girls, Elizabeth, Selina and Catherine ('Kitty') would often come to stay with their aunts at nearby Ashby Place and also spend time at Donington Hall, where they doubtless increased the liveliness of the Hastings schoolroom. Meanwhile their sons, Theophilus and Granville, were at Westminster School with the Hastings boys who delighted to pass on information about the misdemeanours of their cousins.

In spite of all these domestic responsibilities during 1740, the Countess steadily pursued her new desire to meet other Christians. George Whitefield was out of the country throughout this period, but the question of when she first met John and Charles Wesley has been the subject of considerable speculation. In his two-volume work, *The Life and Times of Selina Countess of Huntingdon*, Aaron Seymour suggests that it was as early as 1738 and that the Earl and Countess attended services at the Fetter Lane Society.[1] Although this line has been followed by most

[1] Seymour, *Countess*, vol. 1, p. 19.

subsequent biographers, no documentary evidence exists for the assumption. It is the more improbable because the Countess was not converted until the summer of 1739, and, as we have seen, had not been happy with Whitefield's emphasis. For any of the social rank to which the Earl and Countess belonged to have attended such a gathering would involve courage and commitment. Nor is it likely, with her advancing pregnancy during the latter part of 1739, that Selina would be travelling to London to make new acquaintances. Neither of the Wesley brothers makes any reference to her in his journal nor in any correspondence before 1741. They would surely have done so had she been present. Her knowledge of the early days of the revival would have come from Ingham who was in a position to give her a first hand account of all that had been happening.

The only precise indication of a date for the beginning of Selina's growing friendship with these great men of the revival comes from a letter addressed to Charles Wesley in October 1742. In it the Countess writes:

> Can words now express what I owe you all, double and more than this is due to you, first cause in God's hand for two years of every spiritual blessing I possess.[1]

This would date the start of their friendship in the autumn of 1740. Certainly by February 1741 Selina was writing to John Wesley in tones familiar enough to indicate that a warm acquaintance had now been established.

[1] Manuscript correspondence of the Countess of Huntingdon, John Rylands University Library of Manchester. Letters to Charles Wesley are particularly to be found in the Black Folio, hereafter described as 'Rylands MS', plus number of letter quoted. Here in letter 87, the Countess repeats a fact dating the beginning of her friendship with the Wesley brothers that occurs in a number of letters over the years, both from John Wesley and from the Countess. The last mention of it occurs in a letter to Thomas Haweis written in April 1790, the year before her death, when, in reference to the revival, she speaks of 'our early days now fifty years ago'. Letter 121, Leete Collection, Bridwell Library, Dallas.

From the earliest days of her Christian life the Countess was determined to consecrate all she had to the service of God. In the letter to Charles Wesley just quoted she wrote:

> How do I long to give him the glory for this new creation of body, soul and spirit, a temple of the living God. As to my health, I think nothing about it. My vehement desires in God swallow all up; they exceed even my prayers, tears, all, all . . . I am crucified unto the world, and the world unto me; all events in it are alike but the advancement of God's glory in his saints. My little all has long been his!

In devoting her 'little all' to God's service, Selina gave generous support to Methodist societies meeting in the area around her home.[1] Her first concern, however, lay with those who worked in and around Donington Hall. Whenever she had opportunity she would gather all the domestic staff together and read to them from some religious book from her steadily increasing library,[2] and would couple with this some earnest exhortation to seek salvation.

An anecdote is told of the Countess's attempts to influence those who worked for her. On one occasion, she spoke with a man repairing a wall. She urged him to think about his soul and about the account he must one day give for his life before the judgment throne. Her words seemed unheeded. Many years later, however, on meeting another of her workmen in the garden she spoke to him also. 'Thomas, I fear you never pray nor look to Christ for salvation', she began. 'Your Ladyship is mistaken,' came the reply, 'I heard what passed between you and James when he was mending the wall some years ago, and the word

---

[1] A letter has survived, dated 22 June 1740, from a small Methodist society gathering at Breaston and Draycott, two adjacent Derbyshire villages lying on the farther side of the Trent some five miles north of Donington Hall. It acknowledges a gift of money and books from the Countess (LRO).

[2] Some 70 books from her library, including works by Moravians and French Pietists and most notably William Law, may still be seen in the Cheshunt Foundation Archives, Westminster College, Cambridge.

designed for him took effect on me.' 'How did you hear it?' enquired the Countess. 'I heard it', responded Thomas 'on the other side of the garden through a hole in the wall, and shall never forget the impression I then received.'[1]

In the summer of 1740 the early Methodist movement faced a crisis. Since November of the previous year a situation had been steadily developing which was to shatter the co-operation that had existed between the Moravians and the Wesley brothers. Eventually it was to lead to the first split among the revival leaders. Philip Molther, a young convert who had been a servant in the house of Count Zinzendorf (leader of the Moravians), arrived in England in October 1739. He soon began to introduce a new teaching amongst those who met in society at Fetter Lane: any person who was uncertain whether or not he was a true believer should refrain from using any outward means of grace. He should do nothing but be still, until God gave him an inner assurance of his regeneration. There were no degrees in faith, according to Molther's teaching. Either a person had a full assurance of faith or he had no faith at all. No such thing as a wavering faith existed, and to have any doubts or fears was evidence that there was no true faith in the heart; those experiencing such doubts must do nothing but be still until they receive a full assurance of the forgiveness of sins.

This teaching was a direct negation of John Wesley's emphasis and ran contrary to everything that the brothers had themselves learnt from God. 'I believe,' wrote Wesley, on 31 December 1739, 'there are degrees in faith and that a man may have some degree of it . . . before he has the full assurance of faith, the abiding witness of the Spirit.' The seeker should not just 'be still', but rather, Wesley insisted, 'I believe it is right for him who knows he has not faith to go to church, to communicate, to fast, to use as much private prayer as he can and to read the Scriptures because I

---

[1] Told to Augustus Toplady by the Countess. *Works of Toplady* (London, 1794), p. 503.

believe these are means of grace.'[1] So persuasive were Molther's arguments, however, that although only twenty-one years of age, his ideas spread rapidly amongst the societies, making Wesley's position among them untenable.

Many of Wesley's followers now forsook him and bitter things were said. Benjamin Ingham hurried down from Yorkshire to try to find a point of reconciliation between the two parties but with little success. Even though Ingham was initially clear in his own mind about these issues of faith and assurance, he owed a debt of gratitude to the Moravians and soon began to compromise his own position. Before long he invited the Moravians to come to Yorkshire to begin a Yorkshire congregation with the result that many of his own converts were hindered in their faith by this teaching.

By July 1740 a permanent break with the Fetter Lane Society had become inevitable. On 20 July, after one last attempt to achieve reconciliation, Wesley led a small band of followers out of the Fetter Lane Society and made a disused ammunition factory, known as the Foundery, which he had purchased late in 1739, his new headquarters.[2] From there he began to regulate his 'United Societies', as early Methodism was called, effectively marking its beginning as a separate organisation.

During the autumn of 1740 the Earl of Huntingdon and his wife were both together in London, where they would have worshipped at the Foundery and established a closer relationship with the Wesley brothers. But the split between the Methodists and the Moravians was an embarrassment for Selina, due to her family links with Benjamin Ingham and Lady Margaret. Possibly

[1] Wesley, *Journal*, vol. 2, p. 328–9.

[2] It is improbable that the Countess was present on this occasion as Seymour suggests (vol. 1, p. 36). There is no documentary evidence to substantiate the claim and Wesley would certainly have referred to her presence in his *Journal* had she been there. Wesley does record that Benjamin Seward, whom Seymour says also accompanied him, was in fact there.

wishing to understand the Moravian position more clearly, Selina sent a message to James Hutton, a young printer and London bookseller, whose friendship with the Wesleys had been superseded by his involvement with the Moravians. On 18 November 1740 Hutton reports on this interview in a letter to Augustus Spangenberg, Moravian leader and lecturer at their school of theology at Herrnhaag in Germany:

> Last week I waited upon the Earl of Huntingdon and his lady, at no great distance from London. The Countess, who had sent for me, I found more eager to hear the gospel than anyone I ever saw before. Of poor sinnership and the Saviour[1] she has not much to say; nevertheless she receives the gospel very simply, and believes it. I look daily for its striking deep root in her heart; she has great liking to the Brethren [Moravians]; she does not lack good sense, but has a very violent temper; her lady's maid, however, tells me she has not been in a passion for more than twelve months.

Of Lord Huntingdon's position, Hutton was not quite so sure, describing him as 'not yet awakened, being unable to distinguish between the preaching of the clergy and ourselves'.

The reference to the Countess's 'violent temper' illustrates not only her natural temperament but more importantly the change which grace had effected in her life. This interview in itself gave evidence of this, for Hutton, only twenty-five years of age, took it upon himself to reprove Selina for her attitude towards her husband. He records:

> I spoke very freely to her respecting her conduct towards her lord; telling her she ought to be obedient, cheerful and loving. She listened to me as though she had been my inferior. This astonished me when I considered her as an English Countess and of a choleric and violent temper.[2]

---

[1] Another term for the new Moravian teaching.
[2] James Hutton, *Memoirs*, ed. Daniel Benham (London, 1856), p. 67–8.

This was indeed highly improper on Hutton's part, and in the light of Selina's strong affection for the Earl, as already noticed, hardly necessary.

And so the year 1740 drew to its close. The Countess of Huntingdon was by now establishing friendships and patterns of life that would lay the foundation of her long years of service for the kingdom of God. Already she had experienced something of the cost of Christian discipleship. The die was cast and the scene set for all that was to follow.

# 5

## 'AN INSTRUMENT FOR GOOD'

THROUGHOUT 1741 THE COUNTESS OF HUNTINGDON strengthened her friendship with John and Charles Wesley, associating herself with them to a marked degree. The significance and social cost entailed for one in her position was considerable. The term 'Methodist' was used as an insult, and though the crowds flocked to hear the new field preachers, the higher echelons of society regarded Whitefield, the Wesleys and their followers with contempt. Publications denouncing the Methodists were commonplace. Characteristic of the outcry was the complaint of the vicar of Dewsbury, Yorkshire, who maintained that 'an impious spirit of enthusiasm and superstition has crept in among them'. Describing the infant Methodist movement as 'this monstrous madness and religious frenzy, which like a rapid torrent bears down everything beautiful before it', he was thankful that at present 'the contagion was pretty much confined to the dregs and refuse of the people – the weak, unsteady mob.'[1]

An anonymous writer published a pamphlet in which he described the Methodists as 'crackbrained enthusiasts and profane hypocrites', averring that 'the false doctrines and blasphemies of the Methodists, their field assemblies and conventicles in houses are contrary to the laws of God and man, of church and state, and are tending to the ruin of both.'[2] The

---

[1] Luke Tyerman, *Life and Times of John Wesley* (London: Hodder and Stoughton, 1880), vol. 1, p. 328. Hereafter, Tyerman, *Wesley*.

[2] *Ibid.*, p. 329.

Countess of Huntingdon, on the other hand, regarded her association with the Methodists as an honour. She came into the category of those whom Charles Wesley describes in verse:

> There are who suffer for thy sake,
>     Enjoy thy glorious infamy,
>     Esteem the scandal of thy cross
>     And only seek divine applause.

Throughout the year Selina corresponded with the Wesley brothers from her Leicestershire home. The first letter that appears to have survived is one of encouragement written to John Wesley and dated 2 February 1741:

> Let not your hands hang down, my dear friend. Think what you are set for – the defence of the gospel. Trample on men and devils. The hour is hastening when it will be seen how faithful a Master we serve. Your arm shall break a bow of steel. Believe, believe, all is possible to him that believeth.

Her gratitude for the spiritual help she herself had received from John Wesley shines out: 'I cannot forbear continually giving you the tribute of a grateful heart. We are comforted by your letters . . . You are a chosen vessel to the Lord.' The strength of their early friendship may be demonstrated by the warmth and respect paid by Selina to John Wesley which is evident throughout her correspondence with him. 'My very much beloved Friend in the Lord'[1] is a typical opening greeting.

Although he makes no reference to it in his *Journal*, John Wesley's diary notes reveal that he paid at least six visits to the Countess between April and August 1741[2] when she was staying

---

[1] Seymour, *Countess*, vol. 1, p. 51.

[2] For example: ' June 1 Monday. Prayed, dressed, John xii, the bands; 7.30 rode; 9 Enfield Chase (Lady Huntingdon's) tea, conversed . . . ' and again on Sunday evening six days later, '7.30 rode; 9 Lady Huntingdon's.' Wesley, *Journal*, vol. 2, diary notes, p.460-1.

at Enfield Chase. And in June 1741 he made his first visit to Leicestershire, accompanied by a young man named Thomas Maxfield,[1] doubtless at the invitation of the Countess. Remaining in the area only a week, Wesley was dismayed to discover how strongly the Moravian *stillness* teaching had taken root in the small groups of converts brought to the faith through Ingham's ministry. Visiting Ockbrook, a village community near Derby soon to become a Moravian settlement and remaining so until the present time, Wesley enquired what doctrine was taught there. He received the predictable answer, 'If you will believe, be still. Do not pretend to do good; and leave off what you call the means of grace – such as prayer, running to church and sacrament.'[2]

But another controversy, yet more damaging in its long term effects, was embroiling John Wesley at this time – a controversy which would eventually bring about a serious split in the evangelical revival of the eighteenth century. This was the divergence of view between the Wesley brothers and George Whitefield over the doctrines of election and final perseverance. Coupled with this was John Wesley's growing insistence on the possibility of

[1] Maxfield had been converted under John Wesley's preaching in Bristol during May 1739 and became a member of the first Methodist society meeting at the Foundery in July 1740. His zeal, gifts in prayer and exhortation recommended him to Wesley, but he would only allow ordained men to preach in the societies at that time. During Wesley's absence Maxfield began to preach, the first such occurrence at the Foundery. Although unordained men such as John Cennick and Howell Harris had also been preaching, Wesley expressed his annoyance. But his mother, though long schooled in the correct protocol of the Church of England, intervened on Maxfield's behalf. 'John, you know what my sentiments have been and you cannot suspect me of favouring anything readily of this kind; but take care what you do with respect to that young man, for he is as surely called of God to preach as you are. Examine what have been the fruits of his preaching and hear him also yourself.' After hearing Maxfield preach, Wesley responded with words that marked a significant development in early Methodism: 'It is the Lord; let him do what seemeth him good.' The use of lay preachers, so vital a part of Wesley's endeavour, and later to be adopted by the Countess, had been initiated.
[2] Wesley, *Journal*, vol. 2, p. 464.

believers attaining perfection in this life. A stream of letters had passed between Wesley and Whitefield during the latter's period of absence in Georgia. We catch a sense of Whitefield's grief at the widening gulf between himself and the Wesleys as he writes to James Hutton, the London printer, on 7 June 1740:

> My dear bother, may the Lord be with you! For Christ's sake desire brother Wesley to avoid disputing with me. I think I had rather die than to see a division between us; yet how can we walk together if we oppose each other?[1]

And later that month Whitefield had written to Wesley himself begging him to avoid exposing their differences in his preaching. A further letter from Whitefield, dated 25 September 1740, set out his position yet again and included comments on Wesley's emphasis on Christian perfection: 'I am sorry, honoured sir, to hear by many letters that you seem to own a sinless perfection in this life attainable . . . I know not what you may think, I do not expect to say indwelling sin is finished and destroyed in me, till I bow down my head and give up the ghost.' And then linking this with Wesley's other doctrinal aberrations, he continued, 'What a fond conceit is it to cry up *perfection*, and yet cry down the doctrine of *final perseverance!* But this and many other absurdities you will run into because you will not own *Election*.'[2]

Whitefield's pleas, however, had no effect on the course that Wesley was marking out for the Methodist movement. When all else seemed to have failed Whitefield wrote his long reply to Wesley's *Free Grace* sermon of 24 December 1740, in which he made a robust defence of his doctrinal position and attempted to demonstrate point by point the flawed arguments on which Wesley's sermon was based.

In the spring of 1741 George Whitefield was about to return to England. When he had sailed for America in August 1739 the Countess of Huntingdon had been converted little more than a

[1] *George Whitefield's Letters*, p. 185.    [2] *Ibid.*, p. 211-2.

month. As we have seen, although she had supported Whitefield
in her interview with Martin Benson, no evidence exists suggesting that she knew him personally. It is therefore understandable
that Selina should adopt John Wesley's theological position both
on election and on Christian perfection. She had formed a warm
friendship with the brothers, had attended the Foundery and
listened to their preaching. The fact that both the Wesleys submitted their unpublished journals to the young Countess for her
evaluation is evidence of the respect the brothers felt for her.[1] She
appreciated and commented on Charles Wesley's hymns and
encouraged John to publish his *Journal*. He dedicated his
second journal to her.

Wesley's doctrine on Christian perfection particularly attracted
Selina. The determination and decisiveness of her personality
was stimulated and inspired by the challenge to rest content with
nothing short of perfection as an attainable Christian goal. Referring to a sermon expanded into a pamphlet which John Wesley
had published earlier in that year,[2] she wrote to him on 24 October 1741:

> The doctrine contained therein I hope to live and die by; it is
> absolutely the most complete thing I know. God has helped your
> infirmities; his Spirit was with you of a truth. You cannot guess how
> I in spirit rejoice over it.[3]

Not long after Wesley and Maxfield's visit to Leicestershire in
June 1740, and possibly as a result of seeing the blessing attending Thomas Maxfield's preaching, the Countess decided to send
her own coachman, David Taylor, out on a similar evangelistic

[1] The Countess refers to this in a letter to John Wesley, 15 March 1742.
Cited Seymour, *Countess*, vol. 1, p. 51. Also Rylands MS. Letter 1, 24 Oct-
ober 1741 refers to Charles Wesley's journal that she had been reading. Also
Rylands MS. Letter 3.

[2] 'Christian Perfection', from *Sermons on Several Occasions,* Wesley, *Works,*
ed. T. Jackson (London, 1829–31), vol. 3, p. 203–33.

[3] Rylands MS., Letter 1.

endeavour. His remit from the Countess was not so bold as to extend to actual outdoor preaching. Rather, she commissioned him to visit the houses of the people, read a sermon by Bishop Thomas Ken, sing a psalm and read a prayer.

David Taylor had been converted the previous year, and his passion to reach out to all the surrounding Leicestershire villages with the same message that had transformed his own life carried him far beyond instructions. Great was the Countess's embarrassment when she discovered that Taylor was actually preaching in the open air. Fearful of the offence it may have caused to the local vicar she wrote to him in haste, explaining that her coachman's activities were 'both contrary to my knowledge and approbation'. But her letter had a twist in it. 'You', she remarked pointedly 'must do your duty for the poor people.'[1]

David Taylor could not be restrained, however. One June afternoon it was rumoured that he was to preach at Glenfields, near Leicester. Samuel Deacon, who was scything the long grass on his smallholding in Ratby, not far from Glenfields, heard the report. A farm labourer until recent months, Deacon had prospered to such an extent that by the age of twenty-seven he had saved up enough money to purchase land and begin cultivation. As a loyal son of the Church of England – a bell ringer in fact – Deacon was surprised to learn that Taylor's employer, the Countess of Huntingdon of nearby Donington Hall, actually allowed him to travel around the villages in this way. A novelty it certainly was, but it was more than mere curiosity that made young Deacon throw down his scythe that June day and hurry several miles to Glenfields to hear Taylor's message. It was life-transforming for Samuel Deacon and would lead to years of eminent usefulness for the kingdom of God.[2]

[1] LRO, no date.
[2] Deacon's ministry at Barton-in-the-Beans would lead to a widespread growth of evangelical witness in the area through the testimony of the 'Barton Preachers' and eventually be a major contributory factor in the establishment

After her initial alarm Selina began to appreciate Taylor's efforts, but his zeal soon led him into further trouble. As his converts multiplied he attempted to exercise a greater degree of independence from the Countess and wished to set up small societies as both Benjamin Ingham and John Wesley were doing. More seriously, he was also coming under the influence of the Moravian teaching on stillness, which reduced the effectiveness of his preaching. Writing to John Wesley on 25 March 1742, the Countess complained about Taylor's independent streak: 'I would not trust David with the guidance of my soul, no, not for worlds. I find he is going to build himself a room and break with the ministers, and become a lay preacher. He has more pride than I ever saw in a man. If he will commit his poor sheep into your hands, I will assist in the room, school, etc.; but else I will do nothing.'[1] And again a few weeks later she wrote, 'Your opinion of David Taylor will, I fear, be found true . . . When we lose our plainness, then ends the Christian. A double-minded man, who can bear?'[2]

To what extent Taylor, who had started assisting Benjamin Ingham, had offended against the Countess we are not in a position to say. Born into a social rank that presumed dominion over others as its rightful status, Selina never found the actions of those who contravened her wishes easy to accept. David Taylor's subsequent usefulness as a preacher redresses the imbalance of some of her remarks. He was to have an extensive ministry in Derbyshire, Yorkshire and Cheshire, working with the Wesleys and Benjamin Ingham. John Bennet, whose own remarkable

---

of the New Connexion of General Baptists under Dan Taylor in 1770. See Edwin Welch, 'The Origins of the New Connexion of General Baptists in Leicestershire' (*Leicestershire Archaeological and Historical Society*, LXIX, 1995); also John R. Todd, *By the Foolishness of Preaching* (Barton-in-the-Beans Baptist Church,1989).
[1] Cited Tyerman, *Wesley*, vol. 1, p. 383.
[2] Rylands MS., Letter 109.

SELINA COUNTESS OF HUNTINGDON

work in Derbyshire was much owned by God, was converted through Taylor's preaching.

Selina's concern for those employed in her service and living on her estates was expressed in many practical ways. Daily she could be found visiting them and always seeking to find means to help them. Having suffered much ill-health herself, she had developed a marked interest in medicine and had begun to experiment with a few remedies which she recommended to the sick. Some of these proved highly effective. To Charles Wesley she commented on 5 August 1742:

> I have laboured much among the unawakened. I let none pass by of any rank but I remind them of the fountain that is open for sin and uncleanness. God blesses my labours for their bodily health so much that they come many miles to me on that account and many God sends home aseeking him.

Sometimes her exertions proved almost too much for her own limited strength, however, and she confessed in this letter that she was brought 'by reading, singing and talking to them almost past opening my mouth.' But just when she felt unable to carry on any longer a further opportunity to speak with someone would present itself and the Countess found that God 'with a fresh call lifts me up and gives me new strength to labour for him.'[1]

One group of workers much upon Selina's heart were the miners of Leicestershire. Knowing that George Whitefield and then John Wesley had gained a hearing among the Kingswood colliers in Bristol, she was naturally hopeful that local miners might also be influenced. Donington Hall was in a mining area and the Hastings family itself owned a mine, so she wrote to the local mining contractor expressing her concerns. In reply he explained that 'they are a strong set of obstinate people under no kind of government,' and suggested that mob riots would consti-tute a potential risk. Undeterred, the Countess used her growing influence with John Wesley to press the cause of other miners. A

[1] Rylands MS., Letter 84.

reference in one of his letters indicates that it was she who had urged upon him the need of the colliers in Newcastle. This pressure led to his first visit to the Newcastle area in May 1742, and the consequent establishment of that northern base of Methodism, leading in turn to a significant increase in the spread of the revival.[1]

With a growing family of her own, and possibly remembering her own chequered childhood days and limited educational opportunities, Selina was troubled about the lack of educational facilities for the children of many of the poorer people in the area. She had already shouldered responsibility for a school in Melbourne, three miles south of Donington, started by her sister-in-law, Lady Betty Hastings. Now she extended her efforts by opening a school in Ashby-de-la-Zouch where her other sisters-in-law were living. In nearby Markfield, she opened yet another school placing it under the care of Edward Ellis who had recently been appointed to the local parish church, under the patronage of the Earl of Huntingdon. Ellis had already been educated at Cambridge at the Earl's expense but his recent conversion made him one in spiritual endeavour with the Countess.

The Markfield school was not a success, however. Parents were dilatory about sending their children with any regularity and discipline was hard to maintain. Selina felt obliged to close it down within a year of its opening, complaining that without the co-operation of the parents her best attempts to help the children of Markfield were being thwarted. More than this, the evangelistic aims that she also purposed for the school could not be sustained unless the parents were concerned for the spiritual good of the children. Explaining her problems to Wesley in March 1742, she wrote, 'A school will never answer the end of bringing forth any of the gospel fruits of holiness till the parents are first made

[1] *Letters of John Wesley*, Standard Edition, ed. John Telford (London: Epworth Press, 1931), vol. 2, p. 14. Hereafter, Wesley, *Letters*. See also below, p. 76.

Christian. The parents must lay up for the children, not the children for the parents.'[1]

Despite these problems the Countess did not give up her educational efforts. Shepshed,[2] a quiet and isolated village lying between Loughborough and Ashby attracted her attention. Here, later in 1741, she set up another free school under a certain Mrs Phillips, 'for the learning of the children of the Parish of Shepshead [as the name was sometimes spelt] the English tongue.' But this time she took the precaution of drawing up a careful list of rules that were to apply to both the Melbourne and Shepshed schools and that would overcome the problems she was experiencing in Markfield. If a child was absent for any reason apart from sickness for more than a week he forfeited a place at the school. Strict discipline must be maintained and parents were to permit their children to be corrected. Pupils were to be sent to school 'cleaned, washed and combed.' No child whose father had an income greater than £20 a year was able to attend.[3] How long this school was in existence is not known.[4]

Not only were Selina's days filled with seeking the spiritual and physical well-being of those living in the vicinity of Donington Hall, but the Countess, nearing her mid-thirties, still had the care of a young family and the financial oversight of the estate to occupy her time. Henry was now two years of age, and his sisters, Selina and Elizabeth, four and ten respectively. The three older boys, Francis, George and Ferdinando, away at school in London

[1] Seymour, *Countess*, vol. 1, p. 51.

[2] Though only a small community, Shepshed has figured in the history of the Christian church on several occasions. It was visited in the 1760s by William Darney, one of the early pioneers of the revival, and in 1774 it was the scene of a remarkable revival under William Guy, the preacher at the Particular Baptist Church. For further details see Michael Haykin, *One Heart and One Soul* (Darlington: Evangelical Press, 1994), p. 83.

[3] *Rules for the School in Shepshed* (LRO).

[4] A reference in a letter to Philip Doddridge in 1748 to 'some poor schools of mine in the country' suggests that it may have continued for a number of years (HL).

and Winchester, had many needs, not least for regular visits from their parents, letters from home and a constant supply of school-boy necessities such as new clothes, extra cakes and pocket money. A letter from Francis written in March 1741 was typical of the many that passed between the school and Donington Hall: 'My papa was so good as to say when we left him at Christmas that when we wanted a little money he would desire Mr Wright to give us a little. We are now without any, and if you and papa please, it would be acceptable to us all.'[1]

Lady Frances and Lady Anne living nearby at Ashby Place would often join Selina in her visits to the sick and needy on the estate. Her contacts with Lady Margaret, however, were less frequent than formerly because of the disapproval felt in the family over her impending marriage to Benjamin Ingham. After some dif-ficulty in obtaining a marriage licence the couple were married on 12 November 1741 in Aberford where Lady Margaret and Ingham settled.[2] Few knew that the ceremony was taking place and not for another month did the Earl and Countess hear of the event.

Despite the coolness in relationships prior to the marriage, once the ceremony was over, it was not long before the friendship between Margaret and Selina was restored. 'I find an inclination in my heart to write to your dear Ladyship,' began Margaret rather apprehensively in her first letter after the wedding. Five weeks had elapsed and Margaret was anxious that any misunder-standings should be dispelled. 'I hope you will receive it as I write it, in love. For we have but one common Lord and Master, and all who are united in him will love one another.'

It took longer, however, for Benjamin Ingham to re-establish relationships with Theophilus and Selina Hastings. Firstly he had resented their opposition to his marriage, but a second and probably stronger reason for the decline in contacts lay with his

---

[1] LRO. [2] George Whitefield, who had maintained a warm friendship with Ingham, was married to Elizabeth James two days after Ingham and Lady Margaret were married.

links with the Moravians which were at their closest at that time. Since the disruption at the Fetter Lane Society in London and the resulting damage to the early Methodist work, Wesley had all but cut off links with his old friend. In addition to his temporary acceptance of the Moravian emphasis on *stillness*,[1] Ingham had also expressed strong reservations about Wesley's teaching on Christian perfection. With the Countess warmly associated with the Wesleys in 1741, it is not surprising that he felt unwelcome at Donington Hall. Another hindrance to the restoration of good relations with Selina lay in the fact that her former coachman, David Taylor, was travelling around with Ingham at the time and preaching to his societies, currently numbering about sixty.

Happy in her friendship with John and Charles Wesley and with a growing influence among her servants and neighbours, the Countess of Huntingdon had indeed become 'an instrument for good' – in accordance with a wish she had expressed in an early letter to Charles Wesley. To all her varied attempts to meet the spiritual needs of the people around her, Selina always linked a concern for their temporal and physical welfare. We see, therefore, in the Countess an early example of that desire shown increasingly by evangelicals to improve the social lot of men and women. This would become a strongly marked characteristic of evangelical endeavour in the later eighteenth century and even more so in the nineteenth.[2] But for the time being, Donington Hall was steadily developing into a place where Christian compassion and zeal for the gospel enlightenment of the people went hand in hand; and a home where early Methodist preachers could always be assured of a welcome.

[1] Not all Moravians followed Molther's teaching. John Cennick, who joined them in 1745, maintained an outgoing evangelistic emphasis.

[2] In his *Victorian England, Portrait of an Age*, G.M. Young refers to the transformation in society brought about by the Evangelical Revival of the previous century: 'The Evangelicals gave the island a creed which was . . . the basis of its morality . . . By 1830 their work was done. They had driven the grosser kinds of cruelty underground.' (London: OUP, 1960), p. 4. See also, Kathleen Heasman, *Evangelicals in Action* (London: Geoffrey Bles, 1962).

# 6

## To Rich and to Poor

WHENEVER THE EARL AND COUNTESS OF HUNTINGDON were staying at their Downing Street home they would attend the Foundery to hear one of the Wesley brothers preach. Sometimes Selina would take the opportunity of inviting members of the nobility to accompany her. A letter from the Duchess of Buckingham,[1] who died in March 1742, gives evidence of Selina's early attempts to influence her acquaintances with the gospel message and of the problems she faced due to the overweening pride which characterized many of this class:

> I thank your Ladyship for the information concerning the Methodist preachers; their doctrines are most repulsive, and strongly tinctured with impertinence and disrespect towards their superiors in perpetually endeavouring to level all ranks, and do away with all distinctions. It is monstrous to be told that you have a heart as sinful as the common wretches that crawl on the earth. This is highly offensive and insulting; and I cannot but wonder that your Ladyship should relish any sentiments so much at variance with high rank and good breeding.

[1] When her husband was Marquis of Normanby he had, in 1690, presented the Rev. Samuel Wesley, father of John and Charles, with the living of South Ormsby. He was responsible for erecting the grand house in St James's Park, purchased in 1761 by George III for £21,000 to be a royal residence – Buckingham Palace.

Despite her protestations, however, the Duchess agreed to accompany Lady Huntingdon to the Foundery, and continues in her letter:

> Your Ladyship does me infinite honour by your obliging enquiries after my health. I am most happy to accept your kind offer of accompanying me to hear your favourite preacher[1] and shall wait your arrival. The Duchess of Queensbury[2] insists on my patronising her on this occasion; consequently she will be an addition to our party.

Shortly after this the Duchess of Buckingham was dying, and though Lady Huntingdon attempted to visit her in her last illness, the Duchess declined to see her, saying she felt 'entirely unable to undergo the fatigue of conversation'.

'The fine ladies of Bath'[3] were also included in Selina's early evangelistic attempts. Towards the end of 1741 and during the early part of 1742 she found herself back in Bath, once more under the medical supervision of Dr Cheyne. These 'fine ladies' had been her friends and associates on former visits and with them she had trifled away her time while trying Dr Cheyne's wearisome remedies. Now she spoke to them of the blessings of salvation she had experienced. Despite her doctor's unpleasant prescriptions for her recovery, the Countess had made a personal friend of him. Of a philosophical and religious turn of mind, Cheyne was ready to listen to his patient's conversation and was evidently influenced by her. Selina reports in a letter to Theophilus written in January 1742, 'Today Dr Cheyne has been sitting with me and has been talking like an old apostle. He really

[1] Almost certainly one of the Wesleys at this time.
[2] One of the leading perpetrators of the ladies' attempt to gain entrance to the debate in the House of Lords in 1739.
[3] Seymour, *Countess*, vol. 1, p. 27.
[4] Letter from Lady Margaret who writes: 'I was glad to hear that dear Lady Huntingdon was not ashamed of the cause of Christ among the fine ladies of Bath.'

has the most refined notions of true spiritual religion I almost ever met with. The people of Bath say I have made him a Methodist.'[1]

But the company that gave the Countess the greatest delight was the society of believers that met in Bath, mainly converts of John Wesley's preaching there. Whenever she was able she would also join with the society that met in Wesley's 'New Room', in Bristol, which had been built in 1739. It was probably here that Selina encouraged Thomas Maxfield to expound the Scripture to those gathered. Writing to Wesley on 31 January 1742, shortly before she was due to go home, she commented on what she had heard:

> I never mentioned to you that I have seen Maxfield. He is one of the greatest instances of God's peculiar favour that I know. He has raised from the stones one to sit among the princes of his people. He is my astonishment. How is God's power shown in weakness! You can have no idea what an attachment I have to him. He is highly favoured of the Lord. The first time I made him expound, expecting little from him I sat over against him, and thought what a power of God must be with him, to make me give any attention to him. But before he had gone over one-fifth part, anyone that had seen me would have thought that I had been made of wood or stone, so quite immovable I both felt and looked. His power in prayer is very extraordinary. To deal plainly, I could either talk or write for an hour about him.[2]

With each visit the Countess was growing more uneasy about the real value of Dr Cheyne's medical advice, and although appreciative of his company, she could not dismiss the suspicion that he only kept her there to retain her as his patient. However, she remained in Bath until he finally suggested it would be safe for her to return to Leicestershire early in February 1742. While there Selina met two young women who were also 'taking the

[1] HMC, *Hastings Collection*, vol. 3, p. 32.
[2] Rylands MS., Letter 111.

waters' for the sake of their health. Possibly converted under the preaching of John Wesley or even members of the society that met at the Foundery, Anne and Fanny Cowper were sisters whose earnest faith and spiritual interests quickly captivated the attention and then the affection of Selina Hastings.

So close did the friendship become that when she was due to go home, the Countess suggested that they should both return with her to Donington Hall. As no mention is made of the girls' mother, it is likely that she had died. Fanny, in particular, probably the younger of the sisters, was far from well and needed the care which the Countess, with her interest in medical matters, was able to give. Both were happy to accept the invitation and their father, who seems to have had little sympathy with his daughters' faith, wrote to the Earl and Countess expressing his gratitude for their kindness.

Travelling slowly homeward that February in 1742, the party planned to stop for a few days in Gloucester. As they entered the town who should they see riding out of it towards them but George Whitefield. As we have seen from Selina's robust defence of him in her interview with Bishop Martin Benson in December 1739, she was well aware of the significance of Whitefield's early ministry. She had probably heard him preach from time to time at the Tabernacle in Moorfields,[1] but it would appear that their relationship was little more than formal at this time.

Almost a year had elapsed since Whitefield's return from America, and they had been hard months for him. Soon after his return he had printed the long letter he had written to Wesley in answer to his sermon on *Free Grace*, and, not unexpectedly, this had widened the gulf. Now a distinct coolness existed between the Wesley brothers and Whitefield. When Charles Wesley feared that his brother might be edging towards some sort of an understanding with Whitefield over the issues that divided them, he

[1] Erected as a temporary meeting house for Whitefield's congregations in 1741 and situated not far from Wesley's Foundery.

wrote a stinging letter to John urging him to 'regard not fair speeches; renounce your credulity and George Whitefield until he renounces reprobation.'[1] With all the poet's intensity, Charles had blackened Whitefield's theological position, calling all who taught it 'Priests of Moloch'.

Such was the situation between the leaders of the revival when Whitefield and the Countess unexpectedly met in February 1742. In a letter to John Wesley on 19 February 1742, written after her return to Donington Hall, Selina describes the encounter. Although parts of the manuscript letter are illegible, probably worn away by age, most is still clear. Pleased to see her, Whitefield said that he would be back in Gloucester at eight o'clock that evening and arranged to call on her. Due to her closeness to the Wesleys the Countess was wary of Whitefield and guarded in her comments, particularly when the question of the doctrine of election was raised:

> He held forth above two hours upon the doctrine of election and reprobation and collected all the choicest flowers of all that was to be gathered or said upon the several heads to charm me, telling me withal, (or giving me to understand) I was an elect. I told him upon what he had said that upon the whole I found I should be such a loser by his way of thinking that no consideration that I was yet able to see from anything he had said could have any weight. He seemed surprised and said, How! Could that be! I told him I was so much happier than he was and that not from anything in myself, but on my constant dependence upon Christ.

The next subject which they discussed was the other area of divergence between Wesley and Whitefield, which arose from Wesley's insistence that believers may attain total freedom from sin in this life. The Countess, who accepted Wesley's teaching wholeheartedly, reported to John that she had told Whitefield:

[1] Letter dated 28 September 1741, Tyerman, *Whitefield*, vol. 1, p.482.

I waited and hoped for an absolute deliverance from sin which he was willing to groan under always. He then said, Pray, does your Ladyship live without sin? I told him No! But that there was such a state. He said none had ever yet done it he was sure that ever lived. But I made him own God was both able and willing and that before we died. It was absolutely necessary we should be[lieve?] in it, and in this only we differed. I never could have conceived by anything that had been wrote against the doctrine so strong a prejudice as his whole conversation was.

Yet despite this Selina was not untouched by Whitefield's biblical arguments and had to admit: 'I must say he talked very sensibly. His manner argueth a command of words and smoothly put together.'[1]

Throughout this letter the warm relationship she enjoyed with the older Wesley shines out:

I hope I shall soon hear from you . . . Do think of your Journals being published. From the bottom of my soul and in the most fervent spirit I commend you to our Lord who is able to build up and to carry you through the work he has given you to do: the perfecting all the saints now with you.

Concluding her account, Selina added that Whitefield had been 'much provoked by your brother calling them Priests of Moloch'. Conscious that Charles Wesley might not be happy that she had spoken at such length with Whitefield, she wrote, 'Your brother knows nothing of what passed at G[loucester]'.

With her journey home completed, the Countess flung herself with all her accustomed energy into the task of caring for the children and overseeing affairs on the estates. Day by day she would visit the needy homes of the villagers in the area. Not only were they poor and frequently ill, but Selina was also distressed by the total religious ignorance she discovered on every hand. Gradually

[1] *Ibid.*

a plan began to form in her mind. Perhaps she could bring 'the most extreme poor that are simple of heart' to the Hall on a regular basis, maybe twice a week, feed them, tend their illnesses and teach them from the Scriptures. Then a problem occurred to her. Was she, as a woman, stepping beyond her rightful place if she were to teach the Scriptures in this way? She turned to John Wesley for advice: 'May I explain the Scriptures? When they are fit [that is, sufficiently taught] I shall put them into bands.[1] Speak plainly. I feel no will.'[2]

Meanwhile Fanny Cowper's condition was deteriorating. For three months the Countess watched over the girl with ceaseless diligence but to no avail. Fanny grew only weaker. At last it became evident that she was dying and hasty letters were sent to her father warning him that her life was slipping away. But the nearer Fanny approached to the eternal state the stronger grew her faith and the brighter her joys. Writing to Charles Wesley shortly before Fanny died, Selina described the young woman: 'She sings, reads or prays all day and all night and says, Why should sleep waste her time?' When Charles sent a copy of some of his most recent hymns, she told him, 'Dear Miss Fanny, weak as she is, wanted a pen and ink to copy them out that she might have them by her. We talk of the approaching hour and I pray by her as one whom the Lord has summoned. O happy soul, who will soon be discharged!'[3]

But Fanny had one last request to make. She longed to see John Wesley before she died. Realizing that time was at a premium, the Countess sent an urgent message to the Foundery, pressing Wesley to come to Leicestershire with all haste: 'I beg you will set out as soon as may be after receiving this, as every day she has lived this last fortnight seems a fresh miracle.' Wesley was faced with a conflict of interests. One friend was urging him to come to

[1] Wesley divided his converts into 'bands' which met, men and women separately, for mutual encouragement.
[2] Rylands MS., Letter 107, 29 April 1742.     [3] *Ibid.*

Kent; Charles had written to say he was expected in Bristol. He himself had been toying with plans to visit Yorkshire. Selina's letter decided him and he good-naturedly set out for Leicester-shire without delay reaching Donington Hall on 22 May 1742 after a two-day journey. In his journal he reports:

> About five in the afternoon I reached Donington Park. Miss Cowper was just alive; but as soon as we came in her spirit greatly revived. For three days we rejoiced in the grace of God whereby she was filled with a hope full of immortality; with meekness, gentle-ness, patience, humble love, knowing in whom she had believed.[1]

From Donington Hall Wesley made his way north for his first visit to Newcastle. It is thought that this unexpected decision was reached while he was at Donington; certainly we know that it was Selina who had first suggested the need of the Newcastle miners and also that she commissioned another of her servants, John Taylor, to accompany him on his journey. Taylor, probably the brother of David Taylor, had also been converted while in her service and was to prove more compliant to her wishes. 'I love John Taylor. He is a sweet and humble spirit,' she commented to John Wesley.[2] Like David Taylor, he was to be much used in the work of exhorting and later of preaching.

Fanny Cowper, gratified to have seen Wesley, had not long to live. Selina had grown to love her as a daughter and when Fanny died two weeks later she felt it deeply. So close had the girl become to her older friend that she had asked to be buried in the Huntingdon family vault. Several long letters have survived in which the Countess describes the last days of Fanny's life and her burial. To Charles Wesley she wrote that as she knelt beside her, Fanny had whispered, 'Don't grieve, I am not now doing.' When

[1] Wesley, *Journal*, vol. 3, p. 11.
[2] Rylands MS., Letter 107.

the Countess asked her 'how she found her soul towards God', she had replied, 'O very happy.'[1]

The emotional toll on Selina was high. A depression of spirit seemed to settle on her after Fanny's death that expressed itself in a sense of worthlessness and failure. 'What will you say to my spiritual sufferings on this occasion?' she enquired rhetorically of Charles Wesley. Her assurance of her acceptance with God seemed to waver and she feared lest she 'should be of the number of those that come after the door was shut'.[2] Added to this, she was struggling with the implications of John Wesley's teaching on Christian perfection. Having embraced his ideas wholeheartedly she was finding them impossible to put into practice. Wesley had written to her suggesting that her problem might well be that she had an inadequate view of her own sinfulness.[3] Did he regard her innate awareness of her social status as arrogance? The pressure was leading her into despair. Replying to him she confessed: 'I long to leap into the flames to get rid of my sinful flesh and that every atom of those ashes might be separate, that neither time, place, nor person should say God's Spirit had ever been so clothed.'[4]

Perhaps, thought the Countess, it would be helpful to keep a journal with a regular record of all her thoughts, aspirations and even her failures. Encouraged, no doubt, by reading the journals kept by both the Wesley brothers, she decided that the best way for her to keep such a record would be to write all her material in the form of a regular letter to Charles Wesley. Several lengthy letters representing her attempts to keep such an account have

---

[1] *Ibid.* Fanny's sister, Anne, also died the following year, much to the Countess's grief and embarrassment. Writing to the girls' father, she said, 'I cannot see any symptom abated and humanly speaking she seems out of the reach of our means to bring back . . . May God almighty prepare you for this second great shock, and make us follow our Lord in our lives as she has done.'

[2] Rylands MS., Letter 97, no date.

[3] *Ibid.*, Letter 91.

[4] *Ibid.*, Letter 105, 9 January 1742.

been preserved. The first began shortly after Fanny's death:

> I have till this day since May 22 found no liberty of writing, and
> think if God permit to pursue this method of sending an account of
> each day to my friend, that once in a fortnight one of the journal
> letters may by this means reach him.

Obscure, introspective and difficult to decipher, these letters
must necessarily disappoint a biographer looking for information
on Selina's day-to-day activities. Nor did she intend to include
that sort of information. Rather they were to be a record of her
inward spiritual experiences:

> Wednesday June 3rd [I] had great weight upon my spirits all this
> day and the last night and found no power to speak to [my] com-
> pany this day which has oppressed me beyond all measure. O! my
> baseness and vileness that one day should pass without declaring
> the goodness of God . . . I think nothing shall ever make me hold
> my peace [again].

But the Countess of Huntingdon was essentially a woman of
drive and action and did not have the temperament to keep up the
discipline of such a correspondence for long. The whirl of events
soon made her letters less regular, until they stopped altogether.

Meanwhile the depression that Selina had experienced following Fanny's death was gradually lifting, until it was finally
dispelled by an incident that could easily have had serious consequences. To this Selina refers in a further paragraph of her
'journal': 'By a most severe overturn I was roused and found to
my shame and amazement that I was in the everlasting arms.' This
was an accident that occurred when the chaise in which she and
the Earl were travelling overturned. Early eighteenth century
roads were in a deplorable condition before the introduction of
turnpike trusts which led to some improvement. Many were
merely tracks linking one town to another. Drainage was non-
existent so that roads became impassable for wheeled traffic in

wet weather; surfaces were far from regular and holes were so
deep and treacherous that horses and passengers had been
known to drown in them. Both the Earl and Countess were hurt
in the accident as she later told her son Francis. But it was
Theophilus who appeared to be more seriously injured: 'I
thought his collar bone was broke or [he] indeed killed, for upon
the coach's falling he gave so loud a groan . . . I thought I should
have died at the fright it caused.'[1] The Earl's injuries were, however, less serious than had been at first thought, amounting to
little more than a severely bruised shoulder. Selina too was 'sore
from head to foot' and suffered from shock, but her concern for
her husband's condition made her scarcely aware of her own.
Roused from her depression in so abrupt a fashion, the Countess
resumed her normal occupations. Her children needed her.
Elizabeth was almost into her teenage years and must have also
been affected by Fanny's death. Henry was still little more than
two years old.

To this period belongs the anecdote of a seventy-year-old
woman who lived in one of the cottages on the estate. Having had
some previous conversation with her, the Countess visited her in
her home – little more than a hovel. To her surprise she found the
woman troubled about the future of her soul, fearing what might
happen should she die suddenly. The Countess spoke briefly to
her and offered to return and read to her from the Bible. At
Selina's next visit the woman appeared deeply agitated. To
Charles Wesley she wrote, 'Her agony of mind was so great that
she could not contain [herself] but cried out, "I possibly may die,
and what will become of my soul? O pray for me! O mercy,
mercy!" ' Speaking gently yet firmly the Countess pointed out the
total inadequacy of any good works to save the soul. But that was
not the woman's problem. 'It will not do,' she retorted, 'I am too
bad to be saved.' 'Well, now that you are quite lost, you will find

[1] 5 July 1742, Drew University, Madison, New Jersey.

him who came to seek and save just such as you are', was Selina's reply.

The next day, when the Countess went down to the hut she found the woman still under much anxiety; but that evening an urgent message came to Donington Hall to say that she was in despair and seemed to be dying. Satan's power appeared unleashed, and it took four people to control the desperate woman. Quite suddenly she became still, and lay for many hours wide awake and apparently in a state of calm joy. When the Countess visited her the next morning she cried out, 'O my Lady, my dear Lady, what great things the Lord has done for me! I have no doubt or fear ... I have such tastes of divine love as are not to be expressed.' Not many months of life were left for this woman but during the remainder of her days she gave every evidence of true conversion and when she was dying was able to say, 'The fear of death is gone – O! the name of Jesus, how sweet it is!' This episode must have brought timely encouragement to the Countess.

In August 1742 came the death of John and Charles Wesley's mother, Susanna. The Countess had come to appreciate this grand character whom she had met at the Foundery, where Susanna Wesley was living during the final two years of her life. The Countess had even sent Susanna a gift of Madeira wine on one occasion. Now to John Wesley she wrote kindly: 'The Lord has I believe removed from you one you much loved but I have the pleasure to believe 'twas because he loved her better that he has taken her from you that he "might deliver her from the evil to come".'[1]

For John Wesley himself, the year had seen the opening up of the northern base of Methodism in Newcastle. He wrote to the Mayor of Newcastle, in response to a letter accusing him of raising a tumult in a certain area of the town:

[1] Rylands MS., Letter 117, 4 August 1742.

When I was first pressed by the Countess of Huntingdon to go and preach to the colliers in and near Newcastle, that objection immediately occurred, 'Have they no churches and ministers already?' It was answered [by the Countess], 'They have churches, but they never go to them! And ministers, but they seldom or never hear them! Perhaps they may hear you. And what if you save (under God) but one soul?' I yielded. I took up my cross and came. I preached Jesus, the Saviour of sinners. Many sinners of all sorts came and heard. Many were (and are) saved from their sins. The drunkards are sober, the common swearers fear God, the Sabbath breakers now keep that day holy. These facts are undeniable.[1]

This movement of the Spirit of God was steadily gaining momentum. Although the part played by the Countess was still minor, nor was she seen by others in any leadership role at this time, her dedication and zeal was having an increasing influence, particularly upon the Wesley brothers.

[1] Wesley, *Letters*, vol. 2, p. 14.

# 7

# FAMILY SORROWS –
# CHRISTIAN FRIENDSHIPS

ILL-HEALTH DOGGED THE COUNTESS OF HUNTINGDON throughout much of her adult life in spite of the best medical treatment available, or even possibly because of it. 'I have been so much out of order today', is a comment picked at random from a letter to her husband written at this time, typical of many such expressions. During the early months of 1743, and much against her inclinations, she was obliged to go to Bristol once more where the waters of the Hot Wells had helped her in the past. Here she would be under the watchful eye of Dr Cheyne from nearby Bath. On this occasion she took her three younger children, Elizabeth, Selina and Henry, with her. Always a private person, the Countess rarely mentioned any specific symptoms relating to her illness, but by reading through her letters in which she describes her various fluctuations of health and mood, and the medical advice she received, it has been possible to build up some general picture of her condition and its cause.[1]

Although her earlier problems were undoubtedly linked with the birth of the seven children in quick succession, Dr Cheyne was at a loss to diagnose her continued ill-health. He assured her

For his Oxford B. Litt. Thesis, 'Selina Countess of Huntingdon', Matthew Francis asked his medically qualified brother, Huw W. S. Francis, to read through all the relevant correspondence on this matter. His medical conclusion was that her condition was 'a colic from excessive purgation or congestive dysmenorrhea' (p. 41).

that she had 'no stone, gravel or hurt bowel, nothing but a sharp scorbutic habit and weak nerves'.[1] The 'scorbutic habit' – evidently a condition brought on through lack of sufficient vitamins, comes as no surprise considering her doctor's rigorous regime of vomitings, purgations and a milk diet, but he may well have touched the heart of her problem when he referred to her 'weak nerves'. Given a personality as dynamic, intense and sensitive as Selina's, problems arising from stress and exhaustion may well account for some of her physical symptoms.

During 1743 the Countess was rapidly losing faith in the competence of Dr Cheyne to help her. Writing pointedly to the Earl in May she comments, 'Though Cheyne seems so sanguine I own to you I cannot be so, and I fear but so much of it is in order to keep me to himself, though I know he has a high esteem for me, yet I do not find he knows what to do for me.'[2] Nor was she so sure that taking the waters was of medicinal value, a conclusion that flew in the face of all current medical theory. Clearly Selina was longing to be at home with Theophilus once more and so concludes this letter, 'Therefore, my angel, if you love me, do not press my stay here.'

While the Countess was still recovering at Bristol a sorrow struck the family. On 18 April Robert Hemington, the master in charge of the three Hastings boys at Westminster School in London, wrote to the Earl, who was living at Enfield Chase, expressing his concern about ten-year-old Ferdinando:

> Mr Ferdy is very ill and Dr Burton is of the opinion it will prove the smallpox. He complained a little on Saturday; on Sunday he was very restless and had a fever and great pains all over his body. I shall be careful not to write to my Lady for fear of giving her a surprise in her weak condition.[3]

[1] Francis, p. 57, cited from C. F. Mullett, *Letters of Dr Cheyne to the Countess of Huntingdon* (Huntington Library, California), 1940, p. xvii.
[2] LRO.        [3] *Ibid.*

Letters in quick succession told of the child's deterioration. By Monday 'his fever was violently high and he light-headed all night'. The delirium had become worse by Tuesday, and though they bled the little boy two or three times in the custom of the day, nothing availed to check the virulence of the disease. And on Wednesday 21 April 1743, before his mother had even been told that he was ill, Ferdinando had died of smallpox.

Selina grieved deeply at the loss of her boy. Writing to Charles Wesley a few days after he had been buried in Westminster Abbey, we can sense her struggle:

> Nature says often O! My son, my son! Very pleasant hast thou been, but all the happiness that yet remains in the other five [her remaining children] I have freely offered rather than one single thought should arise in my heart in the course of this trial contrary to the will of God, and I have yet confidence that in this selfsame thing that so I shall be kept.[1]

But the thing that distressed her most of all was that Ferdy had been alone when he died, and had to endure his sickness without the comfort of his mother's presence. Night after night she dreamt about it and as she told her husband:

> Poor Ferdy has been the subject of my dreams many nights – this last particularly for no creature was ever so unhappy about another having to go through his whole sickness and death [alone]. It has made such an impression on me that in the midst of the most remote thoughts it jumps in and damps my spirit.[2]

To add to her trials each of her three children with her in Bristol was also ill. Apprehensively she wrote to Theophilus about three-year-old Henry, 'I am every moment expecting an appearance of the smallpox'; and of Selina who was now six years of age, 'my dear little girl grows worse and worse'. Yet in the midst of her fears her faith triumphed:

[1] Rylands MS., Letter 9.      [2] 31 May 1743, LRO.

Nothing is too hard for the love and mercy of God and therefore I will hope that he will (as he easily can) raise them up again ... [But] sure I am that all is wise and best that happens. I trust in his power to keep my heart from rebelling against him. And let us, my dear, dear soul, submit all to the divine will. He knows what is best.[1]

In the event, Henry did not have smallpox and both the girls recovered strength. By the end of May, Selina was well enough to travel to join the Earl and the two older boys at Enfield Chase. 'I think, if I know my own heart, it will be the last time while I live I shall be from you a night', she told Theophilus. More than this she had decided to terminate her connection with Dr Cheyne. 'I don't find he thinks of anything but vomits,' she complained, 'and these wear me to death.' Instead she planned to put herself under a doctor in Holland, Dr Borhave, whose reputation suggested that he might be more able to help her.

Hard as these days were for the Countess of Huntingdon there were consolations too. On 26 August 1743, while she was still staying at Enfield Chase, she was introduced to Howell Harris. Although he had visited London on four previous occasions, Harris had not met the Countess before that summer. 'On hearing I am to go and see a Lady', he wrote in his journal for 25 August, 'I was inflamed with praise to God'. The son of a carpenter from Carmarthenshire, Harris's family background would normally have precluded him from ever mingling with the social rank to which the Countess belonged.

Converted in the spring of 1735, Harris's zeal for the salvation of his fellow men and particularly for his own Welsh countrymen burdened him continually. Never a day passed but he would preach wherever and whenever he could gain a hearing. Even Whitefield longed to 'catch some of his fire'. Travelling up and down the Principality, Harris formed his converts into small societies as Wesley, Ingham and others were to do and depended solely on the generosity of these new believers for his support.

[1] *Ibid.*

Often abused physically by the rabble and sometimes even in danger of his life, Harris held on his course.

The warm relationships he had established with both the Wesley brothers and George Whitefield, together with his desire for unity between them, brought him to London whenever opportunity arose. So now he was to meet the Countess of Huntingdon for the first time. In his journal for 26 August he records: 'To ... a Lady of quality together with Charles Wesley.'[1] After coming away he was 'exceeding ill' and adds that he slept until 5 o'clock. Perhaps in his nervousness at meeting 'a Lady of quality' he had little guessed that Selina herself was in much need of spiritual consolation. However, the next time he visited her, some ten days later, he was more relaxed. He met her younger children and enjoyed 'heavenly conversation' with her. Before Harris left, Selina, undoubtedly impressed by the dedicated Welshman, gave him £5 – a considerable sum.[2]

At this time the Earl of Huntingdon felt the need of another base in London in addition to his Downing Street house. He may well have been motivated by the prospect of a quiet home, yet still close to Westminster where his sons were at school. A mansion named Chelsea Farm, in the peaceful village of Chelsea on the banks of the Thames two miles from London, was purchased on lease from Sir Hans Loane. Called 'the village of palaces', Chelsea's situation would enable the family to travel into London by boat. Much alteration work was needed to turn the house into a suitable family home, however, and Theophilus, now in his late forties, had not been in the best of health. As usual the burden of the oversight of the work fell on Selina.

The year 1743 was not to close before the Earl and Countess faced another bereavement. Their second son, George, not quite fourteen years of age, also died of smallpox on 20 December. But

---

[1] *Howell Harris, Reformer and Soldier*, transcribed and edited by the Rev. Tom Beynon (Caernarvon: The Calvinist Methodist Bookroom, 1958), p. 50.
[2] *Ibid.*, p. 51.

there was a sweetness in that bitter cup which must have brought strong consolation to Selina in this further loss. George had given evidence of a true saving faith. 'The children of so many prayers and tears, I doubt not, shall one day be blessed', the Countess was to write to a friend in 1747. Certainly she had prayed earnestly for the salvation of her children, and in George she saw an answer to her prayers to a marked degree. To Howell Harris, who had arrived back in London on 15 January 1744, we owe the description of the boy's last days, told him by George Whitefield and recorded in his journal for 17 January: 'At Bro. Whitefield's heard of the amazing liberty a son of Lady Huntingdon had in dying, continuing in prayer three days, and died in full assurance.'[1] George was buried in the same grave as Ferdinando in Westminster Abbey. Though troubled and often bewildered, Selina's faith nevertheless stood the test, and writing to Charles Wesley in the midst of her afflictions she was able to say, 'The cloud would be so dark did I not see my Lord in it; this "must needs be" heaviness may endure for a night but "joy cometh in the morning".'[2]

Fears for the other children and especially Francis,[3] the family heir and a boy of high intelligence and natural charm, drove Theophilus and Selina to take the unusual and controversial step of having their remaining children vaccinated against smallpox. Vaccination, only recently introduced into the country, was still accompanied by considerable risks, and the subject of some

---

[1] *Howell Harris's Visits to London,* transcribed and edited by the Rev. Tom Beynon (Aberystwyth: The Cambrian Press, 1960), p. 41 (hereafter *Harris Visits London*). In Dr Boyd Schlenther's recent biography of the Countess, *Queen of the Methodists* (Durham: Durham Academic Press, 1997) he claims, 'Not one of her own was to accept her evangelicalism', p. 56 – a statement clearly incorrect in the light of this evidence.

[2] Rylands MS., Letter 80.

[3] There is some evidence to suggest that Francis may actually have caught the disease, but recovered. One of Lady Catherine Wheler's sons, cousin of the Hastings boys and attending Westminster School, also died of the infection.

disagreement.[1] Described as 'an operation' in contemporary correspondence, the inoculation of the Hastings children aroused letters of protest from the family, with Lady Frances, the Earl's sister, in particular narrating scare stories of others who had been vaccinated and had then gone mad.

Throughout these years the Countess of Huntingdon, still a young Christian, relied much on her friendship with John and Charles Wesley for direction and encouragement. With Charles she felt a marked empathy of spirit, and as we have seen, this enabled her to share with him the deepest desires of her heart after God. Ever conscious of the spiritual debt she owed to the Wesley brothers, she could declare in a letter to Charles in June 1743, 'I know I owe you all', and add, 'my labours are ... wholly with a view to you and your brother's comfort and advantage.'

With John Wesley, however, she was more guarded than with his brother. Their respect for one another was mutual; to Selina he had submitted his journals for her opinion and she had urged him to proceed with publication.[2] Her support for him was unquestionable. Yet his more brusque approach left her less at ease. Born into a stratum of society that accepted and expected deference as the norm, the Countess had met in the elder Wesley one who found it hard to bow to anyone, high or low, and who

[1] Practised in Turkey since 1713, vaccination for smallpox was introduced into England by Lady Mary Wortley Montagu in 1721. Not until 1746 did the practice become widespread. It was however the subject of considerable misgivings especially among Christians. Jonathan Edwards, the renowned American preacher, died as a result of the smallpox vaccination in 1758, fifteen years after this date. Even as late as 1768 a hospital in Peterborough used for vaccination was burnt down by mob protesters. In some instances epidemics of the disease had actually started after inoculations had gone wrong.

[2] 'I think there is not one thing in the Journal that ought to be omitted. The manner in which you speak of yourself cannot be mended ... The printing in two parts that the history of *Stillness* may be gathered together will be well judged.' In this same letter she ordered a supply of the Wesleys' latest hymn books. Letter to John Wesley, 9 January 1742, Rylands MS. Letter 109, also cited in part by Seymour, *Countess*, vol. 1, p. 46. See also above p. 74, where the Countess urges John Wesley to publish his *Journals*.

had little patience with the social niceties of his day. A custom prevailed which he resented: whenever the Countess was in town a seat was reserved for her in the chapel until the point in the service when the Creed was recited. If she had not arrived by then someone else could fill it. John Wesley disliked the practice: 'I doubt whether this respect to her be too great, but I yield in this point to my brother's judgment.'[1]

In June 1744 the first of the Methodist Conferences, soon to become a regular feature of Wesley's work, took place. Although the Conference sessions were held at the Foundery, the Earl and Countess entertained the six clergymen and four or five laymen who attended in their home, probably at 11 Downing Street. Even though the Earl appears not to have had the same degree of understanding of the gospel as his wife, there is no evidence that at any time he prevented her from taking as full a part in the endeavours of the early Methodists as her health and family commitments would allow. He too would have shared in the obloquy meted out by others of the social rank to which they belonged.

The circle of Christian friends surrounding the Countess was now steadily enlarging. Dr Philip Doddridge, large-hearted pastor of Castle Hill Independent Church in Northampton and tutor of the Dissenting Academy associated with his name, was introduced to her in 1743. Doddridge's attitude to the youthful Whitefield had initially been ambivalent, but gradually his suspicions were allayed, particularly after he met Whitefield in person in May 1739.[2] When Doddridge ventured to take part in a service in Whitefield's Moorfield's Tabernacle on 28 July 1743, a time when the Countess was also in London, a storm of protest broke out from his friends, and not least from Dr Isaac Watts. Watts wrote to his younger friend suggesting that by preaching or praying at the Tabernacle he was 'sinking the character of a minister

---

[1] 22 August 1744, Wesley, Letters, vol.2, p.24.
[2] Whitefield, *Journals*, p. 73.

SELINA COUNTESS OF HUNTINGDON

and especially of a tutor among the Dissenters so low thereby.'[1] Undeterred, Doddridge went so far as to ask Whitefield to preach in his own Northampton pulpit in October of that same year.

A regular correspondence sprang up between the Countess and Doddridge, and he was always a welcome visitor at her London home and later would visit her in Leicestershire. None could meet Philip Doddridge without soon learning to appreciate his soldier friend, Colonel James Gardiner. Upright and manly both in deportment and Christian character, Gardiner had risen to prominence in the armed services. But Gardiner was a man under debt – a debt to the unexpected mercy of God in rescuing him from his sordid lifestyle to live for the glory of God. As a military man he knew his time could be short and he bent all his energies towards compensating for earlier wasted years. The Countess held the Colonel in highest regard:

> I cannot express how much I esteem that most excellent man, Colonel Gardiner. What love and mercy has God shown in snatching him as a brand from the burning! He is truly alive to God, and pleads nothing but the plea of the publican, 'God be merciful to me a sinner', What a monument of his mercy, grace and love![2]

A warm friendship had also begun between the Countess and Gardiner's wife, Lady Frances Gardiner, daughter of the 9th Earl of Buchan.

Another whose acquaintance the Countess enjoyed during the 1740s was the elderly Isaac Watts himself. She may well have met him earlier, but certainly did so in 1744. Diminutive in stature but a spiritual giant, Watts was the leading Independent of the day, whose reputation as a pastor, hymn writer and educationalist was

[1] *The Correspondence of Philip Doddridge,* ed. G. F. Nuttall (Northants Record Society, 1979), vol. 29, p. 185.

[2] Seymour, *Countess,* vol. 1, p. 60. For a life of Colonel Gardiner see 'Remarkable Passages in the Life of Colonel James Gardiner', *Doddridge's Miscellaneous Works* (London, 1839); also my *Sound of Trumpets* (Edinburgh: Banner of Truth, 1999), pp. 2–17.

second to none. Seventy years of age and frail, he had lived for many years with Sir Thomas and Lady Abney, first at their home near Cheshunt in Hertfordshire, and, following Sir Thomas's death, at Abney Park in Stoke Newington, five miles south of Enfield Chase.

'Your Ladyship is come to see me on a very remarkable day,' commented Watts as the Countess entered his study at Abney Park on one occasion.

'Why is this day so remarkable?' enquired Lady Huntingdon.

'This day thirty years [ago]', replied the poet, 'I came hither to the house of my good friend, Sir Thomas Abney, intending to spend but one single week under his friendly roof, and I have extended my visit to the length of exactly thirty years.'

Curtseying with all the dignity she could muster in her widely hooped dress, Lady Abney interjected, 'Sir, what you term a long thirty-years' visit, I consider as the shortest visit my family ever received.'[1]

It may well be that it was the Countess of Huntingdon who softened the attitude of Isaac Watts towards Whitefield, for her own respect for the ardent evangelist was steadily growing. When she was visiting Abney Park on another occasion, the discussion had turned again to the remarkable progress of the gospel under the Methodist preachers. The Countess referred to Whitefield's preaching. Drawing her aside, Watts said, 'Such, my lady, are the fruits that will ever follow the faithful proclamation of divine mercy; the Lord our God will crown his message with success, and give it an abundant entrance into the hearts of men.' Knowing his own labours and service for God were now complete, he took her hand and with obvious affection pronounced an earnest benediction on her as they parted. Then he added, 'I bless God that I can lie down to sleep in comfort, no way solicitous whether I wake in this world or another.'[2]

[1] *Works of Augustus Toplady*, p. 488.
[2] Seymour, *Countess*, vol. 1, p. 200.

Through her continuing friendship with Howell Harris the Countess was drawn to visit the Moorfields Tabernacle more often to hear Whitefield preach before he sailed again for Georgia in the summer of 1744. Now she began to invite some of her aristocratic friends to accompany her to listen to him elsewhere. And it is in this period that we must place the two letters she received from the celebrated Sarah Churchill, Duchess of Marlborough, who died in October 1744. The Duchess wrote:

> I must accept your very obliging invitation to accompany you to hear Mr Whitefield . . . Your concern for my improvement in religious knowledge is very obliging, and I do hope I shall be the better for all your excellent advice. God knows we all need mending and none more than myself. I have lived to see great changes in the world – have acted a conspicuous part – and now hope, in my old days to obtain mercy from God, as I never expect any at the hands of my fellow creatures. The Duchess of Ancaster, Lady Townshend and Lady Cobham were exceeding pleased with many observations in Mr Whitefield's sermon at St. Sepulchre's Church, which has made me lament ever since that I did not hear it as it might have been the means of doing me some good – for good, alas! I DO WANT . . . You are all goodness and kindness, and I often wish I had a portion of it. Women of wit, beauty and quality cannot hear too many humiliating truths – they shock our pride. But we must die; we must converse with earth and worms.[1]

Disillusioned with life and far from well, the Duchess was disappointed when she was unable to accompany Selina to hear the preacher, but was pleased to receive her letters and visits.

Gradually the Countess was shifting her doctrinal position and beginning to embrace the Calvinism of her new friends rather than the emphases she had learnt from the Wesley brothers. In a letter to Charles in June 1743 she could still express reservations

---

[1] *Ibid.*, vol. 1, p. 25. See Appendix 2 for comment on the authenticity of this correspondence.

about the doctrine of predestination; and in this letter her continuing acceptance of Wesley's doctrine of perfectionism is evident, despite her troubled conscience when she seemed unable to attain to the 'triumphant love' of which her friends spoke. By 1744, however, Selina was increasingly drawing benefit from Harris's conversation and ministry, and for a few years her correspondence with the Wesleys appears to have declined sharply.[1] When Harris wrote to Whitefield in March 1744, he spoke of a further meeting with the Countess:

> Thursday night I had the favour of about four hours conversation with my Lady H. but where to begin to relate the mercies . . . and benefits I had there, I can't tell. One so highly favoured and so fitted for that great work and place that I believe the Holy Spirit has called her, I can't tell – She most heartily desired to see you. Her heart I believe is very right with God and one more delivered from her own will and wisdom I have hardly seen. What the Lord is doing among the great, I suppose you have had from her own mouth ere this.[2]

From this letter it is evident both that the Countess was now in regular contact with Whitefield and also that Harris at least had perceived in her one 'fitted for [a] great work and place' in God's purposes – probably the first to recognize this.

Although friendships with men like Doddridge, Watts and Harris were important contributory factors to the shift that was taking place at this time in the Countess's doctrinal position, there was also a deeper reason. As we have seen from her correspondence with Charles Wesley, Selina often lacked assurance of her acceptance with God. 'O the distress of my soul! Who, who can paint it!' was her despairing comment in June 1742. Sometimes she feared lest she 'should be of the number of those that come after the door

---

[1] It is possible that letters from these years have not survived. The correspondence with Charles Wesley is renewed after 1749.

[2] *Selected Trevecca Letters*, 1742–47, p. 135.

was shut.'[1] Now she began to see that by starting with God and his saving purposes for his people, she could find peace of heart and assurance of his power to keep her to the end.

Even though Whitefield had returned to America in the summer of 1744, Selina increasingly attended Moorfields Tabernacle whenever she was in London. Still a large wooden structure intended as a temporary home for Whitefield's congregation, the Tabernacle was situated only a quarter of a mile from Wesley's Foundery. She would, therefore, have had no difficulty in attending services at both places. Writing to Howell Harris towards the close of 1746, Whitefield expressed his appreciation for the beneficial effect of Harris's ministry at the Tabernacle and then added:

> The good Countess of Huntingdon has been there frequently, and has been much pleased, I am told. She shines brighter and brighter every day ... My poor prayers will be daily offered up to the God of all grace to keep her steadfast in the faith and to make her a burning and a shining light.[2]

Throughout this period Selina was necessarily preoccupied with the needs of her family. In 1745 Henry was five, while the girls were seven and fourteen respectively.[3] Francis, judging by his letters to his parents and the width of his interests, was an intelligent youth of considerable talent and charisma. Soon to leave Westminster School and start his studies at Christchurch College in Oxford, the young man was beginning to attract attention among the nobility.

But when Lord Chesterfield began paying his respects to the boy his mother seemed unaware of any potential danger. Her continuing contact with such a man suggests that Selina did not immediately change all the attitudes and values of her earlier years

[1] Rylands MS., Letter 97, no date.
[2] Luke Tyerman, *The Life of George Whitefield* (London: Hodder and Stoughton, 1877), vol. 2, p. 168.
[3] The portrait hanging in the library at Westminster College, Cambridge, painted by Soldi, can be dated at this period.

as a society woman. She had at this time been a Christian little more than four years, and was not immune from the temptations which adulation and flattery can present. So when the Earl of Chesterfield praised the virtues of her son, she seemed blind to his flattery. Writing to her husband she presented a glowing account of Chesterfield's visit. He had called Francis 'a most charming boy', she reported, and added, 'Lord Chesterfield was with me a great while yesterday morning and he did say so much about him that I really believe was never said of any boy before.' Chesterfield, whose lack of moral integrity was becoming increasingly evident at the time, was no true friend to Francis Hastings and his influence on the impressionable youth far from helpful.

The Earl and Countess now divided their time mainly between London and Leicestershire, a lifestyle dictated by both the social customs of eighteenth century nobility and by the need to keep a check on the various properties they rented or owned. From time to time they also travelled to Yorkshire, mainly in the summer months due to the state of the roads in winter. Although checking on the condition of Ledston Hall was the primary purpose of these visits, there were also pleasures awaiting them when they arrived in Yorkshire. With the misunderstandings between Benjamin and Lady Margaret Ingham and themselves largely healed, such a reunion would doubtless bring Selina pleasure, and particularly after the birth, early in 1745, of Ignatius, Lady Margaret's first and only child.

A further joy during visits to Yorkshire was the growing friendship between the Earl and his wife and William Grimshaw, the curate in charge of Haworth – a village high in the Pennines some twenty-five miles west of Ledston Hall. When Ingham first introduced them, an immediate rapport had sprung up between the rugged and unconventional curate and Selina. Grimshaw's own remarkable conversion and his passion for the salvation of the lost made him an instant favourite. To hear of the surprising work of God in Haworth that had its beginnings in 1742 and had now become a floodtide of blessing, would have gladdened the Countess. Now, whenever she was in the area, Grimshaw would ride across and, together with others, would join in days of preaching and fellowship in various locations.

All these things were taking place against the background of the 1745 Jacobite invasion when Charles Edward Stuart, youthful son of the Old Pretender, swept down from Moidart on the west coast of Scotland with his following of four thousand Highlanders. Colonel James Gardiner, friend of Philip Doddridge, died of wounds inflicted in the first major battle of the invasion, fought at Prestonpans, ten miles from Edinburgh. In view of the high regard she had expressed for Gardiner, the Countess must have felt his loss keenly, and particularly in such circumstances.

Heartened by their easy victory at Prestonpans, the Young Pretender's forces marched ever further south. By December 1745 they were on the outskirts of Derby, not ten miles from Donington Hall. There is evidence from the correspondence of the times that the Earl was following these events with an almost obsessive concern. But Derby marked the limit of the Jacobite advance. With none of the hoped-for English support, and the might of the government army gathering for battle, Charles Stuart's generals refused to advance further and on 6 December the Second Jacobite Rebellion was effectively over, as his troops retreated northward again.

With the country still fearful and nervous, accusations of disloyalty and incriminations of supposed Jacobites were frequent. The Methodists were prime targets for suspicion. Their society meetings, only for those of credible Christian profession, laid them open to charges of plotting against the king and of secret Jacobite sympathies. The arrest of the stalwart Yorkshire preacher, John Nelson, press-ganged into the army as an 'idle good-for-nothing', arose from such suspicions. He was only set at liberty because of the personal intervention of the Countess.

Even the Earl and Countess of Huntingdon were not exempt
from suspicion, particularly because of their known support for
the Methodist cause. In November 1745 the Countess wrote to
the Secretary of State, Lord Carteret, declaring her loyalty and
reiterating her plea for justice for the Methodists as victims of
such renewed persecution. Carteret's reply included a double
assurance: first, that the king would not permit any of his subjects
to be harassed on religious grounds and also that he was fully
conscious of the loyalty of the Earl and his wife to the House of
Hanover.

Theophilus himself was not well during 1745 and 1746, and a
number of references in the correspondence of the times suggest
increasing concern for his health. Chelsea Farm was not yet ready
for family occupation and, in view of her husband's health, Selina
pressed on with the necessary alterations. The Earl himself
appears to have been reluctant to take medical advice: perhaps
Selina's experiences had undermined his confidence in the prac-
titioners of the day. A number of letters began to arrive at his
Donington home each begging Theophilus to listen to his
doctors. One letter, written to Selina in June 1746 by a Magdalen
Walmesly, is typical of others expressing the concern of their
friends:

> Whenever Mr Walmesly speaks of his dear old friend, my Lord
> Huntingdon, it is with pain and concern, and a great distrust that
> he cannot hold out long. He would come to Donington Park on his
> hands and knees could he prevail with my Lord to set in, in earnest
> for the recovery of his health. But that he almost despairs of.[1]

In the midst of her anxiety over Theophilus, Selina was taken ill
herself with a fever that left her 'so weak I can hardly hold a pen'.

As the summer of 1746 wore on, the Earl's condition,
described as a 'dropsical disorder',[2] did not improve. At last he
yielded to pressure from his wife and friends to seek medical help

[1] LRO.     [2] A former description of the effects of heart trouble.

and in the autumn travelled to London for that purpose. But before he left Donington Hall he had a strange dream which he recounted to the Countess in the morning:

> He dreamed that death in the appearance of a skeleton, stood at the bed's foot; and after standing a while, untucked the bedclothes at the bottom, and crept up to the top of the bed (under the clothes) and lay between him and his lady.[1]

Naturally, Selina attempted to make light of such a premonition, but it left a deep impression on her mind. A few days later Theophilus set out for London. Perhaps mindful of his dream, Selina could not shake off her fears, though there is no evidence to suggest that she had any reason to think him seriously ill. Her anxiety and affection is evident in a letter she wrote on 4 October soon after he had left:

> I shall long to have some account of how my dear jewel is after his journey, for I think should not your leg[2] be worse by it, I am sure otherwise your health will be better for it. I hope you will, my dear creature, if you should find yourself the least ill, will allow it not to be concealed from me, for nothing could in this world make me so thoroughly unhappy . . . Could my dear creature see the agonies of mind that at times I suffer on account both of your mortal and immortal part . . . it would give you most sensible pain. My dear soul will not think this is in the way of any reproof, but the fruit of my present tears that spring from the most ardent love.[3]

It was to be the last letter Selina wrote to him. On 13 October, only a fortnight after his dream, Theophilus died alone in his home in Downing Street of 'a fit of apoplexy' or, in modern terminology, a stroke.

[1] The Countess told Augustus Toplady about this dream some thirty years later, and he recorded it in his *Anecdotes, Incidents and Historic Passages*, adding that it was 'told me by the Countess at Romford, Essex,' April 12, 1776. *Works*, p. 510.

[2] Swelling of the ankles and legs would have been a symptom of the Earl's illness, a condition often terminating in a stroke.

[3] 4 October 1746, Drew University, Huntingdon Papers.

This was a grief Selina carried with her until the end of her long life. Never could she speak of him without deep and obvious emotion. On 23 October 1746 Theophilus was buried in St Helen's Church in Ashby-de-la-Zouch, and over his grave Selina erected a marble bust of herself mourning her loss. A lengthy epitaph, composed by Lord Bolingbroke, but clearly expressing her sentiments, spoke of the Earl as 'good in every relation of natural and social duty'. Of their love for each other, it claimed they had known:

> the uninterrupted joys of conjugal love, the never failing comforts of cordial friendship. Every care was softened, every satisfaction heightened, every hour passed smoothly away, in the company of one who enjoyed a perpetual serenity of soul, that none but those can feel in this life, who are prepared for greater bliss in the next.

The Earl's spiritual state when he died must remain an open question. The anxiety expressed in that last letter that the Countess wrote to her husband suggests that she herself was troubled about it. The usual words quoted to prove that he was not a converted man are taken from a letter written by John Wesley to a Mary Bishop on 7 February 1778. In this letter Wesley attributes to 'Lord Huntingdon' the words, 'The scriptural scheme of morality is what everyone must admire; but the doctrine of atonement I cannot comprehend.' The Earl had died more than thirty years before the date of that letter and John Telford, editor of Wesley's letters, attributes this comment to Francis Hastings (generally referred to as 'Lord Huntingdon'), rather than to his father. Francis was well-known by that time for his unbelieving lifestyle.[1]

A letter of condolence written to Selina a month after the death of her husband lends credence to the possibility that the Earl may

---

[1] Wesley, *Letters*, vol. 6, p. 298. Unfortunately Seymour, who was also quoting from Wesley, introduced these words into his narrative, stating that they expressed the views of Selina's husband. Hence the wrong tradition mentioned above began. Seymour, *Countess*, vol. 1, p. 50.

indeed have been a believing man. Sir John Thorold, who attended the Earl's funeral and had himself been recently bereaved, wrote:

My fellow-sharer in the cup of sorrow – the words of the great apostle, 'Thanks be unto God who giveth us the victory through our Lord Jesus Christ!' will help to soothe your sorrows. I sympathize with you, but sorrow not as one without hope. There is hope concerning our dear friend: I believe it is well with him.'[1]

The Earl had died intestate, leaving the responsibility for his four children (all still minors) and his vast estates, with the many complications involved in their supervision, solely to his wife. For the moment, however, time seemed to stand still for Selina as she wrestled to come to terms with her loss. Only thirty-nine years of age, frequently unwell herself, and despite her competence, dependent on her husband's affection and presence, she scarcely knew how to face the future. For the next few months she remained in seclusion. In a letter to her friend, Lady Hertford, the original of which is now lost, she suggests that much of that time, especially in those early weeks of her bereavement, was spent in 'a little retreat' close by the Earl's grave.

The death of the Earl marked a watershed in the life of the Countess. Though she may well have felt that her days of usefulness were gone for ever, in reality she stood at the beginning of that outstanding work to which God had called her. Perhaps in those months, hidden from the public gaze, she began to learn those truths which the poet William Cowper would later express in unforgettable words:

Blind unbelief is sure to err,
And scan his work in vain.
God is his own interpreter,
And he will make it plain.

[1] Sir John Thorold was a member of the early Fetter Lane Society, a friend and supporter of both Wesley and Whitefield. Seymour, *Countess*, vol. 1, p. 77.

# 8

# 'I DREAD SLACK HANDS
# IN THE VINEYARD'

'I DREAD SLACK HANDS in the vineyard; we must all up and be doing', wrote the Countess of Huntingdon to Philip Doddridge on 23 February 1747. Exactly four months had elapsed since that October day when Selina had stood beside the grave of her husband. Perhaps her loss had made her wish to withdraw entirely from public life and live out her days caring only for her family and the necessary affairs relating to her husband's estates. But militating against such an inclination, as she told Doddridge in further letters, was her concern for the needs of her generation and a sense she had of the spiritual significance of the days:

> O! How do I lament the weakness of my hands, the feebleness of my knees and coolness of my heart! I want [my heart] on fire always, not for self-delight, but to spread the gospel from pole to pole . . . Some important time is coming! O might I hope it is that time when all things shall be swallowed up by the enlightening and comforting displays of our glorious Redeemer's kingdom.[1]

Eminently practical as always, the Countess was already looking for ways in which she might promote such a work. So now she asked Doddridge to look for a promising young man whom she could finance at his Dissenting Academy in Northampton. Strong though her adherence to the Church of England was, such an offer is one of the many indications of a catholicity of outlook which came with her conversion.

[1] Seymour, *Countess*, vol. 1, p. 79.

Her bereavement, however, was still taking its heavy toll both emotionally and physically. Lady Mary Kilmorey, Selina's sister, and even her own children, young as they were, were troubled to see her 'so weak and ill', as she explained to Doddridge. She therefore yielded to their pressure and agreed to accept medical advice from Dr James Stonehouse of Northampton, a close friend of Doddridge's.

For the time being she continued to live at Donington Hall, but the house and grounds had become the legal property of seventeen-year-old Francis, now studying at Oxford. She planned, therefore, to move across to Ashby Place, built in the shadow of the ruined Ashby Castle, where her sisters-in-law, Frances and Anne had been living since the death of Lady Betty in 1739. Alterations were needed to make it suitable for the family and arrangements for these fell to the Countess. In addition she still had matters that needed attention in connection with her London home at Chelsea Farm.

Six months after the Earl's death the Countess ventured back to the metropolis once more. Here she hoped to renew friendships and perhaps discover God's purposes for her life, now so suddenly and unexpectedly altered. Howell Harris had also come to London from his Trevecca home only three weeks earlier and lost no time in calling on Selina at Chelsea Farm. On 9 April 1747 he records in his diary that he had been among the crowds who witnessed the execution of Lord Lovat, a leading member of the Scottish nobility who had played a prominent part in the recent Jacobite uprising. Sickened by the brutality and insensitivity of the spectators, Harris hurried on to Chelsea. There he found a gathering far different and enjoyed 'free and sweet conversation' with the Countess and her friends for two hours. After he had preached to all present, further conversation followed lasting until ten at night. A sense of the presence of God marked the day: 'We all agree in everything and a flame of love was among us,' he reported.

Sometime during that evening Selina called the Welshman apart to speak with him privately. They discussed various subjects until at last she posed the question weighing on her mind – what should be her role in the future now that her husband had died? Harris added to his diary account for that day:

> She consulted me about which was it best, to live retired and give up all, or fill her place, and I said the latter I thought was right whilst she felt she was able to be faithful and felt the Lord with her.[1]

To 'fill her place' – a place at once unique and packed with potential in the purposes of God that were being worked out in those early days of the evangelical revival – this undoubtedly became the Countess of Huntingdon's *raison d'être* for the rest of her life.

During the weeks that followed the Countess had a number of visits from Howell Harris. Dressed in 'a fine suit of clothes given me in London' and complete with a powdered wig, the Welshman was still scarcely able to credit the company he was now keeping. He noted in his diary: 'What an honour I am called to, from being a poor, mean and despised boy, raised by the Lord gradually from one honour to another.'[2] He also records the fact that it was necessary for him to dress in keeping with the fashion of the day to avoid causing any unnecessary offence for the gospel. Day after day he met more members of the nobility. One name in particular keeps recurring in the chronicles of the times – a Catherine Edwin,[3] close friend of Selina's whom Harris describes as 'all alive for God indeed'.[4] Writing to his wife, Mercy,

[1] 9 April 1747, *Harris Visits London*, p. 137.
[2] 9 June 1747, *ibid.*, p. 145.
[3] Catherine Edwin could have been the wife of John Edwin, an MP, but more probably was an older unmarried lady who was given the courtesy title of 'Mrs' as was common in the eighteenth century. The following year Mrs Edwin inherited Denham Place not far from the Prince's residence at Cliveden.
[4] *Selected Trevecka Letters* (1747-94), transcribed and annotated by G. M. Roberts (Caernarvon: The Calvinistic Methodist Bookroom, 1965), p. 11.

Philip Doddridge evaluated these two women: 'Had these two ladies been bishops, the nation had perhaps been reformed!'[1] Mrs Edwin had established a warm friendship with Frederick, the Prince of Wales, who in turn had shown a degree of spiritual concern.

With his father, George II, now turned sixty, it would seem that the time could be near when the Prince would become King. The prospect of a King sympathetic to the spiritual values of the revival was therefore much upon the hearts of Selina and her friends. Not only would this influence the life of the nation, it would also offer protection to the despised Methodist cause. The Countess, Mrs Edwin, Countess Delitz,[2] the Marquis of Lothian[3] and others made the Prince's conversion a priority in their prayers. Although the Prince admired the Christian principles of these friends, he could only talk lamely of what he would do if he lived to be king, but said 'he could do nothing at present'.[4]

During this period Selina worshipped ever more frequently at Whitefield's Tabernacle in Moorfields and the change in her doctrinal position became more marked. The first clear confirmation of her rejection of John Wesley's teaching on Christian perfection can be dated in 1747. As we have seen, she had struggled to attain such a standard, but with an acute sense of the power of indwelling sin, her shortcomings had sometimes undermined her assurance of salvation. Howell Harris reported in his diary on 9 June, after yet another visit to Chelsea Farm, 'she was against sinless perfection, and the instantaneous gift of sanctification as the Bro. Wesleys hold.'[5]

---

[1] Doddridge continues: 'Mrs Edwin is building for herself a house at Cookham where I hope she will preach her neighbour the Prince of Wales into religion.' *Correspondence of Philip Doddridge*, p. 281.

[2] Countess Delitz, sister of Lady Chesterfield and illegitimate daughter of George I, was a friend and correspondent of George Whitefield's.

[3] A Scottish nobleman who sat at Westminster as a Member of Parliament.

[4] 11 July 1747, *Harris Visits London*, p. 204.

[5] *Ibid.*, p. 145.

By the summer of 1747 the Countess was back at her home in Ashby, but discovered it to be far from the peaceful haven that she felt she needed. For a variety of reasons the people of Ashby were antagonistic to the Hastings family. Possibly they resented the rents levied on their farms and properties, but Selina was convinced that it was her identification with the despised Methodists that angered the people in this strongly royalist area. Writing to Doddridge once more, she describes their animosity towards her:

> Our affronts and persecutions here, for the Word's sake are scarcely to be described . . . Many secret and shameful enemies of the gospel, by his will, appear . . . They call out in the open streets for me, saying if they had me they would tear me to pieces &c., but alas this but proves that it is the Lord that offends them and so must he continue to the unregenerate heart.[1]

When Stonehouse heard of these circumstances, he insisted that if the Countess wished to regain her strength a few months in Bath was the clear answer.

Complying with his advice Selina returned to London before travelling on to Bath. Whilst there she called on the Archbishop of Canterbury, Dr John Potter. Many years before, as Bishop of Oxford, Potter had witnessed the growth of the Holy Club and had actually ordained a number of its members including the Wesley brothers, Benjamin Ingham and James Hervey. But when these men, with the exception of Hervey, began preaching in the fields the Bishop was offended. Now elderly, his sentiments towards Methodism appeared to have softened. When Selina called on the ageing and infirm primate she took the old man's hand in hers and with sincerity and courage warned him that death could come unexpectedly and he must be prepared. Affected by her words the Archbishop responded warmly, 'May the Lord God of Abraham, and of Isaac and of Jacob bless thee!'

---

[1] *Correspondence of Philip Doddridge*, p. 251.

Not long after she had arrived in Bath Selina heard of the death of Dr Potter. He had just written to her and while the letter was still in his hand he had had a sudden and fatal stroke. Dated 10 October 1747, the letter read:

Dear Madam – I have been very ill since I saw you last. I hope soon to hear from you, that your health is better for being in Bath. Continue to pray for me until we meet in that place where our joy shall be complete.[1]

The death of Dr Potter deprived Selina of a friend and the Methodist cause of a tolerant man at the head of the Church of England.

Not only had 1747 been a year of emotional crisis for Lady Huntingdon, but as the months passed she appears to have revived her early interest in the writings of the mystics. Prior to her conversion in 1739 they had influenced her thinking and now she found herself turning back to some of these writers for consolation. Among her books was a copy of François Fénelon's[2] *Dissertation on Pure Love*, and a manuscript translation of various works by Madame Guyon.[3] She had also retained her early friendship with William Law, then living in the Northamptonshire village of King's Cliffe, and spending his days in works of philanthropy. Although Selina had long since turned from Law's emphasis on holiness of life as the pathway to acceptance with God, she continued to correspond with him from time to time. She admired his detachment from the world, his high spiritual expectations and particularly the ideals set out in his classic work *A Serious Call to a Devout and Holy Life*; she had even circulated some of his writings in the form of tracts.[4]

[1] Related to Augustus Toplady by the Countess, *Works, Anecdotes Incidents and Historic Passages,* p. 497.

[2] François de Salignac de la Mothe Fénelon (1651–1715), French mystic, Archbishop of Cambray and writer.

[3] Mme. Jeanne-Marie de la Motte Guyon (1648–1717), French mystic, poet, writer and friend of Fénelon.

[4] LRO. Charlotte Pickering corresponded with the Countess about a tract of Law's that Selina had ordered to be printed in 1746.

If she had been attracted to mystical thinking, as Harris certainly suggests in a letter to Whitefield written in December 1747,[1] an event took place in the spring of 1748 that led to the complete recovery of the Countess's buoyant and out-going spirit. She went on an extended trip into rural Wales to witness the work of God at first hand. Possibly organised by Howell Harris, the party included her sisters-in-law, Lady Frances and Lady Anne and the girls, Elizabeth and Selina, now seventeen and ten years old respectively.[2] A sketchy account in Lady Frances's handwriting is the only record of the tour, but it would appear that four Welsh ministers met the ladies in Bath and accompanied them to the Principality. These were Howell Harris, Daniel Rowland (whom the Countess had met for the first time two years earlier), Griffith Jones[3] and Howell Davies[4] and each took it in turn to preach at the villages through which they passed. Progress was slow; the roads rough and irregular, with potholes merely filled up with pieces of broken brick, while the chaises in which the party travelled were light and frequently un-stable. But everywhere they stopped the villagers listened with attention and the Countess was able to witness first hand the eager response of the people to the preaching of the gospel.

When they reached Howell Harris's Trevecca home a number of other Welsh ministers joined the party, including William Williams of Pantecelyn. And the people poured in from all the surrounding villages and hamlets eager to hear the preaching. Four or five times each day they gathered and Lady Frances records the astonishing and visible effects of the preaching. Many cried out in deep bitterness with obvious anguish of conscience.

[1] 17 December 1747, *Selected Trevecca Letters,* vol. 2, p. 11.

[2] Seymour, *Countess*, places this incident in May 1748, but a careful study of Howell Harris's diary for those dates shows that this must be incorrect. More probably it occurred in April.

[3] Griffith Jones of Llanddowror, senior figure of the Welsh revival, was well known for the founding of the Welsh circulating schools.

[4] Howell Davies, converted in 1737 under Howell Harris's preaching.

When Griffith Jones addressed the people on the text 'What shall I cry?', the power of God was present to an even greater degree. Never had the Countess seen such things before, and she went in and out among the people afterwards asking them why they were in such distress. The reply was usually the same: they feared lest their sins would preclude them forever from the mercy of God.

After spending a number of days at Trevecca the party slowly made its way back to London. Delighted with all she had seen and heard, Selina summed up her experiences:

> I am constrained to exclaim, 'Bless the Lord, O my soul!' I could not but acknowledge, This is the Lord's doing and it is marvellous in our eyes. Many on these solemn occasions ... were brought out of nature's deepest darkness into the marvellous light of the all-glorious gospel of Christ.[1]

With renewed vision and heart aflame with desire to see the progress of the gospel, the Countess of Huntingdon began exploring ways in which she might help to advance the cause of Christ. And in the purposes of God this coincided with George Whitefield's return from Georgia after an absence of four years. He had been sorely missed by the congregation worshipping at Moorfields Tabernacle and by the societies identifying themselves as the Calvinistic Methodists, many brought into being by his preaching. Howell Harris had tried manfully to hold the work together, but his chief loyalty lay with the Welsh Calvinistic Methodists and the time he could give to oversight of the English work was limited. The prospect of Whitefield's return, therefore, infused fresh hope into the hearts of the people.

But someone else was also eagerly awaiting the event. A plan had been taking shape in the mind of the Countess of Huntingdon. As a peeress she had the legal right to appoint two private chaplains whose responsibility it was to minister to the

---

[1] Account in Seymour, *Countess*, vol. 1, pp. 84–6.

spiritual needs of her household wherever she might be living.[1] If she appointed Whitefield to this position she could then invite members of the nobility, politicians and even royalty to her home to listen to her chaplain preach. In this way she could gain a hearing for the gospel of Christ among those of her own rank. Pride, coupled with an apartheid born of social privilege, might otherwise preclude for ever such people from the reach of the evangelical preachers.

When Whitefield disembarked at Deal on 30 June 1748 he made his way to London, reaching the capital on 5 July. Hardly had he arrived before he had a visitor. Howell Harris, 'fearing to offend the Countess', had come at her insistence with a message asking Whitefield to visit her at Chelsea immediately. The four years that had elapsed since the Countess and Whitefield had last met had been highly significant in the lives of both. Whitefield had battled through 'evil report and good report' in America and the Countess, who had lost in death one whom she had loved with all the intensity of her affectionate nature, had embraced Whitefield's own theological position and now stood prepared to use both her strength and means in the work of God.

On 9 July Harris and Whitefield again visited the Countess at Chelsea. A further visit was arranged for 15 July, and on this occasion they arrived at nine in the morning, celebrated a communion service together with others in the house, and then joined the Countess and her family for breakfast. The meal, probably consisting of tea or coffee (now replacing beer as a regular beverage), oysters, cold tongue, and pasties, would have given further opportunities for mutual fellowship. These must have been days of joy and restoration of spirit for Selina; and even more so when another friend arrived in London – Philip Doddridge. Delighted to hear he had come, the Countess invited him to join her friends at Chelsea. 'More cheerfulness I never saw intermingled with

[1] Although two was the specified number of chaplains the Countess could legally appoint, the law was not rigorously applied.

devotion,'[1] Doddridge told his wife, Mercy. In a further letter he added, 'I am told Lady Huntingdon intends to insist on my preaching at her home on Saturday.'[2]

Another invitation to Whitefield to preach at her home reached him on 20 August and in accepting it, he comments:

> As I am to preach, God willing, at St. Bartholomew's on Wednesday evening, I will wait upon your Ladyship the next morning, and spend the whole day at Chelsea. Blessed be God, that the rich and the great begin to have an hearing ear. Surely your Ladyship and Madam E[dwin] are only the first-fruits![3]

Reporting on the occasion, he later wrote to his brother James who lived in Bristol:

> On Tuesday I preached twice at Lady Huntingdon's to several of the nobility. In the morning the Earl of Chesterfield was present; in the evening Lord B[olingbroke]. All behaved quite well and were in some degree affected. Lord C[hesterfield] thanked me, and said, 'Sir, I will not tell you what I shall tell others, how I approve of you,' or words to this purpose. He conversed with me freely afterwards. Lord B[olingbroke] was much moved, and desired I would come and see him the next morning. I did; and his Lordship behaved with great candour and frankness.[4]

Both these men had given the preacher a fair hearing. Chesterfield, who had only recently resigned his position as Chief Secretary of State, commented, 'Mr Whitefield's eloquence is unrivalled – his zeal inexhaustible; and not to admire both would argue a total absence of taste.' Bolingbroke, though he 'sat looking like an archbishop', went further, saying 'Mr Whitefield is the most extraordinary man of our times. He has the most

[1] Seymour, *Countess*, vol. 1, p. 87.
[2] *Correspondence of Philip Doddridge*, p. 280.
[3] George Whitefield's *Works*, ed. J. Gillies, vol. 2 (London, 1771), p.163. Hereafter Whitefield, *Works*.
[4] *Ibid.*, vol. 2, p. 170.

commanding eloquence I have ever heard in any person, his abilities are very considerable, his zeal unquenchable; and his piety
and excellence genuine – unquestionable.' In the light of these
comments, contrasting markedly with the usual innuendoes
passed on the Methodists by men and women of their rank,
the Countess may well have held high hopes of their eventual
conversion.

George Whitefield's favourable reception from two of the most
notable though least religious men in the kingdom, gave Selina
the confidence she needed. She now asked the gifted evangelist to
become one of her personal chaplains. His would be the demanding task of preaching to as many of the nobility as she could invite
to her home at any one time. Although Whitefield did not accept
this responsibility lightly, nor with any degree of self-assurance,
he was nevertheless encouraged at the confidence she had placed
in him. On 1 September 1748 as he set out for Scotland, he wrote
to Selina expressing his sense of the privilege and responsibility at
the appointment:

> I dare not leave town without dropping a few lines gratefully to
> acknowledge the many favours I have received from your Ladyship,
> especially the honour you have done me in making me one of your
> ladyship's chaplains. A sense of it humbles me, and makes me pray
> more intensely for grace to walk worthy of that God who has called
> me to his kingdom and glory. As your Ladyship has been pleased to
> confer this honour upon me, I shall think it my duty to send you
> weekly accounts of what the Lord Jesus is pleased to do for and by me.[1]

On the same day that Whitefield wrote to the Countess, he also
wrote to John Wesley, and it was a letter which marked an important change in his thinking with regard to the leadership of
Calvinistic Methodist Societies. The question of forming societies
had been one of the main topics of discussion when Howell Harris
took Whitefield to see the Countess on 5 July. Harris felt that the

*Ibid.*, p. 168.

gathering together of converts in this way was an essential element in the work. The Countess on the other hand was still uncertain of their value, 'from seeing the bigotry coming in with them'. Now Whitefield had made up his mind. To Wesley he wrote:

> My attachment to America will not permit me to abide very long in England; consequently I should but weave a Penelope's web if I formed societies; and if I should form them I have not proper assistants to take care of them. I intend therefore to go about preaching the gospel to every creature. You, I suppose, are for set-tling societies everywhere; but more of this when we meet.[1]

Recognizing his calling was that of an evangelist, Whitefield was now deliberately and unmistakably laying aside these adminis-trative responsibilities in order to free himself for such usefulness in reaching the people with the gospel of Christ.[2] Benjamin Ingham had done the same six years earlier and for the same reason. The support and confidence of the Countess at this time would have also been a significant factor confirming his decision.

John Wesley could certainly be excused if he felt that Whitefield had now taken precedence over him in the esteem of the Coun-tess. Perhaps sensing this loss he decided to pay her a visit the week after he had received the above letter from Whitefield. The relationship between Selina and the elder Wesley had cooled to a certain extent in the past few years owing in part to the shift in the Countess's doctrinal thinking. Never one to show undue defer-ence to the great, Wesley could be quite outspoken to Selina – a far cry from the treatment to which she had been accustomed from earliest years.

---

[1] *Ibid.*, pp.169–70.
[2] According to Edwin Welch there were 433 Welsh Calvinistic Societies in existence by 1750; whereas in 1747 Whitefield's Societies only numbered 29, with 25 preaching stations. This demonstrates the fact that Whitefield deliberately made little attempt to settle his converts into societies. See Edwin Welch, *Two Calvinistic Methodist Chapels, 1743-1811* (London Record Society, 1975), p. 16–17.

*Astwell Manor House today*

*Pulpit used at Trevecca open-air anniversary services, 1768-91*

*Chelsea Farm, 1829*

*The Countess's younger daughter, Selina, 1762*

*Life-sized portrait of Lady Huntingdon sent to bolster her mission to Georgia in 1773*

*Spa Fields Chapel and House (Guildhall Library, Corporation of London)*

Interior of Spa Fields Chapel

*Trefeca College, 1768 (Evangelical Register, vol. 1)*

Wesley now felt he ought to visit the Countess although he did not particularly relish the prospect. In his journal he wrote, 'Being not able with tolerable decency to excuse myself any longer, I went to Chelsea and spent two or three hours as in times that are past.' Glad to see him, Selina asked him to preach to those present in her house at the time, insisting that he return two days later when she hoped to have a larger gathering to hear him. 'I was too hasty in reckoning,' Wesley confessed. 'Lady Huntingdon pressed me to come again on Friday and I could not handsomely decline it.' Duly he returned, recording, 'I took up my cross once more [an expression both the Wesley brothers used when fulfilling some duty against their natural inclinations], and came to Chelsea a little after 11.' Quite a number were there to hear Wesley preach, including Francis Hastings. The young man had just returned from his period of study at Oxford and was soon to leave home once more for his Grand Tour, as his father had done before him. After preaching a forthright sermon on 'Thou art not far from the kingdom,' Wesley noted that his aristocratic congregation had not taken offence at his outspoken message.

Before leaving he found an opportunity to speak on his own with the Countess. Forthright as ever, Wesley probably showed too little understanding of his friend. 'I trust I delivered my own soul,' he recorded in his journal – a euphemism for having spoken his mind. Considering the fact that Selina was unused to home-truths because of her social rank, we may regard it as being to her credit that Wesley could comment in his journal, 'She took it well', although he admitted that his remarks had caused her some tears. Despite this the Countess urged Wesley to return – if he could not spare an hour, then half an hour would content her. To this he agreed and returned two days later on a Sunday evening, preaching to her household, including once more Francis and also his sister Elizabeth.[1]

[1] Extracts from Wesley's *Journals* cited in *Works of John Wesley,* vol. 26, ed. Frank Baker (Oxford: Clarendon Press, 1982), pp. 330–3.

When Whitefield returned from Scotland at the beginning of November he was immediately engaged to preach twice weekly at Chelsea Farm to the friends, family, acquaintances and members of the nobility who gathered at Selina's invitation. And later that month the evangelist had the opportunity of calling on Isaac Watts, whose life was swiftly drawing to a close. Asking the sick man how he found himself, Whitefield received the memorable reply, 'I am one of Christ's waiting servants.' He had little longer to wait. Only half an hour after Whitefield had left him, Christ took his honoured servant away from all his frailty and trials.

Meanwhile another friend was in trouble. Howell Harris had been preaching through Wales, and had run his physical strength to its limits, sometimes travelling a hundred and fifty miles a week. For the final week of his tour he had given himself scarcely any rest, not even undressing at nights, and occasionally preaching on the mountainsides at midnight to avoid the persecution often meted out on those who listened to him. The vitriolic Sir Watkin William Wynn, a Welsh baronet and magistrate from Denbighshire, had imposed crushing fines of up to £20 on men and women who gathered to hear the Methodist preachers. With his health already undermined by excessive fatigue, Harris was then attacked by a frenzied mob near Bala. He was struck across the head with such violence that he said he felt as if it were breaking in two.[1]

The report of these things motivated Selina into immediate action. Her complaints to the government about the behaviour of Sir Watkin resulted in an instantaneous order for the money confiscated in fines to be duly returned to its owners. Angered and mortified, Wynn vowed to continue his opposition, but within days a fall from his horse ended his spiteful intentions.

As 1748 drew to a close the Countess of Huntingdon, who, as she had said, dreaded 'slack hands in the vineyard', had not only

[1] *Selected Trevecka Letters*, vol. 2, p. 21.

pulled back from a temptation to withdraw from the public work of God but had entered into it more fully. In the appointment of George Whitefield as her chaplain she had taken a step that would have a lasting and significant effect on the lives of many. Writing to his friend Philip Doddridge on 21 December, Whitefield summed it up in these words:

> Last Sunday evening I preached to a most brilliant assembly indeed. They expressed great approbation and some, I think, begin to feel. Good Lady Huntingdon is indeed a mother in Israel. She is all in a flame for Jesus.[1]

---

[1] Whitefield, *Works*, vol. 2, p. 216.

# 9

## 'A Most Brilliant Assembly'

THE COFFEE HOUSES OF LONDON were at the height of their popularity in 1749. Situated mainly in the Strand, Covent Garden and Drury Lane, they provided gossip shops where the literary figures of the day could hold court, each in his own favourite haunt. Dr Samuel Johnson could be found at the *Bedford* where he might be extolling the merits of his newly published poem, *The Vanity of Human Wishes*, considered the best of his poetical works. Richard Sheridan, the playwright, was more likely to be found at the *Piazza*. That same year the actor David Garrick had just produced one of his most popular works, *Irene*, performed at his Drury Lane Theatre. Handel's best-known oratorio, *The Messiah*, had become so popular by 1749 that he established an annual performance at the Foundling Hospital in London.

Throughout 1749 and during the following few years the Countess of Huntingdon's mind was dominated by her new aspiration, and she used every effort to reach these politicians, wits, actors, writers and members of the nobility with the humbling message of the gospel of Christ. And here, her new chaplain George Whitefield was to make a significant contribution. Whenever he was in London Selina arranged for him to preach each Tuesday and Thursday at her Chelsea mansion to as many of her friends and acquaintants as she could gather together – a method of reaching her contemporaries with the gospel that would set a pattern to be copied by a number of her friends. At her request Wesley was also invited to preach at Chelsea Farm, particularly when Whitefield was travelling and preaching in other parts of the country. Glad that his colleague was also able to share in this opportunity, Whitefield wrote to the Countess in February 1749:

> The language of my heart is, Lord, send by whom thou wilt, only convert some of the mighty and noble for thy mercy's sake.[1]

Refreshment on these occasions was limited to drinks of tea or lemonade, but this did not deter some of the most prominent figures of the day from attending. An impressive list of forty or more celebrities was compiled by the Countess's first biographer, Aaron Seymour. Many of these names may mean little or nothing to readers today, yet they were the great and noble of the eighteenth century, men and women who effectively governed the country and to whom all common citizens were expected to show deference.

Most, in common with the Countess and her late husband, had patronized the rival court of Frederick, Prince of Wales, the alienated heir of George II. Among them could be found Selina's aunt, the beautiful Lady Frances Shirley; Lord Chesterfield, together with his long-suffering wife; his sister, Lady Gertrude Hotham, a close friend of the Countess; and his wife's sister, Countess Delitz. In addition, the list included such names as the Earl of Bath, and that of Lady Betty Germaine, whose personal fortune was reputed to be prodigious, quite apart from the wealth accrued by her husband, Sir John Germaine, in a life of gambling and adventure. The Duchess of Montagu – daughter of the Duke and Duchess of Marlborough – was another surprising visitor, as was the Earl of Burlington, famed for his collection of costly artifacts from his overseas travels. The sceptical Lord Bolingbroke, ageing Jacobite peer; Lord St John his half-brother; the beautiful and impulsive Duchess of Queensbury; the eccentric and

---

[1] Whitefield, *Works*, vol. 2, p. 226.

charming Lady Townshend and sometimes even Frederick, Prince of Wales, himself could all be found visiting Chelsea Farm from time to time.

The Scottish nobility was represented by such men and women as the Marquis of Lothian – arrested by Whitefield's early preaching in Scotland and later truly converted; the Earl of Aberdeen; the Earl of Lauderdale; the Marquis of Tweeddale, Secretary of State for Scotland, and Sir James Nimmo with his wife, Lady Jane Nimmo. Some of these had attended Whitefield's preaching during his visits to Scotland and were now happy to crowd into Lady Huntingdon's drawing room. Other politicians besides Bolingbroke and Chesterfield were occasionally to be found among Whitefield's hearers including William Pitt, first Earl of Chatham and future Secretary of State, and Lord North who was to become First Lord of the Treasury.

We must try to imagine the scene. The spacious drawing room of Selina's Chelsea home could scarcely contain its titled clientèle. Hooped skirts supported by whalebone frames added so much width to each noble lady's person that doorways of many a stately home had to be enlarged to facilitate entry. But it was the height of each figure that would have astounded a modern visitor. Headpieces rose to such an elevation that the men were near dwarfed by their female counterparts. Described as 'enormous erections of wool and horsehair and false curls, overlaid with a paste of powder, ornamented with flowers', they could add many inches to a woman's height. And for the men, the powdered wigs, ostensibly to hide grey hairs or a balding head, also provided their wearers with protection against the ever-present dangers of head lice and similar annoyances. Decorations of war and office were noticeably displayed, with the wearing of a sword as a universal habit.

Winsome and eloquent, Whitefield was nevertheless unafraid to speak candidly to these showy representatives of high society. To his friend James Hervey, fellow member of the Holy Club and curate of Weston Favell Church in Northamptonshire, he wrote:

> The prospect of doing good to the rich that attend her Ladyship's house is very encouraging. I preach twice a week and yesterday Lord B[olingbroke] was one of my auditors. His lordship was pleased to express very great satisfaction. Who knows what God may do? He can never work by a meaner instrument. I want humility, I want thankfulness, I want a heart continually flaming with the love of God.[1]

And to another correspondent he exclaimed:

> O how is the power of the Redeemer's resurrection displayed in Lady Huntingdon! She is a mother in Israel indeed. It would please you to see the assemblies at her Ladyship's house. They are brilliant ones indeed. The prospect of catching some of the rich in the gospel net is very promising.[2]

In view of the numbers crowding into her drawing room the Countess decided to take out a lease on another home, this time in Park Street, skirting Hyde Park.[3] This would be more centrally placed than Chelsea Farm, and provide a more convenient venue for the preaching services. Whitefield refers to this in a letter dated 14 November 1748 where he expresses the wish that her new house may be 'agreeable to your Ladyship. That the Redeemer's glory may fill it, and that it may prove a gate of heaven to many of the rich and great.'[4]

In terms of the overall work of God during the mid-eighteenth century it would be true to say that the converts of these gatherings were limited in number and that 'not many wise according to the flesh, not many mighty, not many noble were called'. But there were a significant number – and the Countess rejoiced in

[1] *Ibid.*, p. 221.

[2] *Ibid.*, p. 220.

[3] The fact that there is no further mention of the Downing Street home suggests that the lease was relinquished after the Earl's death.

[4] Whitefield, *Works*, vol. 2, p. 202.

them. Lady Fanny Shirley had tasted all that sordid and superficial society could offer her and had found it left her unsatisfied. She was one of the earliest of Whitefield's converts, and many were the letters he addressed to her in the months that lay ahead:

> I rejoiced to find that it [your letter] bespoke your Ladyship's attachment to the ever-loving, ever-lovely Jesus . . . I doubt not but your Ladyship, with full purpose of heart, will cleave unto him, and in spite of men and devils go on in that narrow way which leads to life eternal. . . . My heart's desire and constant prayer is that you may go from strength to strength.[1]

If ever a woman needed encouragement it was Lady Fanny. The butt of sceptical jokes and unbelieving innuendo, she held on her way, proving the reality of her conversion. Like Selina, Lady Fanny opened her home in Twickenham and invited Whitefield to preach to her friends and neighbours. One of her neighbours showed nothing but contempt for religion and for Methodism in particular. Horace Walpole, brilliant, sardonic and witty, was the youngest son of Sir Robert Walpole. Though a parliamentarian for most of his life, his home at Strawberry Hill, converted into the style of a Gothic castle, became a centre for fashionable learning. From there he wrote most of the letters for which he is still remembered today. And in these letters he poked many a jest at his neighbour, Lady Fanny.

> Here Fanny 'ever blooming fair'
> Ejaculates the graceful prayer;
> And 'scaped from sense – with nonsense smit –
> For Whitefield's cant, leaves Stanhope's wit.[2]

And yet more unkindly this cynic wrote to a friend, 'If you ever think of returning to England, . . . prepare yourself with Methodism . . . this sect increases as fast as almost any religious

---

[1] *Ibid.*, p.284.
[2] 'Stanhope' = Lord Chesterfield, *Letters of Lord Chesterfield to Lord Huntingdon* (London: Medici Society, 1923), p. ix.

nonsense did. Lady Fanny Shirley has chosen this way of bestowing the dregs of her beauty.'[1]

Some were affected by Whitefield's preaching but not converted. David Hume, the agnostic Scottish philosopher had declared, 'Mr Whitefield is the most ingenious preacher I ever heard; it is worth going twenty miles to hear him.'[2] Meanwhile Bolingbroke, hardened and cynical, was able to concede that given the premise that the Bible was true – which he did not believe – he could well accept the doctrines of grace and would be persuaded by Whitefield's earnest words. The preacher's eloquence even touched the old man's pocket, as he donated £5 for the work of the orphanage in Georgia.

But when his half-brother Lord St John was dying, Bolingbroke was affected far more personally. In a letter to Whitefield, then preaching in the west of the country, the Countess described the occasion, telling him that the dying man had begged for a clergyman to be sent to him. He had especially asked for Whitefield to whom, he said, he was deeply indebted. Lord St. John's dying words hopefully demonstrate the reality of his conversion: 'To God I commit myself. I feel how unworthy I am; but Jesus Christ died to save sinners; and the prayer of my heart now is, God be merciful to me a sinner.' Continuing her letter, Selina wrote: 'This, my good friend, is the first fruits of that plenteous harvest which I trust the great Husbandman will yet reap among the nobility of our land. Thus the great Lord of the harvest has put honour on your ministry.'

She was, however, under no illusions over Bolingbroke's spiritual state even though she had maintained contact with him:

[1] Seymour, *Countess*, vol. 1, p. 108.
[2] Speaking of Whitefield's preaching Hume wrote: 'In the most simple but energetic language [he] described what he called the Saviour's dying love to sinful men, so that almost the whole assembly was melted to tears. This address was accompanied with such animated yet natural action that it surpassed anything I ever saw or heard in any preacher. J. B. Wakeley, *Anecdotes of George Whitefield* (London: Hodder & Stoughton, 1879), p. 210.

My Lord Bolingbroke was much struck with his brother's language in his last moments . . . . O that the obdurate heart of this desperate infidel may yet be shook to its very centre . . . I tremble for his destiny. He is a singularly awful character; and I am fearfully alarmed lest that gospel which he so heartily despises, yet affects to reverence, should prove eventually the savour of death unto death to his immortal soul.[1]

The triumphs of the gospel in Lord Chesterfield's immediate family, however, must have heartened the Countess. Lady Chesterfield, gentle and unselfish, and her sister the Countess Delitz, both of them illegitimate daughters of George I by his mistress the Duchess of Kendal, were both numbered amongst those reborn into the family of God. Lady Chesterfield walked a hard path. Devoted to her faithless husband, she acceded to his wishes that she would accompany him to some of the court functions that were his delight.

The story is told of an occasion at a royal function when Lady Chesterfield was wearing a lovely dress with silver flowers on a brown background. A special and costly gift from her husband, the dress attracted the attention of the King on account of its modesty of style in contrast to the fashions of the times. Approaching her, the King, who was in fact her half-brother, said jocularly, 'I know who chose that gown for you – Mr Whitefield; and I hear you have attended on him this year and a half.'

'Yes, I have,' responded Lady Chesterfield, 'and I like him very well.' Later, however, she grieved that she had let slip a valuable opportunity to have spoken more forthrightly to the King.[2] When Whitefield heard the story he wrote to tell the Countess of Huntingdon about it, adding, 'O that all were clothed in the bright and spotless robe of the Redeemer's righteousness! How beautiful would they then appear in the sight of the King of Kings!'[3]

[1] Seymour, *Countess*, vol. 1, p. 98.
[2] Whitefield, *Works*, vol. 2, p. 317.      [3] *Ibid.*, p. 312.

Chesterfield's own sister, Lady Gertrude Hotham, already a widow at the time, was another early convert from the world of social graces and place-seeking to Jesus Christ. Together with Countess Delitz and Lady Fanny Shirley, these three high-born ladies had also opened their homes to Whitefield and other preachers, and especially so when Selina was back in Ashby or in Bath. Like her they paid a high price of social ridicule for their allegiance to the cause of Christ.

Lady Gertrude's eldest daughter was similar in age to Francis Hastings and had already attracted the young man's attentions. She too responded to Whitefield's preaching and became a bright example of Christian conversion. But her earthly course was to be short. Soon afterwards she was terminally ill and when James Hervey called at her home he wrote telling Selina that the sick girl was 'ripening fast for glory', and that he expected 'to hear every day of her abundant entrance into the joy of her Lord.'[1]

The young Earl of Bath, William Pulteney, an upright, generous and outwardly moral character, was a leading and powerful politician of the day. He too was frequently found listening to Whitefield's preaching, and was deeply affected and later converted.[2] His attendance at the Countess's drawing room gatherings was so regular that Horace Walpole sniped in one of his letters:

Whitefield preaches continually at Lady Huntingdon's at Chelsea. Lord Chesterfield, Lord Bath, Lady Townshend, Lady Thanet and others go continually to hear him; nor shall I wonder if next winter he is run after instead of Garrick.

[1] Seymour, *Countess*, vol. 1, p. 161.
[2] He was later to declare of the preaching that transformed his life, 'Mocked and reviled as Mr Whitefield is by all ranks of society, still I contend that the day will come when England will be just and own his greatness as a reformer and his goodness as a minister of the most High God.' Seymour, *Countess*, vol. 2, p. 379.

But when the Earl of Bath began to court Colonel Gumley's eldest daughter, the old Colonel cannot have foreseen the consequences it would have for himself. Soon after the marriage, the Earl took his new father-in-law to hear the preaching that had so profoundly influenced his thinking. As Colonel Gumley listened to Whitefield's message and spoke with the Countess, he too became a Christian. Writing to his wife, Philip Doddridge told her that he had met Gumley at the Countess's home, and added 'he is really a second Colonel Gardiner' – a high accolade coming from one who had valued that outstanding Christian so highly. Walpole, on the other hand, commented cynically, 'Gumley . . . is grown Methodist. His wit is at its wit's end.'

Lady Townshend, rich, eccentric and erratic was loud in her fulsome praises of Whitefield's preaching, but her rapid swings of religious allegiance left her wide open to the taunts of the sceptics. After her footman reported that he had seen her attending a celebration of the Mass, Horace Walpole sneered contemptuously, 'She certainly means to go [to the after life] armed with every *viactum*, the Church of England in one hand, Methodism in the other, and the Host in her mouth.'[1] When Lady Townshend appeared to be dying, the Countess told Whitefield of her condition. He wrote to the unpredictable woman urging her warmly and yet boldly to cast aside her doublemindedness and cleave to Christ only for her eternal security.

A far different type of woman was Lady Suffolk. Proud, beautiful and self-important, she belonged to the select circle that made up the entourage surrounding the poet, Pope. After Lady Fanny's conversion Lady Suffolk had become the focal point of Lord Chesterfield's attentions. Invited by a friend to attend a meeting at one of the Countess's homes, she was present on one occasion without Whitefield's knowledge. In the course of his message he described the pride, vanity and deceit of the natural heart with

[1] *Ibid.*, vol. 1, p. 105.

such accuracy that Lady Suffolk thought the preacher was deliberately insulting her and aiming his remarks specifically at her. The offended beauty could scarcely contain herself until Whitefield had finished his message. Then at the first possible moment she flew into a rage with the Countess, insulting her with abusive language. The infuriated woman finally gave a graceless apology to Selina and left the house never to return. Even on her deathbed many years later Lady Suffolk refused a visit from the Countess.

Yet there were others whose response to Whitefield's preaching brought delight to Selina and lasting glory to God. A later convert, but one of outstanding significance for his future contribution to the progress of the gospel, was the statesman, Lord Dartmouth, later to become Colonial Secretary, President of the Board of Trade and President of the Royal Society. Had he been the only convert from Selina's attempts to reach the aristocracy, her efforts would have been well repaid in this significant and influential friend of the gospel.[1] In 1755 Selina invited Dartmouth to her Park Street home to hear Whitefield preach. Young, capable and already an influential politician, he was converted and from that time on became another prepared to suffer the 'glorious infamy' of being known as a Christian. To him the poet William Cowper referred in his poem *Truth*:

> We boast some rich ones whom the gospel sways,
> And one who wears a coronet and prays.

In addition we may mention two sisters, Mrs Carteret and Mrs Cavendish, both married into wealthy eighteenth century families. Converted at the same time, they kept the faith under difficult circumstances and later, dying soon after each other,

[1] Disowned and treated with contempt by some of his high-ranking relatives, particularly his uncle, Henry Legge, Chancellor of the Exchequer, Lord Dartmouth appealed to the Countess to try to effect some reconciliation. Her words to his family eased the situation to such an extent that his relatives even came to her Park Street home to hear Whitefield preach.

SELINA COUNTESS OF HUNTINGDON

expressed a sole confidence in the atoning death of Christ. When Henry Venn visited Mrs Carteret on her deathbed she grasped his hand and prayed earnestly that 'the Lord Jesus would blot out every spot and stain in his most precious blood and clothe her in his own most glorious righteousness.' Mrs Cavendish had repeated her favourite hymn many times over, 'There is a fountain filled with blood . . . ' and had spoken much of the everlasting covenant on which she pinned all her hopes of heaven.

Social status made it hard for these men and women to accept the humbling message of the cross. Yet the genuine and obvious change in the lives of those who professed conversion brought credit to the cause of Christ. Writing to the Countess at the end of January 1749, Whitefield commented:

> Surely your Ladyship will never know till the day of judgment the great ends God had in view in calling your Ladyship to London. I rejoice in the prospect of seeing your Ladyship happy amidst a crowd of your spiritual children . . . You will suffer many pangs for them; but all shall work for your Ladyship's present and eternal good.[1]

As no biography of the Countess was attempted until a century after these events had taken place, probably only a few names of those converted or influenced may have survived the passage of time. There could well have been many more. Whitefield's letters, written to encourage some of these young converts in the faith, make reference to a number whose identity it is hard to establish.[2] On 10 November 1748 he writes to a fellow preacher: 'About thirty have desired to come [to Lady Huntingdon's home], and I suppose they will bring thirty more. I have heard of

[1] Whitefield, *Works*, vol. 2, p. 225.
[2] When Dr John Gillies of Glasgow first compiled and published Whitefield's letters in 1772 most of Whitefield's correspondents were still living. To protect them Gillies removed many names from the letters, referring to the recipients and others by initials only. This has deprived biographers and historians of the opportunity of identifying many of these people.

two or three more dear Christians among the *Great Ones*.'[1] And again in 22 February 1749 he writes to a Lady G— 'Of the honourable women, ere long I trust, there will not be a few who will dare . . . to confess the blessed Jesus before men . . . .You, honoured Madam, I trust, are one of this happy number.'[2]

It cannot be doubted that even Frederick, Prince of Wales had been touched by the gospel. On one occasion he had enquired why he had not seen the Countess in his court recently. Lady Charlotte Edwin had replied cynically, 'Why, I suppose she is praying with her beggars.' 'Lady Charlotte,' replied the Prince, 'when I am dying I think I shall be happy to seize the skirt of Lady Huntingdon's mantle to lift me up with her to heaven.'[3] Bolingbroke himself was of the opinion that 'his Royal Highness is fast verging towards Methodism'.[4]

In view of these facts it is the more surprising that both the late Dr Edwin Welch and Dr Boyd Schlenther, in recently published biographical studies of the Countess of Huntingdon, have played down the lasting works of grace accomplished at this time through her drawing room meetings. Following the same line as Welch, Dr Schlenther says, 'In the end blue blood ran thin in the enterprise, and her aunt, Lady Fanny Shirley, was her only "parlour" convert.'[5]

Such a work of God as had already taken place amongst the nobility of England cannot have failed to have acted as a leaven on

---

[1] Whitefield, *Works*, vol. 2, p. 200.   [2] *Ibid.*, p. 236.

[3] In later years Lady Charlotte Edwin (not to be confused with her sister-in-law Lady Catherine Edwin) became concerned for own spiritual condition and frequently attended Whitefield's preaching at Tottenham Road Chapel.

[4] Sometimes Frederick would go privately to hear Whitefield preach and when he was dying, Lord Lyttleton, who had access to him, told the Countess that he had been reading Doddridge's *Rise and Progress of Religion in the Soul*, presented to the Princess of Wales by Doddridge himself at the Countess's encouragement.

[5] Edwin Welch, *Spiritual Pilgrim*, p. 70 and Dr Boyd Schlenther, *Queen of the Methodists*, p. 41.

that fastidious and degenerate society. Many of those influenced or converted became regular hearers of Whitefield, first at Moorfields and later at Tottenham Court Road Chapel. In his *Life of George Whitefield*, Luke Tyerman sums up this eventful period in the Countess's life and evaluates its effect in these words:

> The gatherings in Chelsea and North Audley [home of Countess Delitz] were profoundly interesting spectacles; and never till the Day of Judgment will it be ascertained to what extent the preaching of the youthful Whitefield affected the policy of some of England's greatest statesmen and moulded the character of some of England's highest aristocratic families.[1]

We could also add that the evangelical revival of the eighteenth century might never have gained the acceptance that it did apart from the endeavours of the Countess of Huntingdon. Where once Methodism had been disparaged, and its adherents sneered at, a new attitude slowly began to prevail. The titled and prominent in society now came to speak with more deference of the labours of the Methodist preachers and gradually the political and social life of the country was shaped by such changed attitudes among the nobility. The unbelieving and amoral notions expressed by Horace Walpole, Bolingbroke, Chesterfield and others might otherwise have permanently shaped the psyche of the nation. The Countess used her unquestionable influence in the highest circles of the land and even in the royal court to throw the cloak of her protection over the prominent preachers of the day and over the fledgling Methodist movement itself. And by this means Christian doctrine with its resulting standards of morality influenced the mindset of a people well into the Victorian era and beyond.

---

[1] Tyerman, *Whitefield*, vol. 2, p. 212.

# 10

# 'THE STRENGTH OF HER SOUL
# IS AMAZING'

EACH PERIOD OF UNUSUAL ACTIVITY or pressure in the life of the
Countess of Huntingdon seemed to be followed by a time of illness. Perhaps her intense personality made her the more
vulnerable to both physical and stress-related ailments. So now
after the exhilaration of recent days it is not surprising to learn
that she suffered a prolonged period of ill-health. As the waters of
the Bristol Hot Wells had been helpful in the past, Selina chose to
spend time in the city together with her sisters-in-law, Lady
Frances and Lady Anne during the summer of 1749. While there
the three ladies became aware of a class of people that evoked
their pity in a special way – prisoners incarcerated for minor debt,
who were often obliged to leave their families in a state of destit-
ution. Due to rigorous and inequitable penal laws, men and
women who owed only a few shillings were flung without mercy
into insanitary prisons, with walls dank and slimy, and nothing to
lie on but filthy straw. There they could be left to die of gaol fever.
Together the three women would visit the debtors' prison and
Selina is known to have relieved at least thirty-four debtors who
owed £10 or less during this period. She would make good the
debt herself and so restore the prisoner to his family.

When Howell Harris arrived in Bristol early in August 1749 the
Countess was still there. Although she had now swung decidedly
behind Whitefield and the Calvinistic Methodists, she had a
natural aversion to the divisions that lay just beneath the surface

and which threatened the work of God. Added to this, her strong Church of England background left her apprehensive of any move that might lead to a break with the Established Church. Harris's arrival gave Selina the opportunity to discuss these matters of concern. George Whitefield was also in Bristol and together they talked over the problems and the outlook for a greater degree of unity between themselves and the Wesley brothers. As it happened John and Charles Wesley were also both in the area, so it seemed a timely moment to suggest a hastily convened conference between the four men. Harris describes the occasion:

> After praying we opened our hearts about the points in dispute, and saw a possibility of coming to terms, confining to a practical way of preaching and keeping off from the controversial way, to adopt each other's expressions as much as possible, each to give up all we can ... Agreed ... to abide in the communion of the Established Church till thrust out. I mentioned my fears lest he (J.W.) should affect to be head and to be a party.[1]

Whitefield, according to Harris's report, also 'mentioned his objection to his [Wesley's] monopolising the name of Methodist to himself only'.[2] Though it was a brave endeavour, this impromptu conference appeared to have achieved little at the time. Charles Wesley wrote across his paper setting out the terms for their increased harmony, 'Vain agreement.' In his journal he recorded, 'Our conference this week with Mr Whitefield and Mr Harris came to nought.'[3]

Yet it was not entirely fruitless, for in the coming months there was a closer measure of co-operation between the preachers of the revival. A mere six weeks later Whitefield could write to the Countess from Newcastle, 'In my way hither I met Mr Charles

---

[1] *Harris Visits London*, p. 229.    [2] *Ibid.*

[3] *The Journal of the Rev. Charles Wesley, M.A.* ed. Thomas Jackson (reprint, Grand Rapids: Baker Book House, 1980), vol. 2, p. 63.

W[esley] who ... introduced me to the pulpit in Newcastle ... I have preached now in their room four times, and this morning I preached to many thousands in a large close.'[1] Meanwhile Charles could say: 'George Whitefield and my brother and I are one – a threefold cord shall no more be broken.'[2]

Returning to Ashby in the autumn of 1749, Selina was pleased when Whitefield joined her once more that November. Since February he had been travelling the country: Gloucester, Portsmouth, Wales, Bristol, Newcastle, Haworth, Leeds, and wherever he went the crowds gathered to hear him preach. In accordance with his intention he had written often, telling the Countess of the progress of his endeavours: such letters to her were common at this period, though they became less frequent in time. Whitefield's visit would have lifted Selina's spirit for he had much to tell of the exhilarating days he had recently spent in the north of England, where he could report that 'the glorious Emmanuel is riding on in the chariot of his gospel, from conquering to conquer.'[3]

Back in London he was soon immersed once again in preaching to the crowds that thronged Moorfields Tabernacle. A letter from Whitefield to the Countess on 30 November 1749 includes significant words on how he viewed his patroness:

> The Lord's smiling upon my poor labours sweetens all. I have begun to preach at six in the morning. We have large congregations even then ... However, a leader is wanting. This honour hath been put upon your Ladyship by the great head of the church. An honour conferred on few, but an ernest of a distinguished honour to be put on your Ladyship before men and angels, when time shall be no more.[4]

This is a noteworthy recognition by Whitefield of the Countess's growing influence in the revival and of the gifts of

[1] Whitefield, *Works*, vol. 2, p. 283.
[2] Tyerman, *Whitefield*, vol. 2, p. 278.
[3] Whitefield, *Works*, vol. 2, p. 286.      [4] 30 November 1749, *ibid.*, p. 294.

leadership she was beginning to exercise. We may safely affirm that she had indeed begun to 'fill her place', as she had expressed it in her conversation with Howell Harris in April 1747.

As winter gave place to spring in 1750 Whitefield set out once more on his travels, planning an extended tour north through Yorkshire, to Newcastle and on to Edinburgh. On his way, however, he called at Ashby Place. Northampton also lay on his route, so after a brief visit to his friends there, Doddridge, Hervey and Stonehouse, he travelled on, arriving in Ashby during the second week of May 1750. Here he was relieved to find the Countess better in health than he had expected, and could write to a friend, 'For a few days I have been at good Lady Huntingdon's, who though weak in body is always abounding in the work of the Lord.'[1] The warm welcome from Selina and her sisters-in-law stood in sharp contrast with the reception he received from some of the people of Ashby. In spite of all the kindness that the titled ladies had attempted to show, regularly inviting the poorest of the people into the kitchens for free meals and medicines, the Hastings family was no more popular than it had been before. Ugly scenes developed as Whitefield preached and, reporting to Doddridge later, he wrote:

> The kind people of Ashby stirred up some of the baser sort to riot before her Ladyship's door, while the gospel was preaching; and on Wednesday evening, some people in their return home narrowly escaped being murdered.[2]

The Countess had to appeal to the local magistrate to restore order before serious crime was committed, but she did not press her lawful rights or insist on the penalties due to the perpetrators of the trouble. Writing to her later Whitefield expressed the hope that 'your Ladyship may live to see many of those Ashby stones become children of Abraham.'

[1] *Ibid.*, p. 349.     [2] *Ibid.*, p. 350.

Leaving Ashby Whitefield travelled on northward and whenever opportunity afforded he wrote to the Countess. Reaching
Edinburgh early in July 1750, he found two letters awaiting him
from her. In them she reported that the trouble in Ashby rumbled
on. 'Ungrateful Ashby!' Whitefield exclaimed in his reply. 'Surely
your Ladyship may shake off the dust of your feet against them.
This was the command that the meek and lowly Jesus gave to his
apostles when the gospel was not received.'[1]

While her chaplain was travelling north Selina had visits from
two other friends. First came James Hervey, Whitefield's friend
from his Oxford days, whom she had met for the first time earlier
that year. He had not been well and during April had responded
to her invitation to spend a few weeks at Ashby Place in order to
recuperate his strength. A warm admirer of his writings, the
Countess had a high opinion of Hervey and of the way he pointed
the believer away from his own attainments to the imputed righteousness of Christ.

In May 1750, soon after Hervey had left, Philip Doddridge called
and, like Whitefield, found the Countess much restored in health.
With a growing admiration for the large-hearted Dissenter, Selina
continued to take a close interest in the work of his Academy in
Northampton. Doddridge, however, was troubled about the decay
in spiritual zeal among Dissenting churches and he shared his concerns with her. Though outwardly prosperous, many Dissenters
were drifting into rationalism and Unitarianism; while internal
bickerings resulted in dwindling congregations.[2]

[1] *Ibid.*, p. 370.
[2] Untouched in the main by the revival, and often critical of the evident work
of God that had been in progress for some thirteen years by this time, Dissenters had tended to become socially respectable and were at a low ebb spiritually
in consequence. Delivered from the threat of persecution, particularly after the
death of Queen Anne in 1714, many appeared to have forgotten those truths
for which their forefathers had struggled and suffered. In his work, *The Dissenters, From the Reformation to the French Revolution* (Oxford: Clarendon
Press, 1985), Michael Watts comments, 'It was not only the 'hill called lucre'

As they discussed the situation the Countess would have agreed with Doddridge that a revived and godly ministry seemed the only solution to the problem. For some years she had felt the urgent need of training men for the all-important task of preaching and already several students were attending Doddridge's Academy at her expense. Now she was prepared to finance another on a generous yearly grant. Not a man normally given to eulogy, Doddridge wrote in glowing terms of the Countess's Christian character in a letter to his friend Benjamin Fawcett in Kidderminster:

> Lady Huntingdon, for whom I desired your prayers, is wonderfully recovered. She walked with me in the garden and park and almost wearied me, such is her recruit of strength; but the strength of her soul is amazing. I think I never saw so much of the image of God in a woman upon earth. Were I to write what I know of her, it would fill your heart with wonder, joy and praise . . . She has God dwelling in her and she is ever bearing her testimony to the present salvation he has given us, and to the fountain of waters which she feels springing up in her soul.[1]

By early October 1750 Whitefield had made his way back to the Midlands to spend a further few days with the Countess and her sisters-in-law at Ashby Place. Here he discovered that even in 'ungrateful Ashby' some had been converted since his last visit in spite of the widespread opposition in the town. From a letter

---

which confronted Christian as he crossed the Plain of Ease; beyond the hill lay Doubting Castle. And beyond the problems of social adjustment that faced the Dissenters in an age of toleration lay more serious problems of religious adjustment raised by the transition from the enthusiasm of the mid-seventeenth century to the rationalism of the eighteenth. In as far as Dissenters were now looking to Locke rather than to Calvin for intellectual support for their faith; in proportion to their readiness to seek inspiration from the spirit of reason rather than the Spirit of God, their zeal flagged and their congregations dwindled.' pp. 391–2.

[1] Doddridge to Fawcett, 26 June 1750, Seymour, *Countess*, vol. 1, p. 154.

written on 11 October to Countess Delitz we catch a glimpse of those days of Christian fellowship that were a delight to Whitefield. We also see his growing awareness of Selina Hastings' contribution in the revival:

> Good Lady Huntingdon goes on acting the part of a mother in Israel, more and more. For a day or two she has had five clergymen under her roof, which makes her Ladyship look like a *good Archbishop* with his Chaplains around him. Her house is indeed a Bethel. To us in the ministry it looks like a college. We have the sacrament every morning, heavenly conversation all day, and preach at night. This is to live at Court indeed.[1]

But this was not merely an artless description of life at Ashby Place. Behind it lay a strategy for Christian service which had long been taking shape in the mind of the Countess. As a loyal member of the Church of England she wished above everything else to see the Church reformed from within. The Methodist societies were gathering together men and women born anew by the power of God but none of the early leaders of the revival saw this as anything other than a movement within the Church. No services were held in the Methodist preaching houses during the stated times of the parish church services. Any thought of separation from the Established Church into the ranks of Dissent would have appalled them. But the situation threw up real problems. With a moribund Church, and clergy often passionately opposed to the Methodist societies, there was an increasing need for men of evangelical persuasion to be ordained.

Yet who would ordain 'Methodist' clergymen? Here the Countess saw a role opening up for her. By means of her influence in the highest places of the land she determined to bring pressure on the bishops to ordain men who held to the truths of the gospel, that there might be evangelical preaching at the very heart of the Church of England. So it was that she invited men who felt called

[1] Whitefield, *Works*, vol. 2, p. 381.

to the ministry to her home at Ashby Place. When she was convinced both of their gifts and dedication to the gospel of Christ she began to rally support among her friends to campaign for ordination. If one bishop refused to comply with the request she would try another. Describing this strategy, Luke Tyerman comments:

> There can be little doubt that this was the grand scheme now revolving in the mind of the illustrious Countess . . . Whitefield tried to raise up converted clergymen and the Countess procured them ordination and [later] built them chapels. The idea was grand – perhaps inspired – and the working it out was unquestionably the principal means of effecting the marvellous change that has taken place since then in the Established Church.[1]

Two men were ordained at this time through Selina's efforts. One was Martin Madan. A personable, wealthy and able young lawyer, Madan had been at Westminster School and later Oxford at the same time as Francis Hastings. Gifted with the power of mimicry, he had attended a service at which John Wesley was preaching in order to impersonate the idiosyncrasies of his style for the entertainment of his friends. But when Wesley gave out his text, 'Prepare to meet thy God', the young man's conscience was awakened and the Spirit of God convicted him. He returned to his friends, who immediately asked him to 'take off the old Methodist.' 'No, gentlemen,' he replied, 'I cannot, but he has taken me off.' He began to identify himself publicly with Methodists and it was not long before Madan was introduced to the Countess. To her he confided his wish to enter the Christian ministry but his new connection with this despised cause was proving a barrier hard to be overcome. Through her efforts Madan was ordained and began a useful ministry in Lombard Street, London.

Moses Browne was the other for whom the Countess tried to secure ordination at this date. Unlike Madan, he had no univer-

---

[1] Tyerman, *Whitefield*, vol. 2, p. 192.

sity training, nor was he from a wealthy family background, but his talent and spiritual zeal commended him to Selina. The first bishop to whom she wrote had no time for would-be clerics with Methodist connections. To the second she sent three signed testimonials as a recommendation but once again met with a polite refusal. Finally she rallied many of her titled friends to give Browne financial support, and at last, after a seemingly interminable delay, a third bishop was persuaded to accept Browne. This experience became a prototype of such endeavours for many years to come. Another for whom she had also attempted to gain ordination was her friend Howell Harris himself. But for the Welsh exhorter, there remained only rebuffs from the bishops.[1]

During the winter of 1750 and the early months of 1751 the Countess faced further acute illness. The problem appears to have been one of those virulent and probably unidentified infections that so often swept through homes and communities at that time, carrying off men, women and children to early graves. 'Lady Huntingdon continues very ill. I fear we shall lose her,'[2] wrote Doddridge to a friend on 22 December. Thirteen-year-old Selina, the Countess's younger daughter, was also ill with the same infection, as was her sister-in-law, Lady Frances Hastings. Throughout January 1751 the Countess's condition deteriorated until few of her friends held out much hope for her recovery. When her state appeared critical Whitefield was hastily summoned. He scarcely knew whether he would find her still alive by the time he reached Ashby Place; but a surprising situation confronted him on his arrival.

---

[1] Howell Harris's refusal to relinquish his itinerant preaching appears to have been the main obstacle. Reiterating his position in his diary on 3 June 1748, he had stated, 'I mentioned to Lady Huntingdon our willingness to submit (as to myself) wholly to the Bishops if they will but give one point: liberty by licence for me to go about to preach the gospel to poor sinners that perish, and to have private societies to build up such as are awakened.' But this was too much for the prelates and an impasse had been reached over the ordination that the Welsh exhorter had so coveted.

[2] Letters to Rev. Samuel Wood, *Correspondence of Doddridge*, pp. 345–6.

SELINA COUNTESS OF HUNTINGDON

'I got safe to Ashby where I found good Lady Huntingdon very sick, though I trust not unto death', he wrote. But Lady Frances had died, and as Whitefield reported, 'She seemed as it were to smile at death, and may be said, I trust, truly, 'to fall asleep in Jesus.'[1] Always in the background, yet devoted to the service of Christ, Frances Hastings, together with her sister Anne, had been Selina's constant friend and companion. Converted in 1739 under the preaching of Benjamin Ingham, she had maintained a consistent Christian testimony and when the Countess had improved enough to realise the severity of her loss, she missed her sorely.

Sufficiently recovered, Selina complied with the advice of her friends and travelled to Bristol. Thankful to have arrived safely despite bitter weather conditions, she wrote to Whitefield and his supportive reply illustrates the pastoral relationship that had been established:

Underneath your Ladyship are his everlasting arms; you cannot sink with such a prop. Your Ladyship must be made conqueror, yea, more than conqueror through his love that is engaged to bring you through whatever sufferings may be before you.[2]

From Athlone on his second visit to Ireland, Whitefield continued to send encouraging letters to Bristol, informing Selina of his work.[3] In June 1751 he wrote:

May patience have its perfect work and your Ladyship come out of the furnace like gold tried seven times in the fire! ... For this week past I have been preaching twice almost every day in some country towns, and yesterday I sounded the gospel trumpet here. Everywhere there seems to be a stirring among the dry bones.[4]

[1] Whitefield, *Works*, vol. 2, p. 397.
[2] *Ibid.*, 26 February 1751, p. 400.
[3] For a detailed account of this visit see C. H. Crookshank's *History of Methodism in Ireland* (reprint, Clonmel: Tentmaker Publications, 1994), vol. 1.
[4] Whitefield, *Works*, vol. 2, p. 411.

And in a letter to her from Glasgow on 12 July 1751, he added:

Though I preached near eighty times in Ireland and God was pleased to bless his word, yet Scotland seems to be a new world to me. To see the people bring so many Bibles, turn to every passage when I am expounding and hang as it were upon me to hear every word, is very encouraging . . . This I suppose will find your Lady-ship yet in the furnace, but Christ is in the midst of the bush, and in the fiery furnace too. He will quench the violence of the flames, or cause the fire of his love to burn higher.[1]

By the end of August Whitefield had boarded *The Antelope* to return to America once more after an absence of three years.

As *The Antelope* carried the preacher far away from English shores, the Countess also faced the loss of another whose friendship she had valued. Philip Doddridge had for some time been displaying the symptoms of consumption. All that eighteenth-century medical knowledge could suggest was tried to improve his ailing health. At last his doctor, James Stonehouse, came to the conclusion that the only hope for him lay in a voyage to Lisbon, where the warmer climate would allow a period of recovery over the winter months. Doddridge and his wife decided to try this expedient, journeying to the coast at Falmouth by way of Bristol and the Hot Wells.

As soon as Selina, who was in nearby Bath at the time, heard of their arrival at the end of August 1751, she arranged for a coach and six to convey her personal physician as speedily as possible across to Bristol to see if anything more could be done to help the sick man. More than this she began to lobby her well-placed friends for funds to finance the trip to Lisbon. Within a few days she had raised £300, of which £100 was her own personal contribution. Writing to Doddridge she begged him to come across to Bath with his wife so that she could care for him for a few days before they embarked at Falmouth for Lisbon.

*Ibid.*, p. 418.

Forever etched upon her memory were the scenes that followed. The Countess had sincerely thought that she would die first and that Philip Doddridge, whose life and spiritual contribution seemed of paramount importance, would be left to serve his God for many years to come. But at the age of forty-nine Doddridge was dying. Coming into his room unexpectedly on the morning he was due to leave for Falmouth, Selina found him weeping with the Scriptures open in front of him. The words that had moved him so deeply were from the book of Daniel, 'O Daniel, a man greatly beloved.'

'You are in tears, Sir,' she said simply.

'I am weeping,' responded Doddridge, 'but they are tears of comfort and joy. I can give up my country, my relations and friends into the hands of God; and as to myself, I can as well go to heaven from Lisbon as from my own study in Northampton.'[1]

And so he did. He died at Lisbon on 26 October 1751. Not until February 1752 did Whitefield hear the news and comment: 'Dr Doddridge, I find, is gone; Lord Jesus prepare me to follow after!'[2] Meanwhile Selina confessed that 'the death of my dear Doddridge has affected my heart in a most unusual manner.' Whenever she thought of him and of the loss that the Christian church had sustained, she would find herself moved to tears. Drawn back from the verge of the grave herself, she now felt a yet greater responsibility to serve her generation while opportunities remained. As she had once written to Doddridge not long after the Earl's death: 'My heart wants nothing so much as to dispense all – all for the glory of him whom my soul loveth.'[3]

[1] Told to Augustus Toplady by the Countess twenty-four years later. *Works of Augustus Toplady* (1794), p. 498.
[2] Whitefield, *Works*, vol. 2, p. 429.
[3] Seymour, *Countess*, vol. 1, p. 79.

# 11

# THE COUNTESS AND THE
# WESLEY BROTHERS
# 1749-55

'YOUR MOST AFFECTIONATE, LOYAL AND FAITHFUL FRIEND' was a
description the Countess often used of herself as she ended a
letter to one of her friends. She had demonstrated the truth of
these words at the close of Philip Doddridge's life, and in her
kindness to his widow, Mercy, ensuring that she would lack no
material provision.

Although Selina Hastings had established friendships among
the Dissenters and others of a Calvinistic persuasion such as
George Whitefield and Howell Harris, she did not in any way
abandon her former friends, John and Charles Wesley. Nor did
she forget the early debt she owed them for their support and
fellowship during the first years of her Christian life. To her,
therefore, it was an occasion of much joy when on 8 April 1749
Charles Wesley married a young Welsh woman, Sarah Gwynne,
whose father was a wealthy Breconshire magistrate.

Commonly known as Sally, Marmaduke Gwynne's twenty-
three-year old daughter was an excellent choice of life partner for
the English poet of the revival. Supportive and unselfish, she was
able to cope with his intense mood swings and with his total dedication to the labour of bringing the gospel of Christ to the men
and women of England. But the courtship had not been a smooth
one. Charles had faced initial difficulties with his brother but

even more with Sally's mother who was anxious that her daughter should be supported in a manner appropriate to one who had previously known only circumstances of ease and luxury. Charles Wesley suggested that he could secure an income of £100 a year from royalties accruing from his hymns and from his brother's sermons – a generous provision when most country clerics were 'passing rich with forty pounds a year'.[1] Even this proposal failed to satisfy Mrs Gwynne. Who could tell, she argued, whether the whole Methodist movement would collapse and then who would wish to purchase the Wesleys' publications? When an impasse seemed to have been reached the Countess intervened on Charles's behalf. She undertook to make up the shortfall should ever the money earned by the publications fail to reach the required sum.[2] On this condition the marriage was allowed to proceed. Not only had Selina helped Charles Wesley, she also gained a new friend in Sally. Like herself, Sally came from a privileged background, a circumstance that formed a natural compatibility between them. Only two years older than her own eldest son, Francis, she found in Sally one whom she could love almost like a daughter.

Charles and Sally Wesley set up home in Charles Street, Bristol, in September 1749 and this may well have influenced Selina in her decision in 1752 to lease a further house in Clifton. An attractive area overlooking west Bristol, it was a natural choice for it was also near the Hot Wells that had proved beneficial to her health. Clifton became Selina's main home for much of the 1750s and whenever she was able she would call on Charles and Sally Wesley. Later she wrote: 'I often think and wish for those happy mornings we all spent together in Charles Street.'[3] She too had a love of hymns, poetry and music and had even composed some

[1] Oliver Goldsmith, *The Deserted Village, An Anthology of Longer Poems,* ed. Moles & Moon (London: Longmans, 1963), p. 27.
[2] Rylands MS.,Letter 62, November 1756, refers to this undertaking at a time when Charles was short of money, and she was enclosing a gift.
[3] *Ibid.*, Letter 24.

hymns herself.[1] Together they would sing Charles's hymns, doubtless to Sally's accompaniment on her harpsichord. A fair-haired son called Jacky, born to the Wesleys in the autumn of 1752, added to the pleasure of her visits. Charles in turn often called on the Countess at her Clifton home, preaching and administering the sacrament to the gathered household there.

The Countess supported Charles Wesley in his ministry, following his progress with frequent letters as he travelled the country. To him she felt able to confide some of her most personal spiritual experiences. It would seem that throughout these early years of her widowhood Selina relied on the strength and advice of such upright Christian men as the Wesley brothers, Howell Harris[2] and George Whitefield to a marked extent. So on 7 October 1752 she writes to Charles: 'Upon the fifth instant in the evening I experienced an uncommon degree of the glorious presence of our Lord. It continued from evening till midnight.'[3] Such letters afford interesting sidelights into Selina's personal life. On another occasion she told him:

> Your letter was full of spiritual comfort and instruction. I trust God will abundantly reward those prayers you offer for me. I value them more than thousands of worlds. By these my youngest daughter is given me back for a time. O! may I be deeply sensible by being deeply humbled for two such great mercies.[4]

While her friendship with Charles Wesley and his wife was deepening, Selina's contacts with John were becoming more formal and guarded during this period. Both had a forceful, even

---

[1] Howell Harris spoke of such evenings of singing and fellowship when he visited the Countess in London (e.g. *Harris's Visits to London*, p. 137). At her suggestion John Wesley had published *A Selection of Moral and Sacred Poems from the most Celebrated English Authors* in 1744, and dedicated the collection to the Countess.

[2] Howell Harris withdrew from itinerant preaching during the 1750s, reducing the Countess's contacts with him.

[3] Rylands MS., Letter 24.

[4] *Ibid.*, Letter 21.

domineering streak in their make-up which easily resulted in tensions between them. More than this, Wesley could see the Calvinistic wing of the revival grouping itself ever more closely around the Countess.

Relationships between John Wesley and his brother, Charles, had also been strained since Charles had intervened precipitously in October 1749 to prevent his brother marrying Grace Murray, the Newcastle widow to whom he was engaged. The brothers had drifted further apart after John's subsequent marriage to Molly Vazeille, widow of a sea captain. Contravening their agreement to consult each other before embarking on any courtship, John had married before his brother had time to interfere. 'Happy is the wooing, not long in doing', wrote Charles hopefully when he heard about the marriage although he was disturbed over his brother's choice. Attempting to accept both the situation and his new sister-in-law, Charles 'called on my sister [Molly], kissed her and assured her I was perfectly reconciled to her and my brother.'[1] But it did not last long, and Molly Wesley soon became intensely jealous of Charles.

Fearing that Charles might be drifting towards the same doctrinal position as that of the Countess and George Whitefield, John, who was preaching in Ireland, wrote to his brother from Athlone in August 1752:

> I almost wonder that I hear not one word from you . . . Does everyone forget me as soon as we have the sea between us? . . . Our preachers here have . . . openly affirmed that you agree with Mr Whitefield touching perseverance, at least, if not predestination too.[2]

Charles, for his part, had become concerned with aspects of his brother's leadership. With his strong attachment to the Church of England – an attachment shared by the Countess – he feared the

[1] Charles Wesley, *Journal*, vol. 2, p. 78–9.
[2] *Works of John Wesley*, ed. Baker, vol. 26, p. 498.

direction in which John might be leading the burgeoning Methodist societies. Towards the end of 1752, Charles wrote to Whitefield about his anxieties. The letter is lost and this whole year is missing from Charles Wesley's journal, but judging from Whitefield's reply, Charles may have been suggesting a closer collaboration with him. This would confirm the rumours John Wesley had heard in Ireland. Whitefield's answer, dated 22 December 1752, reads in part as follows:

> I have read and pondered your kind letter . . . and now sit down to answer it. And what shall I say? Really I can scarce tell. The connection between you and your brother hath been so close and continued, and your attachment to him so necessary to keep up his interest, that I would not willingly for the world do or say anything that may separate such friends . . . .I am glad you are with our elect Lady; she will shine in heaven as a common friend. O how amiable is a truly catholic spirit! Lord, make us all partakers of it more and more.[1]

And on the same day Whitefield also replied to a letter from the Countess:

> I shall observe your Ladyship's hints about Mr Wesley . . . but I am easy, having no scheme, no design of supplanting or resenting, but I trust a single eye to promote the common salvation without so much as attempting to set up a party for myself.[2]

John Wesley had always had an abiding fear of the doctrine of predestination, conceiving that its acceptance was likely to lead to antinomianism. So now he endangered the fragile unity that had existed for the last few years between the leaders of the revival by publishing a pamphlet entitled *Predestination Calmly Considered*.[3] According to his biographer, Luke Tyerman, this was one of Wesley's 'most cogent and exhaustive' treatments of the subject, aimed at 'utterly demolishing the Calvinistic theory'.[4]

[1] Whitefield, *Works*, vol. 2, p. 464.    [2] *Ibid.*, p. 466.
[3] Published 1752.
[4] Tyerman, *Wesley*, vol. 2, p. 148.

Wesley went further and, at his annual Conference that met in Leeds on 22 May 1753, he attempted to deal with the question of 'predestinarian preachers'. These were to be excluded in future from all Methodist pulpits connected with his societies. The Conference then requested that a 'loving and respectful letter' should be written to Whitefield, warning him against allowing any of the Calvinistic Methodist preachers to contravene Wesley's teachings in public or private to any members of Wesley's societies. These teachings included the doctrine of predestination, Christian perfection and the possibility of true believers being finally lost.

In the letter to Whitefield on 28 May 1753, Wesley included paragraphs which could only be described as containing matters of some personal abuse.[1] Not unexpectedly this brought Whitefield a considerable measure of distress. Not only did he deny all the accusations brought against him but also decided to go into print to vindicate himself. The Countess followed all these developments with concern. Her earnest wish was that all her friends should be united in the cause of the gospel, so when she heard that Whitefield was planning to print a reply to Wesley's letter, she was initially disturbed, but then wrote to Charles Wesley:

> Mr Whitefield writes me word he has not time to copy the letter he intends to print. I am glad of it as I hate everything that does not make for peace and I never saw anything wrote offensively that I did not disapprove. Charity is the more excellent way ... Conferences clear up more in an hour than a paper war after seven years ... I do think it is best for us all to keep clear of anything that may be followed with a scrap of any kind.[2]

The proposed response was never published. Probably her chaplain's time-consuming zeal to preach the gospel, coupled

[1] *Ibid.*, p.167.
[2] Rylands MS., Letter 23.

with the present rebuilding of Moorfield's Tabernacle, contributed to his change of mind.

The Countess's own relationship with John Wesley was still strained in 1753. Writing to Sally in September of that year she complained, 'I have not heard one word of Mr J. Wesley, and if he is not willing I should, I am satisfied.'[1] In addition the tension between the Wesley brothers had worsened. Contact between them had dwindled, and any collaboration in preaching schedules almost ceased. At last at the end of October John wrote to Charles with an ultimatum: 'Take one side or the other', he challenged. 'Either act readily in connection with me, or never pretend to it. At present you are so far from this that I do not even know when or where you intend to go.' He suspected that Charles had been planning his itineraries in consultation with the Countess instead of with himself. Concluding his letter, he claimed, and probably rightly, 'I may say without vanity, that I am a better judge in this matter [where Charles should concentrate his efforts] than either Lady Huntingdon, Sally, Jones or any other, nay than your own heart.'[2]

In the midst of these disagreements an event occurred that put an end, at least temporarily, to such tensions. John Wesley became seriously ill. A cold he had caught in November 1753 after preaching at Leigh-on-Sea had rapidly developed into a severe cough giving evidence of acute inflammation of the lungs. When he showed no improvement, the usual eighteenth century remedy of fresh air and donkey's milk was suggested. After five weeks of country air at the home of his friend, Ebenezer Blackwell in Lewisham, he was a little better, though he had, in fact, written his own epitaph to prevent expressions of adulation among his followers should he die.

[1] *Ibid.*, Letter 22.
[2] *Works of John Wesley*, vol. 26, p. 527. There were a number of early Methodist preachers by the name of Jones. This may have been a Thomas Jones, described as 'an awakened clergyman' to whom the Countess refers in several letters at this time.

As soon as Charles Wesley heard of his brother's condition, he rode hastily to Lewisham where he found John somewhat better, but 'still in imminent danger, being far gone and very suddenly, in a consumption'. Charles, with a customary emotional reaction, wept when he saw his brother and begged his forgiveness for the differences that had developed between them. John, for his part, urged his brother and Molly to be reconciled to one another; and a better relationship was restored between them. Whitefield meanwhile had gone to Bristol after a preaching tour in the south-west. Here he was to officiate at the opening services of a new chapel built in the city for his congregation, from subscriptions raised by the Countess and her friends. Hearing the news of John Wesley's illness and thinking that his fellow-preacher was dying, he wrote a tender-hearted farewell to a man whom he sincerely respected and loved, despite their differences:

> If seeing you so weak when leaving London distressed me, the news and prospect of your approaching dissolution hath quite weighed me down. I pity myself and the church, but not you. A radiant throne awaits you and ere long you will enter into your Master's joy.[1]

Charles Wesley soon left Lewisham and went to stay with a friend near the Foundery from where he undertook all his brother's London responsibilities. But no sooner had he arrived than he received two letters in quick succession addressed in a hand he knew well. Dated 3 December 1753 and written in much haste, the Countess was informing him that Sally had been taken ill and her condition could well be smallpox. A quiet heroism marks the next few days of Selina's life as she called constantly at Charles Street to care for her sick friend. Scarcely ten years had passed since Ferdinando and George had died of the same illness. Never strong herself, she took a serious risk as she spent many hours with Sally.

[1] 3 December 1753, Whitefield, *Works*, vol. 3, p. 44.

Hopeful that it might not be too severe a case, the Countess did not wish to alarm Charles unnecessarily. With little confidence in medical opinion, Selina suggested that the best option in her view was 'diluting liquors, keeping warm and not interrupting nature'. She promised to write to Charles giving him regular reports on his wife's progress: 'You shall hear from me tomorrow night again, and I beg by the first post to know, should it prove the smallpox, whether you would have your little boy removed.'

Sally's condition deteriorated sharply, however, and for several days her life hung in the balance. Realising the degree of her danger, Selina urged Whitefield to proceed to London immediately to relieve Charles of his duties there so that he could return to Bristol to be with Sally. Whitefield himself was becoming increasingly apprehensive lest the Countess was putting her own life in jeopardy by her attentions to her sick friend. Knowing that no warnings of his could cause this determined woman to forsake Sally, he could only conclude, 'But your Ladyship hath long since learnt that as your days so shall your strength be. I pray the Lord of all lords to lengthen out your important life.'[1]

When he arrived back in Bristol on 6 December Charles gazed in consternation at his pretty wife; the illness had so disfigured her that he scarcely recognised her:

I found my dearest friend on a restless bed of pain, loaded with the worst kind of the worst disease . . . Good Lady Huntingdon attends her constantly twice a day . . . She had expressed a longing desire to see me just before I came, and rejoiced for the consolation; I saw her alive, but O how changed![2]

With Charles back home and Sally's mother also present, the Countess could safely relinquish her daily visits, but her mind was often with her friend. Writing to Charles she asked for news:

[1] *Ibid.*, vol. 3, p. 50.
[2] Charles Wesley, *Journal*, vol. 2, p. 100.

I long to hear how dear Mrs Wesley does as the night is so bad (and as I could be of no real use), I have begged an account. The distress of your mind will render quiet more agreeable to you, and I trust that God will give you the desire of your heart back from the grave. Assure her of my love and prayers and to Mrs Gwynne, my best and kindest services. May the grace of Jesus Christ sustain your spirit.[1]

In the midst of this situation the Countess herself received disturbing news. A messenger arrived from Ashby Place where her own two children were living to tell her that thirteen-year-old Henry had been bitten by a mad dog and was in danger of contracting rabies. His mother was understandably alarmed. 'I do most earnestly beg your prayers for him and for me', she wrote to Charles Wesley, then still at the Foundery. As we have seen, the Countess had quite a store of medical knowledge herself, so she sent the messenger back to Leicestershire with 'a remedy that has never failed yet', and instructions to bring the boy to Bristol immediately. Within a week, however, she could tell Charles that the news of Henry was 'every hour more favourable'.

As 1753 came to an end, Sally Wesley, still weak from her smallpox, had a further heavy affliction to endure. Despite all precautions, her sixteen-month-old son, Jacky, had also contracted the illness. Sally watched helplessly over the child as he struggled against the disease but early in January 1754 he lost the battle against this highly virulent infection. As the Countess was visiting the Hot Wells on the day following Jacky's death, she was surprised to meet John Wesley himself, who had come to Bristol to take advantage of the waters. She was glad to find him 'not near so ill as I expected'. From him Selina learnt of the child's death. Once again the Countess called immediately on the bereaved mother whom she found 'sorely wasted and weak in body.' On the same day she wrote to Charles – a letter expressing the deep sympathy of one who had trodden that same hard path herself:

[1] Rylands MS., Letter 27.

As a parent and a friend I feel for you most sincerely, but as a Christian . . . I must believe this little dear child is only delivered from the evil that is coming over a wicked and most apostate nation . . . The chances against us parents for happiness is a hundred to one and the dear little creature is happy for eternity and your grief can be only for one moment.[1]

Selina had proved a 'most affectionate, loyal and faithful friend', and a courageous one too. Following John Wesley's recovery, relations improved between the brothers and with the Countess as well. Correspondence was now renewed between them so that Selina could write to Charles in March 1754:

I was greatly obliged by your brother's and your letters. I should have wrote the last post but indeed I am so hurried and all my family in their turns have been so ill that I have been ready to sink under it, not being very well myself.

Throughout these years Selina continued to correspond regularly with Charles Wesley. She recognised that sometimes the forcefulness of her personality – that God-given trait which made her what she was – seemed too much for some to cope with. To him she confessed, 'I am so blunt that I fear I please none but you, who am as much as ever your friend.' Cheered by his letters and visits when she was at her Clifton home she could write to Charles in May 1755: 'I cannot express the comfort your letter gave me.'

Tensions had begun to rise again during 1755 between the Wesley brothers, partly because of the acute personal problems John Wesley was facing in his marriage, but more because of the internal unrest which was on the increase among Wesley's lay preachers. Inbuilt into the Methodist system that he had been developing since the earliest days of the revival was the unresolved tension between loyalty to the Church of England and the resurgent evangelicalism that threatened its unity. Society

[1] *Ibid.*, Letter 33.

meetings had always been intended to supplement and not to replace the stated services of the Church. But once John Wesley had set foot down the road of 'irregularity', introducing unordained preachers, crossing parish boundaries, building preaching houses for Methodist gatherings, organising band meetings and class meetings, it was only a matter of time before the compatibility of such things with church protocol would be questioned. Now there was pressure from within the ranks of the preachers either to break away from a decadent church and join the ranks of Dissent, or at least to conduct their own communion services. Ever more clear-sighted than his brother, John Wesley recognized, at least in principle, that a future separation might well be inevitable; but for the present the only way ahead was to call a conference to discuss the whole issue.

This Conference met on 6 May 1755 in Leeds, with three ordained men present, John and Charles Wesley and William Grimshaw, and sixty-three lay preachers. For three days the issue of separation was thrashed out and, although no details have survived, John Wesley wrote in his Journal: 'Whatever was advanced on one side or the other was seriously and calmly considered; and on the third day we were all fully agreed in that general conclusion, that (whether it [separation] was lawful or not) it was no ways expedient.'[1] Although the result had been in line with Charles Wesley's wishes, he was far from happy, perhaps feeling that his brother's pragmatism would one day inevitably lead to separation from the Church. Whatever the cause, he left the Conference early, insisting he would never attend another – a threat he did not in fact carry out. Nor did he tell anyone that he was leaving. On his way back to Bristol he called in at Donington Hall where the Countess was overseeing improvements on her son's property. Without doubt the crisis facing Methodism was discussed fully, and in Selina Charles Wesley found one whose loyalty to the Church was unquestion-

[1] Wesley, *Journal*, vol. 4, p. 115.

able, but whose reactions were perhaps more measured than his own.

Writing to his brother on 28 June 1755, John Wesley was anxious that Charles should lift his eyes beyond the externals of church order to the all-important matters of truth and holiness. 'I dare not spend my time and strength on externals', he wrote. 'If, as my Lady Huntingdon says, all outward establishments are Babel, so is this establishment. Let it stand for me. I neither set it up nor pull it down. But let you and I build up the city of God.'[1] Conscious of the degree of anxiety Charles felt over these issues, the Countess also wrote on 23 December with another suggestion:

> I wish you would see Mr Whitefield and talk matters over with him ... His heart is honest and he has a truly brotherly love for you ... I think if your brother found you in friendship then it would keep him in order more than anything I know ... Mr Whitefield has no design of staying in England or dividing any interests. This I know to be a fact. He is more and more detached from all things but that of public labour ... May our Lord bless and direct you and take this as the effort of my best judgment and most unfeigned friendship.[2]

Despite times of tension, misunderstanding and even suspicion, the Countess had maintained an 'unfeigned friendship' with both John and Charles Wesley throughout the early 1750s. Although her influence had been steadily increasing among the men who represented the Calvinistic wing of the revival, her genuine love of both the Wesley brothers and the debt she undoubtedly owed them, cemented the bonds of friendship and surmounted any temptation to allow a permanent breakdown in relationships.

---

[1] *Works of John Wesley*, vol.26, p. 565.
[2] Rylands MS.,Letter 52.

# 12

# AN EMERGING PATTERN

WHEN GEORGE WHITEFIELD WROTE to Countess Delitz in October 1750 comparing Lady Huntingdon to 'a good archbishop with his chaplains around him', he had touched on an all-important factor in her thinking at this time. Predominantly a loyal member of the Church of England, she was anxious to keep the Methodist movement within the bounds of the Established Church. Like Charles Wesley, she too feared a day when Methodist lay preachers might begin to drift into Dissent for lack of opportunity to exercise their ministry, not only in preaching, but also in administering the sacraments to their people. She therefore bent her constant endeavours towards the reformation and renewal of the Church.

As we have seen, her first thought was to seek the improvement of its ministry by applying pressure on the bishops to ordain evangelical men to its pulpits. No easy task at any time, it proved yet harder as the years passed, for most of the bishops had become deeply suspicious of the men whom she recommended, rightly believing they would be of Methodist persuasion. In a letter written many years later to Archbishop Cornwallis she explained that her purpose in all her endeavours had always been 'to stop the overflowings of infidelity and vice, and this as far as I could by ministers of our own Church.'[1]

Throughout the 1750s another idea was steadily gaining prominence in the mind of the Countess. If she, with her

[1] Cheshunt Foundation Archives, Westminster College, Cambridge.

[154]

privileges as a peeress, were able to assist in financing new buildings or in purchasing the lease of existing ones, this would
provide places of worship where evangelical men could preach
without the strictures often imposed upon them by the hierarchy
of the Church. Among her earliest initiatives was a spacious
preaching house in Bristol erected and opened in November
1753.[1] Financed largely by the contributions of Selina and her
friends, it was designed to accommodate the crowds who were
clamouring to hear Whitefield preach.[2] Another sizeable chapel
had been erected in Norwich during 1755, again financed mainly
out of the Countess's generous contributions. This was intended
for the people who wished to hear James Wheatley, a preacher
who had formerly worked with Wesley.[3]

As the number of chapels built from subscriptions raised by the
Countess and her friends increased, so the need for men willing
and able to fill their pulpits became a pressing need. Howell
Harris, on whose help she had often called in the past, was no
longer able to assist her. Exhausted by years of travelling throughout the Principality, often short of money, rarely eating
adequately, never allowing himself proper sleep, we cannot be
surprised that even so dauntless an evangelist as Harris could
complain at this time, 'My nature is so worn out and spent, and
my body so impaired that I have not sufficient strength.'

[1] Matthew Francis, in his thesis on the Countess, claims that the very first
chapel she financed was in York in 1750, accommodating those who wished to
worship there after a visit from George Whitefield. Built in a small garden in
College Street, it was unadorned and seated about 200 on benches without
backs.
[2] Referring to this chapel Whitefield wrote to a friend on 1 December 1753,
'On Sunday I opened the new Tabernacle. It is large, but not half large
enough: would the place contain them, I believe near as many would attend as
in London.' Whitefield, *Works*, vol. 3, p. 41.
[3] Wheatley, who had been preaching in association with Wesley since 1742,
had been accused of questionable moral behaviour in 1751 and expelled from
Wesley's list of lay preachers. Now deeply penitent he had taken up his ministry again.

Erratic by nature, in better times Harris had been able to hold in check certain traits of character that now seemed to gain control of him. He became censorious of his fellow workers, demanding recognition for his part in the revival and expressing critical and harsh comments about others. He sincerely felt that because he had been the 'first in the field' as he put it – the first to undertake itinerant preaching and to gather his converts into societies – he therefore merited the foremost place in the leadership of the Welsh Association.

Throughout the years there had been simmering trouble between Harris and the other acknowledged leader in the work, Daniel Rowland. As time passed Harris's diaries were increasingly peppered with references to his own primacy on the Welsh scene and progressively more critical of others. An aberration of doctrine regarding the person of Christ[1] also became a feature of his preaching and writing at this time. In addition, his unwise behaviour in allowing a woman known as Madame Griffith to accompany him on his travels was a cause of serious concern. At last a crisis had been reached and in July 1750 Howell Harris was formally expelled from the Welsh Association that met at Llantrisant. A sad division in the work of the Welsh branch of the revival ensued, with the majority supporting Rowland. The two leaders went their separate ways and had little to do with each other for the next eleven years. Harris retired to his Trevecca home, making it the base of all his future endeavours.

The loss of Howell Harris brought an added urgency to the Countess's search for men who could preach in her home and in the pulpits where she had an increasing influence. Whitefield had been her personal chaplain since the end of 1748, but he was necessarily either in America or engaged in preaching in many parts of Britain. So now her thoughts were directed to William Romaine. We must therefore look briefly at the background of

---

[1] He taught that God the Father was also suffering and dying in the person of his Son – a form of Patripassianism.

this remarkable preacher who begins to figure prominently in the story of the Countess of Huntingdon.

Born in Hartlepool in 1714, Romaine was of Huguenot stock. His father's family had fled to Britain in the period of intense persecution following the revocation of the Edict of Nantes in 1685. Yet, in spite of such a background, he was without spiritual light. Coming to London in 1747 young Romaine had one aim: to cut a stunning figure in the metropolis by obtaining an influential pulpit and by publishing a learned treatise which he had prepared. Describing himself later as 'a very very vain, proud young man', Romaine had a bitter lesson to learn when he found both himself and his gifts ignored. He had decided to return home to Hartlepool when, due to an apparently chance meeting, he obtained a lectureship at St Dunstan's-in-the-West. At this time God began to work secretly in young Romaine. He went to many different churches and heard as many sermons but none seemed to answer his soul's need. At last God dealt directly with him:

> I became very vile in my own eyes. I gave over striving; the pride of free will, the boast of my own heart were laid low and Self was debased; the Scriptures became a new open book, and every page presented the Saviour in new glory.[1]

With renewed heart and enlightened mind Romaine's preaching soon began to attract the people. Though he subsisted on a mere £18 a year from his lectureships, gifts from those whose lives had been transformed by his ministry supplemented his income. St Dunstan's-in-the-West was situated in an influential position in Fleet Street near the law courts, and though the increasing effectiveness of his preaching soon aroused the hostility of the local vicar, Romaine continued undaunted. A further opportunity for Romaine came in 1750 when he was appointed to assist the ministry at St George's, Hanover Square – again an important church in the centre of the developing and influential

[1] Thomas Haweis, *The Life of William Romaine* (London, 1797), pp. 30–1.

west of London as it then was. The Countess of Huntingdon, ever a keen observer of the religious scene, was well aware of William Romaine's ministry. With her strong desire to see evangelical men placed at the heart of the ministry of the Church of England, she was quick to recognize the value of Romaine's position.

As the numbers of his hearers grew, so did the opposition. Regular parishioners objected to finding their seats occupied by strangers to the parish, and Romaine's ministry was under threat. 'If the power to attract be imputed as a matter of admiration to Garrick [the actor], why should it be urged as a crime against Romaine?' asked the Duke of Northumberland adroitly. But nothing availed to appease the disgruntled parishioners, and in 1755 the incumbent of St George's dismissed his lecturer.

Yet still the people wanted the opportunity of hearing their favourite preacher and at this point the Countess of Huntingdon stepped in. She invited William Romaine to become one of her chaplains, and opened up her home in Park Street to his hearers. Knowing that it would be below the dignity of the nobility to mingle with the ordinary citizens, two separate gatherings were established. For his regular hearers she encouraged Romaine to make use of her kitchens and ancillary rooms where his people could gather and hear him without any disturbance. And for the nobility his weekly ministry to her titled hearers became a feature of his life for a number of years. Not only was Romaine willing to preach in Selina's London home, he also began to minister in other pulpits where her influence gained him a hearing.

Another whose services the Countess began to call upon to preach at her home meetings at this time was Martin Madan. As we have seen, she was directly responsible in gaining ordination for Madan who had now been appointed as chaplain of the Lock Hospital. Instituted in 1746 and situated near Hyde Park, in present day Grosvenor Square, the hospital was unique for the times. With doctors giving their services gratis, it was designed to provide a refuge for fallen and destitute women whose illnesses excluded them from most public welfare services. Madan, whose preaching and activities had already caused a considerable stir among his erstwhile companions and legal clientele, would sometimes say, 'I have long been accustomed to plead at the bar the cause of man; I stand here to plead the cause of God and to beseech sinners to be reconciled to him.'

Early in January 1756, when the Countess was staying in Bath, she took the opportunity of encouraging aspiring preachers and ordained men by inviting them to her home. She had done this on several previous occasions in the past but now such events were to become a feature in Bath, particularly in the winter months which the Countess often spent there. Preachers from various parts of the south-west gathered and were her guests for a number of days. There they had opportunities for discussion, with days of fellowship and prayer, coupled with numerous occasions for preaching to enthusiastic congregations who congregated quickly whenever word was passed around of the venue where one or other of her guests would be preaching.

At the same time George Whitefield, who had returned to England in May 1755 after a year's visit to America, was exploring a further means of evangelism. Aiming to reach the fashionable members of the London theatre-going community with the gospel message, he informed the Countess on 31 December 1755:

> A noble chapel is now opened in Long Acre where I am to read prayers and preach twice a week. Hundreds went away last night who could not come in; but those that could, I trust, met with Jesus.[1]

The explanation was that a Dissenting meeting house, Long Acre Chapel, had been rented by one of Whitefield's converts who had asked Whitefield to preach there. The chapel was

[1] Whitefield, *Works*, vol. 3, p. 153.

well-placed for reaching the theatre world; it also provided an easily accessible venue for the many titled hearers who had been influenced by the meetings at the Countess's homes and in those of other members of the nobility such as Lady Fanny Shirley, Lady Gertrude Hotham and Countess Delitz.

Soon Whitefield could report 'a glorious stirring among the dry bones.' But then violent opposition broke out. Theatre magnates, perhaps fearing the effect of a converting work among their clients, stirred up the mob to disturb the worship by every means in their power. Whitefield wrote to the Dean of Westminster, Zachary Pearce, in whose diocese the chapel lay, informing him of the disturbances, including the fact that large stones had been flung through the windows, injuring members of the congregation. The Dean chose to ignore the demonstrators and did nothing to suppress the rioting.

Despite all that Whitefield and his supporters could do the situation only grew worse. The Countess put him in touch with several in high office who had power to put an end to this unacceptable situation but to no avail. When Whitefield began to receive death threats he realised that it was imperative to find alternative premises for the congregation that had been built up. His next letter to Selina, now back in Bristol, brought news of a large and strategically placed plot of land in Tottenham Court Road – not far from Long Acre Chapel – an area then on the outskirts of London surrounded by fields and gardens. Here he could build a further Tabernacle to meet the requirements of the people.

Gradually the outline of an impressive new chapel began to take shape against the London skyline. With two galleries on each of three sides, it was to be seventy feet square. The Countess took a lively interest in the progress of Whitefield's Tabernacle and, in order to guard his congregation from any further interference, Whitefield applied to the House of Commons for a licence to place the building under her protection. Both the Countess and

Whitefield would have been disappointed at the negative ruling that he received to his proposal. On 4 June 1756 Whitefield wrote giving her the text of the reply:

> No nobleman can licence a chapel or in any manner have one put in his dwelling house; that the chapel must be a private one, and not with doors to the street for any persons to resort to at pleasure, for then it becomes a public one; that a chapel cannot be built and used as such without the consent of the parson of the parish and when it is done with his consent, no minister can preach therein without licence of the Bishop of the diocese.[1]

Following this unfavourable response Whitefield decided to register Tottenham Court Road Chapel as a Dissenting meeting house under the protection of the Toleration Act. Though a retrograde step in the eyes of loyal members of the Church of England, it would at least afford Whitefield a measure of protection from such interference as he had experienced at Long Acre. This ruling was, however, a foreshadowing of things to come, for the Countess had assumed that as a peeress her policy of opening her chapels to the public would not be brought into question.

These circumstances also further highlighted the unresolved tension between the Church of England and the vibrant Methodist movement in its midst that was steadily becoming less easy to ignore. Methodists were often refused communion at their local parish churches or, even if they were not, they found it unacceptable to partake in churches where the truths that they believed were disregarded or even disparaged. Despite the all-important Methodist Conference of 1755 where these issues were supposedly thrashed out and settled at least for the foreseeable future, the situation was far from satisfactory. Several Methodist preachers had already become Dissenters and others were deeply dissatisfied with the strictures placed on their ministry by the Wesley brothers. One of their number, Edward Perronet, son of

[1] *Ibid.*, p.182.

Vincent Perronet, close friend of both brothers, had published a long and stinging exposé in verse form of the weakness and decadence of the Church of England.

Primarily concerned over the issue was Charles Wesley, who had become almost frenetic in his determination to keep the links with the Church of England securely in place. Inevitably, therefore, John Wesley, whose outlook on the whole question was far more pragmatic and realistic than that of his brother, considered it necessary to make this an important topic of discussion once more in the forthcoming Conference to be held in Bristol in August 1756. Knowing the depth of Charles Wesley's concern over the issue, the Countess wrote to him shortly before it was due to begin saying, 'I hope every blessing you wish or desire may attend the Conference.'

In the event, John Wesley took a firmer line than before against separation, declaring in his Journal: 'We largely considered the necessity of keeping in the Church, and using the clergy with tenderness; and there was not one dissenting voice. God gave us all to be of one mind and of one judgment.'[1] Meanwhile Charles Wesley had set off on a tour of the societies in the north of England with the specific agenda of bolstering up their flagging loyalty to the Church, a tour that proved to be his last. In addition to more than fifty itinerant preachers, the Conference had been attended by the same three ordained men as in 1755: the two Wesleys and Grimshaw, but this time with the addition of a fourth, there for the first time – Henry Venn, a young curate from Clapham. His name was to become closely linked with that of Selina, Countess of Huntingdon.

Born in 1724, Venn had studied at Cambridge and though a candidate for the ministry, his great interest was cricket, a game at which he excelled. After his ordination in 1747, however, he gave up playing, insisting that he would not wish any of his parishioners to be able to say to him, 'Well struck, Parson!' Though

[1] Wesley, *Journal*, vol. 4, p. 186.

upright, sincere and with a love of good books, Venn was still a stranger to heart religion at this time. But now he began to feel a deeper concern, and particularly as he read William Law's classic, *A Serious Call to a Devout and Holy Life.* Like Wesley, Whitefield, Grimshaw and many others Henry Venn experienced a period of striving to please God by religious devotion with fastings, prayers and other duties. Law's book had awakened him to his obligations, but it provided no answer for the guilty conscience for it did not point to the atoning work of Christ. But God met him and we read that 'in the meadows behind Jesus College he had such a view of the goodness, mercy and glory of God as elevated his soul above the world and made him aspire towards God as his supreme good, with unutterable ardour and enjoyment'.[1]

Still far from clear in his understanding, Venn found a true friend in Thomas Haweis,[2] who had been converted under the ministry of Samuel Walker in Truro. Then a curate at St Mary Magdalene in Oxford, Haweis was in London taking a short break from his duties. Finding Venn hard pressed with his many commitments, he spent time assisting him. Long and animated discussions took place between the two, centring particularly on the issue of Calvinism as opposed to Arminianism. 'Allow me, my dear Haweis, to be something more than a stone,' Venn remonstrated in the middle of one of their discussions concerning God's sovereign control in the affairs of men. Gradually Venn began to understand the truths that his friend was seeking to demonstrate, and Haweis commented, 'He very shortly after learned that it was of stones God raised up children unto Abraham and that it is his grace alone which takes away the heart of stone and gives a heart of flesh.'[3]

---

[1] *Life and Letters of Henry Venn,* with a Memoir by the Rev. John Venn (Edinburgh: Banner of Truth, 1993), p. 16.

[2] He pronounced his name 'Haws', rhyming it in a comic verse with 'paws'.

[3] A. Skevington Wood, *Thomas Haweis* (London: S.P.C.K., 1957), pp. 75–6.

But early religious ideas are not easily cast off, and in his preaching Henry Venn urged upon his people standards of Christian perfection that he had learnt from William Law. Then just at this time he was taken seriously ill and for several months was unable to preach. During a period of convalescence he reflected deeply on the course of his life and ministry. On his recovery Whitefield invited Venn to accompany him, together with Martin Madan, on a preaching tour in the south-west of the country, and during this period these men were all hospitably entertained at Clifton, two miles from Bristol, by the Countess of Huntingdon.

Ever a shrewd observer of the men who gathered in her home for days of fellowship and preaching, Selina was quick to notice the lingering effects of the mystical writers upon Venn's thinking and ministry. She too had struggled under the burden of such teaching[1] and had known the oppression of conscience to which it led. Concerned for her new young friend and anxious that he might be released from the bonds that still in measure fettered him, she wrote him a long and forthright letter after he had returned to Clapham.

A remarkable letter, it demonstrated the Countess's grasp of Christian doctrine and was the instrument God was to use to bring Henry Venn to a new measure of spiritual understanding. It can be regarded as foundational to his future life and ministry:

O, my friend! we can make no atonement to a violated law – we have no inward holiness of our own; the Lord Jesus Christ is the Lord our Righteousness. Cling not to such beggarly elements, such filthy rags – mere cobwebs of Pharisaical pride – but look to him who hath wrought out a perfect righteousness for his people. You find it a hard task to come naked and miserable to Christ, to come, divested of every recommendation but that of abject wretchedness

[1] This comes out in much of Selina's early correspondence with Charles Wesley. See in particular Letter 105 cited in chapter 6.

and misery, and receive from the outstretched hand of our divine Immanuel the riches, the super-abounding riches of redeeming grace. But if you come at all, you must come thus, and like the dying thief, the cry of your heart must be, 'Lord, remember me.' There must be no conditions – Christ, and Christ alone, must be the only Mediator between God and sinful men – no miserable performances can be placed between the sinner and the Saviour. Let the eye of faith ever be directed to the Lord Jesus Christ . . . And now, my dear friend, no longer let false doctrine disgrace your pulpit. Preach Christ crucified as the only foundation of the sinner's hope. Preach him as the Author and Finisher, as well as the sole object of faith – that faith which is the gift of God. Exhort Christless impenitent sinners to fly to this city of refuge – to look to him who is exalted as Prince and a Saviour, to give repentance and the remission of sins. Go on thus, and may your bow abide in strength![1]

Henry Venn's acceptance of her words speaks highly of his Christian character. Whitefield was soon able to report to the Countess:

Your exertions in bringing him to a clearer knowledge of the ever-lasting gospel have indeed been blessed. He owes your Ladyship much, under God, and I believe his whole soul is gratitude to the divine author of his mercies and to you, the honoured instrument in leading him to the fountain of truth.'[2]

---

[1] Seymour, *Countess*, vol. 1, pp. 225–6.
[2] *Ibid.*, p. 225.

# 13

# FAMILY CONCERNS

ALTHOUGH THE COUNTESS OF HUNTINGDON was becoming increasingly involved in the wider work of the revival throughout the 1750s, yet the concerns of her family still required her time and attention. Henry had his tenth birthday in December 1749 and Selina was twelve. Eighteen-year-old Elizabeth, vivacious and sociable, had grown into an attractive but restive young woman, who showed an increasing degree of impatience with the strictures of her home life.

For her elder daughter, however, Selina had a plan. Through her support of Frederick, Prince of Wales, she had gained a considerable measure of influence in the royal household. So in March 1749 Elizabeth had been appointed Lady of the Bedchamber to the two young princesses, Amelia and Caroline. But her period in this position was short-lived. Horace Walpole suggests a possible though unconfirmed reason: 'The Queen of the Methodists got her daughter named for Lady of the Bedchamber to the princesses; but it is all off again, as she will not let her play at cards on Sundays.'[1]

Back with her mother, Elizabeth found the intense atmosphere of home irksome to her spirit. Describing her mother as 'righteous overmuch', she could say of herself, 'I have not a grain of the solitary in me. I enjoy the society of my fellow mortals exceedingly.' She had found the glittering attractions of court life a strong

[1] Walpole to Horace Mann, 4 March 1749, Seymour, *Countess*, vol. 1, p. 460.

temptation. The death of Frederick, Prince of Wales, in 1751 meant that Elizabeth was not likely to gain any further position at court, so marriage seemed the only means of escape to the young woman. In the early spring of 1752, Elizabeth was engaged to Lord Rawdon, an Irish peer considerably older than herself. Her mother was not unduly troubled by Elizabeth's prospective marriage. Lord Rawdon was a religious man and she saw this development as the hand of God in the life of her headstrong daughter. Writing to Charles Wesley early in March 1752 she reports:

> I am sure it will be a great pleasure to you to hear that Lady Betty was yesterday married to a most sensible and worthy man, Lord Rawdon of Ireland. He has a very great fortune but above all a man disposed to great seriousness and which, from the respect I have for him, I trust will end in true and exemplary piety.[1]

A letter written by Elizabeth to her brother Francis shortly after her marriage bears out the young woman's impatience with her home life: 'I lived a life of duty with my mother,' she confessed. 'I own it grew wearisome at length, and was a strong inducement to my marrying – my situation in Ireland is happy – extremely so, in separating us so far asunder.'[2]

Meanwhile Francis, who had turned twenty in 1749, was on his Grand Tour. Lord Chesterfield, as we have seen, took an attentive interest in the boy, regarding himself as a replacement for the father Francis had recently lost. Wherever the young man travelled Chesterfield followed him with letters of advice and direction, designed to develop the youth's potential and make him into a nobleman of distinction and worldly graces. The flattering compliments he paid to Francis were enough to turn any young man's head. Writing to a friend to ask her to accommodate the youthful traveller, he introduced him with these words:

[1] Rylands MS., Letter 21.
[2] HMC, *Hastings Collection*, vol. 3, p. 14.

He is one of the finest peers of England, whose family is celebrated in the most ancient records. His merits and talents are at least equal to his descent; he is distinguished from all our young nobility by his personal erudition; in short he wants nothing to make him perfect but what he will acquire with you.[1]

Even though Francis was abroad, his mother thought of him with concern and looked for news of him. But no news came. He was so engrossed with his new way of life, learning French, dancing, fencing and horse riding, that he had little time or inclination to write. At last after six months had passed Chesterfield addressed the situation: 'I have heard it whispered that you have not wrote to Lady Huntingdon above once since you left England . . . If it be true I take the liberty of begging you, for your own sake, to write to her from time to time with marks of affection.'[2] The truth was that Francis was drifting further and further into a self-indulgent and careless way of life. Nor could he receive any help, in this respect at least, from the man who had set himself up as his mentor.

The Duchess of Somerset,[3] a long-standing friend of Selina's, while expressing her satisfaction at Elizabeth's marriage, was less than sanguine about Francis Hastings. 'What an affliction is Lord Huntingdon's dislike for religion!' she exclaimed in a letter to a friend, 'and what have not my Lords Chesterfield and Bolingbroke to answer for!' Although the Countess made no direct reference to it in her letters, we learn from contemporary correspondence that Francis had been forming illicit relationships with women whom he met on his travels.

Lord Chesterfield, on whom the Duchess of Somerset pinned much of the blame, could only advise him to avoid the physical and social consequences of his sin.[4] It little mattered how he

[1] A. H. New, *The Coronet and the Cross* (London, 1858), p. 78.
[2] *Letters of Lord Chesterfield to Lord Huntingdon* (London: Medici Society Ltd., 1923), p. 7.   [3] Formerly the Duchess of Hereford.
[4] *Chesterfield to Huntingdon*, p. 23.

lived, Chesterfield maintained, as long as the results of his immoral lifestyle did not impede his progress in society. He wished Francis would move on from Caen, where he had been staying, and that he would visit Paris. The young man seemed reluctant, and so Chesterfield enquired, 'Is there another Berenice to be dismissed when you leave Caen or several? The more, the more easily parted with.'[1]

How little can the Countess have realized the consequences of allowing Chesterfield to befriend her son! Though lower in social ranking than Selina herself, Chesterfield, with his erudition, his ingratiating manner and his magnificent hospitality both deceived and flattered her. Always prepared to discuss religion, he had allowed her to think that he might yet be won for the Christian gospel. 'It was a dangerous alliance', comments a later writer, 'between the blasé, cynical, aristocratic roué, and the sheltered, well-bred, innocent youth . . . From that time the mother had the bitterness of seeing her son estranged by deepening infidelity from the faith that was life itself to her.'[2] More than this, Chesterfield had ulterior motives for his attentions to Francis Hastings. He had hopes that Francis would reciprocate his friendship by assisting Chesterfield's own illegitimate son to make headway in high society.

On a brighter note, the Duchess of Somerset whose letter was written in 1752, gives the first evidence that the Countess's younger daughter, Selina, was a source of spiritual consolation to her mother: 'Lady Selina is a great comfort,' she reports, 'and is a most amiable, pious and affectionate character.'[3] Henry, too, was making satisfactory progress. A description of the twelve-year-

[1] *Ibid.*, p. 13.
[2] A. D. Belden, *George Whitefield, the Awakener* (London: Low, Marston & Co.), p. 167. Augustus Toplady described Chesterfield as 'a decent civilised fornicator' and 'a father who was at once capable of guiding a son into the ruinous paths of vice, and of pretending at other times to give him a few squeamish cautions against it.' Toplady's *Letters*, *Works* (1794), pp. 858, 866.
[3] *Coronet and Cross*, p. 109.

old, written by his mother to Elizabeth, was probably over-complimentary:

> Your brother left me three days ago for school. He grows so like your dear father that I look on him with more delight than I can express. He has never given even occasion for correction and his tutor says he will more and more answer the most sanguine expectations. His heart is at present set upon going to be a good scholar from school, and his sobriety is astounding. I cannot express how great a blessing I look upon this from the hand of almighty God. I will write if possible before I go to Clifton to live. May our gracious Lord bless you and make you sensible of the favour of his which is better than life itself.[1]

Like any mother the Countess was always eager for news of her family, whether from Henry, away at school, from Elizabeth in Ireland, or even the occasional letter from Francis. Second only to her all-consuming concern for the spread of the gospel, she could declare to Elizabeth in the letter quoted above, 'Family news is all I call interesting after the one object of my heart.'

Throughout the early years of the 1750s Francis travelled on the continent. He had remained in Paris two years longer than had been expected, detained by an obsessive friendship with an eighteen-year-old French opera dancer, Louise Lany. Following the birth of their son, Francis left the girl and her child in order to continue his Grand Tour. Chesterfield's advice had been that a temporary liaison with such a person as Louise Lany was 'not unbecoming', but any long-term relationship would be 'disgusting'.[2] After spending some time in Madrid, Francis Hastings at last made plans to return home in 1755.

During his travels the young man, now twenty-six years of age, had accumulated an impressive collection of art treasures, busts, statues and books. To house all these artifacts he asked his

[1] HMC, *Hastings Collection*, vol. 3, p. 18.
[2] *Chesterfield to Huntingdon*, p. 52.

mother to organize substantial alterations and extensions to Donington Hall. Selina was immediately involved in the expenditure of time and strength, paying for plans to be drawn up and employing workmen to make the appropriate changes in time for her son's return. The property had been unoccupied for almost ten years; some parts had fallen into disrepair and were even reputed to be rat-infested. Repairs and the new extension proved more expensive than the Countess had budgeted for. 'I have lived in dust and mortar for five months with the house about my ears that it might not quite fall on his [Francis's] head', she told Charles Wesley. A reduction in plans was inevitable and Selina was uncertain as to whether Francis would be satisfied with the alterations she had made. In the event he was not. His mother's decided liking for Gothic architecture had led her to introduce this style into the new wing being erected, but to Francis's critical eye it failed to tone in with the existing building. Writing to his sister, Elizabeth, he said he planned to undo much of what had been done. Horace Walpole, cynical as ever, ridiculed the Countess's efforts, describing the extension as 'two tawdry rooms like assembly rooms at Blackheath.' Certainly Chesterfield felt he needed to admonish his young friend to be careful not to criticize his mother, at least not in public:

> In all events let me beg of you, my dear Lord, to say nothing to Lady Huntingdon upon her miscalculation that may produce the least coldness between you ... Her character is a very popular one, her enthusiasm has raised it with many people and lowered it with none. Your character ... must not have that little speck, which the least coldness between your mother and you would throw upon it, in the opinion of the majority.[1]

When George Whitefield disembarked at Newhaven in May 1755 after a six-week voyage back from America, the Countess was still at Donington Hall. He quickly made enquiries and,

[1] *Ibid.*, p. 108–9.

learning of her whereabouts, wrote to tell her of his activities. But before he was able to make her a visit, Selina was once more called to face the bitterness of bereavement in her immediate family circle. Her remaining unmarried sister-in-law, Lady Anne, died at the beginning of July after a short illness. 'Alas,' wrote Whitefield, when he heard the news, 'how many have your Lady-ship lived to see go before you! An earnest this, I hope, that you are to live to a good old age, and be more and more a mother in Israel!'[1]

The Countess was in the midst of making the extensive funeral arrangements for Lady Anne when news came that her young friend Sally Wesley had given birth to a daughter just eighteen months after the death of her first son, Jacky. The Countess wrote to Charles immediately:

> My present great distress cannot stop me returning thanks to God for his great goodness for dear Mrs Wesley and you. I did hope our Lord would bring her safe through and hope her little girl will live and be a great blessing to you both . . . . Till after the last office of the funeral is over I must expect no rest. A house full of people upon this occasion is my care as well.[2]

'A house full of people', although normally one of Selina's pleasures, could prove a strain at such times, and especially when her guests were not in sympathy with her spiritual views. Too often, as she told Charles Wesley, she had 'a table full of people and the subject is nothing than that of eating and drinking and they all of the world'.[3] One welcome guest, however, was Benjamin Ingham who invited her to come up to Yorkshire for a break. This Selina accepted, glad also to be away from Donington Hall for a time. 'None but those concerned with workmen knows the disputings that attend them,' she had complained to Charles

[1] Whitefield, *Works*, vol. 3, p. 128.
[2] Rylands MS., Letter 42.
[3] *Ibid.*, Letter 48.

Wesley. But before she left, even while the coach was waiting at the door, she took time to write another quick note to Charles and Sally for she had just received news that their baby daughter, Martha Maria, had died at five weeks of age. A grief common enough in those days of high infant mortality, it was no less painful for that.

In Yorkshire the Countess was glad to renew fellowship with her northern friends, particularly men like William Grimshaw. She soon learned, however, that Ingham's societies were in a state of flux, troubled by the same issues regarding separation from the Church of England that had been perplexing the Methodist societies. The small groups of believers that had been gathered together as a result of Ingham's ministry now numbered more than eighty. Centred mainly in Yorkshire and Lancashire, they were bound together by regular visits from Ingham and his fellow workers. Quite unexpectedly the largest society with a membership of over eighty withdrew unilaterally from the Church and declared themselves Dissenters. This action forced Ingham's hand and he felt he had no option but to regularize the situation by placing all his societies in the ranks of Dissent. During the period of Selina's stay in Yorkshire, Ingham called a Conference to set in place a new structure for his work, with Ingham himself elected to the position of General Overseer. Next he ordained his two fellow workers, an action that troubled Selina as a loyal churchwoman. She conceded, however, that he had little alternative in the circumstances imposed upon him. Laughingly she would refer to him as 'the Bishop'.

Returning from Yorkshire, the Countess travelled to London as quickly as the roads permitted, probably with a coach and six. Certainly the speed her coachman achieved startled the Duchess of Somerset when they passed each other on the road. 'I was surprised,' recorded the latter to a friend 'to meet Lady Huntingdon on the road last Saturday fortnight; she was on her way to London, but her coach drove by so fast that I had only time to send Lomas after her with my compliments; she seemed to me to look as well as ever I saw her.'[1]

Another matter was causing the Countess grave concern in the mid-1750s. Henry was far from well. Now fifteen he had brought Selina as much joy as her elder son had brought sorrow. Though dutiful in his studies, Henry appeared to lack the flair of his older brother, at least in the estimation of Chesterfield who commented disparagingly to Francis, 'You can make nothing liberal of him, nor is there occasion for it.' But Selina viewed him in a different light. She watched over Henry, praying earnestly that he would respond personally to the Christian message and would one day enter the ministry.

But now the boy was ill with some unknown disorder that was steadily affecting his eyesight. His mother brought him to London to obtain the best medical advice available. The first reference to Henry's condition comes in a letter from Whitefield written to the Countess on 4 June 1756. 'Man appoints, but God disappoints,' he wrote. 'In hopes of seeing your Ladyship I hastened to Bristol, but found your Ladyship had been to London whilst I was there. Sorry I was for the occasion of your Ladyship's journey, yet glad to hear that Master Hastings was so well recovered.'[2] As 1756 wore on, however, it became evident that any degree of recovery was only temporary. Not only was Henry gradually going blind, his entire health appeared to be breaking down. Having exhausted all that London medical opinion could suggest, Selina knew of one more expedient that she felt she must try.

In 1753 a certain Dr Richard Russell had published a medical treatise on the causes and treatment of glandular consumption. This had set in motion a new fashion among the moneyed classes: sea bathing. For Russell maintained that bathing in salt water could be of considerable benefit in the case of a number of

[1] *Coronet and Cross*, p. 119.
[2] Whitefield, *Works*, vol. 3, p. 182.

ailments and particularly for glandular conditions. Until that time England's coastal towns were little more than straggling villages scattered along the shoreline where fishermen struggled to sub-sist. But now sea bathing soared in popularity and coastal towns became important health resorts, competing with the spa towns of Bath, Bristol and Cheltenham.

So in the spring of 1757 the Countess decided to take Henry to Brighthelmstone – or Brighton as it was later to be called – in the hope that sea-bathing might prove a curative for the steadily deteriorating condition, not only of his sight but of his general health. Roads to Brighton were undeveloped and the journey to the south coast must have been an exhausting one. Describing a similar journey not many years later, Augustus Toplady wrote:

> If you should ever stand in need of violent exercise come down hither [to Brighton] by way of Reigate and Cuckfield . . . the road is the roughest, the country the coarsest and the vehicle the uneasi-est that can well be imagined. I never yet had so complete a shaking and was literally sore from head to foot for twenty-four hours after my arrival here, occasioned by such a series of concussions as I really thought it impossible for any carriage to impart.[1]

How surprised must the Countess have been on her arrival when a woman she had never met before addressed her in the street with the words: 'Oh Madam, you are come!'

'What do you know of me?' asked the Countess in surprise.

'Madam, I saw you in a dream three years ago, dressed as you are now', answered the woman. She then proceeded to tell of a dream she could never forget in which she had seen a tall woman dressed just as the Countess was now dressed, and had under-stood that when this woman came to the seaside town of Brighthelmstone she would be the means of doing much good.[2]

[1] Toplady, *Works*, Letter 42, p. 873–4.
[2] This incident was recorded by Toplady who was told it by the Countess on 30 August 1776. *Works*, p. 509.

This incident was one that would lead to developments far other than the Countess could have ever imagined. It must have left her with the strong impression that perhaps God had some hidden purpose in bringing her to this small town on the south coast. When she called on the woman soon afterwards she discovered one whose heart God had prepared to accept the message of his grace. Time was at a premium, however, for this woman had only a few months to live.

Nor was she the only one to whom the Countess spoke of these things. Hearing of a soldier's wife who had just given birth to twins and was not expected to live, Selina responded quickly, helping the young woman as much as she was able. And she also addressed a greater need – the need of her soul. The dying mother wept as she began to understand her sinful state before God and begged the Countess to return and teach her from the Scriptures before it was too late. Next door to the soldier's wife's lodgings was the public bakehouse and as few homes could boast the luxury of an oven, the local people would bring their dough ready kneaded to bake in the communal oven. A crack in the wall between the bakehouse and the apartments of the soldier's wife meant that those awaiting their turn to bake their bread could hear snatches of the conversation that was going on next door. Listening through the crack, others benefited from the teaching Selina was giving. Gradually word was passed around the neighbourhood of the tall stranger from London, reputed to be a peeress, who was telling of a way of forgiveness for sin. Other women then asked for admittance to this bedside Bible class.

Numbers increased and before long the small room was filled with eager hearers on the occasions of Selina's visits. But one day as she entered the apartment she noticed a shadowy figure seated in a far corner, apparently hoping to escape notice. Joseph Wall, a local blacksmith, noted for his immoral lifestyle and foul-mouthed speech, had been urged to come and listen. As none but women had attended before, the Countess hesitated, scarcely knowing whether to ask him to leave or not. Deciding to ignore him, she proceeded as usual, praying with the women and urging them to seek God for mercy and forgiveness while opportunity remained. The arrow of God's word pierced the conscience of the coarse blacksmith and Joseph Wall became a new man in Christ. A changed life was to demonstrate the reality of his conversion.[1]

In addition to Henry's illness another situation had arisen in the Countess's immediate family circle that brought her distress. From the context of a reply from George Whitefield to a letter which Selina had asked him to destroy after he had read it, we can only assume that Francis, who had now returned home from the Continent, had been guilty of further open sin that brought shame to his mother. In his letter of October 1757 Whitefield tried to counsel and console his friend:

> I burnt, but I believe I shall never forget the contents of your Lady-ship's letter. Who but the Redeemer himself can possibly describe the yearnings of such a tender parent's heart? Surely your Ladyship is called to cut off a right hand and pluck out a right eye; 'But it is the Lord, let him do what seemeth him good.' This was the language of Eli, whose sons were sinners before the Lord exceedingly ....May the Lord Jesus raise up your Ladyship many comforters! Above all, may he come himself. He will – he will![2]

Henry's condition was not responding to sea-bathing or any other medical treatment, and to Charles Wesley, who had also

[1] For twenty-nine years Joseph Wall lived a consistent Christian life. A day or two before his death he declared that he 'would not change his state with a king,' and as he died in June 1786 was heard to whisper, 'Come, Lord Jesus, come quickly'. Seymour, *Countess*, vol. 1, p. 313.

[2] Whitefield, *Works*, vol. 3, p. 214. From this letter Aaron Seymour, the Countess's first biographer, wrongly assumed that the reference was to Henry and that he had died as an unbeliever in September 1757. However, references to Henry in letters from the Countess dated 1758 show this to be incorrect.

shown concern for the Countess in this period of family anxiety, she wrote in February 1758:

> My very kind Friend, Your letters were a great comfort to me
> ... My sorrows have taken such hold upon me that I was not able
> to look up – from whence cometh my help? ... Yet I would not
> have had one sigh or tear less for the friendship of the world ... My
> poor son's sight grows worse ... and I am in the midst of much I
> wish otherwise ... but his heart and spirit conquered by grace is
> my one wish about him now. O could this be given me my heart
> would rejoice in the midst of my present grief about him.

The news from Elizabeth in Ireland was not good either. But Selina was able to keep the situation in proportion, and commented as she concluded her letter to Charles:

> My daughter Rawdon [Elizabeth] has been happily brought
> through the birth of a son who lived just to suffer much - a few
> hours and then died. Lady Selina [her younger daughter] is, I
> praise God, well. You see how I speak of blessings with thankful-
> ness to you as I would my sorrows with patience.

The Countess did not remain in Brighton throughout this period but returned with her family to her London home in Park Street from time to time. While there she once more opened up her drawing room for the preaching of the gospel – occasions that Whitefield referred to as 'spiritual routs'. More members of the nobility than ever before flocked to hear those whom the Countess invited to preach to these gatherings. Whitefield rejoiced in the obvious success of her endeavours. But he also realized that they took place against a backdrop of painful personal circumstances:

> I rejoice in the increase of your Ladyship's spiritual routs. I can
> guess at the consolations such uncommon scenes must afford to
> your Ladyship's new-born soul. No wonder you are distressed
> from other quarters ... Nature recoils, when constrained to take

the cup; and it may be from a near and dear relation's hand: but infinite Wisdom knows what is best.[1]

Such joys were a prelude to a great sorrow. Henry was clearly dying and nothing seemed able to arrest the course of his disease. Distressed and perplexed, Selina was determined not to question the goodness of her God in this severe dispensation. In August 1758 she dropped Charles Wesley a short note when the end seemed close: 'All things work together for good and in this blind hope, under all the most unintelligible events, I rest secure, and am determined to make no explanations for myself or others.' In September 1758 eighteen-year-old Henry, on whom she had pinned many hopes, died in Brighton.

At fifty-one years of age Selina had lost her husband and three of her six children. But there was a strong consolation in her present grief. Henry had shown evidence of true faith before he died. A letter to Charles Wesley written a few weeks after her bereavement refers both to her grief and to her consolation:

I shall surprise you more when I tell you my testimony of my dear child's happiness was not, nor is not, transient. No, I see him, I feel him in that inseparable union with God that neither time, place or frame or temper alters; and yet when the sensations of the joy in that union abates, his death, his manner of death, his long and sore affliction, is felt with a sensibility that nothing but the like feeling can describe.[2]

Not many months would elapse before the Countess must have begun to recognise a divine purpose behind her suffering. That small group of women who joined the bedside Bible class as Selina taught the soldier's wife had now become a society of men and women transformed by the grace of God. Here was the nucleus of a church in Brighton. Perhaps she could erect a building where services could be conducted for them. With the town's

[1] *Ibid.*, p. 237.
[2] Rylands MS., Letter 67, December 1758.

rocketing popularity as a health resort it would be an ideal location, and if she added her own living accommodation to the proposed chapel, she could invite men with clear evangelical principles to preach without fear of ecclesiastical interference.

Painful as the circumstances of the last two years had been, the foundations had now been laid for the significant endeavours that would occupy much of the remaining years of the life of the Countess of Huntingdon.

# 14

## CROSS CURRENTS

As 1759 DAWNED the Countess braced herself to put her bereavement behind her. Hearing that John Wesley was on his way back to London, she arranged to meet him in Bristol and accompany him to Bath where he would preach to invited guests at her accommodation. Although members of the nobility were not his favourite type of hearers, Wesley complied with his old friend's wishes, preaching for her on several occasions. Early in February the Countess herself returned to London.

During 1758 Great Britain had faced some serious setbacks in the Seven Years War – a war currently being waged across a number of fronts, with Britain predominantly in conflict with France. In view of this, a national day of prayer and fasting had been called for 16 February, a Friday, when special preaching services were to be held in every place of public worship. The Countess attended services at both Moorfields Tabernacle and the nearby Foundery, listening to sermons by Whitefield and Wesley respectively, and commented, 'O that the prayers and supplications which so lately ascended from so many quarters may be heard and answered and abundant blessings be poured upon our sinful country.'[1]

The concern of the Countess and her friends went deeper, however. The early impetus of the revival had waned to some

[1] Seymour, *Countess*, vol. 1, p. 396.

extent by the late 1750s and, in common with the Wesleys,
William Grimshaw and others, she believed that a spiritual
malaise was gripping the nation, provoking God to deal with it in
judgment. Understanding the military setbacks in this light,
Selina asked that a further fortnight of prayer and preaching
might be held at her Park Street home. Whitefield, Romaine,
Madan, John and Charles Wesley, Thomas Maxfield, Venn and a
newer friend, John Fletcher[1] (whom Charles Wesley had introduced to Selina the previous summer), all took part. They each
shared in preaching, exhorting and conducting sessions of
prayer. Following these days John Wesley wrote to the Countess:

> The agreeable hour which I spent with your Ladyship the last week
> recalled to my mind the former times, and gave me much matter of
> thankfulness to the Giver of every good gift. I have found great
> satisfaction in conversing with those instruments whom God has
> lately raised up. But still, there is, I know not what, in them whom
> we have known from the beginning, and who have borne the
> burden and heat of the day, which we do not find in those who have
> risen up since, though they are upright of heart.[2]

During this period of special prayer reports filtered through of
some extraordinary happenings in the small village of Everton,
near Bedford – a village with a population of little more than two
hundred. Here a certain vicar, John Berridge by name, had
already been preaching for more than a year with exceptional
power. This seemed a direct answer to their prayers and the
Countess was naturally most interested to learn more about the
situation. She learnt that John Berridge, who had been ordained
into the Church of England fourteen years earlier, had formerly
been a diligent though unsuccessful preacher. Exhort his people

[1] Swiss-born John Fletcher, who acted as family tutor for a Shropshire
Member of Parliament, Thomas Hill. Ordained into the ministry of the
Church of England in 1757, Fletcher helped the Wesley brothers whenever his
duties brought him to London.
[2] Wesley, *Letters*, vol. 4, p. 57.

as he would, it had produced no life-changing effects. At last he had come to realize that his message was defective and that he himself was at fault for he had been depending on his own good works to save his soul. With this realization came an all-important transformation as, to use his own words, he 'fled to Jesus for refuge'. The change in both his life and preaching was radical. Burning all his previous carefully composed sermons, Berridge now began to preach in a fundamentally different way:

> I asked them, if they had ever broken the law of God once in thought, word or deed? If they had, they were then under the curse; 'for it is written, cursed is every one that continueth not in all things that are written in the book of the law to do them.' . . . If I keep all God's laws today this is no amends for breaking them yesterday. If I behave peaceably to my neighbour this day, it is no satisfaction for having broken his head yesterday.[1]

Such preaching had had an immediate effect on the people of Everton, and not on them alone, for the news spread quickly from village to village. Soon the crowds thronged to Everton, walking many miles to be under the sound of such a message.

Anxious to discover more, Selina asked Wesley if he would go to Everton to see the situation for himself. Although Wesley had visited Everton on several previous occasions, he complied with her request. His report was entirely favourable:

> Mr. Berridge appears to be one of the most simple [single-minded] as well as most sensible men of all whom it has pleased God to employ in reviving primitive Christianity . . . They come now twelve or fourteen miles to hear him; and very few come in vain. His word is with power; he speaks as plain and home as John Nelson, but with all the propriety of Mr. Romaine and tenderness of Mr. Hervey.[2]

[1] *Works of the Rev. John Berridge*, ed. R. Whittingham (London, 1864), p. 350.
[2] Wesley, *Letters*, vol. 4, p. 58.

This was commendation indeed to the Countess of Huntingdon. In John Berridge God was raising up a new friend for Selina
– a friend whose name would be for ever linked with hers in the
work of the gospel. To some extent he would take the place of
friends like Philip Doddridge and also of James Hervey who had
died two months earlier in December 1758.

In May 1759, however, an increased level of phenomena began
to accompany Berridge's preaching: some hearers fainted and
appeared almost lifeless for many hours; others spoke as if in a
trance; others experienced violent contortions; while yet others
were in raptures of joy as they knew and felt their sins forgiven.
Uncertain what to make of accounts she was hearing, Selina now
asked two other friends to go to Everton to investigate. William
Romaine and Martin Madan, although hesitant at first, were soon
convinced by all they saw and heard that this was a genuine movement of the Spirit of God – although undeniably Satan had also
taken advantage of the depth of emotions expressed by some
converts to counterfeit the true. Selina now planned to visit
Everton herself as soon as she had opportunity.

During the summer months of 1759 the Countess returned
to Brighton, for although the place held painful memories for
her, the encouragement of those eager to hear the preaching of
men such as Romaine and Whitefield outweighed any natural
reluctance. First to preach there that year was Whitefield who
addressed an eager crowd, standing under a tree in the middle of
a field. His sermon on God's words through Ezekiel the prophet
to the wayward people of Israel, 'Turn ye! Turn ye! Why will you
die?', was the means of the conversion of two young men: one
was Thomas Tuppen who had come to mock the preacher and
the other Edward Gadsby whose long and exemplary Christian
life was to become a byword even before his death nearly thirty
years later.

The Countess was convinced that she must erect a chapel for
the people of Brighton. Apart from the parish church, only one

small Baptist cause and an Independent meeting house served their needs. Although she had considerable resources, much of it was tied up in property and it was not easy for her to raise the ready money necessary for such a venture. Unable to fund the project herself Selina applied to her friend Lady Gertrude Hotham, with a request for the loan of £500.[1] Even so, funds were still short and the Countess is reputed to have sold £698 worth of her personal jewels to finance the enterprise.[2] Land was then purchased in North Street and work began to erect the chapel – the first to be planned and built solely at the initiative of the Countess. Like all other early Methodist chapels, it was not intended to replace the parish church but rather to supplement its services by providing extra preaching meetings at times other than those of the regular hours of worship.

On her return to London in the autumn of 1759 the Countess was anxious to continue her work among the aristocracy. Whitefield was often away on his preaching tours; both Romaine and Madan were hard pressed with other commitments, and Henry Venn had left Clapham for Huddersfield. So Selina began to look around for some other man of evangelical faith and ability who could help her. Her eyes turned to the young Swiss preacher, John Fletcher, who was still in London assisting John Wesley. After discussing the matter with Charles Wesley, she asked him to approach Fletcher with an invitation to come and visit her. Fletcher responded and on 15 November told Charles:

I passed three hours with a modern prodigy – a pious and humble Countess! . . . She proposed to me something of what you hinted to

[1] A legal document setting out the details of this loan on 16 February 1762 can be seen in the Cheshunt Foundation Archives. To repay it the Countess claimed £2000 owing to her from Lady Betty Hastings' will. This money had been left first to Lady Betty's personal companion, Sarah Hole, and upon her death to the Countess.

[2] A document in the Cheshunt Archives, probably dating from about 1791, lists the jewels that she sold and includes thirty-seven pearls at £4.15s each, a gold box and other items. For a full list see Seymour, *Countess*, vol. 1, p. 314.

me in your garden; namely, to celebrate the communion sometimes at her house in a morning, and to preach when occasion offered. Charity, politeness, and reason accompanied her offer; and I confess, in spite of the resolution which I had almost absolutely formed, to fly the houses of the great, without even the exception of the Countess, I found myself so greatly changed, that I should have accepted on the spot.[1]

After discussing the proposal with the Wesley brothers, John Fletcher agreed to undertake the responsibility in spite of much misgiving. Twice a week he took his turn, conducting communion services and preaching to the somewhat intimidating assembly of grandees at Selina's Park Street home.

Early in 1760 the Countess faced another, though quite different family crisis. As we have already noted, Selina had inherited a certain Shirley trait – a temper that often proved hard to control. But control it she usually did, and if she failed she would grieve over the fact. Far different was her cousin Lawrence Shirley, who had become the fourth Earl Ferrers in 1745. With the earldom he had also inherited the Shirley property at Staunton Harold. From all reports a likable enough young man, Lawrence Shirley had set off on his Grand Tour at the age of twenty, but 'the drunkenness and brutality that the young lord picked up on his European travels seem to have found in him a congenial soil where they grew up thick and fast.'[2]

Returning home Ferrers gave vent to violent outbursts of passion whenever circumstances were not entirely to his liking. His servants scarcely endured life at Staunton Harold long enough to receive their pay, as he would kick out at them and lash them with his horsewhip. When pretty Mary Meredith agreed to marry the ill-tempered Earl she cannot have realized what she was

[1] Luke Tyerman, *Wesley's Designated Successor* (London: Hodder & Stoughton, 1882), pp. 474–8.
[2] M. N. D'Auvergne, *Tarnished Coronets* (London: T. W. Laurie, 1937), p. 180.

doing. As usual, any salacious gossip to be picked up was repeated by Horace Walpole, and in due course he was not slow to allege that the Earl took his pistols to bed with him and constantly threatened to kill his wife before morning. The situation must have been dire, for Mary acted against the social customs of the times and appealed to the House of Lords for a legal separation. This was granted to her and a hapless man by the name of John Johnson was appointed as steward to ensure that Mary received her rightful income from her husband's estates.

Lawrence Shirley assumed that Johnson would be prepared to bend the law in his favour to cheat Mary of her due. In this he was mistaken and revenge on Johnson followed swiftly. Obeying his master's summons to come to his apartments at Staunton Harold in January 1760, the unsuspecting steward may not have noticed that the place was almost deserted. All but three of the servants had been ordered to leave the premises for the day. With cool deliberation Shirley locked the door of his room when Johnson entered, then ordered him to sign papers to the effect that he had intentionally wronged his master and was a scoundrel. When Johnson refused the Earl whipped out his pistol and ordered his unfortunate steward to make his peace with God. Regardless of the old man's pleas for pity the Earl shot him without further ado.

Immediately after committing his crime Earl Ferrers regretted what he had done, but it was too late, Johnson died the next day. Lawrence Shirley was brought to court for murder and tried before the House of Lords on 17 April 1760. Charles Wesley rallied to the support of his friend, Selina, joining with her and others in both public and private prayer for the Earl, and attending his trial in person together with George Whitefield. An awesome occasion, the trial was conducted in the presence of a full House complete with bishops, earls, dukes and most of the royal family – 'One of the most august assemblies in Europe', reported Charles in a letter to Sally. But he was far too grieved to be impressed, 'The pomp was quite lost on me', he added.

The scandal burst on the country like a thunderclap: never before had a peer of the realm been tried for murder. A plea of insanity was tabled as the only hope for mitigating the death sentence, but the circumstances of the murder were too well planned to allow such a ploy to gain credence. After many hours of deliberation and several adjournments to allow the Earl further time to consider his defence, each member of the House of Lords present for the trial was asked for his verdict. All one hundred and six declared the Earl guilty.

The Countess's critics exploited the situation with a degree of sardonic pleasure. A strain of madness ran in the family, they said, expressing itself in murder in some and religious mania in others. Nor was she the only member of the family to suffer reproach at this time. Another cousin, Walter Shirley, vicar of Loughrea in Ireland, was five years younger than his brother, Lawrence. He had been converted two years previously, probably under the preaching of John Wesley on a visit to Ireland. Before that Shirley had been more interested in his hunting dogs than in the souls of his people, but all had then changed. Aligning himself with the despised Methodists, he had already known a measure of persecution, and now bore his share in the calumny meted out to the Countess. The tragedy brought the cousins closer together as they both did all in their power to bring Lawrence to a sense of his sins in the sight of God. Day after day they visited him in the Tower as he awaited execution. The criminal quickly tired of the exhortations of his brother, Walter Shirley, yet appeared more disposed to listen to his cousin, Selina.

Whitefield paid two visits to the Tower but although the condemned man listened politely to the preacher, he was impervious to his words. Whitefield concluded that 'his heart was stone'. The Earl's conduct on the day of execution demonstrated the rightness of that assessment. Dressed in a suit of light satin embroidered with silver – his wedding suit, in fact – the condemned man rode in his personal landau drawn by six horses.

Vast crowds thronged the streets to watch him pass and hurried to gain a vantage point from which to witness the execution at Tyburn. 'His courage rose,' reported Walpole, 'and even an awful procession of above two hours with that mixture of pageantry, shame, ignominy, nay, and of delay, could not discount his resolution.' Apart from a brief prayer at the last, the flamboyant Earl died in shame on a scaffold draped in black at the expense of his distressed family.

Her cousin's crime and execution brought profound distress to the Countess. She remained among her friends in London until the end of June. Conscious of the opportunity that such a family dishonour afforded, John Wesley chose this time to write a long letter to Selina's elder daughter, Elizabeth, in Ireland. So sure was he of the reality of her early profession of faith that he addresses her as a backslider rather than an unbeliever:

MY LADY - It was impossible to see the distress into which your Ladyship was thrown by the late unhappy affair without bearing a part of it, without sympathizing with you. But may we not see God therein? May we not both hear and understand his voice? We must allow it is generally 'small and still'; yet he speaks sometimes in the whirlwind. Permit me to speak to your Ladyship with all freedom; not as to a person of quality, but as to a creature whom the Almighty made for himself, and one that is in a few days to appear before him.

You were not only a nominal but a real Christian. You tasted of the powers of the world to come . . . But you fell among thieves, and such as were peculiarly qualified to rob you of your God. Where are you now? . . . Do you now say (as you did almost twenty years ago)

> *Keep me dead to all below,*
> *Only Christ resolved to know;*
> *Firm, and disengaged, and free,*
> *Seeking all my bliss in Thee? –*

Is your taste now for heavenly things? Are not you a lover of
pleasure more than a lover of God?

Oh that the time past may suffice! Is it now not high time that you
should awake out of sleep? Now God calls aloud! My dear Lady,
now hear the voice of the Son of God, and live! The trouble in
which your tender parent is now involved may restore all that
reverence for her which could not but be a little impaired while you
supposed she was 'righteous over-much.' Oh how admirably does
God lay hold of and 'strengthen the things that remain' in you! . . .
I am, my Lady, Yours, John Wesley[1]

This faithful letter could well have been the means of turning
Elizabeth's heart back once more to the truths she had once pro-
fessed. There is contemporary evidence to indicate that both
Elizabeth and her husband became warm supporters of the
Methodists in Ireland at this time.[2]

Perhaps as a means of relief after the trauma of recent days, the
Countess chose the summer of 1760 to visit Everton and to see
and hear for herself all that had been happening there. The
physical phenomena that had formed so prominent a part of the
awakening the previous year had now waned to a considerable
extent. Accompanied by Martin Madan and Henry Venn, Selina
spent three days in the village as Berridge, together with Madan
and Venn, conducted services.

[1] Wesley, *Letters*, vol. 4, pp. 87–8.

[2] Wesley was in Ireland at the time of the execution and wrote from there.
When he arrived at Moira where Elizabeth and her husband lived he found them
anxious that he should be allowed to preach in the parish church which lay
directly opposite their home. When the vicar refused, Lord Rawdon sent a
bellman around the town to announce that Wesley would be preaching on a
gravestone in the churchyard. Wesley, *Letters*, vol. 4, p. 379. By the end of the
1760s the couple had opened the great hall of their home for Methodist
services, attended regularly themselves and encouraged both tenants and
servants to attend. They also welcomed and entertained the preachers –
a circumstance that strongly suggests that Elizabeth had been restored spiritually.
See C. H. Crookshank, *History of Methodism in Ireland,* (reprint, Clonmel:
Tentmaker Publications, 1994), vol. 1: *Days of Revival.*

No sooner had the Countess returned to London from Everton than she discovered a situation that alarmed and disgusted her, relating to her chaplain, George Whitefield. During his absence from the capital on one of his preaching excursions, Whitefield had become the victim of jokes and innuendo in a play called *The Minor* that had been staged in the Haymarket New Theatre. This play, described as 'an infamous production' and 'an almost unparalleled outrage against all propriety', was the brainchild of a Samuel Foote, the producer and principal actor. He took it in hand to mock and discredit the Methodists, with Whitefield, characterized as 'Dr Squintum', as his chief target of abuse. Claiming that 'ridicule is the only antidote against this pernicious poison' [of Methodism], Foote employed offensive language and implied immoral and scandalous behaviour, both in Whitefield and in those who listened to him.

The Countess immediately sprang to the defence of her chaplain. First she contacted the Lord Chamberlain calling for the play to be suppressed immediately. When his Lordship declined to take any action she approached Garrick, the actor. He professed to find the work offensive, but when he discovered that there was money to be made in its performance, he weakly gave way and allowed *The Minor* to be performed at his own theatre in Drury Lane. Whitefield, untouched by the slurs designed to destroy his character, was in Yorkshire enjoying 'great days of the Son of Man', to borrow his own expression. Here he was joined by the Countess who came to spend time with Ingham and Lady Margaret. She was accompanied by William Romaine, whose family home at Hartlepool drew him to the area whenever opportunity arose, and by Henry Venn, who was returning to Huddersfield.

Ever since Ingham's societies had declared themselves Dissenters in 1755 there had been repeated conferences on the subject of church order. Now separated from ecclesiastical regulations imposed by Canon Law, every item of congregational life had become an issue for Ingham's people: the hymns they should sing, the discipline to be adopted, the relative position of Ingham and his elders – all seemed to be in the melting pot. Ingham would undoubtedly have discussed the issues at length with the Countess and, on 27 September, she and Romaine sat in on a Conference of leaders of all Ingham's societies, watching as they cast lots, as was their custom, to choose new church officers. With her frequently expressed desires for Christian unity, she may well have warned Ingham that his work could suffer unless a degree of authority was brought to bear on the situation. Following the Conference Ingham conducted his guests on a tour of some of his eighty societies throughout the counties of Yorkshire and Lancashire, with Romaine and himself preaching to the people in the different chapels. Romaine was impressed with the spirituality of Ingham's people – a tribute to the ministry under which they had been converted. 'If ever there was a church of Christ upon earth that was one', he commented later. 'I paid them a visit and had a great mind to join them. There was a blessed work of God among that people.'[1]

Returning to Aberford they were joined by William Grimshaw. Robust, outspoken and with a passion for the souls of the lost corresponding to Selina's own, Grimshaw had earned a place in the affections of all the men surrounding the Countess at this time. We may date an anecdote relating to the curate of Haworth in this period. Francis Hastings, probably staying in his Yorkshire home, Ledston Hall, came across to Aberford to visit his mother and found Grimshaw there. Always ready for a religious argument and with plenty of head knowledge of the Christian gospel, the young man tried to draw Grimshaw into a dispute. Knowing how deeply her son's unbelief and way of life grieved the Countess, Grimshaw replied, 'My lord, I do not refuse to argue because I have nothing to say, or because I fear for my

[1] *Evangelical Magazine*, 1814, pp. 301–8.

cause. I refuse because argument will do you no good. If you really needed information I would gladly assist you. But the fault is not in your head but in your heart, which can only be reached by divine power. I shall pray for you, but I will not dispute with you.' As the young Earl afterwards admitted, such plain speaking was more effective than if Grimshaw had entered into a fracas with him.

While Selina was still in Yorkshire a letter arrived from John Fletcher informing her that his patron, Sir Thomas Hill, had arranged for him to be presented to the living of Madeley in Shropshire as both his sons, Fletcher's former pupils, were now at Cambridge. Fletcher, who had been preaching regularly in connection with the Countess, admitted quaintly, 'Were I to have my choice, I would prefer waiting at the pool under your roof . . . and I will own to your ladyship that the thought of giving this up is one of the chief difficulties I have now to encounter.' But he was sure God was directing him to this new sphere of service, and so continued, 'The church is vacated; the presentation to it brought unasked for into my hands . . . What does your ladyship think? I long to go and consult you in Yorkshire.'[1] Although losing Fletcher's help would be a setback for the Countess, she too could see a divine overruling behind this appointment in days when evangelical men had great difficulties in obtaining parish pulpits. Perhaps this, together with events taking place at Everton, were tokens for good, harbingers of renewed blessings from God for the land, an answer to the prayers offered in her home early in 1759.

[1] Tyerman, *Wesley's Designated Successor*, p. 56.

# 15

# DOORS OF
# OPPORTUNITY

'TO THE EVERLASTING PRAISE OF OUR DEAR JESUS be it known to you that his work of grace prospers in these parts. Our congregations are generally large: new members are added to our societies, and our old ones go on in full assurance, and some of them in the triumph of faith to heaven.' This bright picture of the work of God in the north of England was written by William Grimshaw to the believers in the Newcastle society in January 1761.[1] It introduces us to a new movement of the Spirit of God that did indeed begin at this time and continued throughout the early years of the 1760s. The floodtide of blessing grew wider and deeper as the months passed, not only in the north but across the country. By October of that year John Wesley found congregations of believers 'hungering and thirsting after righteousness', and wrote, 'It seems God was pleased to pour out his Spirit this year on every part of England and Ireland, perhaps in a manner we have never seen before, certainly not for twenty years.'[2]

But one man, remarkably used by God in the revival up until this time, was unable to share in the opportunities which this new work of God presented. Illness that had often followed George Whitefield as he laboured beyond the limits of his strength now silenced the preacher for most of the year. Recurring throat

[1] Letter cited in my *William Grimshaw of Haworth* (Edinburgh: Banner of Truth, 1997), p. 264.
[2] Wesley, *Journal*, vol. 4, p. 477.

infections left him seriously unwell and reports even circulated that he had died. 'I strive to put out to sea as usual but my shattered bark will not bear it,' he commented ruefully in June 1761. So when the attractive chapel in North Street, Brighton, built at the Countess's own expense, stood complete and ready for opening that July, Whitefield was unable to preach or even take part. Martin Madan officiated instead, for he, together with Romaine, Fletcher, Berridge and Venn had preached to the increasing congregation there since 1759. It must have been a moment of gladness for Selina who had seen the work grow from a few poor women studying the Scriptures together to a well-established and vibrant Christian congregation.

Men and women came from far and near to attend services in the North Street chapel including farmers and manual workers from the Sussex countryside. Some who came from as far away as Cuckfield and Wivelsfield – more than ten miles from Brighton – now urged the Countess to consider building another chapel further inland for the spread of the gospel in that area. Willing enough to oblige, Selina knew of no suitable location where such a chapel could be built. But at this very juncture the owner-occupier of a mansion that had once belonged to the Shirley family offered to lease the spacious home to her so that she could turn the great hall into a place of worship. Situated in a place known as Ote Hall, near Wivelsfield, it was an ideal solution to the problem. Because it would cost no more than the rent and the alterations, the Countess could go ahead on this second project without delay and so provide for the needs of the people in rural Sussex.

Before the end of 1761 Ote Hall was ready and opened for worship. As in Brighton, the Countess transformed some rooms into private apartments for herself, her daughter Selina, her nieces and her guests. William Romaine, with no parish responsibilities, was more able to help the Countess at Ote Hall than others. After one visit he reported:

Such a time I scarce ever knew as we had at Oathall. I met the society twice and had spoken to them one by one before we had the sacrament; we were about a hundred communicants at the Lord's table. It was a feast indeed . . . Surely Oathall is a highly favoured place, where the Lord himself delighteth to dwell.[1]

Two notable conversions may be traced back to the early days at Ote Hall: while both were soldiers, in every other respect they were far different from each other. 'Old Abraham', who had reached the advanced age of one hundred years, was a man who had escaped death on many a battlefield of Europe. Restless in spirit yet hardly knowing why, the old soldier had tried every place of worship he knew in the area of Sussex where he and his wife lived. Although prejudiced against Methodists, he decided to slip into a meeting at Ote Hall. A fine-looking and well-built clergyman, who, Abraham discovered, was named Henry Venn, was conducting the service. As the preacher concluded, the old soldier turned to the one sitting next to him and declared, 'Ah, neighbour, this is the very truth of the word of God that I have been seeking for, and never heard it so plain before. Here will I abide.' And he did. For six more years the old man was spared to grow in grace, his snow-white hair making him a conspicuous member of the congregation. The Countess took a deep interest in Abraham, visiting him in his cottage and speaking earnestly to his wife. But though the latter showed some response, she gave no evidence of true faith.

Captain Jonathan Scott had also seen service in hard-fought battles – but most notably the Battle of Minden in 1759 when the English forces at last routed the French – a turning point in the Seven Years War. Constantly faced with life-threatening situations, the captain had experienced periods of temporary religious concern. At this date he was stationed with his regiment

[1] New, *Coronet and Cross,* p. 154. Romaine uses a variant spelling for Ote Hall.

in Sussex and not long after Ote Hall opened for preaching services he was caught out in a thunderstorm. Seeking shelter from the elements, he knocked at the door of a farmstead. After treating the soldier hospitably, the farmer, a member of the society which met at Ote Hall, pressed him to come and hear an exceptional preacher at the newly opened chapel. Intrigued, Captain Scott agreed to come. There in the pulpit he saw a clergyman of medium height with quick, sharp yet kindly eyes set in a thin but deeply lined face. The preacher's suit of blue cloth looked rather cheap to Captain Scott, while his coarse blue stockings and grey unpowdered wig gave the impression either of insufficient means or of a studied indifference to appearance. Soon, however, all this faded into insignificance as William Romaine's words penetrated the heart of the listening soldier. The text that day was John 14:6 and, as Romaine spoke, the truth of God's word took hold of Captain Scott, making him a new man.

Like Captain Gardiner before him, Scott soon took every opportunity, not only of testifying to his regiment, but of preaching wherever he was stationed. Writing to the Countess, John Fletcher described a meeting with the captain:

> I went last Monday to meet Captain Scott – a captain of the truth – a bold soldier of Jesus Christ . . . For some months he has exhorted his dragoons daily; for some weeks he has preached publicly at Leicester in the Methodist meeting-house to numerous congregations . . . I believe this red coat will shame many a black one. I am sure he shames me.[1]

Continuing in the army, Scott bore a courageous witness among the rough men with whom he was associated. Whitefield had confidence in him and invited him to preach at the Tabernacle. Soon after this Scott sold his commission and for the next forty years devoted himself to the service of a higher King. Preaching

[1] Tyerman, *Whitefield,* vol. 2, p. 502.

mainly in Lancashire and the Midlands, he was responsible for planting many new churches and has been described as 'the most pertinacious and successful of itinerant preachers in Lancashire, Shropshire, Staffordshire and particularly Cheshire'.[1] Scott's life of usefulness in the gospel may be regarded as a direct fruit of the vision and sacrifice of the Countess of Huntingdon in her determination to open up preaching centres for the people.

As the Countess's chapels began to increase, so did the administrative labour of ensuring that the pulpits were supplied with preachers – a task she undertook singlehanded at this time. The men on whom she could call early in the 1760s were few in number so she had to organize a system of constant replacements. If Berridge were preaching for two months in Brighton, someone had to care for his people. So while Madan went to Everton for that purpose, Romaine would have to serve for him at the Lock Hospital. Or if Fletcher came to Ote Hall, Venn might find himself asked to go to Madeley for a few weeks. Accustomed to issuing orders to her domestic staff, the Countess could sometimes sound more than a little peremptory in her instructions on such arrangements. Usually her friends were happy to comply, but with the needs of their own congregation a first responsibility, some found they had to refuse her pressing invitations. A letter from Berridge, who was never unduly overawed by the Countess, illustrates the point:

> My Lady, I cannot see my call to Brighthelmstone; and I ought to see it for myself, not another for me. Was any good done when I was there? It was God's doing, all the glory be to him . . . I am not well able to ride so long a journey; and my heart is utterly set against wheel-carriages on these roads. Indeed I see not my call; I cannot think of the journey; and therefore pray your ladyship to think no more of it. I write plainly, not out of forwardness, I trust,

[1] R. Tudur Jones, *Congregationalism in England* (London: Independent Press, 1962), p. 156. Scott was also responsible for building many chapels, particularly in Congleton, Townley and Macclesfield.

but to save your ladyship the trouble of sending a second request, and myself the pain of returning a second denial. You threaten me, madam, like a pope, not like a mother in Israel, when you declare roundly, that God will scourge me if I do not come; but I know your ladyship's good meaning . . . Whilst I was looking towards the sea, partly drawn thither with the hope of doing good, and partly driven by your Vatican bull, I found nothing but thorns in my way; but as soon as I turned my eyes from it, I found peace.[1]

Whether the Countess shared Berridge's sense of humour, we do not know. She certainly did not appear to resent his way of speaking.

Rumours were rife about the financial rewards these men enjoyed as a result of their services. Jealous minds assumed that her two chaplains, Romaine and Whitefield, as well as the other preachers, were secretly amassing small fortunes as a result of their labours. Thomas Haweis, later to become a chaplain to the Countess himself, is categorical on this point:

I believe I may venture to say that his [Romaine's] labours were without the least expectation of any remuneration, and that all he ever got from Lady Huntingdon barely paid his journeys and his expenses. I mention this because many have circulated the basest stories respecting him and Mr. Whitefield. But I may venture to say that neither of the former were ever a shoe-latchet the richer for any service done her Ladyship.

But in case any should come to the opposite conclusion and judge the Countess mean in not recompensing these men more adequately, Haweis added:

Not that this is meant to impeach her ladyship's boundless liberality. Never perhaps did mortal make nobler use of what she possessed, live less attached to earth or dispense it with more open hand. I have often said she was one of the poor who lived upon her

[1] Berridge, *Works*, p. 455.

own bounty, and if she grudged anything, it was to herself . . .
Never did human being sit more loose to money or more jealously
watch over the distribution of it . . . I leave this testimony to her
worth in this respect, that every shilling she possessed should be
employed for the glory of God. But with all her fortune and
self-denial her finances were inadequate to her calls, and it was
impossible that she could have done the noble acts that marked her
character if she had not found such men as these with disinterested
zeal.[1]

A further testimony to the Countess's unstinted generosity,
even to the point of stringent self-denial, comes from the pen of
her friend William Grimshaw who sent a 'begging letter' on
behalf of one of his young converts, Titus Knight, who had established an Independent church in Halifax. His people were too
poor to finance a much needed building but Grimshaw knew of
one who would help if she could:

> I have had two visits from Mr Knight . . . The people among whom
> he is sowing the seed of the kingdom are poor and their means are
> very limited, yet the Lord has put it in their heart to build a house
> for his word. Now I have come to the point – can your Ladyship
> spare a mite to aid these worthy souls? The demands on your gen-
> erosity I know to be great, and on that account I feel a repugnance
> at asking, because I am persuaded you would give even to the gown
> on your back if the case required it . . .'[2]

Needless to record, the Countess did help the struggling cause
and the chapel was built.[3]

To suggest, therefore, that Selina was less than open-handed
towards her chaplains and helpers would be misleading. A letter
from Fletcher, written shortly before his settlement at Madeley

---

[1] Haweis, *Life of Romaine*, p. 85–6.
[2] Quoted more fully in my *Grimshaw*, p. 235.
[3] Known as Square Chapel, Halifax, this was the church in which J. H.
Jowett was later brought up.

and after he had spent some weeks preaching in Brighton, refers
to a generous gift he had just received, a gift that would 'deprive
[him] for many months of the unspeakable advantage of living
upon Providence'.[1]

Throughout his early years in Madeley, Fletcher turned
constantly to the Countess for advice, and not advice only but
also for consolation when trials seemed to weigh him down and
his mind was distressed by spiritual failure. In January 1761 he
wrote:

> I had a secret expectation to be the instrument of a work in this part
> of the church; I did not despair of soon being *a little Berridge*; and
> thus warmed by sparks of my own kindling I looked out to see the
> rocks broke in pieces . . . but to the great disappointment of my
> hopes I am now forced to look within and see the need I have of
> being broken.

And in another letter he wrote: 'Conscious that few people can
sympathise with me in so feeling a manner as your Ladyship, I
shall make no apology for pouring out my complaints before you
in this letter.'[2]

The term 'a mother in Israel', first used of Deborah in the book
of Judges, has been applied, and justly, to many women over the
centuries of Christian history, but its use seems particularly apt in
reference to the Countess. Perhaps her wealth, her social status,
her strength of character and intellectual calibre were factors that
initially attracted some. But it was other qualities that drew men
– often themselves wise and experienced Christians – to her for
advice and consolation. Ronald Knox comments on this surprising situation:

> She did not domineer over them, did not put herself forward as a
> prophetess in the style of Madame Guyon. She devoted herself to

[1] Seymour, *Countess*, vol. 1, p. 234.
[2] *Ibid.*, p. 240.

praying for the effectiveness of their preaching . . . No, it is difficult to accuse her of going beyond her measure. And yet the ascendancy she seems to have established over their minds may well leave the reader gasping.[1]

Although her grasp of Christian doctrine and innate practical wisdom were also clearly reasons for this, it was the godliness of her life, her width of compassion and her deep concern for the progress of the kingdom of God that lay at the root of her influence.

It was, therefore, to the Countess of Huntingdon that Benjamin Ingham turned late in 1761 as he surveyed in anguish the wreckage of his own life's work. The cause of the trouble, later described by William Romaine as 'that horrid blast from the north', had its beginning in 1760. Ingham, who been reading a treatise entitled, *The Testimony of the King of Martyrs*, written by a Scottish divine, John Glas, had been attracted to the views of church government set out there. So impressed was he by all he read, that he had sent his two elders up to Scotland to study the life and worship of the Glasite churches at first hand.

These churches, under the direction of John Glas and his son-in-law Robert Sandeman, believed in the independence of each congregation, but also insisted in a plurality of elders, together with various customs that they thought were practised in the New Testament churches. Feet washing, the community of goods and the greeting of one another with a 'holy kiss' were among their rituals. But when James Allen and William Batty, the two elders sent by Ingham, returned from Scotland and tried to implement such ideas in their own societies, the results were catastrophic. The rock on which Ingham's work foundered more than any other, however, was the Glasite demand for total unanimity for each church decision. As the Inghamite societies argued over each possible change to their order of worship and church

---

[1] Ronald Knox, *Enthusiasm* (Oxford: Clarendon Press, 1950), p. 487.

government, divisions and conflicts increased proportionally. At last in November 1761 James Allen, complaining that Ingham had too much authority, stormed out of a conference, saddled his horse and rode off. He established a separate church of Glasite views, an act that signalled the splintering of all the Inghamite societies which had previously worked together harmoniously. Some drifted back into the Church of England while others joined the various Methodist groups. Out of eighty flourishing societies only thirteen were left adhering to Ingham. Summing up the situation, Seymour wrote, 'Disputes without end arose, excommunication upon excommunication followed; they condemned one another for hair-breadth differences, and were thus split like a wrecked ship into a thousand pieces.'[1]

Stunned by the break-up of his life's work, a deep depression settled on Ingham's spirit. 'I am lost, I am lost,' he would cry out as he thought of all that had happened. And it was to his sister-in-law, Selina, that he turned for consolation. Her letters to him were a lifeline. Writing in response, Ingham expressed his gratitude: 'A thousand and a thousand times do I bless and praise my God for the words of comfort and consolation your Ladyship's letters conveyed to my mournful heart, dismayed and overwhelmed as it was with the pressure of my calamities. Righteous art thou, O Lord, and just are thy judgments.'[2]

During the summer of 1762 Selina again visited Yorkshire, drawn by the needs of Benjamin Ingham and Lady Margaret, and by her love for many of the sterling Yorkshire Christians – men such as Richard Conyers, vicar of Helmsley, William Grimshaw and his fellow workers. Whitefield was by this time considerably improved in health. A visit to Scotland at the beginning of the year had raised his spirits, and a month in Holland during June had proved beneficial. Now declaring 'all my old times are

[1] Seymour, *Countess*, vol. 1, p. 275.
[2] Luke Tyerman, *The Oxford Methodists* (London: Hodder & Stoughton, 1873), p. 153.

revived again', he set off for Yorkshire to join the Countess. It was a unique occasion because the visit coincided with John Wesley's Conference held in Leeds that year. In company with Ingham, Venn (who had come across from Huddersfield), Romaine, Madan, Grimshaw and John Wesley, Selina found much to stimulate her zeal.

Together they travelled around the towns and villages of Yorkshire, the preachers taking it in turn to address the expectant people. These were days of almost unparalleled openness to the gospel in the area. Persecution had been reduced to a background rumble of discontent, while doors of opportunity opened wide on every hand. Writing to the Countess in November 1762, shortly after her return to Brighton, Grimshaw could say of his own work, 'The societies are everywhere in a good state. The Lord is adding to them many seekers of the blessed Jesus – many lively souls who have come to a sense of the pardoning love of God and are eagerly hungering after your inestimable Redeemer and mine.'

The presence of the Countess of Huntingdon with these earnest gospel preachers seemed to kindle their hopes and endeavours to a flame. Grimshaw looked eagerly for her to return:

> When will your Ladyship revive us with another visit? What blessings did the Lord shower upon us the last time you were here! and how did our hearts burn within us to proclaim his love and grace to perishing sinners! Come and animate us afresh – aid us by your counsels and your prayers – communicate a spark of your glowing zeal, and stir us up to renewed activity in the cause of God . . . .All long for your coming amongst us again.

Grimshaw was convinced that God had much for Selina yet to do. Although she was in fact a year older than he, he had a premonition that his own days were soon to end. So he writes in this letter:

May He bless you, sanctify you, and make you abundantly useful in your day and generation! He has raised you up for the accomplishment of a mighty work in the land. I may not live to witness it, but I shall assuredly see some of the triumphs of the cross, the blood-bought slaves, the ransomed captives, rescued from the tyranny and slavery of the great enemy of souls, in the chapels of your Ladyship, all arrayed in robes of dazzling white, and washed from every defilement in the fountain opened for sin and uncleanness, praising and blessing Him who hath made them kings and priests unto God and the Lamb for ever. Yes, when I am before the throne – then I shall see, and hear, and know what you have been made the instrument of accomplishing upon earth; and at last we shall meet as two poor worthless sinners, stripped of every fancied good, to bless and praise him through eternity![1]

[1] Seymour, *Countess*, vol. 1, p. 284.

# 16

# TRAVELLING ON

IN COMMON WITH OTHER MEMBERS of the eighteenth century nobility, the Countess of Huntingdon rarely stayed in any one place for more than a few months. Before her conversion she had travelled with her husband to London for at least part of 'the season' each year – between April and June when Parliament was in session. During the summer months they would spend time at their properties in Leicester or Yorkshire and during the autumn and winter months could often be found at the spa towns such as Bath, Bristol or Cheltenham where members of the aristocracy would regularly congregate. After her husband's death the Countess still travelled, and although health, custom and preference continued to play a part in determining where she would be at any given time, she had an overriding motive for her journeys – the concerns of the kingdom of God. These had become 'the one object of my heart', as she expressed it in a letter to her daughter Elizabeth.

During much of 1761 and 1762 the Countess had been based in Brighton or at nearby Ote Hall as the development of the two new churches engrossed her time and attention. She had also visited Yorkshire, as we have seen, and had, of course, spent time in London. Now fifty-five years of age, Selina continued to undertake these long and uncomfortable rides. Sometimes she had to travel roads frequented by highwaymen; then her coachman would drive the team of horses faster in order to avoid trouble. Even London could present as many dangers as lonely country roads. Thieves were plentiful and youths, ostensibly employed to carry lanterns ahead of visitors to light them to their destination, would sometimes rob their clients instead. It was in London, early in 1762, that the Countess herself was held up and robbed by a highwayman as she crossed the city. A wealthy German, Count Kielmansegge, who was travelling in England at the time noted the fact in his diary:

> We took the road around the town which was more convenient than going through the City; but we provided ourselves with an armed servant on horseback, because my lady Huntingdon had been robbed a few days previously of her watch and money by a highwayman in those parts.[1]

Back in Brighton later in 1762 Selina found satisfaction in the warmth and spiritual devotion of the society which was increasing steadily in size. Letters from her Yorkshire friends also told of continued growth and blessing in the north. But at this same time John Wesley began to experience serious difficulties among his London societies. Thomas Maxfield, a trusted assistant who had worked harmoniously with him for twenty-three years, had been one of the few Methodist lay preachers to have succeeded in gaining ordination and had held a position of considerable influence among the London societies. So when Wesley learnt that Maxfield was propagating an extreme form of perfectionist teaching and causing confusion among the societies, he was deeply concerned.

The root of the problem, however, could be traced back to Wesley's own emphasis. During his Holy Club years he had striven after exacting standards of holiness in an attempt to please God through his good works. After his conversion he freely acknowledged that justification could only come by faith, but he still insisted that desires after holiness were a necessary evidence of a true work of grace in the soul. Wesley went further than this,

---

[1] Count Frederick Kielmansegge, *Diary of a Journey to England, 1761–1762* (London: Longmans, 1902), p. 243.

however, and was soon reintroducing some of his earlier concepts into his teaching, particularly an emphasis on Christian perfection or 'perfect love' as he preferred to term it.

Although Wesley himself never claimed to have attained such perfection, this was to become one of the hallmarks of the Arminian Methodist movement and a repeated source of dispute through the years. Relying mainly on an interpretation of verses in 1 John, he claimed that 'a Christian may be so far perfect as not to commit sin', and be 'freed from evil thoughts . . . and from evil tempers.'[1] As we have seen, the Countess was initially a warm supporter of this position. Reading the sermon from which these quotations are taken when it was first published in 1741, she had pronounced it 'absolutely the most complete thing I know' and a doctrine that 'I hope to live and die by'.[2] Her subsequent repudiation of the teaching sprang from an increasing understanding of biblical teaching coupled with her own experience of repeated failure. She knew she fell far short of what she ought to be.

On a number of occasions throughout the years Wesley had defined and then redefined his view on perfection in an attempt to accommodate his critics. Always, however, the predominant note remained the same: although Christians are not free from ignorance and error, they can become free from outward acts of sin by 'a simple act of faith'; although this, he insisted, remained in conjunction with an on-going work of sanctification in the believer's life.[3] In 1763 he wrote in answer to an enquiry about his teaching, 'But is there not sin in those that are perfect? I believe not; but, be that as it may, they feel none, no temper but pure love . . . and whether sin is suspended or extinguished, I will not dispute; it is enough that they feel nothing but love.'[4]

---

[1] *A Plain Account of Christian Perfection, Sermons on Several Occasions* (London: Wesleyan Methodist Bookroom), pp.579–80.

[2] Rylands MS., Letter 1.

[3] See footnote 2, p. 210.

[4] Wesley, *Letters*, vol. 4, p. 213.

# Travelling On

Almost all the other leaders in the eighteenth century revival, with the exception of John Fletcher, rejected this teaching. Grimshaw, who was probably closer to Wesley than any other and designated his successor in the leadership of Methodism should John and Charles Wesley both die first, was unequivocal on the matter. Writing shortly before the trouble in London, he declared:

> My perfection is to see my imperfection; my comfort to feel I have the world, flesh and devil to overthrow through the Spirit and merits of my dear Saviour; and my desire and hope is to love God with all my heart, mind, soul and strength, to the last gasp of my life. This is my perfection. I know no other, saving to lay down my sword and my life together.[1]

Now came the news from London that Maxfield and some two hundred members of the London society, were not only claiming to be perfect, but were following such teaching through to its logical conclusion: they were therefore superior to all who had not reached this standard and needed none to instruct them. Nor could they ever fall from their exalted position. The societies were in an uproar over these assertions and the situation was made palpably worse when a fanatic by the name of George Bell became yet more extravagant, saying he could raise the dead and cure the blind. He even predicted that the end of the world would take place on 28 February 1763.

Grimshaw wrote laconically to Charles Wesley, 'Last Monday should have been the Day of Judgment. Therefore to have answered your letter sooner would have been a waste of labour, time and paper . . . But who was mistaken? God or Bell?' He feared, however, that it was John Wesley's teaching on Christian perfection that was largely at the root of the trouble. 'Sinless perfection I disclaim . . . I fear, though I will not certainly affirm, [it]

[1] Letter to Charles Wesley, 31 October 1760, cited in full in my *William Grimshaw of Haworth* (Edinburgh: Banner of Truth, 1997), p. 237.

has given birth and being to all those extravagant, presumptuous, scandalous and irreligious vagaries among our London brethren.'[1]

Even Charles Wesley, previously a warm advocate of his brother's position, became far less sure of it. Troubled by the behaviour of these 'perfect' Christians, and probably influenced by the Countess and by Grimshaw, who had become his close friend and correspondent, he no longer contended for his brother's emphasis. Grieved at his brother's uncertainty about his own strongly held views, John Wesley wrote to Charles in March 1763 anxious that they should speak with united voice. 'Some thoughts occurred to my mind this morning, which I believe it may be useful to set down, the rather because it may be a means of our understanding each other clearly, that we may agree as far as ever we can and then let the world know it.' He then set out his present, but somewhat ambivalent views to his brother, concluding with the plea, 'If it is possible let you and me come to a good understanding, both for our own sakes and for the sakes of the people.'[2]

---

[1] *Ibid.*, p.267.

[2] '1. By perfection I mean the humble, gentle, patient love of God and man ruling all the tempers, words, and actions, the whole heart and the whole life.

I do not include a possibility of falling from it, either in part or in whole. Therefore I retract several expressions in our hymns which partly express, partly imply, such an impossibility. And I do not contend for the term 'sinless,' though I do not object against it. Do we agree or differ here? If we differ, wherein?

2. As to the manner, I believe this perfection is always wrought in the soul by faith, by a simple act of faith; consequently in an instant. But I believe a gradual work both preceding and following that instant. Do we agree or differ here?

3. As to the time, I believe this instant generally is the instant of death, the moment before the soul leaves the body. But I believe it maybe ten, twenty, or forty years before death. Do we agree or differ here?

I believe it is usually many years after justification, but that it may be within five years or five months after it. I know no conclusive argument to the contrary. Do you?' Tyerman, *Wesley*, vol. 2, p. 443.

From her home in Brighton the Countess heard disturbing rumours of this confusion among Wesley's London societies. Knowing that she would consider that the troubles he was experiencing sprang directly from his own teaching, Wesley wrote to her on 20 March 1763. The letter expressed his sense of isolation as the crisis continued:

My Lady, For a considerable time I have had it much upon my mind to write a few lines to your Ladyship; although I cannot learn that your Ladyship has ever inquired whether I was living or dead. By the mercy of God I am still alive, and following the work to which he has called me; although without any help, even in the most trying times, from those I might have expected it from. Their voice seemed to be rather, 'Down with him – down with him, even to the ground.' I mean (for I use no ceremony or circumlocution) Mr. Madan, Mr. Haweis, Mr. Berridge, and (I am sorry to say it) Mr. Whitefield. Only Mr. Romaine has shown a truly sympathising spirit and acted the part of a brother[1] . . . As to the prophecies of these poor, wild men, George Bell and half a dozen more, I am not a jot more accountable for them than Mr. Whitefield is; having never countenanced them in any degree, but opposed them from the moment I heard them. Neither have these extravagances any foundation in any doctrine which I teach. The loving God with all our heart, soul, and strength, and the loving all men as Christ loved us, is and ever was, for these thirty years, the sum of what I deliver, as pure religion and undefiled.[2]

Meanwhile a scene far different was being enacted in the north of England in the bleak Pennine village of Haworth where William Grimshaw's ministry, begun twenty-one years earlier,

[1] Romaine, though concerned about Wesley's problems, had no sympathy with his views. Writing to the Countess on 26 March, five days after Wesley had written, he commented, 'I pity Mr John from my heart. His societies are in great confusion; and the point which brought them into the wildness of rant is still insisted on as much as ever.' Seymour, *Countess*, vol. 1, p. 330.

[2] Seymour, *Countess*, vol. 1, p. 329.

had changed the face of West Yorkshire and far beyond through the power of the gospel he had preached. On 20 March 1763, the same date as Wesley was writing the above letter to the Countess, William Grimshaw mounted his pulpit to preach to his people for the last time. A typhus epidemic was sweeping through the town, and Grimshaw who had been visiting a sick parishioner succumbed to the virulent infection.

Only fifty-four years of age, Grimshaw had sensed for some time that his life's service for God might be drawing to a close. When Benjamin Ingham heard of his friend's serious illness he rode across immediately from Aberford to visit him. 'My last enemy is come,' declared Grimshaw as Ingham entered the room. 'The signs of death are on me, but I am not afraid – No, no, blessed be God, my hope is sure and I am in his hands.' With a heavy heart Ingham wrote to the Countess to tell her that it seemed that their valued friend and fellow worker would soon be taken from them.

When Ingham next visited Haworth on 2 April, Grimshaw was sinking swiftly, but Ingham had brought with him a message from the Countess to lift the spirits of the dying man. Touched by her thought for him in his need, Grimshaw raised himself up and replied in words that expressed something of the deep affection in which he held Selina:

> Tell her Ladyship, that dear elect woman, that I thank her from the bottom of my heart for all her kindnesses to me during the years that I have known her. With my dying breath I implore every blessing, temporal and spiritual, to rest upon her. May the God of Abraham, Isaac and Jacob bless her – bless her in body, soul and spirit. I can never repay the spiritual good I have reaped at her hands. O may she be eminently useful in her day and generation![1]

Four days of suffering were left for this valiant Christian until on 6 April 1763 he could say to the one who was caring for him, 'I

[1] For further details see my *Grimshaw*, pp. 284–96.

have nothing to do but to step out of bed into heaven. I have my foot on the threshold already.' With his death later that same day the church of Jesus Christ lost a balanced, wise and devoted leader and the Countess yet another esteemed friend.

Little more than two weeks later the Countess faced a severe trial, at once more personal and therefore more acute. She was visiting Romaine in London when news came from Ote Hall that her daughter, Selina, now twenty-five years of age and engaged to be married to her cousin, had been taken seriously ill. Selina was a bright and attractive young woman: described by Lord Chesterfield as a 'perfect beauty'. A surviving portrait painted in 1762 shows a pensive and tender looking girl with features remarkably like her mother's at a similar age. She was a constant solace to her mother, particularly in view of Henry's death five years earlier, coupled with the disappointment over Francis and the fact that her other daughter, Elizabeth, was far off in Ireland. Dutiful and loving, young Selina had therefore become the focal point of her mother's affections; but more than this, she was a spiritual companion, sharing the same faith and ideals.

Returning immediately, the Countess watched over her daughter as the high fever continued unabated for a further two and a half weeks. Ill as she was, no one seriously expected that the young woman would not recover. Yet she herself seemed to know that this illness would be her last. We give her mother's own account of her daughter's death, written in a letter to William Romaine:

> It pleased our dear God and only Saviour to take from me, May 12, 1763, at three quarters after four in the morning, my dearest, my altogether lovely child and daughter, Lady Selina Hastings, the desire of my eyes and continual pleasure of my heart . . . She often desired me to pray by her, and with great earnestness accompanied me . . . She often called on the Lord Jesus to have mercy on her, and complained of her impatience, though no one ever heard a

complaint pass her lips, notwithstanding her sufferings were very great . . . During the last four days; these sentences at times fell from her: 'Jesus, teach me! – Jesus, wash me! – cleanse me, and purify me!' . . . Another time she said – 'I am as happy as my heart can desire to be.' The day before her death, I came to her and asked her if she knew me. She said, 'My dear mother!' I then asked her if her heart was happy? She said ' . . . I am happy, very, very happy!'. . . She often said, to be resigned to God's will was all, and that she had no hope of salvation but in the mercy of Jesus Christ alone.[1]

This bereavement was hard indeed for the Countess to bear. Throughout her daughter's illness she had searched the Scriptures for tokens of God's intention to restore Selina to health once more and believed that it would be so. Yet in spite of her disappointment and sorrow she was still able to declare, 'In the midst of judgment he has remembered mercy.' Writing to one of the Countess's nieces, Romaine commented, 'Although my Lady bears this so well, yet she feels it. She is but a woman, and though a gracious one, yet grace does not destroy nature. She is a parent and at present incapable of writing.'[2]

Letters of consolation began to arrive at Ote Hall. The Earl of Dartmouth wrote from his Blackheath home a few days after Selina's death:

Little did we imagine when we had the pleasure of seeing her so lately in London that she was so near the confines of the eternal world. But we know not what a day or a night may bring forth. Though nature must feel the loss of such a darling object, now must your Ladyship's grief be mingled with joyful satisfaction . . . that the noble evidence she gave of the grace and hope of the Gospel, and the loving-kindness and mercy of the Saviour manifested in her dying moments. Oh, my dear Madam, Lady Selina is

[1] Rylands MS., Letter 73.
[2] Seymour, *Countess*, vol.1, p. 334.

now singing the praises of redeeming love before the throne of God
and of the Lamb.

Continuing in this letter, Lord Dartmouth spoke of the debt
that he and his wife owed to her:

> We are deeply indebted to your Ladyship, more deeply than we can
> express. Our obligations are of a nature never to be repaid by us;
> but you will be rewarded openly before an assembled world, when
> we shall swell that innumerable train of children which the Lord
> hath given to you.[1]

Henry Venn also wrote sympathetically, as did John Berridge,
but in a different vein. Anxious lest the Countess should allow
her sorrow to distort her judgment or that she should lose sight of
the eternal perspective, he expressed himself in words that may
sound unfeeling to modern ears. A month had passed since her
bereavement and Berridge felt she had grieved long enough; it
was time to put her desolation of heart behind her:

> My Lady, I received your letter from Brighthelmstone, and hope
> you will soon learn to bless your Redeemer for snatching away your
> daughter so speedily. Methinks I see great mercy in the suddenness
> of her removal . . . O! what is she snatched from? Why, truly, from
> the plague of an evil heart, a wicked world, and a crafty devil,
> snatched from all such bitter grief as now overwhelms you,
> snatched from every thing that might wound her ear, afflict her eye,
> or pain her heart. And what is she snatched to? To a land of ever-
> lasting peace . . . where 'every inhabitant can say, 'I am no more
> sick' . . . O Madam! What would you have? Is it not better to sing
> in heaven, 'Worthy is the Lamb that was slain', than crying at

[1] *Ibid.*, p. 335. Dartmouth, who warmly acknowledged his spiritual debt to
the Countess, was becoming an increasingly influential friend of the evangelical cause. Not only did he open his home for the preaching of the gospel, but
he used his immense wealth to help those in need. He also bestowed livings in
his gift on evangelical men, so promoting the reformation of the Church of
England. He remained a life long friend of Selina's.

Oathall, 'O wretched woman that I am!' Is it not better for her to go
before, than to stay after you? and then to be lamenting 'Ah, my
mother,' as you now lament, 'Ah, my daughter?' . . . Lament if you
please, but Glory, glory, glory be to God, says John Berridge.[1]

As when the Earl had died the Countess, ever a deeply affectionate and intense personality, clearly needed privacy and quiet
to come to terms with such a loss. But by September 1763, four
months after Selina's death, even so kindly a correspondent as
John Fletcher felt it was time for her to turn from her bereavement:

Blessed be God for giving us the unspeakable satisfaction to see
Lady Selina safely landed, and out of the reach of vanity. This is
mercy rejoicing over judgment of a truth . . . Come, my Lady, let us
travel on, sticking close to our heavenly Guide; let us keep a hold of
the hem of his garment by firmly believing the arms of his wise
providence and everlasting love are underneath us; let us hasten to
our friends in light . . . Lord Jesus, come quickly, and let us all be
lost together in thy love and praise.[2]

So now the Countess began indeed to 'travel on'. The antidote
to her sorrow lay not so much in putting her bereavement behind
her, as in focussing on the delight that Selina was now experiencing in a better world and in throwing her energies once more into
the work of God.

---

[1] Berridge, *Works*, p. 446.
[2] Seymour, *Countess*, vol. 1, p. 337.

# 17

# New Chapels, New Friends, New Unity

THE 1760S PROVED TO BE A DECADE OF INVENTION and advance across a wide front in Britain. In 1764 a cotton weaver living near Blackburn in Lancashire devised and patented a new spinning frame that would enhance the quality, speed and texture of cotton production. While James Hargreaves' 'Spinning Jenny' opened the door to a revolution in the cotton industry, a twenty-nine-year-old Glaswegian had been experimenting with the use of steam as a source of power. In 1765, during the course of his work, James Watt discovered a method of condensing steam, a prerequisite for his steam engine, patented in 1769.

As in the world of industry and engineering, so in the life of the Countess of Huntingdon, this decade was one of rapid expansion: a prelude to her life-work. With two preaching centres already established in Sussex, the preachers willing to help Selina started to explore further openings for gospel preaching in towns, radiating outwards from Brighton. Men such as Romaine and Madan had travelled to Worthing, twelve miles to the west, but found little there to encourage them. In Lewes, eight miles inland from Brighton, the reception was different, and soon the Countess began to look around for possible sites where she could build a chapel or buy an existing one.

To organize regular preaching services in an increasing number of places laid a heavy burden of responsibility upon the Countess in view of the few able to undertake the work. Since her daughter's death the preaching at Ote Hall had been suspended but now the Countess was anxious to resume it. The fact that this could happen must demonstrate an obvious weakness in the Countess's endeavour, for its entire structure depended upon her ability to provided the necessary ministry. But help was at hand and the names of others ordained into the Church of England now appear in the records as those expressing their willingness to preach at her chapels in conjunction with their own regular ministries. Thomas Haweis, recently expelled from his church in Oxford for his uncompromising evangelicalism, and currently helping Martin Madan at the Lock Hospital in London, was one; Joseph Townsend, converted through the influence of his sister Judith, another. Walter Shirley, brother of Lawrence Shirley who had been executed for murder, also began to work closely with his cousin.

The Countess's arrangements did not always run to her liking. John Berridge had found the long journey on horseback a daunting prospect and could not necessarily see it as God's will that he should leave his own prospering work. Others whom she invited could never be persuaded to come. Even though Selina was convinced that the sea air would be beneficial to Richard Conyers' ailing health, the fear of transgressing the laws of his Church prevented him from leaving his own parish in Helmsley. Some who promised to come failed to arrive. Writing to Howell Harris, now restored to health once more and in charge of a self-supporting community of more than a hundred people in Trevecca, the Countess complained that one of her best men had let her down:

> Mr Madan never came or wrote as he had engaged and hundreds [were] disappointed and the work . . . hindered by the repeated and repeated disappointments. Through the faithfulness of dear Mr Townsend I trust all shall work together.[1]

[1] *Selected Trevecka Letters*, vol. 2, p. 91.

One man on whom Selina could always rely was William Romaine and much of his time during 1763 and 1764 was spent preaching for the Countess in her Sussex chapels. With increased opposition to his ministry, there seemed little likelihood that her chaplain would ever gain a London pulpit. Even the future of his lectureship at St Dunstans now appeared doubtful. But just at this time a London church, St Ann's, Blackfriars, became vacant. Unlike most churches where the new incumbent was appointed by a patron, the position at St Ann's was determined by the votes of parishioners. As soon as the Countess heard that a new rector was being sought, she immediately began exerting pressure wherever she could. The importance of obtaining a London pulpit for the evangelical cause superseded all other considerations in her view. The outcome of her efforts, and that of others, we shall later see.

Although she did not see as much of John and Charles Wesley as she once had, the Countess remained in contact with them and continued her correspondence with Charles and Sally. After the debacle of George Bell and his prophecies, all Methodist work had suffered a temporary set back. John Wesley, nettled that his own teachings on perfection were widely held to be responsible, assumed that the Countess had not invited him to preach at Brighton or Ote Hall because of his views. A letter of 8 January 1764, revealed the depth of his hurt and indignation:

My Lady – Shall I tell your Ladyship just what is in my mind, without any disguise or reserve? I believe it will be best so to do. And I think your Ladyship can bear it. 'When Lady H.' (says my brother) 'invites me to Brighthelmstone, will you bear me company?' I answered, 'Yes', being under no apprehension of his claiming my promise suddenly. And indeed I was perfectly indifferent about it, being in no want of employment. It was therefore little concern to me that Mr Whitefield, Madan, Romaine, Berridge, Haweis were sent for over and over, and as much notice taken of my brother and me as if we had been of couple of postillions. It only confirmed me in the judgement I had formed for many years that I am too rough a preacher for tender ears. 'No, that is not it; but you preach perfection.' What! Without why or wherefore? Among the unawakened? Among babes in Christ? No! To these I say not a word about it. I have two or three grains of common sense. If I do not know how to suit my discourse to my audience at these years, I ought never to preach more.

But I am grieved for your Ladyship. This is no mark of [a] catholic spirit, but of great narrowness of spirit. I do not say this because I have any desire to preach at Brighthelmstone. I could not now, if your Ladyship desired it. For I am engaged every week, till I go to Bristol, in my way either to Ireland or Scotland. But this I wish, even your perfection – the establishment of your soul in love. I am, my Lady, your Ladyship's affectionate and obedient servant, John Wesley.[1]

Such a letter must have disturbed the Countess and made her anxious to strive yet once more for a spirit of love and understanding in the leadership of the revival. Despite any doctrinal differences, she had a strong and overriding concern for unity amongst the increasing number of ordained evangelical men whom God was raising up. So when she and John Wesley met again some months later this subject was uppermost in her mind.

As a direct consequence of their conversation Wesley wrote a long circular to fifty clergymen, appending a personal comment to each letter. Sketching the progress of the revival from the beginning, he alluded to the constant problems arising from their lack of unity: 'As labourers increased, disunion increased . . . till at length those who were not only brethren in Christ but fellow labourers in his gospel had no more connection or fellowship with each other than Protestants have with Papists.' He then referred to the grounds on which fellow believers should be

[1] MS. letter in Cheshunt Foundation Archives, Westminster College, Cambridge.

united, citing three essential and primary truths: original sin, justification by faith and holiness of heart and life. And how might such unity be effected? Wesley's remedy for the bickering that could so easily mar their testimony was one with which no right-minded Christian could disagree:

> Never speak disrespectfully, slightly, coldly or unkindly of each other. Never repeat each other's faults, mistakes, or infirmities . . . never say or do anything to hinder each other's usefulness either directly or indirectly . . . Speak respectfully, honourably, kindly of each other; defend each other's character . . . This is the union I long have sought after.[1]

In addition to the fifty or more clergy to whom he addressed this letter, Wesley also sent copies to the Countess and to Lord Dartmouth. 'Who knows,' he added in a personal note to Selina, 'but it may please God to make your Ladyship an instrument in this glorious work, in effecting a union among the labourers in his vineyard?' Encouraged by her positive response he wrote again, expressing his innermost desires for unity, 'I own freely, I am sick of disputing. I am weary to bear it. My whole soul cries out "Peace, peace!" At least with the children of God, that we may all unite our strength to carry on the war against the "rulers of the darkness of this world".'[2]

John Wesley received only three replies to his circular letter and his initiative seems to have met with an apathetic response. Selina, however, felt unable to let the matter rest and decided to summon as many friends of the revival among the clergymen of the Church of England as she could to meet together in Bristol. As an extension of her practice of organizing regular gatherings of clergy at her home in Bath, this mini-conference attracted a wider cross-section of her friends including men such as Fletcher of Madeley, Joseph Townsend from Wiltshire and Howell Harris.

[1] Wesley, *Letters*, vol. 4, pp. 237–8.
[2] *Ibid*, p. 239, 20 April 1764.

Some might think that the Countess was going beyond her biblical remit in organising such conferences. Perhaps she was, but we may regard her position in this and in other respects as a unique one in the purposes of God for an abnormal situation. She herself was well aware of the scriptural teaching on such issues and, as we have seen, had asked John Wesley's advice in 1742 as to whether or not she might give biblical instruction to a small group of women in her home. Never did she put herself into a position where she was instructing preachers or teaching the Scriptures publicly.

In 1764 a bold and absorbing new venture was forming in Selina's mind: the building of another new chapel, not merely in some Sussex village but this time in Bath itself. It would be the culmination of long years of testimony in that centre of social amusements. Without delay – and all that the Countess conceived she carried out with astonishing speed – she bought a plot of land measuring 163 feet by 60 in a part of Bath known as *The Vineyards,* adjacent to a road then running through open countryside. Builders, plasterers and tilers were soon employed and work on the new chapel begun.

Bemused and not a little hostile, the locals watched as a chapel of ambitious proportions and unexpected architectural design took shape before their eyes. In Georgian Bath, the Countess chose to employ her favourite style of architecture – the Gothic. Little wonder that it aroused comment. With its crenellated frontage, tall arched windows and intersecting tracery, the chapel was designed as a building in which the aristocratic residents of Bath would feel at ease. Evidently her efforts were not favourably received and writing to Charles Wesley in June 1764, she complained:

> My chapel is above ground and I find I am heartily wished to die before it is finished. I am sure of your prayers for its progress, but I think it is remarkable I have not had a line from one creature to

rejoice at its being built, but of that and all things else it is a matter quite between my heart and our only best friend and that being supreme I can want no more.[1]

As Lord Chesterfield watched the growth of the new chapel with its elegant windows and turrets an idea struck him. His country mansion, Bretby Hall, in Derbyshire was little used. Noticing the Countess's propensity for building chapels, he decided to offer her the loan of Bretby Hall. With a ready-built chapel and spacious living accommodation it would be ideal for her purposes. Although such a proposition, coming from a man like Chesterfield, must have caused Selina some hesitation, she agreed to arrange a visit to Derbyshire, accompanied by two friends, William Jesse,[2] vicar of West Bromwich, and Joseph Townsend. Drawbacks there undoubtedly were, but the Countess decided to arrange preaching meetings based at Bretby Hall, and there, against the backdrop of hills and woods in the heart of Derbyshire countryside, large preaching services were held.

Eager crowds from the surrounding villages gathered to listen to the preachers, adding to the considerable number of men and women already on the domestic staff of such a country estate. Newly returned from America, Whitefield joined them, and days of blessing followed. Reporting to a friend on all that they had experienced, Romaine wrote:

> We had there a most refreshing time. Fifteen pulpits were opened and showers of grace came down. Sinners in great numbers were awakened and believers comforted.[3]

---

[1] Rylands MS., Letter 75.

[2] Described by the Countess in a letter to Lord Dartmouth as 'dear honest-hearted Jesse . . . a humble, devoted soul who is much in his Master's work.' The Countess's recommendation led Dartmouth to offer Jesse the living of West Bromwich.

[3] *Letters from Romaine, published from original manuscripts*, by Thomas Wills (London, 1796), p. 61.

A group of converted men and women then formed the nucleus of a new society, gathering regularly at the Bretby Hall[1] chapel. Thomas Maxfield, who had now joined those assisting the Countess, gave regular pastoral oversight to the society at that time.[2]

Back in Sussex, the initiative begun in Lewes several years earlier was coming to fruition. Early in 1765 the Countess hired a room in which Romaine and others could preach. When the undertaking was met with angry censures from the local clergy, Selina decided that here too she would need to build a chapel (with the usual living accommodation attached) to secure her work from the clamour of disapproving voices. The opening services were held in August 1765, conducted by Thomas Pentycross, an earnest and well-liked young man, whom Whitefield affectionately called 'our dear Penty'. Henry Peckwell also took part.[3] Both are preachers whom we shall meet again in the unfolding drama of Selina's endeavours.

As her chapels increased, so the Countess cast her net yet wider for needed assistance, calling on such old Welsh friends as Howell Harris, Peter Williams and Howell Davies. Venn, Berridge, Fletcher, Shirley, Madan, Haweis and Romaine all travelled extensively for Selina, despite their own personal commitments. Still the man-power was not enough to meet the demand. The labour and correspondence involved in arranging for many different pulpits monopolized much of Selina's time and

[1] Rebuilt in 1777 by the Fifth Earl of Chesterfield into a magnificent mansion, Bretby Hall is still standing, and has now been adapted and sold as separate luxury apartments.

[2] Maxfield had been expelled from Wesley's societies because of his extreme views of perfectionism in 1762. The Countess had 'rescued' him, showing him kindness and gradually he had come to a firm Calvinistic persuasion and served with her whenever he was able, until he obtained a regular London pulpit.

[3] Peckwell was to become one of the most outstanding and erudite of the eighteenth century preachers. He had been encouraged and supported financially by the Countess until his own resources became more adequate.

strength. But at this period the name of Jenetta Orton is found linked with Selina's. Jenetta, a young woman from a society family background, became a constant companion and friend for the fifty-eight-year-old Countess. Converted through the preaching of Thomas Haweis, she assisted Selina with her many arrangements, travelling with her and shouldering some of the ever-increasing burden of correspondence.

On 6 October 1765 the new chapel in Bath was at last ready and opened for worship. Three magnificent eagles with outspread wings – still to be seen today – formed a trio of lecterns at the front of the chapel, one on each side of the central lectern or pulpit. On the pedestal of each eagle-lectern a set of initials was engraved, WS, TH and SH, representing three whom the Countess had loved dearly: her father, Washington Shirley, her husband, Theophilus Hastings and her daughter, Selina Hastings.

Among her friends, Whitefield, Venn, Shirley and Townsend accepted the invitation to participate in the opening services. Whitefield preached in the morning and Townsend at night. Reporting on the occasion Whitefield wrote, 'the great Shepherd and Bishop of souls consecrated and made it holy ground by his presence'. Crowded with both aristocracy and ordinary citizens, with the curious and the concerned, the opening of the Vineyards chapel in Bath was a source of widespread interest in the city. The Countess was anxious to capitalize on the interest that had been created and to maintain a high standard of preaching. Urgent letters were sent across the country, begging, even insisting, that her friends lay down their present work and take it in turns to preach at Bath. Kindly obeying her dictates, Madan was the first to come, followed by Whitefield, and by the end of October Fletcher had arrived from Madeley. His preaching, which the Countess described as deep and awesome, probed the artificiality and self-importance of many of his sophisticated hearers.

With her ever-widening circle of influence, names now crowd the canvas of Lady Huntingdon's busy life – names that ranked both among the godly and the influential of her day. Many appear only to pass soon from sight, but others came to play a significant part in her developing story. Sir Richard Hill of Hawkestone in Shropshire had been converted ten years earlier through his conversations with John Fletcher, who was still living nearby at the time. Brought to despair through a sense of sin yet with none to help, Richard Hill had contacted Fletcher, about whom he had heard strange and contradictory reports. As Fletcher corresponded with the young nobleman and lent him books, Hill was converted. Soon he began to associate with the friends of the gospel despite the embarrassment and disapproval of his family.

Richard's younger brother Rowland, studying at St. John's College, Cambridge, was converted shortly afterwards. When he aspired to do some preaching his parents threatened to disown him and to withdraw their financial support. Probably at the suggestion of Whitefield, Rowland Hill travelled to Bath to share his predicament with the Countess. She received him gladly and wrote twice to his parents interceding on his behalf. Jane Hill, sister of Richard and Rowland, had also been converted and had in turn been instrumental in the conversion of another young woman, Willielma Campbell – Lady Glenorchy.

Willielma Campbell's future course was to be in some respects similar to Selina's own. Only twenty-four years of age when she first met the Countess in October 1765, Willielma, still a young Christian, had been unwell and her husband was anxious to divert her mind from 'the religious turn' she appeared to have taken. What better place than Bath for such a purpose? But he had not reckoned on the presence of Selina Hastings in the city, nor on the fact that a chapel had just been opened and that its pulpit was being supplied by men of spiritual passion and earnestness. Fully aware of the allurements of high society with all its potential perils, the Countess befriended the younger woman, advising and helping her. Writing after her return to Edinburgh, Lady Glenorchy expressed her gratitude for Selina's friendship, adding, 'I hope the Lord permits it as a spur to me to be watchful and to keep near to him who alone is able to keep me from falling.'[1]

A short time later Willielma's sister, also in her mid-twenties, arrived in Bath with her husband. Recently bereaved by the death of their two-year-old daughter the couple also felt that a period in Bath might divert their minds and raise their spirits. But trouble followed on trouble and not long after their arrival the husband, Lord Sutherland, was taken ill with a virulent fever. Distraught with anxiety his wife watched by him night and day. When the Countess heard of the situation she did all she could to help. Earnest prayer was offered on their behalf and many of the care-less and lighthearted of Bath watched and waited to see what would happen. Weakened by her long vigil at her husband's bed-side, Willielma's sister succumbed to the infection herself and died little more than two weeks after her arrival. Her husband struggled on but a fortnight later he too died. The tragedy shook the complacent nobility of Bath. 'I never saw such a universal concern at the death of any persons before', wrote the Countess. 'Many seem cut to the heart – others plunged in the deepest grief. It has been a most awful event, and has brought many to the chapel who had hitherto refused to enter it.'[2] Whitefield was in Bath at the time and it is not hard to imagine that he made effec-tive use of the occasion.

Two years had passed since Wesley and the Countess had tried to effect a greater unity amongst all branches of the Methodist work. Now they made a further attempt to strengthen the bonds of love that sometimes became frayed between them. In the summer of 1766 Whitefield, the Wesley brothers and the Coun-tess all met together to discuss ways of promoting unity. Writing to Sally about the occasion Charles commented: 'Last night my brother came. This morning we spent two hours together with G.

[1] Seymour, *Countess*, vol. 1, p. 471–2.
[2] *Ibid.*, vol. 1, p. 473.

Whitefield. The threefold cord, we trust, will never more be broken. On Tuesday next my brother is to preach at Lady Huntingdon's chapel in Bath. That, and all her chapels, . . . are now put into the hands of us three.'[1] It would appear that Selina had agreed to pass over some of the burden of responsibility for her chapels to Wesley and had arranged for him to preach at them when he was in the area. Whitefield too was to be free to preach among Wesley's societies.

The Countess wrote to Wesley that September: 'I do trust this union that is commenced will be for the furtherance of our faith and mutual love for each other. It is for the interest of the best cause that we should all be found first faithful to the Lord and then to each other.'[2] In his *Journal* for Sunday, 17 August, 1766, Wesley recorded, 'It was the earnest request of [the Countess], whose heart God has turned again, without any expectation of mine, that I came hither [to Bath] so suddenly.' And the following day he added, 'Many were not a little surprised in the evening at seeing me in the Countess of H.'s chapel. The congregation was not very large, but serious, and I fully delivered my own soul.'[3]

In August 1766 Wesley's annual Conference was due to take place in the city. Writing to Charles the Countess reported, 'I have a letter from your brother who wishes my stay for the Conference and I do hope you will be at it and prevail with any or all of the clergy you meet with to be at it. I believe it will be an important season.' Clearly Wesley was anxious to use the prevailing goodwill between himself and the Calvinistic Methodists to follow up on his recent initiative to promote greater unity. To have

[1] Charles Wesley, *Journal*, vol. 2, p. 246.
[2] Rylands MS., Letter 103.
[3] Wesley, *Journal*, vol. 5, pp. 182–3. Asking him to preach again in October the Countess wrote, explaining that it would be a most important occasion because it was the 'height of the latter season when the great of this world are in the reach of the sound of the gospel'. They usually attended in the mornings while 'the inhabitants' attended at night. Letter 103, Rylands MS. Wesley preached, therefore, on 5 October – a Sunday, and on the following Thursday, 9 October.

the Countess present would therefore be 'an excellent service in confirming any kind of friendly disposition which the Lord might plant in the hearts of his servants', as Wesley had told Selina in his invitation.[1]

On 5 October Wesley was once again preaching at the Countess's chapel in Bath. Probably unknown to him, however, an unexpected visitor was in the congregation that morning – none other than the cynic, Horace Walpole, whose ill-health had brought him to the city. The account he gave of the occasion in a letter to his friend John Chute provides us with the best description of the chapel as it was in that first year after its opening:

They have boys and girls with charming voices that sing hymns in parts to Scotch ballad tunes; but indeed so long that one would think they were already in eternity . . . The chapel is very neat, with true Gothic windows . . . At the upper end is a broad *hautpas* of four steps, advancing in the middle; at each end of the broadest part are two of *my*[2] eagles, with red cushions for the parson and clerk. Behind them rise three more steps, in the midst of which is a third eagle for a pulpit. Scarlet armed chairs to all three. On either hand a balcony for elect ladies. The rest of the congregation sit on forms. Behind the pit, in a dark niche, is a plain table within rails; so you see the throne is for the apostle [i.e. the pulpit took precedence over the communion table]. Wesley is a lean elderly man, fresh-coloured, his hair smoothly combed, but with a *soupçon* of curl at the ends. Wondrous clean, but as evidently an actor as Garrick. He spoke his sermon, but so fast, and with so little accent, that I am sure he has often uttered it, for it was like a lesson. There were parts and eloquence in it; but towards the end he exalted his voice, and acted very vulgar enthusiasm . . . Except a few from curiosity, and some honourable women, the congregation was very mean [made up of the poorer sections of the community].[3]

[1] Wesley, *Letters*, vol. 4, p. 244.
[2] A cynical reference to the initials on the pedestals.
[3] *Private Correspondence of Horace Walpole*, London, 1820, vol. 3, pp.191-2.

Of interest is this early reference by Walpole to the singing in the chapel. The Countess had always had a love for hymns, and as we noted previously, Charles Wesley had sent her some of his earliest work for her comment. When her friend Fanny Cowper was dying in 1742, it was one of Wesley's hymns that brought her consolation. So now, for the opening of her Bath chapel, a hymnbook containing two hundred and thirty-one hymns selected by the Countess herself had been produced.[1] The service itself followed the regular *Book of Common Prayer* sequence with its repetition of prayers and responses, but the central position of the pulpit reflected the Countess's priorities in any service of worship.

During the winter months of 1766 and into 1767 Selina was back in Brighton. The increasing numbers who wished to attend the North Street Chapel forced her to the conclusion that though the building had been open for little more than five years, it would need to be considerably enlarged and refurbished. Work on this project went speedily ahead and by early spring the rebuilt chapel was ready to be opened. Anxious that the occasion might prove one of joyful fellowship among all her friends and a symbol of the new initiative for union among them, Selina wished as many as possible to attend. To Charles Wesley, who had been unwell, she wrote on 4 February 1767:

> I am refitting my chapel here for many reasons that appear needful for the furtherance of the work and when it is opened I could not help wishing to have all the old friends together at one love feast before I finished my course. Your brother and Mr Whitefield are nearby in London and Mr Harris here and nothing but you

[1] This was, in fact, the second edition of her hymnbook. The first was produced the previous year (1765), and was used at the opening of the chapel in Lewes. This one, printed by E. Farley in Bath, was divided into three parts: *Society hymns* (127), *Children's hymns* (13) and *Congregational hymns* (91). Her hymnbook went through many editions each bearing the words, 'Collected by her Ladyship'.

wanting. Should your heart wish to share this blessing I really expect from this feast as a fresh dedication of our remaining days to the Lord. I trust the day of Pentecost may fully come and crown all the last works with fresh glory upon them.[1]

In the event the enlarged chapel was reopened on 20 March 1767 with Martin Madan preaching in the morning and Whitefield in the evening. But in keeping with her desire that the occasion should be one of personal and corporate rededication to the service of God, the Countess set apart the previous day for special prayer. The morning she spent on her own, and in the evening all her friends who had assembled at her request joined in united prayer.

As John Berridge surveyed the advance in the work to which the Countess had committed her time, strength and financial resources, he wrote encouragingly, 'Go on, my dear lady, build and fight manfully, and believe lustily. Look upwards and press forwards. Heaven's eternal hills are before you, and Jesus stands with arms wide open to receive you.'[2] And so she did.

---

[1] Rylands MS., Letter 76.
[2] Berridge, *Works*, pp. 504–5.

# 18

## 'A School of Prophets
– That Is the Thing!'

At a time when the Countess needed yet more preacher friends who were prepared to itinerate, William Romaine's days of travelling were to be severely curtailed. As we have seen, the living of St Ann's, Blackfriars, had unexpectedly become vacant and his friends, including the Countess, had done all in their power to secure the pulpit for him. Some parishioners on whose votes the outcome depended were wary and uncommitted, knowing of Romaine's links with Methodism. Others were fearful of an incursion of hearers from other parishes. The Countess watched and waited with concern as Romaine's initial election was countermanded by his opponents and the case was forced to go to a suit in Chancery.

William Jesse of West Bromwich was with the Countess at Ote Hall when the news finally came through early in 1766 that the living of St Ann's had been secured for Romaine. 'We have had quite a little jubilee on the confirmation of our dear brother Romaine's election', Jesse reported. 'Never have I seen more heart-felt joy and gratitude than was expressed on that occasion by her Ladyship. I verily believe that if Mr Romaine had not gained his election the disappointment and vexation would have well nigh killed her.'[1] A strategic Church of England pulpit had been secured in the heart of the capital.

---

[1] New, *Coronet and Cross*, p. 177.

With his new and much increased responsibilities Romaine would no longer be able to serve the Countess as before. At the same time Thomas Haweis had become embroiled in a dispute with the unprincipled patron of his living at Aldwinkle in North-amptonshire, a situation that was seriously curtailing his usefulness and also affecting his friend, Martin Madan. Whitefield too was not as available as in former years. When Wesley met him in 1766 he described him as 'an old, old man' at fifty-two years of age, worn out by his tireless labours. Sometimes the Countess was quite unable to find preachers able and willing to undertake the extra responsibilities involved in supplying the preaching stations she had set up. When this happened they would have to remain closed, depriving the people of gospel ministry. Clearly the need for more preachers was imperative.

To meet this pressing necessity, the Countess had a plan – a plan that had been forming in her mind for many months or maybe years. Since her early friendship with Philip Doddridge she had been interested in theological education, and had supported his work by financing students at his Academy. Now her own need for such an institution, 'a nursery for preachers' as she described it to Charles Wesley, became paramount: a place where men of evangelical conviction could be trained and then sent out to supply the vacant pulpits.

As early as 1764 she had shared these concerns with Howell Harris during a visit to Abergavenny, only to discover that he too had been thinking along the same lines. Fifteen years earlier the distant prospect had been the subject of his prayers.[1] In 1761, soon after he had resumed his preaching tours, he had written in his diary, 'Crying for Trevecka; then it passed through me that a great building was to be there for . . . an academy for preachers. Lord, thou art able and I leave it to thee.'[2] Again in 1763 he had

[1] 3 January 1749: 'I had especial freedom to cry for a school at Trevecka to train young men to the Lord.' *Harris Visits Pembrokeshire*, p. 158.
[2] Harris, *Reformer and Soldier*, p. 114.

referred to the 'need of building a new grand house for an academy or school for new young preachers'.[1]

Here then were two minds with a single purpose, uniting both the vision and the financial means to accomplish that vision. After their meeting in Abergavenny, Harris conducted Selina to his Trevecca home to show her a sixteenth century building known as Trefeca Isaf, situated close to his own settlement.[2] He had rented this rundown farmhouse from his brother, Thomas, the previous year together with part of the adjoining lands, possibly intending it for the college that he had long envisaged. Showing this farm complex to the Countess, Harris expressed his willingness to sub-let both buildings and land to her on a twenty-five year lease for an annual rent of ten guineas, with a view to establishing a training school for preachers.

Before 1764 had ended the Countess had been making preliminary enquiries for a suitable tutor and early in 1765 more definite plans were discussed. With Harris's institution already at Trevecca, skilled men would be on hand to help with any building or alterations needed at Trefeca Isaf. Not only would students be housed in quiet surroundings, but Harris himself would also be nearby and able to keep a watchful eye on the work. A letter from the Countess to Harris on 15 January 1765 contains an early reference to the joint venture: 'Except the college is really established in the true and primitive spirit, I would rather wait ever so long. Our Saviour's time will render all easy.'[3]

Work to enlarge and adapt Trefeca Isaf for its new purpose eventually began on 1 December 1767. Ten months earlier Howell Harris had undertaken the journey from Wales to

[1] *Ibid.*, p. 197.
[2] Built in the year 1576 for a woman named Rebecca Prosser, Trefeca Isaf means Rebecca's abode. It stood 500 yards further along the road in the Talgarth direction than Howell Harris's establishment. 'Trevecca' has been variously spelt but we have chosen to use this spelling throughout unless it is spelt otherwise in the reference quoted.
[3] Edward Morgan, *Life of Harris* (1852), p. 237.

Brighton to be present at the opening of the extended chapel in North Place. Doubtless the visit gave the Countess and the Welsh preacher opportunity to discuss plans for the proposed alterations. Shortly after Harris had left, the Countess prepared to embark on an itinerary that would take her first to Trevecca, then into Shropshire, across to Derbyshire, on into Yorkshire and finally to Edinburgh – her first visit to Scotland.

Towards the middle of April 1767 Selina set out together with Jenetta Orton and another young friend, Lady Anne Erskine. They spent a few days near Gloucester on the way, and discovering Whitefield in the area, would have enjoyed hearing him preach once more. Soon after arriving at Trevecca, the party was joined by John Fletcher who had also been taking a lively interest in all the Countess's plans for a college. With Fletcher as their guide they set off for Madeley in Shropshire, a journey of almost seventy miles.

Days of fellowship followed in the Madeley vicarage and especially when the colourful soldier-preacher, Captain Scott, converted at Ote Hall, joined them. Writing to a friend on 27 April 1767 Fletcher describes his guest: 'I have just received your letter upon my arrival from Wales with dear Lady Huntingdon, who is of a truth, a tried stone, built upon the corner stone . . . a soul devoted to Jesus.'[1] It was probably during this visit to Madeley that the Countess first considered asking Fletcher whether he would accept the position of future president of her new college – an appointment that illustrates her wish that the undertaking should serve the entire Methodist work, not merely the Calvinistic wing.

Now turned sixty years of age and suffering indifferent health, Selina Hastings was embarking on the most demanding project of her life. The prospective college would have to be fully furnished, but yet more important was the recruitment of suitable students.

---

[1] Tyerman, *Wesley's Designated Successor,* p. 118.

So Selina's next step was to draw up a list of qualifications she would expect to find in any young man who applied to enter the college: qualifications of godliness, zeal, general ability and suitability for all that was involved in the task of travelling and preaching. She hoped that the more able of the candidates would proceed for ordination, preferably in the Church of England, after completing a course of training at Trevecca.

When she had completed her list, Selina sent it around to different ministers and friends, asking them to consider whether any young men known to them might qualify as prospective students. On receiving it, John Fletcher discovered an additional personal request attached: it was that he should examine the candidates to decide on their suitability. He replied on 24 November 1767:

My dear Lady,

I received the proposals which your ladyship has drawn up for the examination of the young men who may appear proper candidates for the Trevecca academy; and I gratefully acknowledge your kindness in allowing me to propose suitable young men resident in my parish.

Our Israel is small, my lady, and if among six hundred thousand only two faithful men were found of old, the Joshuas and Calebs cannot be numerous among us. After having perused the articles, and looked round about me, I designed to answer your ladyship, *'Out of this Galilee ariseth no prophet.'* With this resolution I went to bed, but, in my sleep, was much taken up with the thought and remembrance of one of my young colliers, who told me, some months ago, that for four years he had been inwardly persuaded he should be called to speak for God.

I looked upon the unusual impression of my dream as a call to speak to the young man, and at waking desired to do so at the first opportunity. To my great surprise, he came to Madeley that very morning, and I found upon enquiry that he had been as much drawn to come as I to speak to him. This encouraged me to speak of your ladyship's design, and I was satisfied by his conversation that I might venture to propose him to your ladyship for further examination.

His name is James Glazebrook, collier and getter of ironstone in Madeley Wood. He is now twenty-three – by look nineteen. He has been awakened seven years. He has been steady from the beginning of his profession . . . Notwithstanding his strong desire to exhort, he has not yet attempted to do so; and his not being forward to run of himself, makes me have the better hope his call is from God. He has no mean gift in singing and prayer.

With regard to the superintendency of the college, or the examination of the candidates, I know myself too well to dream about it; nevertheless, so far as my present calling and poor abilities will allow, I am ready to throw my mite into the treasury.

Writing to Howell Harris on 17 December 1767, Selina recorded her progress:

I have waited that long in order to be as particular as possible and to show you how the Lord has hitherto blessed the undertaking at Trefecca. Seven young men I have heard of that I believe really are precious souls. Mr Fletcher sends [one], Dr Conyers another two; then from London dear Mr Whitefield I believe has found us a master. His heart is much in it, and I fancy sees the necessity of training a ministry spiritual and wholly given up to the Lord.[1]

The provision of suitable books for the students was another aspect of the project that concerned the Countess. Again she wrote to Fletcher asking advice. Unsure whether he was best qualified to help because few of his studies had been undertaken in England, Fletcher suggested that the Countess should approach Joseph Townsend or Charles Wesley. However, certain books he felt would be of importance:

[1] *Selected Trevecka Letters,* p. 115. The very difficult handwriting has made this letter hard to decipher.

Watt's 'Logic,' and his 'History of the Bible, by Questions and Answers,' which seem to me excellent books of the kind for clearness and order. Mr. Wesley's 'Natural Philosophy' contains as much as is wanted, or more. Mason's 'Essays on pronunciation' will be worth their attention. 'Henry and Gill on the Bible,' with the four volumes of Baxter's 'Practical Works', Keach's 'Metaphors,' Taylor on the 'Types,' Gurnal's 'Christian Armour,' Edwards on 'Preaching,' Johnson's English Dictionary, and Mr. Wesley's 'Christian Library,'[1] may make part of the little library.[2]

The itinerary on which the Countess had set out, and that was to have included her visit to Edinburgh, had to be cut short after she reached Yorkshire because of further illness in the summer of 1767. A letter of sympathy from Fletcher now back in Madeley indicates the regard in which Selina was held:

My very dear and honoured Lady,

The God of Abraham, Isaac, and Jacob, who tried Israel, and led them through many a wandering to the good land – this faithful God has met with you, a rod is in his hand, but that hand bears so deep a print of love, that the design of his visitation cannot be mistaken . . . . My hearty prayer for your ladyship is that you may drink the cup the Lord holds out to you as a new token of his unchangeable love . . . I have often heard your ladyship speak of *'the fellowship of his sufferings'*. The Lord will have you improve in that heavenly knowledge; therefore he gives you so long a lesson at this time. The lesson is hard, I grant; but the Master is *so loving*, and the scholar so used to severe exercises, that it is no wonder you are placed on the highest form. No cross – no crown! The heavier the cross, the brighter the crown![3]

As soon as she was well enough to travel Selina returned to Bath, but before she had fully regained her strength she learnt of

[1] Mainly abridgements of Puritan and other works.

[2] For a full list of Fletcher's suggestions see *Wesley's Designated Successor*, p. 132.

[3] *Ibid.*, p. 120.

the deaths of two of her friends, taken in quick succession. In September 1767 she heard with sadness of the death of Henry Venn's young wife, a death that left him with five children to care for. Venn's close friends were the Countess's two nieces Elizabeth Medhurst and Kitty Wheler who lived in Leeds. They showed much kindness to the bereaved preacher and from his letters to them we learn more of the circumstances surrounding the death of this godly Christian woman.[1] Irreparable as such a loss was, Venn was still able to triumph in the knowledge of God's overruling purposes. The Countess quickly invited him to come and stay in Bath. Though grateful for the invitation Venn wrote declining on 15 October 1767:

> The only return I can make your Ladyship for the very tender sympathy you show for me in my present trial, is prayer to him who has already so much use of you as an instrument, that he would do so more and more . . . Did I not know the Lord to be mine . . . into what a deplorable condition should I have been now cast . . . I have lost her when her industry, and ingenuity and tender love and care of her children were all just beginning to be perceived by the two eldest girls . . . I have lost her when her soul was as a watered garden, when her mouth was opened to speak for God. Nevertheless I can say, All is well! Hallelujah! for the Lord God omnipotent reigneth.[2]

Throughout this period the numbers crowding into the Vineyards chapel in Bath had been steadily increasing. Lord and Lady Buchan, whose daughter, Lady Anne Erskine, was now Selina's constant companion, had been regular in their attendance. Gradually the truth proclaimed by the preachers who visited Bath began to affect them both deeply. Lord Buchan, who had come there for his health, was clearly dying. When the end seemed near

[1] Details of Mrs Venn's last illness can be found in letters to the Countess's nieces in *Letters of Henry Venn*, pp. 135–144.

[2] Seymour, *Countess*, vol. 2, p. 7.

he asked Selina if she would call on him. As she entered the room, he spoke words that must have brought her joy: 'I have no foundation of hope whatever, but in the sacrifice of the Son of God; I have nowhere else to look; nothing else to depend on for eternal life and salvation.' As the last hours of life slipped past his joys grew brighter. 'Had I strength of body, I would not be ashamed before men and angels to tell what the Lord Jesus hath done for my soul,' he whispered. And his dying words were, 'Happy . . . happy . . . happy'.[1]

This triumphant death on 1 December 1767 had a profound impact on both the serious and the frivolous of Bath. Still weak from her own illness, Selina nevertheless used the occasion to the greatest possible advantage. For five days as Lord Buchan's body lay in state in the Vineyards chapel, Whitefield preached twice daily to the incessant stream of mourners who came to pay their last respects. 'Many, I trust, are obliged to say, "How dreadful is this place!" Such a like scene I never expect to see again on this side eternity,' commented Whitefield.[2]

As soon as the Countess was well enough, she was back at her desk writing letters and planning for the prospective college at Trevecca. A long letter to Howell Harris written on 4 June 1768 gives a fascinating picture of all the arrangements with which she concerned herself. Ever a gifted organizer, her abilities were now needed to the full. Hannah Bowen, the trusted and well-loved housekeeper at Harris's establishment, had been asked to work at the college. But now the Countess wondered 'whether she is too young a woman and being more amiable than the generality of her orders it might be a great temptation to her and more so to the twenty young men that she must of necessity be much with.' Perhaps an older woman would be preferable. Then a cook was needed and a boy to run errands and fetch coal: 'more than those three I will not hear of and but these two women, unless on a

---

[1] *Ibid.*, vol. 2, p. 15.          [2] *Ibid.*

washing day.'[1] Of course the students would be expected to help in the day-to-day running of the establishment.

Ideally the Countess felt that at least two tutors would be essential. One she had already engaged, a Welshman, who could help Welsh students with the English language. The reference to another she had in mind, a man who could teach arithmetic, Latin and the Greek Testament, is now illegible in the original letter. Fletcher himself would oversee the religious studies when he made his periodic visits to the college. With Harris on the spot to aid the students in their early pulpit endeavours, the Countess's long held plans and hopes were coming to fruition. Writing to Harris again two weeks later, she gives further details about the Welsh tutor she had engaged. Describing him as a man who was willing to serve for nothing but 'a crust and Jesus Christ', she continued, 'I have got the most proper master that is possible. His name is Williams. He was awakened by you and can teach the grammar in Welsh and Latin and all the rules of English and I can only wait for Mr Fletcher's approbation to send him down to you.'[2]

Not all her friends, however, were convinced that Lady Huntingdon was doing the right thing in attempting to set up a college at Trevecca. John Berridge, a man never afraid to speak his mind to the Countess, had many doubts about the project. When he received a copy of the proposed guidelines governing the selection of students, he wrote expressing his misgivings:

> The soil you have chosen is proper. Welsh mountains afford a brisk air for a student; and the rules are excellent; but I doubt the success of the project; and fear it will occasion you more trouble than all your other undertakings besides. Are we commanded to make labourers or to 'pray the Lord to send labourers'? Will not Jesus choose, and teach, and send forth his ministering servants now, as

[1] *Selected Trevecka Letters*, vol. 2, pp. 119–20.
[2] *Ibid.*, p. 123.

he did his disciples aforetime? . . . We read of a school of prophets in the Scripture but we do not read that it was God's appointment. Elijah visited the school, which was at Bethel, and seems to have been fond of it; yet the Lord commands him to fetch a successor not from the school . . . but from the plough. Are we told of a single preaching prophet that was taken out of this school? . . . That old prophet who told a sad lie to another prophet was of this school, and might be the master of this college, for he was a grey-haired man (1 Kings 13:11). Whilst my heart is thus prattling to you very simply, like a child, it stands in no fear of offending you; and if your project be right, the Master keep you steadfast, and you will only smile at my prattling.[1]

It was indeed hard to be offended with Berridge. Despite her friend's misgivings, the Countess still pressed ahead with her 'school of prophets', though the vicar of Everton's fears that the project could bring many problems were to prove well-founded.

[1] Berridge, *Works*, p. 449–50.

# 19

## HOPES FULFILLED

IN MAY 1768 CAPTAIN JAMES COOK set out in the *Endeavour* on an epic voyage of discovery, a voyage that took him far into the southern Pacific Ocean where he confirmed the existence of the vast Australian continent – previously the subject of myth and conjecture. 1768 also marked the beginning of a new venture in the experience of the Countess of Huntingdon, now approaching her sixty-first birthday: the opening of Trevecca College.

A notable event took place in March 1768, however, that added urgency and momentum to the Countess's endeavours. Six students from St Edmund Hall, Oxford, described as 'enthusiasts who talked of regeneration, inspiration and drawing nigh unto God', were expelled from the university for evangelical beliefs. Trouble had been brewing for some years since the dismissal of Thomas Haweis from his Oxford curacy at St Mary Magdalene in 1762 for no other offence than that his fearless evangelical preaching was attracting ever-increasing congregations. To dismiss Haweis might be easy but to purge the university of the powerful influences of the gospel was a more difficult matter. Although the pulpits of the town were closed to Methodist preaching, those students whose hearts God had touched met secretly to read the Scriptures and to pray, often in the home of a widow, Mrs Durbridge – a friend of George Whitefield.

Among mid-eighteenth century Oxford's twenty colleges and five halls, St Edmund Hall had gained a reputation for fine stand-ards, discipline and high religious ideals, partly through the influence of its principal, Dr George Dixon. Far different was the vice-principal, John Higson. Proud and vengeful by disposition, he was also full of bitterness and bluster against certain students who by their superior knowledge of the Scriptures had shown up his ignorance. During his lectures he had attempted unsuccessfully to draw them away from the principles of the Reformation and the Thirty-nine Articles. At last Higson, a man with a known record of mental imbalance, could bear it no longer. Reporting seven of his students to Dixon, he demanded that they be disciplined. Dixon, supposing that his colleague was suffering from strain, pointed out the exemplary conduct of the young men in question and suggested he had no case against them because all that they had said could be substantiated from Scripture. Higson then took the extreme step of appealing to the Vice-Chancellor of the university, Dr Durrell, who set in place a formal trial of the seven students.

The trial was a travesty of justice. According to Whitefield, the students were 'hissed at, pushed about and treated in a manner that the vilest criminal is not allowed to be treated either at the Old Bailey or any court of justice in the kingdom.'[1] Accused of being sub-standard in their academic attainments, of coming from humble backgrounds, but most significantly of offering extempore prayers and even attempting to preach without ordination, six of the seven students originally accused were expelled from St Edmund.[2]

The Countess followed the case with close interest. Some of the students arraigned in this way were personally known to her and may well have been recommended by her to pursue their studies

[1] Whitefield, *Letter to the Vice-Chancellor*, 1st edition, p. 19, cited by S. A. Ollard, *The Six Students of St Edmund Hall* (London: Mowbray & Co., 1911), p. 19.

[2] The six students expelled were: James Matthews (an older student, aged thirty at the time), Joseph Shipman, Erasmus Middleton, Benjamin Kay, Thomas Grove and Thomas Jones.

at St Edmund. She insisted, however, that there was no truth in the story being propagated by the press that she had encouraged these men to leave their livelihoods as tradesmen and had financed their university courses so that they might gain ordination, and so forward her cause. In high annoyance she wrote:

> With the foul invectives of common newspapers I have nothing to do, neither am I accountable for the impudent falsehood of those who have maliciously asserted that I have inveigled six ignorant young men from their trades in the country, and maintained them at the university. All these, and many other absurd and ridiculous accusations, insinuations and statements are utterly false . . . and without the least foundation in truth to support them; but the Lord God is witness between me and my accusers in this matter.[1]

The conduct on the part of the university in expelling the six students made Selina and her friends realize yet more acutely the importance of providing alternative educational facilities for young men of evangelical persuasion. More than this, the pamphlet war that ensued created something of a national sensation, with participants both for and against the students. At least twenty-three separate publications addressed the issue, some running into multiple editions. First to appear on 11 April 1768 was a trenchant letter from George Whitefield who had always taken an interest in the welfare of Christian students. Addressing his letter to the Vice-Chancellor, Whitefield wrote a spirited defence of the students' conduct, and particularly of their use of extempore prayer and private exhortations. This letter evoked an immediate response from an undergraduate who sprang to the defence of the university hierarchy.[2]

Next came the most important publication on the issue, a pamphlet by Sir Richard Hill with a full defence of the students, but also introducing another element into the controversy: the issue

[1] Seymour, *Countess*, vol. 1, p. 426.
[2] *Ibid.*, p. 424.

of the clear Calvinistic nature of the Thirty-nine Articles.[1] In turn this widened the debate and called attention once more to the fraught doctrinal issues that had so often threatened to divide the work of the revival. Another major contribution to the argument, not merely in defence of the students, but again on the Calvinism of the Articles came from an anonymous writer who styled himself 'Clerus'. With forceful polemic this writer defended the formularies of the Church against the claim that they were Arminian in character.[2] The writer was soon discovered to be none other than thirty-year-old Augustus Toplady, the newly appointed vicar of Broadhembury in Devon.

During this same period Rowland Hill was also coming under pressure in Cambridge. No-one, as he later remarked, could even spare him a cordial smile on account of his stand for truth, apart from the old shoe-black at the gate of St John's who 'had the love of Christ in his heart'. John Berridge at nearby Everton soon heard of Hill and befriended the student who had now gathered a group of like-minded students around him. But when the young man began preaching in nearby villages and in Cambridge itself, the university authorities became seriously concerned. The situation deteriorated still further when Hill persisted in preaching whenever and wherever opportunity afforded. Even his parents threatened to disown him. At this point Rowland Hill asked Whitefield for his advice. Knowing from his own experiences something of what Hill was facing, Whitefield took time and trouble to advise him. Were it not for the fact that he was the son of a baronet, it is likely that in March 1768 he too would have suffered the same fate as the Oxford students at St Edmund Hall.

While the religious world, still in a commotion, reacted and argued over the persecution meted out to students of Methodist convictions, the Countess suffered yet another bereavement.

---

[1] *Pietas Oxoniensis,* published June 1768.
[2] Augustus M. Toplady, *The Church of England Vindicated from the Charge of Arminianism* (London, 1769).

Lady Margaret, wife of Benjamin Ingham and youngest sister of her husband, Theophilus, had been instrumental in Selina's own conversion and she had loved her gentle sister-in-law dearly. Dying on 30 April 1768 at the age of sixty-seven, Lady Margaret's passing was marked with the same serenity as her life. Describing his wife's last days, Benjamin Ingham wrote:

> When she had no longer strength to speak to me, she looked most sweetly at me and smiled. On the Tuesday before she died when she had opened her heart to me and declared the ground of her hope, her eyes sparkled with a divine joy, her countenance shone, her cheeks were ruddy. I never saw her look so sweet and lovely in all her life. All about her were affected: none could refrain from tears, and yet it was a delight to be with her.[1]

On her coffin words were engraved that recall Count Zinzendorf's great hymn:

> Christ's precious blood and righteousness
> Her clothing were, her wedding dress.

Shortly after Lady Margaret's death Selina returned to Tunbridge Wells, which she had visited from time to time since 1763. Like Brighton, the town was growing steadily in popularity as a health resort, fast rivalling Bath as a playground for the rich and indolent. Ever alert for opportunities for the spread of the gospel, the Countess had managed to borrow a large Presbyterian church for her preachers and was increasingly sure that God had purposes of mercy for the people of Tunbridge Wells.[2] In April 1768 she decided to buy property in a popular area of the town known as Mount Ephraim where she purposed to build yet another chapel. In one of the very few letters from Selina to Whitefield which have been preserved, she writes to tell him of it:

[1] Seymour, *Countess*, vol. 1, p. 302.
[2] Seymour provides further details of the circumstances leading to the opening of a chapel in Tunbridge Wells, *Countess*, vol. 2, p. 125.

Very low and ill have I been since I came to this place or [I] should have wrote to you. Such I continue, but an old servant does not cease doing his master's work because he is not so well able to perform it, but continues to work on till he can work no longer . . . I. have agreed to the spot I think which has evidently been kept in store for the purpose of an altar to him.[1]

In this letter Selina expressed her wish that her chaplain should come to her as soon as he was able. With typical kindness the busy preacher hastened to Tunbridge Wells, preaching there as often as he could. Later the Countess wrote: 'Very many were cut to the heart – sinners trembled exceedingly . . . truly God was in the midst of us to wound and to heal. Such happy indications . . . induce me to hope that he will deign to smile on my poor efforts for his great name and the good of the people in this place.'[2]

While the Countess was in Tunbridge Wells, two young men called to see her. James Matthews and Joseph Shipman were both among the six students expelled from St Edmund Hall and were now wondering about their own future. Perhaps there might be a place for them in the new college at Trevecca? Gladly Selina welcomed the students and during their stay was clearly appraising them as to their abilities and calling for the work of the ministry.

Two anecdotes are told of their stay in Tunbridge Wells. It so happened that Selina's son, Francis, was visiting his mother at the time. Not only did Francis reject the faith, but he had imbibed all the rationalist tenets of the day and spurned any notion of divine revelation or the supernatural. To influence her son, who, like everyone else, had heard of the expulsion of the six students, the Countess arranged for them both to talk privately with Francis. Joseph Shipman, the more gifted and articulate of the two, spoke with Francis first, followed by his friend James

[1] Rylands MS., Letter 115.
[2] Seymour, *Countess*, vol. 2, p. 126.

Matthews. Francis, lucid and well-prepared with his arguments, quickly confused and outwitted Shipman who was forced to leave the room without undermining any of the sceptic's opinions. When Matthews entered, however, Francis was faced with a man even less able to confound him in debate. Instead of trying to do so, Matthews recounted God's dealings with his soul. The nobleman listened in silence. He attempted no argument. When his mother questioned him later he answered, 'I liked the last best. Taking the first upon my own ground I could combat him tolerably well; but the latter has been in paths to which I am a stranger. I have no doubt he is an honest and good man.'[1]

In a further trial of the two students, Selina gave advance notice of a preaching service to be conducted in front of the house. Only as the expectant people assembled did she tell Shipman and Matthews that she would be glad if one of them would preach to the gathered crowd. Both immediately protested their inability, saying they had never preached before. It availed little. Thrusting a Bible into Shipman's hand, the Countess challenged the young man either to address the people or to go out and tell them that he was too afraid to trust his God for help: 'The Lord will be with you – do the best you can', were her final words. In the event Shipman's preaching, on 'My Spirit shall not always strive with man', was used by God to the conversion of one who was to become a key figure in the work in Tunbridge Wells. Further preaching endeavours followed for Joseph Shipman who soon displayed real ability and would become one of the first students to study at Trevecca. For Matthews, whose bashfulness and diffidence made it evident that he should not proceed into the ministry, the Countess recommended that he return to his former trade of a weaver.

Though most of her friends were encouraging as the time approached for the opening of Selina's 'school of prophets', John

[1] New, *Coronet and Cross*, p. 226. New records that when Francis was dying some twenty years later, he enquired after Matthews.

Wesley was less than enthusiastic. Even his admiring biographer, Luke Tyerman, admits that a measure of jealousy might have played a part in his comments and attitude at this time.[1] As early as 1748 Wesley had been making plans to include a five-year academic course for young men at Kingswood School in Bristol, the school that now catered mainly for the children of his itinerant preachers. After the debacle of the expulsions from Oxford, he too had felt the urgency of providing alternative education for men holding Methodist convictions. Now he drew up more detailed plans for a four-year course of study that would make the student 'a better scholar than nine in ten of the graduates at Oxford and Cambridge'.[2] So when the Countess forged ahead with her plans it is not surprising that Wesley should express a degree of chagrin. Writing to his brother Charles on 19 May 1768, after he had received the same set of proposals governing the institution and running of the college as Berridge had done, Wesley doubted the viability of the project and expressed himself with a touch of sarcasm:

> I am glad Mr Fletcher has been with you. But if the tutor fails what will become of our college at Trevecca? Did you ever see anything more queer than their plan of institution? Pray, who penned it, man or woman? I am afraid the visitor [Fletcher] too will fail.[3]

Perhaps Wesley foresaw that there was a basic incompatibility of views between the Countess and Fletcher which could well mean that they would not be able to work together for long. He also feared Selina's influence on his friend. A letter to him written two months earlier seems a veiled exhortation to avoid the company of the Countess and her preachers. Responding to a remark of Fletcher's that he felt deadness of spirit, Wesley wrote:

[1] 'Was there a tinge of jealousy in this? We know not'. Tyerman, *Wesley*, vol. 3, p. 35.
[2] H. D. Rack, *Reasonable Enthusiast* (London: Epworth Press, 1989 p. 357, citing Wesley's *Short Account of Kingswood School,* 1768.     [3] *Ibid.*

I do not wonder at it at all especially considering with whom you have chiefly conversed for some time past . . . you have for some time conversed with the genteel Methodists . . . In order to truly profitable conversation may you not select persons clear of both Calvinism and antinomianism; not fond of that luscious way of talking?[1]

But despite the misgivings of some and the criticisms of others, the Countess pressed on with her plans for the college. She installed windows at Trefeca Isaf in the style of her favourite 'Strawberry Hill' variant of Gothic architecture, a style introduced by Horace Walpole. Howell Harris's men worked ceaselessly in order to complete the alterations and to supply the new college with furniture in time for the opening, intended to coincide with the Countess's sixty-first birthday on 24 August 1768.

Writing to a friend on 21 July, Harris was enthusiastic about the progress. Two of his young men had papered the dining room and study, together with a further three rooms, but 'the dormitory, garrets, boarding and stairs will take them, I suppose, a fortnight yet.' Selina seemed disinclined to delegate even the smallest decisions regarding the new college and so Harris continues, 'I wish you would write if you know my Lady's determination about papering the chapel which she mentioned about two months ago . . . The kitchen will be tiled tomorrow and next week I hope the work will be finished in the Chapel.' A path linking the college with Harris's settlement gave him particular pleasure, and concluding his letter, he wrote, 'I think the old house looks now very well within and without, and I trust indeed our Saviour will preside there.'[2] Harris kept a careful account of the outlay for the project which he knew the Countess would reimburse in due course.[3]

[1] Wesley, *Letters*, vol. 5, pp. 83–4.
[2] *Selected Trevecka Letters*, vol. 2, pp. 123–4.
[3] By 1769 the cost had reached £764.

Howell Harris mentions fifteen as the number of students who were to begin their studies at Trevecca. Among them were James Glazebrook, the miner recommended by Fletcher; the two young men whom Dr Richard Conyers from Helmsley had mentioned and Joseph Shipman, ex-student of St Edmund Hall.[1] At the opening each man was dressed in a new suit of clothing made from bales of heavy duty material that the Countess had ordered from a local tailor.[2] The resident tutor was, as we have seen, a Welshman by the name of John Williams.[3]

Not until the night before the college was due to open did the work on the building finally reach completion. All Selina's friends received invitations to attend the services to mark the important occasion. Surprisingly few details of the opening ceremony have been preserved. Whitefield preached on the occasion – a difficult engagement for him to fulfil for it came only two weeks after the death of his wife, Elizabeth. He took for his text, 'In all places where I record my name, I will come unto thee and bless thee.'

---

[1] Actual numbers and names of students at any given period are hard to ascertain as surviving lists are fragmentary. The most comprehensive list has been compiled by G. F. Nuttall, 'The Students of Trevecca College 1768-1791', *Transactions of the Honourable Society of Cymmrodorion*, 1967. This list is incomplete, however, as many more names of students have come to light in recent years. A list of the earliest students can be found in a letter from Fletcher to the Countess in which he includes the following surnames: Glazebrook, Waite, Davenport, Rowley, Aldridge, Cosson, Hull, Ellis, Hewer, Pecore, Mead, Goodrich, Cook, Gibbons. With the inclusion of Joseph Shipman we would have the 15 mentioned by Harris. A number of these men will be mentioned in forthcoming chapters. Cheshunt Foundation Archives.

[2] Samples of cloth sent to the Countess with the relative costs per yard can still be seen in the Cheshunt Foundation Archives.

[3] Seymour began the tradition that Joseph Easterbrook was the first tutor at Trevecca and most accounts of the early days of the college follow this line. It was however a misunderstanding on Seymour's part, based on a reference to him in one of Fletcher's letters. Easterbrook was a youth of seventeen at the time who hoped to train for the ministry and therefore spent time at Madeley with Fletcher. He subsequently became vicar of Temple Church, Bristol. See Tyerman, *Wesley's Designated Successor*, p. 131.

The following day he spent time with the students, encouraging
them and urging them to be faithful to their calling. On the Sunday he preached to crowded congregations, mainly gathered to
the front and to the side of the college. Commenting on the whole
occasion, he was able to say, 'What we have seen and felt at the
college is remarkable!'

Who else was present we do not know for certain. Circumstantial evidence makes it clear that Fletcher attended, but one
notable absentee was John Wesley. He had suggested he would be
present if at all possible, but although preaching not far away, he
turned and travelled into Devon as the day approached. While
Charles Wesley was also absent he had written excusing himself.
He was serving the Bath chapel at the time. To him she could
reply, 'I had no reason to complain of your absence though I had
to lament it.'

A number of the Welsh ministers were there and tradition has it
that William Williams' great hymn, *Guide me, O thou great
Jehovah*, first written in 1745, was translated into English by
Peter Williams for the opening of Trevecca. To hear those Welsh
hills echoing and re-echoing to the sound of a thousand voices
singing

> I am weak, but thou art mighty,
> Hold me with thy powerful hand . . .

must have filled the Countess of Huntingdon with joy and
confidence as at last she saw the fulfillment of her long cherished
hope.

# 20

# Calm before the Storm

Life at Trevecca soon began to fall into a regular routine. Possibly the best description of the appearance of the College in its earlier days can be found in the words of a contemporary, Sir Thomas Cullam, a man with little sympathy for the evangelical revival, who called in unexpectedly in 1775:

The House, modern gothic, stands in a pleasant spot, about $3\frac{1}{2}$ miles out off the Road, on the Right, exactly half way between Brecknock [Brecon] and Hay. At present it contains 7 students, whom I happened to find at their Studies, which were in the New Testament, both in Greek, Latin, and English. They were about 20 years of age, dressed chiefly in black, very grave and attentive to their Business. Their Master was a decent man, about 30 years of age. The Schoolroom is a very pleasant Apartment with a Collection of Books in it. Over the Chimney is a painting of Frank [Francke], a German Divine . . . and there were 20 Desks in the Room. The Chapel is a neat pretty room. A handsome Eating Room, used when her Ladyship is among them, for thither she sometimes comes, and makes a short Residence. The Common Eating Room is small. The Walls of the whole House are adorned with Scripture Passages, and that selected over the Chimney in the Eating Room is, 'Feed my Sheep.' Her Ladyship's Apartment is very small, but the whole is extremely neat, and all the Rooms cheerful, calculated to improve much more lively and pleasant sentiments than seemed to reign there.[1]

[1] Cited by Welsh, *Spiritual Pilgrim*, p.117, from writings of Sir Thomas Gery Cullam, 1775. The original is lost but this transcript has been preserved in the National Library of Wales, Aberystwyth.

After the opening ceremonies a succession of the Countess's friends visited the college during the following weeks. First to come was Charles Wesley who spent some days with the students. After him came an earnest and able young preacher who had been itinerating for the Countess, Cradock Glascott. Fletcher himself came next and stayed until November. But Fletcher was far from happy with what he found when he arrived. The novelty and elation among the students, due in all likelihood to their new circumstances, had in Fletcher's view quenched the Spirit of God. Only 'a round of duties and a form of godliness' seemed to distinguish Trevecca from any other academy, or so he told the Countess. In his words 'a spirit of levity, irony and trifling sat in the temple of God and the humble wrestling spirit of prayer had disappeared.'[1]

Fletcher immediately did all in his power to rectify the situation. After preaching a sermon on Psalm 24 to arouse the consciences of the young men, he spent an evening rebuking them one by one:

> I told them that if things went on at this poor trifling formal rate I would advise your Ladyship to pick out half a dozen of the most earnest and send the rest about their business that room might be made for a better set.

Fletcher then set aside the following Wednesday as a day of prayer and fasting. But on the Monday night one student knocked timidly at his door. He wanted to confess that 'he had trifled with God and deserved the hottest hell'. That was a beginning of an unusual work of the Spirit among the students of Trevecca. With confessions and praises, tears and rejoicing the young men renewed their dedication to the service of God. None was untouched. Even Betty Hughes, the housemaid, crept in

[1] Possibly the Countess had been ill-advised over some of the young men she had admitted to the College. On the other hand, natural exuberance among a group of young men working and studying together is well-known.

unnoticed and, when all the students had gone to their rooms, confessed that she too felt 'tempted and dry' and feared lest she should be passed by when others were being blessed. The following day Howell Harris and a number from his community arrived at the college; they too were moved to join in the prayers and gladness experienced by the students. A child employed as a shoeblack pleaded: 'Come Lord Jesus, come to a little boy, come to a wicked boy, give me a new heart, Lord, a new heart before I go to hell.'

One young man in particular was influenced. Joseph Shipman, whom the Countess had inveigled into preaching by thrusting him out of her front door at Tunbridge Wells, had been a difficult student from the first. Nothing suited him: not the food, the Welsh air, nor the standard of instruction. Full of complaints, he wrote often to the Countess urging his special needs. But all this was now changed. Fletcher noted how he prayed that God might forgive him for the way he had grieved the Countess. In Shipman's preaching too the effect was noticeable as he began to preach 'much deeper than the surface of the doctrine'.

These were memorable days and the longer term effect, as Fletcher was to tell the Countess, was to give the students a 'love for prayer, an end of divisions and a degree of zeal for God and brotherly kindness, watchfulness and an apparent concern for souls.'[1] 'I am glad to hear of the plentiful effusion from above on Talgarth,' wrote John Berridge to Selina as reports filtered through to Everton of the blessings of those days in November 1768. 'Jesus has now baptised your college and thereby shown his approbation of the work', he continued, reversing his former gloomy prognosis of the future of the new enterprise. But he had a warning: 'You may therefore rejoice, but rejoice with trembling. Faithful labourers may be expected from thence, but if it be Christ's college, a Judas will certainly be found amongst them.'[2]

[1] John Fletcher to the Countess, 10 November 1768, Cheshunt Foundation Archives; hereafter C.F. Archives.
[2] Berridge, *Works*, p. 504.

The year 1769, though filled with its normal quota of trials, problems and also a further time of illness, proved to be a period of relative calm for Selina as she saw several of those enterprises to which she had given her time, strength and money come to fruition. Back in London for the winter months, she opened her London home, currently at Portland Row, Cavendish Square, for the preaching of the gospel. New guests now occupied the comfortable upholstered chairs. Gone for ever, taken away by death, were some who had once crowded her drawing rooms at Park Street and Chelsea Farm to hear Whitefield and others preach.

As Selina thought of these things her desire to use every opportunity to reach those of her own social status was as strong as ever. Almost sixty-two years of age and far from strong, she knew her time could also be short: 'O that I may be more and more useful to the souls of my fellow creatures. I want to be every moment all life, all zeal, all activity for God, and ever on the stretch for closer communion with him',[1] she wrote. Well could she have echoed the words of her friend Charles Wesley:

> Our residue of days and hours
> Thine, wholly thine, shall be;
> And all our consecrated powers
> A sacrifice to thee.

These desires became ever more pertinent as the Countess realized that George Whitefield was now an ill man. When Wesley saw him at the Countess's home on 27 February 1769 he commented, 'His soul appeared to be vigorous still but his body was sinking apace; and unless God interposes with his mighty hand, he must soon finish his labours.'[2] As the weather grew warmer Whitefield's health began to improve once more. But now he was anxious to return to Georgia where he hoped to oversee and bring to completion the building of two new wings on the

---

[1] Seymour, *Countess*, vol. 2, p. 101.
[2] Wesley, *Journal*, vol. 5, p. 303.

Bethesda orphanage which were intended as an academy for students: a project he had long desired to see accomplished.

Before sailing Whitefield undertook one more preaching tour of the southwest: Chippenham, Gloucester, Painswick, Rodborough. These were towns that had witnessed amazing triumphs of the gospel in the past as Whitefield had preached with impassioned oratory to vast crowds. Accompanying him on this tour were Selina and her two friends, Anne Erskine and Jenetta Orton. Never happier than when expending his strength preaching the gospel, Whitefield exclaimed in a letter to a friend, 'It is good to go into the highways and hedges. Field preaching! Field preaching, for ever!'

A final important engagement fell to Whitefield before he booked his passage on board the *Friendship* in early September 1769 for his thirteenth voyage across the Atlantic. At last the new chapel in Tunbridge Wells was ready to be officially opened and Selina was anxious that he should be the main preacher. A neat attractive building, it was described in *Lloyd's Evening Post* as 'the most complete piece of Gothic architecture that has been constructed for many years.'[1] The project had clearly been the centre of considerable interest in the town, and the Countess had sent out invitations to friends from near and far to attend the occasion. Nor was she disappointed. From early in the morning on 23 July the people began to gather. The early-comers passed the time in singing hymns under Selina's window, and she commented, 'It is impossible to express the delight and satisfaction I experienced on being awoke[n] at an early hour in the morning by the voice of praise and thanksgiving; my heart was powerfully affected, and never can I forget the sensations of pleasure I then felt.'[2]

[1] Cited by Tyerman, *Whitefield*, vol. 2, p. 561 from *Lloyd's Evening Post* for 31 July 1769.
[2] Seymour, *Countess*, vol. 2, p. 128.

Whitefield's sermon, an example of all that was best in the great evangelist's preaching, was based on Jacob's words at Bethel, 'How dreadful is this place! This is none other than the house of God, and this is the gate of heaven.' He prayed earnestly that the very spot might prove the gate of heaven to some sinner that day, that someone might acknowledge it to have been their spiritual birthplace. And God heard his prayer. At least one young woman, brought along unwillingly by her mother, found the call of God an irresistible one.

A spiritual feast day, the people enjoyed at least three other sermons preached from a small eminence outside the new chapel. A young Irishman, Richard de Courcy, was among the preachers that day. Educated at Trinity College, Dublin, de Courcy had become Sir Walter Shirley's curate at Loughrea. His ardent preaching had soon drawn the crowds to hear him; but it had also drawn intense opposition from the prelates of the Irish Church. Banned from the pulpit, he resorted to preaching from a tomb-stone as Wesley had done before him. When the Countess heard from her cousin of de Courcy's problems, she invited him to England so that he might itinerate among her increasing number of chapels.

Whitefield preached his last sermon at Tottenham Court Road Chapel the following Sunday, and the tenor of his remarks made it clear that he anticipated that he would never see his London friends again. 'I do not look upon myself at home until I land in my Father's house,' he said. 'My greatest trial is to part with those who are as dear to me as my own soul. O keep close to God, my dear London friends.'[1] Selina Hastings, ever a shrewd observer of her friends, would have realised that when the *Friendship* carried her longest serving chaplain away from English shores on 4 September, it was unlikely that they would meet again in this world.

[1] Tyerman, *Whitefield* , vol. 2, p. 563.

Throughout the year the Countess had kept in close contact with events and arrangements at Trevecca, corresponding with Howell Harris with regard to problems that arose. Details of diet concerned her: 'Love to Hannah Bowen', she wrote in June 1769 'and she may provide chickens and ducks.' It seemed that some of the students had already worn out their clothes, a fact that puzzled her as they had all been newly-made little more than nine months earlier. Above all, she was concerned for the spiritual life and zeal of the students: 'O for a day of power on these young men there; may free grace so overpower their own souls as to preach salvation gloriously and freely to every sinner they meet!'[1]

William Williams of Pantecelyn, signing himself 'Billy Williams', wrote with courtesy and diffidence to Selina on 6 August 1769. Describing himself as 'one who never wrote a letter to a Lady before', he gave perceptive advice on her choice of students for her fledgling college and on the curriculum needed for prospective preachers:

> Many parents that wish well to their children would be glad to put them into your college, some only for pious education, others on a farther view of training them up for the ministry, without weighing whether they are called or not thereto, and others from that base end of rising up their children to be men without emptying their own pockets in so doing.

Clearly Williams felt that a 'faculty' of one resident tutor – and that one not thoroughly qualified – was inadequate for such an enterprise. So in this letter he recommended that the Countess should also aim to employ 'a pious master well versed in the Greek and Latin languages'. The tutor would then be free to lecture in 'logic, rhetoric, natural and moral philosophy and other sciences decent and edifying for the gospel minister.' A

---

[1] *Selected Trevecka Letters*, vol. 2, pp.133–4.

few paying scholars, Williams suggested, might well augment the finances of Trevecca.[1]

As we have seen earlier, two tutors had been the Countess's original wish. Now in response to William Williams's letter she began again to look for someone able to teach Latin and Greek in order to free the tutor, John Williams, for the more specialized subjects needed for the ministry. Fitting together the fragments of information available about these early days is by no means easy, but it would seem that this was the period when she made a surprising decision. She would employ the help of a twelve-year-old boy, John Henderson, to teach the classical languages. Henderson's father had been one of Wesley's lay preachers, and his only son, John, was sent to the Kingswood School in Bristol. John was described as 'having a memory so strong that he retained all he read; and his judgment so solid that he arranged, examined and digested all that he remembered and thus made it his own'. Never had he been known to cry or indulge in childish behaviour, but was 'born as it were a thinking being'.[2]

---

[1] William Williams began this letter with a touch of the poet's rhetoric, 'I have been roving and ranging over the rude mountains and precipices of Wales in search of poor illiterate souls chained in the dens of darkness and infidelity.' Ending the letter he wrote, 'I know not how to conclude for I never wrote to a Lady before, except it be in the words of an old decrepit presbyter of mean parentage to the elect lady: "Having many things to write unto you" [2 *John* 14]. Your Ladyship's most humble servant and poor brother, Billy Williams.' C.F.Archives.

[2] Later Henderson became a student at Pembroke College, Oxford. His width of knowledge was extraordinary, covering history, rhetoric, logic, ethics, and metaphysics. He had studied medicine, geometry, astronomy and various other disciplines. He was familiar with many modern languages, including Persian and Arabic. Like other men of genius he was also an eccentric. He went to bed at daybreak and began his day in the late afternoon. At night he always wore a wet shirt! He was, however, pleasant company and a good conversationalist. A trunk full of Henderson's manuscripts, the result of many years of study, was lost when a housemaid lit the fires with them. He never referred to his loss, but died soon after at the age of thirty-two. For further details of the career of this prodigy see Tyerman, *Wesley's Designated Successor*, p. 145-8.

A set of exercises, drawn up by John Fletcher and written in a long letter to the students, gives some insight into the standard of attainment required of Trevecca students in these early days:

1. I desire you to turn the 39 Articles in as good classical Latin as you possibly can.
2. Write an English letter to a Deist to convince him of the truth of the Scriptures.
3. Draw a parallel between John's baptism and Christ's, and prove the superiority of the latter over the former.
4. Make an English theme upon the mischief of unsanctified learning.[1]

In addition, as we have seen, Fletcher had recommended a minimum library for Trevecca, including books on grammar, logic, rhetoric, church history, philosophy, geography and practical divinity.[2] A dictionary belonging to Selina was loaned to the college, but fearful that some careless student might borrow it and forget to return it, she wrote on the flyleaf, 'This dictionary belongs to Lady Huntingdon, therefore let none steal it from the study, a practice too frequent among students, but knavery is inconsistent with the character of the gospel minister.'

Probationary students were required to preach in front of the other students and then receive both their critical comment, advice and encouragement. This was an ordeal for a young man

[1] Other exercises recommended by Fletcher included, '5. Draw up an address to Jesus for the gift of the Holy Ghost, urging the strongest reasons you can think of to engage him to grant it to you. 6. Try in a letter to convince one who has not the spiritual kingdom set up in his soul that he never had the true Christian faith or is backslidden. 7. Read pathetically aloud the 3rd part of Baxter's *Saints' Everlasting Rest* and tell each other your thoughts concerning it. Save your exercises for my perusal.' Fletcher to students at Trevecca. C. F. Archives.

[2] Few of the early text books remain. Probably most were disposed of when the college moved from Trevecca to Cheshunt in Hertfordshire after the Countess's death in 1791. Part of the Countess's personal library is kept in the Cheshunt Foundation Archives.

unaccustomed to public speaking and proved too much for some. Samuel Eyles Pierce could not forget his first experiences:

> I mounted the rostrum and read the words of my text. I had not been five minutes before . . . I said, 'I can say no more.' A senior student cried out, 'You had better then come down.' So I did, hoping never to go there again.[1]

In August 1769 the Countess prepared to undertake the two-hundred mile journey from Tunbridge Wells to Trevecca for the first anniversary of the opening of the college. Seldom can there have been such a gathering of exceptional preachers in so isolated a location. Men such as Daniel Rowland, William Williams, John Fletcher, Walter Shirley, Peter Williams and Howell Davies joined Howell Harris in preparation for the days of preaching and fellowship that lay ahead. Services began on 18 August and continued over the weekend and on the Monday and Tuesday. On the Wednesday, the actually anniversary of the college, John Wesley himself arrived, perhaps a little concerned to show a measure of support for his old friend's endeavour in view of his absence the previous year. He records his impressions in his Journal.

> Wed. 23 – I went on to Trevecca. Here we found a concourse of people from all parts, come to celebrate the Countess of Huntingdon's birthday, and the anniversary of her school, which was opened on August 24 of last year. I preached in the evening to as many as her chapel could well contain; which is extremely neat, or rather, elegant; as is the dining room, the school, and all the house. About nine Howell Harris desired me to give a short exhortation to his family. I did so; and then went back to my Lady's, and laid me down in peace.

[1] *A True Outline and Sketch of the Life of S. E. Pierce; Minister of the Everlasting Gospel* (London, 1824) p. 54. Cited by D. E. S. Brown, Ph.D. thesis, University of Winconsin-Madison, 1992, p. 119. Pierce later became a hyper-Calvinist.

Thurs. 24 – I administered the Lord's Supper to the family. At ten the public service began. Mr. Fletcher preached an exceeding lively sermon in the court, the chapel being far too small. After him Mr. William Williams preached in Welsh, till between one and two o'clock. At two we dined. Meantime, a large number of people had baskets of bread and meat carried to them in the court. At three I took my turn there, then Mr. Fletcher, and, about five, the congregation was dismissed. Between seven and eight the lovefeast began, at which I believe many were comforted. In the evening several of us retired into the neighbouring wood which is exceeding pleasantly laid out in walks; one of which leads to a little mount raised in the midst of a meadow, that commands a delightful prospect.[1]

Only George Whitefield was missing. Due to sail the following week, he was unavoidably detained in London preaching and taking leave of his congregations and fellow workers. The whole event brought much joy to Selina. 'Though necessarily much hurried with outward things my mind was preserved in peace', she recorded. Describing it as 'a season of refreshing . . . a time never to be forgotten', she was particularly moved by the singing of one of Charles Wesley's hymns: 'Words fail to describe the holy triumph with which the great congregation sang.' Even after most of the other visitors had left, Walter Shirley and John Fletcher remained conducting services for the rest of the week. This occasion had represented for the Countess that union of purpose and fellowship for which she had striven for many years.

Despite the unusual blessing on the college nine months earlier, a situation had been simmering that now erupted. First a measure of friction had arisen between the Countess herself and Howell Harris. Though restored to his old fire and earnestness of spirit, Harris had never found it easy to work in close co-operation with others. The problem concerned the tutor, John Williams. Academically it had proved that he was scarcely

[1] Wesley, *Journal*, vol. 5, pp. 334–7.

capable of the task assigned to him. In April 1769 Fletcher was complaining to Selina that her tutor would 'soon be overtaken by the most backward student'. But as early as February, Howell Harris was accusing Williams not only of seeking the affections of his young daughter, Betty, but of being less than honest with Hannah Bowen, the housekeeper, who had also developed a strong affection for him. On Easter Sunday 1769 Harris had been 'very home' to Williams, accusing him of setting the students a bad example, 'opening the way for them to turn to courtship'; of being unfair to Hannah by initially concealing his true affections and of courting Betty without Hannah's knowledge. Earlier he had complained that Williams was acting without sufficient propriety in his relationship with Betty, and had not even asked her father's permission before making his advances. Betty Harris, like many young women, resented her father's interference in her personal affairs, and announced that she was leaving home. Trouble rumbled on for some months and by September it had reached crisis point.

Shortly after the anniversary services were over the Countess was obliged to address the problem. She had anticipated this sort of situation when she first engaged Hannah, fearing she might be too young and attractive to be housekeeper in the college. Now she thought she had no alternative but to dismiss both Williams and Hannah. Hannah, who would have thought this unreasonable, exhibited 'a bad spirit, demanded and had her wages'.[1] Harris took her back to his institution until her future could be determined but considered that the Countess had acted beyond her station as a woman in the matter. According to his sometimes over-coloured account, not only had she dismissed her tutor, but

---

[1] Dr Boyd Schlenther suggests that Hannah was actually pregnant, but this is a misreading of Harris's diary, which says that Hannah had become over-conscious of her appearance and somewhat haughty. She was, writes Harris, preoccupied with 'looking at her flesh, and self grown so big that she could not bow here as formerly . . . but must have her own way.' For entire account see *Harris, Reformer and Soldier*, p. 220–9.

had also 'given him over to Satan'. If this were indeed the case, Harris certainly had grounds for his objection, for in his words, 'She was no apostle and at the head of no Church to excommunicate.' Although this would appear a cavalier and excessive reaction on Selina's part, it also demonstrates the seriousness with which she viewed the effects of Williams's lack of wisdom on the Trevecca students.

Not unnaturally the Countess now turned her eyes to the Kingswood School to find a permanent tutor who could serve at Trevecca in place of John Williams. Twenty-year-old Joseph Benson was Wesley's classics master, and a young man of upright and godly character. Under his influence a number of the children at Kingswood had been awakened to their spiritual needs during the summer of 1768. But during 1769 Benson had become increasingly unsettled at Kingswood. Misunderstandings had arisen between him and John Wesley, who had taken it in hand to rebuke his young classics master sharply, an occurrence that produced a long and spirited letter of self-defence from Benson. Recognizing both the Countess's need of a new tutor and Benson's own need of a change, Fletcher had recommended him to consider the vacant position at Trevecca. Not only so, but Wesley himself had proposed the same change for his classics tutor.[1] In his private diary for 27 November 1769 Benson confirmed his personal agreement with the suggestion: 'I have recently seen my way plain to leave Kingswood and conclude on going to Trevecca' – clear evidence that the final decision was his.

Despite it being his own proposal that Benson was the right man for Trevecca, Wesley's annoyance at the importance Selina attached to the institution spilled over in a letter to Benson:

Trevecca is much more to Lady Huntingdon than Kingswood is to me. It mixes with everything. It is my college, my masters, my

[1] Tyerman, *Wesley's Designated Successor*, p. 157.

students. I do not so speak of this school. It is not mine, but the Lord's. I look for no more honour than money from it.[1]

Wesley's next sentence, however, addresses another point of irritation that was producing a growing barrier between the Countess and himself: his teaching on Christian perfection. Although it had already generated confusion and disagreement, this teaching had become increasingly a central plank in Wesley's theology following the new wave of blessing that his societies had known since the early 1760s:

> But I assure you, you must not even mutter before her anything of *deliverance from all sin. Error errorum*, as Count Zindendorf says; 'heresy of heresies.' 'I will suffer no one in my society that even thinks of perfection.' However I trust you will not only think of [it] but enjoy it.

Benson had assured Wesley that he would abide by a previous commitment and remain at Kingswood until March 1770, but Wesley was still no better pleased. On 27 January 1769 he wrote to Benson: 'If the school at Trevecca is the best that ever was since the world began, I am glad of it, and wish it may be better still. But do not run away with any of my young men from Kingswood: that I should blame you for.'[2]

In January 1770 Benson paid his first visit to Trevecca and the Countess engaged him to begin his duties the following March in accordance with his commitment. Concerned that no spirit of dissension might creep in to mar the sometimes fragile unity now prevailing, she wrote to Benson on 14 December prior to his first visit: 'May your heart and their hearts so unite in the love of Jesus as to lose every difference that might cause [you] to differ and become one breath of loving praise to the Lord for time and eternity.'[3]

---

[1] Wesley, *Letters*, vol. 5, p. 166.      [2] *Ibid.*, p.178.
[3] From a private manuscript held by Mr P. Conlan (Bromley, Kent).

From Benson's pen we learn of some of the events at Trevecca in those early days and particularly whenever John Fletcher visited the college. When he arrived the students would push their books to one side and listen to the glowing exhortations of the vicar of Madeley. 'Prayer, praise, love and zeal ... were the elements in which he continually lived', commented Benson. And the students could not listen to him for long before 'they were all in tears and every heart caught fire from the flame that burned in his soul.' Believing that a heart devoted to God was the best qualification for an effective ministry, Fletcher would say to the students 'As many of you as are athirst for this fulness of the Spirit follow me into my room.' For two or three hours these young men, together with Fletcher, could be found kneeling together earnestly beseeching God for the coveted blessing – until some found their knees so sore they could remain kneeling no longer. At one time, continued Benson, he had seen Fletcher 'so filled with the love of God, that he could contain no more, but cried out, 'O my God withhold thy hand or the vessel will burst'.[1]

From the beginning the Countess planned that the college should not serve any one section of evangelical life exclusively. The appointment of John Fletcher as President was a clear indication of this. She would have known of his Arminian position when she invited him to take the post. Although her predominant purpose was to provide ministry for churches within the Establishment, yet many of her students served Dissenting churches, and as ordination into the Church of England became yet more problematic, an increasing proportion of Trevecca students entered the Dissenting ministry. Despite any early difficulties at the college, the presence and oversight of a man of Fletcher's spiritual stature began a tradition of zeal and service which must have gladdened Selina and given her confidence that all her best hopes for the institution were being fulfilled.

[1] James Macdonald, *Memoirs of the Rev. Joseph Benson* (London, 1822); also cited by Seymour, *Countess*, vol. 2, p. 103.

Meanwhile, as we have seen, the Countess left Trevecca on 20 September 1769 and travelled slowly towards Bath and Bristol where she spent the early part of the winter. Here at her invitation Henry Venn joined her early in October as he had agreed to supply her Bath pulpit for a few weeks. His letters to his friends in Huddersfield give a unique and contemporary account of the extraordinary scenes that accompanied his preaching in the Bath chapel:

On Sunday evening last [4 November] there was such a crowded audience, Mr Shirley told me, as there never was before. The chapel doors were set open; and people stood in the court, as far as the houses.

On Selina herself he wrote to James Kershaw the following day:

I am favoured with the pleasing sight and with the animating example of a soul inflamed with love to a crucified God – that stumbling block to them that perish. In Lady Huntingdon I see a star of the first magnitude in the firmament of the church ... No equipage – no livery – no house – all these given up that perishing sinners may hear the life-giving sound and be enriched with all spiritual blessings. Her prayers are heard, her chapel is crowded, and many sinners amongst the poor are brought into the City of Refuge. I feel from Lady Huntingdon's example an increasing desire both for myself and for you and all our friends that we may be active and eminent in the life of grace.[1]

And so, much improved in health, the Countess was encouraged on all sides by the progress of the work for the kingdom to which she had dedicated her resources of money and strength.

John Berridge had a warning for her, however. 'The Master will always new-shave your crown before he puts a fresh coronet upon your head.' This was a comment based both on his own observation of God's ways and on the link he had noticed between the

[1] *Letters of Henry Venn*, pp.159–60.

periods of significant advance in the Countess's endeavours and the trials she so often faced. He spoke better than he knew. 1769 had indeed been a time of joy and fulfilment, but 1770 would prove one of the most fraught and stressful years in the experience of the Countess of Huntingdon.

## 21

# THE PARTING OF THE WAYS

ON 1 DECEMBER 1767, JOHN WESLEY was sitting alone in a coach completing a journey from London to Norwich, a distance of some hundred and ten miles. With time on his hands and no company to distract his attention, he began to meditate on an issue to which his mind often returned: the connection between religious profession and holiness of life. As in any new work of the Spirit of God there were those who had made high-sounding claims of spiritual experiences and yet whose subsequent life gave little evidence of the genuineness of such assertions. Some who had claimed to have attained to 'Christian perfection', in accordance with Wesley's own teaching, had negated the truth of their words by unattractive conduct. When Grimshaw heard that thirty or more had made these claims in Leeds and Otley, he could only comment, 'Time will prove it. I wish they knew their own hearts.' At the other end of the spectrum, there were some of Calvinistic persuasion who were using the doctrine of the imputed righteousness of Christ as a cover for a careless attitude to God's holy laws.

Another factor adding to the confusion was the widespread growth of a teaching that became known as Sandemanianism.[1] Its emphasis on a mere mental assent to truth as a means of salvation

[1] Robert Sandeman, son-in-law of John Glas, had propagated this teaching in his book, *Letters on Theron and Aspasia* (1757), an answer to James Hervey's work setting out the doctrine of the imputed righteousness of Christ. Sandeman's teaching was casting an increasing blight over many churches at this time.

was breeding an increasing generation of professors of religion whose unchanged lives gave little indication of the new birth. Writing to the Countess of Huntingdon the month after his coach journey to Norwich, Wesley had referred to this situation:

> I have been lately surprised to observe how many who affirm salvation by faith have lately run ... full into Mr Sandeman's notion that faith is merely an assent to the Bible, and not only undervaluing but even ridiculing the whole experience of the children of God. But so much the more do I rejoice that your Ladyship is still preserved from that spreading contagion, and also enabled plainly and openly to avow the plain, old, simple, unfashionable gospel.[1]

As Wesley turned over all these things in his mind he came to some surprising conclusions despite his own undoubted adherence to that 'plain, old, simple, unfashionable gospel'. These he wrote down in his journal that night:

> That a man may be saved who cannot express himself properly concerning imputed righteousness.
> Therefore, to do this is not necessary to salvation.
> That a man may be saved who has not clear conceptions of it. (Yea, that never heard the phrase.) Therefore, clear conceptions of it are not necessary to salvation. Yea, it is not necessary to salvation to use the phrase at all.
> That a pious churchman who has not clear conceptions even of Justification by Faith may be saved. Therefore, clear conceptions even of this are not necessary to salvation.
> That a mystic, who denies Justification by Faith (Mr Law, for instance) may be saved. But, if so, what becomes of *articulus stantis vel cadentis ecclesiae*?[2] If so, is it not high time for us to return to the plain word, 'He that feareth God, and worketh righteousness, is accepted with him'?[3]

[1] Wesley, *Letters*, vol. 5, p. 74.
[2] Nehemiah Curnock, editor of Wesley's *Journal*, translates this 'the grand doctrine by which the church stands or falls'.
[3] Wesley, *Journal*, vol. 5, pp. 243–4.

Of these reflections, the last two are more reminiscent of John Wesley's Holy Club days, than of his evangelical enlightenment.

It was now 1770 – two years after Wesley's meditations in the coach – years in which he continued to be concerned over the discrepancies between the professions and practice of those who claimed high experiences of Christian grace. Wesley was still unwilling to accept that his own emphasis on 'perfect love' could have exacerbated the problem of such inconsistencies. Instead he laid the larger proportion of the blame on Calvinistic doctrine, equating it with the antinomianism that was doubtless present in some circles. But whether he recognized it or not, antinomianism was also prevalent among his own societies.[1] A further doctrine that troubled Wesley was that of the imputed righteousness of Christ. He held that such an emphasis suggested to the believer that once he had been granted this righteousness, he need not seek after personal holiness on his own account. This would lead inevitably to spiritual slackness.[2]

As we have seen, Wesley had written a warning letter to John Fletcher in 1768 when he had complained of dryness of spirit and of the unprofitable conversation he discovered among some Christians. Wesley's letter had contained the strong suggestion that the problems that lay at the root of Fletcher's malaise, could be traced to the influence of men such as Romaine, Madan and even Whitefield – all friends of the Countess.[3]

The relationship between Selina and John Wesley had passed through periods of strain over the years. Yet their underlying desire to work in harmony with each other for the common good

---

[1] John Fletcher was later to speak of the 'antinomian principles and practices which spread like wild fire in his [Wesley's] societies', adding, 'We stand in particular danger of splitting on the Antinomian rock.' Fletcher, *First Check to Antinomianism, or A Vindication of the Rev. Mr Wesley's Last Minutes* (Devon, 1834), p. 9.

[2] See *Christ Stabb'd in the House of His Friends*, John Wesley, ed. Albert Outler (New York: Oxford University Press, 1964), p. 380.

[3] Wesley, *Letters*, vol. 5, pp. 83–4.

had always prevented any lasting breakdown of communication. They shared many characteristics. Both were natural leaders; both determined, authoritarian and sometimes outspoken. In his own bantering style Berridge could refer to his friends as 'Pope John and Pope Joan.'[1] Even though doctrinal differences had widened the gap between them, this alone was not responsible for the mounting tension at this time, for the Countess still maintained warm relations with both Charles Wesley and John Fletcher.

John Wesley was essentially a man of the people. He was most at ease addressing the common man and least relaxed amongst the aristocracy. 'We need great grace to converse with great people,' he had commented in his journal in April 1758, adding, 'except in some rare instances, I am glad to be excused.'[2] He had an in-built resentment for the deference paid to the Countess and to her wishes in the affairs of the societies. He felt, with some justification, that without her social standing and financial resources she could not have gained the prestige and influence that she possessed.

As we have noted, Wesley himself had long wished to open an academy for the further education of young men of Methodist persuasion. What he had hoped to do, the Countess had now achieved in the opening of Trevecca College. Even the fact that she referred to the institution as a 'college' would have riled Wesley. Few of the Countess's students had received much education, nor did any Dissenting academy aspire to such a description before 1786. To dress her students in academic caps and gowns[3] would have seemed to the Oxford don like assuming status to which they were not entitled.

[1] Edwin Sidney, *The Life of the Rev. Rowland Hill*, 3rd edition (London, 1835), p. 440.

[2] Wesley, *Journal*, vol. 4, p. 259. Wesley may also have been conscious of the spiritual danger of mingling too much with high society.

[3] See *Harris, Reformer and Soldier*, p. 221.

When a situation arose, described by Fletcher as 'the Brecknock division',[1] Wesley's patience with the Countess of Huntingdon and Trevecca College seemed to snap. He chose the summer of 1770 to write a letter to Selina pointing out her defects, her sins and the matters at issue between them. In his view the letter was long overdue. Writing to Benson in November 1770 Wesley explained why he had written as he had:

> For several years I had been deeply convinced that I had not done my duty with regard to that valuable woman; that I had not told her what I was throughly assured no one else would dare to do, and what I knew she would bear from no other person, but possibly might bear from me. But, being unwilling to give her pain, I put it off from time to time. At length I did not dare to delay any longer, lest death should call one of us hence. So I at once delivered my own soul, by telling her all that was in my heart. It was my business, my proper business, so to do, as none else either could or would do it. Neither did I take at all too much upon me; I know the office of a Christian minister. If she is not profited, it is her own fault, not mine; I have done my duty. I do not know there is one charge in that letter which was either unjust, unimportant or aggravated, any more than that against the doggerel hymns which are equally an insult upon poetry and common sense.[2]

The letter was deeply offensive to the Countess. We have no means of knowing its exact contents apart from Wesley's own comments, and those of his contemporaries who actually saw it, because Selina, who was understandably distressed by it, destroyed it soon after receiving it. John Fletcher spoke of it as 'unkind' although 'well-meant', and a letter the Countess had

---

[1] Wesley's biographer, Tyerman, said he had not been able to discover any facts about this dispute. As Brecknock (or Brecon) was near the college, it may have involved some clash between Trevecca students and Wesley's preachers. *Wesley's Designated Successor*, p. 181n.
[2] Wesley, *Letters*, vol. 5, p. 211.

found 'highly insulting';[1] while Howell Harris described it as 'a very bitter letter' that had charged the Countess with 'self and having fallen to pride etc.'[2] Walter Shirley went further, declaring that he could 'never have conceived that he [Wesley] would have carried his self-sufficiency and pride to so immoderate a pitch as has appeared in the last letter he wrote to your Ladyship.'[3] Not only had Wesley named the Countess's sins and weaknesses, but, as Shirley mentions, he had also poured scorn on the hymnbook that she had compiled, complaining that she had included hymns which could only be described as doggerel. For a man to write such a letter to any woman would have been inadvisable. This rebuke was particularly hard for the Countess to accept in view of her temperament, her social background, and the deference she had been taught to expect as the norm from her earliest days. Howell Harris had commented in his diary in 1765 that 'she does not love reproofs or to be told her faults' – but few people do! Although Selina had accepted Wesley's admonitions in the past,[4] this letter came into a different category and marked the end of the long and cordial friendship she had enjoyed with the elder Wesley.

Even though he knew he had wounded his long-standing friend, Wesley expressed no regrets about what he had done. He wrote to Joseph Benson on 28 December 1770, 'This morning I have calmly and coolly read over my letter to Lady Huntingdon. I still believe every line of it is true; and I am assured I spoke the truth in love. It is a great pity for anyone who wishes her well to skim over the wounds which are there searched. As long as she

[1] Tyerman, *Wesley's Designated Successor*, p. 181.
[2] Howell Harris's unpublished Trevecca diaries, cited by J. E. Hull, 'The Controversy between John Wesley and the Countess of Huntingdon', Ph.D. Thesis, University of Edinburgh, 1959.
[3] Westminster College, C. F. Archives, 19 May? [MS damaged], 1770.
[4] See above p. 113. An example of this is when Wesley visited her at Chelsea in 1748, and 'delivered his own soul'. Even though she wept, he could record that 'she took it well'.

resents the office of true esteem her grace can be but small.'[1] Writing a year later to another friend, he reiterated his confidence that he had acted rightly in 'delivering his soul' in such a way:

> Perhaps we may see a new accomplishment of Solomon's words, 'He that reproveth a man shall afterward find more favour than he who flattereth with his tongue.' But, be that as it may, I have done my duty; I could no otherwise have delivered my soul. And no offence at all would have been given thereby had not pride stifled both religion and generosity.[2]

Charles Wesley, whose esteem and friendship with the Countess had run deep for nearly thirty years, wrote to the Countess expressing his support for her and his regret at his brother's actions, although he had not seen the letter himself.

Given this background of annoyance on Wesley's part, with hurt, resentment and withdrawal on the part of the Countess, we may more readily appreciate the tension in personal relationships that existed even prior to Wesley's twenty-seventh annual Conference that opened in London early in August 1770. Since the expulsion of the St Edmund Hall students and some of the pamphleteering that had followed, which had claimed that the Articles of the Church of England were essentially Calvinistic, Wesley had steadily been losing patience with the men of these convictions. So he chose his 1770 Conference to air once again the doctrinal differences which had long existed within the Methodist movement. But his comments at the Conference had a more serious dimension. In his anxiety to remedy the problem of inconsistent professors of religion, Wesley introduced his preachers to elements in his thinking that he had clearly been mulling over since his lonely coach ride to Norwich two years earlier. When the Conference was over he took the unusual step of printing the *Minutes*, which read in part as follows:

---

[1] Wesley, *Letters*, vol. 5, p. 215.     [2] *Ibid.*, vol. 5, p. 251–2.

Take heed to your doctrine.

We said in 1744, We have leaned too much towards Calvinism. Wherein?

1. With regard to *man's faithfulness*. Our Lord Himself taught us to use the expression; and we ought never to be ashamed of it. We ought steadily to assert, on His authority, that if a man is not 'faithful in the unrighteous mammon' God will not give him 'the true riches.'

2. With regard to *working for life*, this also our Lord has expressly commanded us. 'Labour' (literally, 'work') 'for the meat that endureth to everlasting life.' And, in fact, every believer, till he comes to glory, works for, as well as *from*, life.

3. We have received it as a maxim that 'a man is to do nothing in order to justification.' Nothing can be more false. Whoever desires to find favour with God should 'cease from evil and learn to do well.' Whoever repents should do 'works meet for repentance.' And if this is not *in order* to find favour, what does he do them for?

Review the whole affair.

1. Who of us is *now* accepted of God?

He that now believes in Christ with a loving and obedient heart.

2. But who among those that never heard of Christ?

He that feareth God and worketh righteousness, according to the light he has.

3. Is this the same with 'he that is sincere'?

Nearly, if not quite.

4. Is not this salvation by works?

Not by the *merit* of works, but by works as a *condition*.

5. What have we, then, been disputing about for these thirty years?

I am afraid about words.

6. As to *merit* itself, of which we have been so dreadfully afraid, we are rewarded 'according to our works' – yea, 'because of our works'. How does this differ from *'for the sake of our works'*? And how differs this from *secundum merita operum*, as our works deserve? Can you split this hair? I doubt I cannot.

7. The grand objection to one of the preceding propositions is drawn from matter of fact. God does in fact justify those, who, by their own confession, 'neither feared God nor wrought righteousness.' Is this an exception to the general rule? It is a doubt, God makes any exception at all. But how are we sure, that the person in question never did fear God or work righteousness? His own saying so is not proof; for we know, how all that are convinced of sin undervalue themselves in every respect.

8. Does not talking of a justified or a sanctified *state* tend to mislead men? almost naturally leading them to trust in what was done in one moment? Whereas we are every hour and every moment pleasing or displeasing to God, 'according to our works'; – according to the whole of our inward tempers, and our outward behaviour.[1]

As we might expect the contents of these *Minutes* burst like a thunderclap on many of the preachers and friends of the evangelical revival. Blurring distinctions held precious by Christians since the days of the Reformation, Wesley brought down on his own head a barrage of criticism. Since the earliest days of the revival there had always existed a divergence of views about the nature of justification by faith,[2] but the terms Wesley employed in his *Minutes* were such as many of his friends found unacceptable. As a recent biographer explains:

Not only did he emphasise the goal of holiness with an enhanced role for works, but he impatiently dismissed what Calvinists regarded as essential technical points about 'merit' as being mere hair-splitting and 'disputes about words'. This echoed the attitude of a few years earlier in his solitary meditations in his coach. What matters is the achievement of holiness whatever the means. To a

[1] Tyerman, *Wesley*, vol. 3, pp. 169–70.
[2] Justification, for Wesley, was an acquittal from all condemnation on account of the merits of Christ's blood. Like earlier Anglicans, he did not believe it included the forensic imputation of the righteousness of Christ to his people. This in turn led to his inability to accept the doctrine of the final perseverance of believers.

Calvinist he seemed to be allowing merit to works, as though we are saved at least partly by our works, even if this depends in some ultimate sense on grace. In all his oscillations between Calvinism and Pelagianism (never, indeed, ever reaching either extreme), this was the point at which Wesley came nearest to the latter position.[1]

The Countess was deeply troubled. John Fletcher too was disturbed, not so much about the contents as about the wording, which he regarded as 'unguarded and not sufficiently explicit'.[2] But in the view of Selina and her friends this was 'another gospel'.[3] She came to the radical conclusion that John Wesley had defected from the faith. These *Minutes* appeared to be Roman Catholic in their emphasis and could therefore be interpreted as subversive to the very fundamentals of the evangelical message. Without waiting for explanations and still sore over the letter she had received, Selina wrote to Wesley stipulating that until he renounced the teaching set out in the *Minutes* he would no longer be welcome to preach in any of her chapels. At the time she wrote, the second anniversary of Trevecca was due to take place in two weeks time and Wesley had been preparing to travel to Wales with her in accordance with an invitation she had given him the previous year. With the invitation withdrawn, he travelled to Cornwall instead.

A long way off from such concerns the irenic George Whitefield's earthly course was running swiftly to its close. On 29 September 1770, far from well, he was persuaded to preach to the expectant people as he stopped overnight at Exeter on his way to Plymouth, New England. 'Sir, you are more fit to go to bed than to preach', remonstrated a friend.

[1] H. D. Rack, *Reasonable Enthusiast* (London: Epworth Press, 1989), p. 454.
[2] Tyerman, *Wesley's Designated Successor*, p. 178.
[3] Over twenty years earlier Howell Harris had noted in his diary how clearly the Countess expressed herself 'against justification by works'. *Harris Visits London*, p. 145. We may also recall her letter to Henry Venn where she spoke explicitly about this issue, see pp. 164–5.

'True, sir,' responded the preacher, and then addressing himself to his God he spoke these unforgettable words: 'Lord Jesus, I am weary in thy work, but not of it. If I have not yet finished my course, let me go and speak for thee once more in the fields, seal thy truth and come home and die.' Whitefield may well have already heard of the '*Minutes* controversy' for he chose as the subject for his address the relationship between faith and works in the plan of salvation.[1] In the course of that two-hour sermon we are told by one who was present, 'He suddenly cried out in a voice of thunder, "Works! Works! A man get to heaven by works! I would as soon think of climbing to the moon on a rope of sand!"'

The next day Whitefield, exhausted with the effort and clearly ill, travelled on to Newburyport. He had just sufficient strength to exhort the waiting people as he stood on the stairs, candle in hand, before retiring for the night. But the ardent evangelist had preached his last sermon. By six o'clock the following morning Whitefield's work was indeed done, as God took his servant home.

News of Whitefield's death reached England five weeks later on 5 November, and although Thomas Maxfield hastened to write immediately to the Countess at Trevecca, she had already seen it in a newspaper before the letter arrived. Howell Harris too had read the news and was not surprised when Selina came across to his home. In his diary for 10 November he wrote, 'Yesterday (after I had seen it in the paper) Lady Huntingdon came to my room all in tears at the death of a dear and faithful servant of the Lord.' She then asked Harris to give an address on her chaplain's life and death, which he agreed to do and 'had a great and to me unusual flow of affection in prayer and discoursing (often

[1] If news of Whitefield's death only took four and a half weeks to reach England (30 Sept.– 5 Nov.), it is most likely that Whitefield had heard of Wesley's *Minutes* because more than seven weeks had elapsed since the Conference.

weeping).'[1] The death of Whitefield brought distress to many but in a special way to Selina. She had often relied on his judgment and especially on his pastoral concern during the last twenty years.

At Whitefield's own request, John Wesley was to preach the memorial sermon for his friend. The request had been a final act on Whitefield's part to demonstrate the union he had fostered between himself and the one whom he had regarded as his 'father in the faith'. Scheduled to begin at half past five on the afternoon of 18 November 1770, the time of the service was brought forward to four o'clock because every seat had been filled for over an hour. As he preached to the immense congregation, Wesley concentrated on Whitefield's life, the records he had left in his journals and the importance of taking to heart the death of such a man and of benefitting from his example. Avoiding any mention of the areas of difference between them, he spoke only of those things that they had held in common:

> These are the fundamental doctrines which he [Whitefield] everywhere insisted upon; and may they not be summed up in two words – the new birth and justification by faith? These let us insist upon with all boldness, at all times, in all places. Keep close to these good, old, unfashionable doctrines, how many soever contradict and blaspheme.[2]

The fact that Wesley was to preach the memorial sermon posed a serious problem for the Countess. Feeling unable to attend the service at Tottenham Court Road Chapel, she invited Henry Venn to preach a similar sermon in Bath on the same day. Aware of Selina's grief at the loss of her friend and chaplain, Charles Wesley wrote her a letter of condolence. Included in the letter was a request that she should write a brief appreciation of her chaplain – a tribute she was glad to make. Her reply has been preserved and reads in part as follows:

[1] *Harris Visits London*, p. 19.
[2] Tyerman, *Wesley*, vol. 3, p. 77.

I thank you for your kind consideration of me. I am glad my friend
David went before me and that that voice had arose in his heart that
very often does in mine, 'Lord remember thy poor widow and all
her troubles.' All I can say is it is the narrow way and life is in it. I
hope it will be no matter of dispute between you and your brother
on my account.

I wish I could say anything to add to the best impressions of my late
dear friend Mr Whitefield. One part of his character, ever the most
to be admired by me, was the most artless mind – an Israelite
indeed in whom there was no guile . . . There is not one soul living
either in temporals or spirituals who [he] ever meant to deceive for
any purpose, and that it was his great point ever in godly sincerity
and simplicity to have his whole life approved in this world. No
prospect of pretended good could make him do evil - this is my
testimony of him in this respect. I account for this from the clear
revelation of Jesus Christ to his soul by the Holy Ghost . . .
[He]had a single eye for the Lord and whatever was mistaken for
this end was deficiency in judgment, considered rationally and
temporally. Anyone that knew as well as I his true spiritual knowledge of eternal things must be absolutely sure of this. My dear
friend, believe me, there is little of this left in the world, though it is
the whole of all religion and this every hour does certainly prove to
me . . . May mercy be the cry of every soul for this blessing. These
are my best hints as they came most under my own knowledge and
for which my heart was unnaturally attached to him and I trust ever
will be.

My love to dear Mrs Wesley. Thank her for her kind sympathy. I
am, my dear Sir, your truly affectionate and sincere friend, S.H.
College, 20 November 1770.[1]

Whitefield's death was a severe loss. Even the appointment of
the Countess's cousin Walter Shirley as her personal chaplain in
his place could not compensate. Undoubtedly she had over-
reacted to Wesley's *Minutes*, as she herself later came to see. Had

[1] Rylands MS.

Whitefield been there, he would surely have reminded her that for over thirty years Wesley had preached justification by faith alone throughout the length and breadth of the land and had suffered physical and verbal abuse in consequence.

'I am fully persuaded that there is more misunderstanding between my Lady and Mr Wesley about words and modes of expression than about things and essential principles',[1] wrote John Fletcher in a long account of the *Minutes* controversy of 1770. Certainly there was a measure of misunderstanding, accompanied by lack of clarification, but if words are to be taken at their face value, we are not surprised that the Countess and many others from the Calvinistic wing of the revival should believe that there were indeed 'essential principles' of the evangelical gospel at stake. Describing her strong reactions, Fletcher wrote, 'I look upon Lady Huntingdon as an eminent servant of God, an honest, gracious person, but not above the reach of prejudice; and where prejudice misleads her, her warm heart makes her go rather too fast.'[2] While admitting that the Countess was 'a truly excellent person herself', Fletcher unwisely disclosed that in the heat of her agitation, distress and 'mistaken zeal', she had even described Wesley in a private conversation as 'a papist unmasked, a heretic, an apostate'.[3]

Although this controversy had been simmering for two years, it had now found a focal point in the *Minutes* of Wesley's 1770 Conference. The weight of responsibility for the grievous dispute, with the division among friends that was to ensue, must rest largely on Wesley's shoulders, but the Countess too was accountable for some of the events that followed. She should have sought an elucidation of the unfortunate wording of the *Minutes* before embarking on a course of action that would make the rift with John Wesley permanent and set in motion a train of regrettable consequences far beyond her control. 1770 indeed proved to be the parting of the ways.

---

[1] Tyerman, *Wesley's Designated Successor*, p. 182.    [2] *Ibid.*, p. 178.
[3] *Ibid.*, p.195.

# 22

# THE AFTERMATH

THE SECOND ANNIVERSARY CELEBRATIONS of Trevecca college fell in August 1770 and gave a temporary respite from the *'Minutes'* controversy. The Countess was able to put the disquiet of recent days behind her as together with many others she commemorated God's help and provision for the fledgling college. The burden of expense had been high and, for the second time, John Thornton, businessman, philanthropist and warm friend of the gospel, had sent a gift of £500. Lady Glenorchy, the young woman Selina had befriended and influenced during her visit to Bath in 1765, sent a gift of £400. Thanking her for her generosity, the Countess told Lady Glenorchy of the blessing of God on the college:

> The college, as dear Mr Berridge says, has been baptised with the baptism of the Holy Ghost; great grace rests upon all within its walls, and eminent success crowns their labours in the towns and villages around. To God alone be all the glory – the work is his – and he will carry it on in his own way . . . I thirst for an entire devotedness to him, and his cause and interest in the world. O! that I had a thousand hands, a thousand hearts; all should be employed for him - for he is WORTHY![1]

The celebrations followed a similar pattern to those of the previous year with at least ten preachers, each distinguished in his own right, arriving at Trevecca in the third week of August. The Countess rented over twenty rooms from Howell Harris's

---

[1] Seymour, *Countess*, vol. 2, p. 112.

Trevecca institution where she could entertain her preachers, friends and guests. These included Daniel Rowland, Henry Venn, Walter Shirley, John Berridge, William Williams and of course, John Fletcher, the president. Eight days of preaching, singing and mutual fellowship ensued. On Friday, 24 August, the actual day of the anniversary, there was an early morning celebration of the Lord's Supper, before preaching services in both English and Welsh began. These continued over the weekend with Venn, Berridge and others taking part, making the whole a memorable occasion.

As her friends dispersed the Countess had to turn her mind once more to the position of the college in the light of the controversial *Minutes* published earlier in the month. Joseph Benson, newly appointed tutor at Trevecca, was in a quandary because his theological convictions were in line with Wesley's own. Reporting on the Countess's reaction to the *Minutes* in a letter to Fletcher, Benson wrote, 'My Lady wept over them and lost some nights' sleep on the occasion. At last she told me she must burn against them and whoever did not readily avow against them must quit the college.'[1] Still only twenty-two years of age, Benson valued his position at Trevecca, but his respect for Wesley was high – his view of John Fletcher even higher. To him Fletcher was 'as an angel of God'; 'An angel in human flesh, so fully raised above the ruins of the fall that though by the body he was tied down to earth, his whole conversation was in heaven.' At last he told the Countess on 1 January 1771 that he could not repudiate John Wesley's *Minutes*. He promptly forfeited his position at the college. The Countess, however, gave her young tutor a warm recommendation:

> This is to certify that Mr Joseph Benson was master for the languages in my college at Talgarth for nine months, and that, during that time, from his capacity, sobriety, and diligence, he

[1] Rylands, unpublished MSS., John Fletcher volume.

acquitted himself properly in that character; and I am ready at any time to testify this on his behalf whenever required.

College, January 17, 1771.      S. Huntingdon.[1]

Benson meanwhile went to stay with a friend at nearby Hay-on-Wye. While he was there he received a letter from Wesley, commenting on the situation:

> Dear Joseph, I am surprised at nothing. When persons are governed by passion rather than reason, we can expect little good. I cannot see that there was anything blameable in your behaviour. You could not do or say less with a clear conscience . . . You are welcome to stay at Kingswood till you are better provided for.[2]

Fletcher, not unexpectedly, was also troubled at the young tutor's dismissal, believing it to have been arbitrary and unfair. Writing to Benson on 7 January 1771, he tried to calm the tension:

> Take care, my dear Sir, not to make matters worse than they are; and cast a mantle of forgiving love over the circumstances that might injure the cause of God, so far as it is put into the hands of that eminent lady, who has so well served the Church of Christ. Rather suffer in silence, than make a noise to cause the Philistines to triumph. Do not let go your expectation of a baptism from above. May you be supported in this and every other trial! Farewell![3]

On the same day, Fletcher wrote to the Countess, and his letter indicates that the issues in question had now widened to include the central disagreement between Calvinists and Arminians: election or free will. He could see that this had serious implications for him. 'If "every Arminian must quit the college", I am actually discharged also', he told her.[4]

---

[1] Tyerman, *Wesley's Designated Successor*, p. 175. It is probable that the boy tutor, John Henderson, left Trevecca at the same time.

[2] Wesley, *Letters*, vol. 5, p. 217.

[3] Tyerman, *Wesley's Designated Successor*, p. 176.

[4] *Ibid.*, p. 175.

As he faced the real possibility that he would indeed have to resign as president of Trevecca, Fletcher wrote again to Benson two days after his previous letter: 'I am determined to stand or fall with the liberty of the college. As I entered it a free place, I must quit it the moment it is a harbour for party spirit.' And of the Countess herself he added, 'Remember that great lady has been an instrument of great good, and that there are great inconsistencies attending the greatest and best of men.'[1]

Travelling to Trevecca in March 1771, Fletcher found all peaceful, but when he preached to the students the following day he experienced no liberty of spirit. Gradually he became convinced that 'the college was no longer my place, as I was not likely to do or receive any good there, especially as Calvinism strongly prevailed.' As he discussed the situation with Selina and particularly the offensive wording of the *Minutes*, she wept once more over what she viewed as Wesley's apostasy from the faith. Detailing his conversation with the Countess to John Wesley in a letter dated 18 March 1771, Fletcher reported her as saying she had 'an honest fear that you had fairly and fully given up the grand point of the Methodists, free justification . . . The heresy appeared horrible, worth being publicly opposed, and such as a true believer ought to be ready to burn against.'[2]

Fletcher now believed he had no course of action other than to resign and this was underlined when the Countess required each of the students to state in writing his own position on the relationship between faith and works in the scheme of salvation. Fletcher, too, recorded his views, and, as he later reported to Wesley, had attempted to show 'the absurdity of inferring from these *Minutes* that you had renounced the Protestant doctrine and the atonement'.[3] About one third of the students were Arminian in their beliefs, while others tended to an extreme Calvinistic position, holding Dr John Gill's views on 'eternal justification'. All of both persuasions were required to leave the college.[4]

[1] *Ibid.*, p. 176–7.　　[2] *Ibid.*　　[3] *Ibid.*, p. 178.　　[4] *Ibid.*, p. 183.

Fletcher was of the opinion that such a dismissal of all holding
to either of these views was contrary to the principles on which
Trevecca had been established. These had specified that the
college was open to all who could unite on the common doctrine
of man's total fall in Adam. 'I thought that my lady had no right
to impose such a law – a law so contrary to her first proposals – till
it had received a proper sanction by a majority of the votes both
of masters and students.'[1] Tendering his resignation, Fletcher
recommended another to take his place – Rowland Hill whom he
described as 'a moderate Calvinist'. In Fletcher's view Hill could
restore a balance to the college, while upholding the doctrinal
principles the Countess held dear. Commenting sadly to Benson
on the situation at Trevecca, John Fletcher wrote, 'What are our
dear lady's jealousies come to? Ah, poor college! They are without a master, but not without a mistress.'[2] Selina had been placed
in a position she had neither anticipated nor wished for and one
which appeared beyond her powers to control.

The Countess was shaken both by Fletcher's resignation and
by the fact of his basic agreement with Wesley. She valued him
highly and knew full well his deep spirituality of heart and conduct. Her attitude towards the 1770 *Minutes* softened immediately and she told Fletcher that she would write to Wesley and ask
for an explanation of his meaning, 'that she and the college may
see you are not *an enemy to grace* and may be friends at a distance
instead of open adversaries'.[3]

However, Selina did not write to Wesley. Instead she consulted
further with her cousin, Walter Shirley, Thomas Powys and
others to decide on a course of action in the light of the circumstances. Powys then drew up the following letter to be sent to all
who were unhappy with Wesley's doctrinal stance:

[1] *Ibid.*, p.182. If the Countess had established a Council to govern College
affairs, composed of such men as William Williams, John Fletcher, John
Berridge and Walter Shirley, the responsibility for such decisions would have
been a shared one.     [2] *Ibid.*, p. 209.     [3] *Ibid.*, pp.177–8.

Sir, Whereas Mr Wesley's Conference is to be held at Bristol, on Tuesday the 6th August next, it is proposed by Lady Huntingdon and many other Christian friends (real Protestants) to have a meeting at Bristol at the same time, of such principal persons, both clergy and laity, who disapprove of the under written 'Minutes'; and, as the same are thought injurious to the very fundamental principles of Christianity, it is a further proposed that they go in a body to the said Conference, and insist upon a formal recantation of the said Minutes; and, in case of a refusal, that they sign and publish their protest against them. Your presence, Sir, on this occasion, is particularly requested; but, if it should not suit your convenience to be there, it is desired that you will transmit your sentiments on the subject to such persons as you think proper to produce them. It is submitted to you, whether it would not be right, in the opposition to be made to such a dreadful heresy, to recommend it to as many of your Christian friends, as well of the dissenters as of the Established Church, as you can prevail on to be there, the cause being of so public a nature.

I am, Sir, your obedient servant,
Walter Shirley.[1]

To her chaplain's signature, Selina added her own. It was to be sent throughout the country together with a copy of the offending *Minutes* of 1770.

The Countess's relationship with John Wesley was not the only casualty from these unfortunate circumstances. Anticipating that her long-standing friend, Charles Wesley, would take her part over against his brother, she wrote him a covering letter on 8 June 1771, as she sent him a copy of Shirley's circular letter. In it she reaffirmed her desire to hold fast 'the fundamental principles of the Church to which I belong', including 'the sufficiency of that glorious sacrifice for sinners as the whole of my salvation, abhorring all merit in man'. She then added, 'As you have no part in this

*Ibid.*, p. 188.

matter, I find it difficult to blame your brother to you, while as an honest man I must pity and not less regard you, as you must suffer equal disgrace and universal distrust from the supposed union with him.' This was too much for Charles Wesley. He wrote at the bottom of the letter, 'Lady Huntingdon's LAST. Unanswered by John Wesley's brother.'[1] So ended another friendship that had brought comfort to the Countess.

Wesley himself, who was over in Ireland on an extended preaching tour, found time to write once more to Selina from Londonderry on 19 June 1771. He had probably not yet seen a copy of Shirley's circular, as it was not until 24 June that Fletcher wrote sending him one.

My dear lady, Many years since I saw that 'without holiness no man shall see the Lord.' I began following after it, and inciting all with whom I had any intercourse to do the same. Ten years after God gave me a clearer view than I had before of the way to retain this, namely, by faith in the Son of God. And immediately I declared it to all . . . I have continued to declare this, for above thirty years; and God has continued to confirm the word of his grace. But during this time, wellnigh all the religious world hath set themselves in array against me, and among the rest, many of my own children, following the example of one of my eldest sons, Mr Whitefield. The general cry has been, 'He is unsound in the faith; he preaches another gospel.'

But it is said, "O, but you printed ten lines in August last which contradict all your other writings. Be not so sure of this. It is probable, at least, that I understand my own meaning as well as you do; and that meaning I have yet again declared in the sermon last referred to [Whitefield's memorial sermon]. By that interpret those ten lines, and you will understand them better; although I should think that any one might see, even without this help, that the lines in question do not refer to the condition of obtaining, but of

Cited in T. Jackson, *Life of the Rev. Charles Wesley, MA* (London: Mason, 1841), vol. 2, p. 256 .

continuing in the favour of God. But whether the sentiments contained in those lines be right or wrong, and whether it be well or ill-expressed, the gospel which I now preach God does still confirm by new witnesses in every place; perhaps never so much in this kingdom as within these last three months. Now, I argue from glaring, undeniable fact; God cannot bear witness to a lie. The gospel, therefore, which he confirms must be true in substance.

To be short: such as I am, I love you well. You have one of the first places in my esteem and affection. And you once had some regard for me. But it cannot continue if it depends upon my seeing with your eyes; or on my being in no mistake. What if I was in as many as Mr Law himself? If you were, I should love you still, provided your heart was still right with God. My dear friend, you seem not to have well learned yet the meaning of those words which I desire to have continually written on my heart, 'Whosoever doeth the will of my Father which is in heaven, the same is my brother and sister and mother.'

I am, my dear lady, your affectionate John Wesley, June 19 1771.[1]

This was the clarification that the Countess and her friends had needed. Three weeks later, on 10 July, Wesley elucidated his position further by sending out a long circular letter, this time to his preachers explaining and vindicating his position in similar terms. By 'salvation', he maintained, he had not meant salvation from sin at the beginning of the Christian life, but final salvation, for 'without holiness no man shall see the Lord'.[2]

As the date for Wesley's Bristol Conference drew near, Selina, by now calmer about the situation, realized that to intrude in the intended way into a private Conference was in fact presumptuous even though important issues were at stake. On 2 August, four days before the Conference was due to begin, she wrote a letter apologizing for what she now saw as 'an arbitrary way of proceeding'. 'As Christians,' she continued, 'we wish to retract what a

1 Wesley, *Letters*, vol. 5, pp. 258–60.
² *Ibid.*, pp. 262–5.

more deliberate consideration might have prevented.' However, she still maintained that 'the principles established in the Minutes were repugnant to the whole plan of man's salvation under the new covenant of grace and also to the clear meaning of the Established Church . . . to whose foundations the highest respect and honour are due.'[1]

Walter Shirley added his apology, acknowledging that 'upon the whole the circular letter was too hastily drawn up and improperly expressed'. He added, however, 'I cannot but wish most earnestly that this recantation of the circular letter may prevail as an example for the recantation of the Minutes.' 'Had the apparent error', he was later to write, 'been of less magnitude, did it not seem to shake the FOUNDATION itself, we should have been less zealously affected concerning it.'[2]

There was no time to contact all those who had received Shirley's first letter summoning them to Bristol, but there was little enthusiasm for the initiative in any case. Wesley's Conferences were private affairs and attendance was by invitation only. Possibly due to a degree of embarrassment only a handful of men journeyed to Bristol to register their protest. Wesley recorded in his journal for 6 August:

> We had more preachers than usual at the Conference in consequence of Mr Shirley's circular letter. At ten on Thursday morning he came with nine or ten of his friends. We conversed freely for about two hours; and I believe they were satisfied we were not so 'dreadful heretics' as they imagined, but were tolerably sound in the faith.[3]

Shirley first read aloud to the delegates at the Conference both his and the Countess's letters of apology. He then presented Wesley with a declaration he wished him to sign. Wesley studied

---

[1] Walter Shirley, *A Narrative of the Principal Circumstances relative to the Rev. Mr Wesley's Late Conference held in Bristol, August 6 1771* (Bath: W. Gye, 1771), p. 8.          [2] *Ibid.*, p. 5.
[3] Wesley, *Journals*, vol. 5, p. 425.

the document and then rewrote it making a few inconsequential amendments. This declaration he and fifty-three of his preachers then signed. It read as follows:

> Whereas the doctrinal points in the Minutes of a Conference held in London August 7, 1770 have been understood to favour Justification by Works: now the Rev. John Wesley and others assembled in Conference, do declare that we had no such meaning, and that we abhor the doctrine of Justification by Works as a most perilous and abominable doctrine: and, as the said Minutes are not sufficiently guarded in the way they are expressed, we hereby solemnly declare, in the sight of God, that we have no trust or confidence but in the alone merits of our Lord and Saviour Jesus Christ, for Justification or Salvation, either in life, death, or the Day of Judgment: and, though no one is a real Christian believer (and consequently cannot be saved), who doth not good works, where there is time and opportunity, yet our works have no part in meriting or purchasing our salvation from first to last either in whole or in part.

Wesley, for his part, then asked Shirley, as the representative of those who had been unhappy with the *Minutes*, to make a public recognition that they had been mistaken in their interpretation of them. Hesitant at first, Shirley then gave Wesley the acknowledgement for which he had asked:

> Mr Shirley's Christian respects wait on Mr Wesley. The declaration agreed to in Conference August 8, 1771 has convinced Mr Shirley he had mistaken the meaning of the doctrinal points in the Minutes of the Conference held in London August 7, 1770; and he hereby wishes to testify the full satisfaction he has in the said declaration, and his hearty concurrence and agreement with the same.

Had that been the end of this unfortunate affair, it would have been consigned to a page or two in the records of the times and soon forgotten. The Countess, who had not appeared in person at Wesley's Conference, would have been able to restore a normal relationship with her old friend once more. Unfortunately it was not so.

John Fletcher, fired by what he felt was the unjust criticism levelled against his friend, John Wesley, took it upon himself to write a long *Vindication of the Minutes of 1770*. He set out to demonstrate that this was indeed a satisfactory statement of Christian truth, and all who had protested against it had misunderstood its intent. With compelling arguments he contended for Wesley's case. Completed on 29 July, this document was in fact in Wesley's hands before the Conference began. He had read it, approved its contents and sent it to the printer. It was in the process of being set up for printing while the Conference was in session.

On 9 August, the day after the Conference had closed, Walter Shirley was informed that Fletcher's *Vindication* was going through the press. He, together with Fletcher's long-standing friend, John Ireland, did all in their power to have the work suppressed, offering to pay any cost incurred to the printer. Wesley, however, was unwilling that it should be stopped. Assuring Shirley that he had 'removed all tart expressions', he insisted that the printing went ahead.

As soon as Fletcher himself heard of the declaration signed at the Conference, and the new measure of accord between the contending parties, he knew instantly that his *Vindication* could do no good but would inevitably rekindle the flames of controversy. It must be suppressed at all costs. 'My dear sir,' he wrote to John Ireland, 'what must be done? I am ready to defray by selling to my last shirt the expense of printing my *Vindication*, and suppress it. Direct me, dear sir. Consult with Mr Shirley and Mr Wesley about the matter.' Despite every effort to suppress the publication, Wesley was adamant. It must go forward. And so it did. In the words of Luke Tyerman, 'Thus, by Wesley's firmness, Fletcher's manuscript, without any delay, was printed and published.'[1]

---

[1] Tyerman, *Wesley's Designated Successor*, p. 193.

On 14 August 1771 Wesley wrote to the Countess in answer to
her letter sent at the beginning of the month explaining and defending his position once more:

When I received your Ladyship's of the 2nd instant, I immediately
saw that it required an answer; only I waited till the hurry of conference was over, that I might do nothing rashly. I know your Ladyship would not 'servilely deny the truth'. I think neither would I;
especially that great truth, Justification by Faith, which Mr Law
indeed flatly denies (and yet Mr Law was a child of God), but for
which I have given up all my worldly hopes, my friends, my reputation; yea, for which I have so often hazarded my life, and by the
grace of God will do again. 'The principles established in the Minutes' I apprehend to be no way contrary to this, or to that faith . . .
which was once delivered to the saints. I believe who ever calmly
considers Mr Fletcher's Letters [the Vindication] will be convinced
of this . . . Those letters (which therefore could not be suppressed
without betraying the honour of our Lord) largely prove that the
Minutes lay no other foundation than that which is laid in Scripture, and which I have been laying, and teaching others to lay, for
between thirty and forty years. Indeed, it would be amazing that
God should at this day prosper my labours, as much if not more
than ever, by converting as well as convincing sinners, if I was
'establishing another foundation, repugnant to the whole plan of
man's salvation under the covenant of grace, as well as the clear
meaning of our Established Church and all other Protestant
Churches.' This is a charge indeed! But I plead, Not guilty. And till
it is proved upon me, I must subscribe myself, my dear Lady,
Your Ladyship's affectionate but much injured servant,
John Wesley.[1]

Fletcher's *Vindication*, called *Checks to Antinomianism*, took
the form of five letters addressed to Walter Shirley, in which he set
out to clear Wesley's name, demonstrating his faithfulness as a

[1] Wesley, *Letters*, vol. 5, p. 274–5.

preacher. Admitting that the Methodist leader may have unwittingly misled his readers, Fletcher pleads for honesty and an objective assessment of the intention behind the words rather than their obvious meaning. It was a masterly defence in which Fletcher summed up the whole by appealing for peace. This single publication, to which Walter Shirley responded with an account of events from his point of view,[1] led relentlessly onwards until a number of good men were involved in altercations one with another. Bitter and unchristian words were written and printed that some would afterwards regret.

Although the Countess of Huntingdon took no further part in the disputes, she followed all the publications on each side and grieved over the disharmony and bad feeling engendered between those who should have been united in believing the centralities of the faith. Her affection for the students at Trevecca took precedence over all else from now on. Writing to Howell Harris on 26 March 1771, shortly after Benson and Fletcher had left the college, she said: 'My heart is much united to my great charge there, and the college means more to me before the Lord than anything else in this whole world.'[2]

The controversy had, however, several long-term effects both on the Countess and on her work. Firstly Selina had lost in the space of twelve months her four closest friends and fellow workers, men on whom she had relied probably more than she realized. Whitefield had died, but as much if not more than the loss of Whitefield, was the deprivation the Countess suffered in the withdrawal of the friendship of Charles Wesley. Able to share her deepest feelings and spiritual experiences with Charles over a period of thirty years, Selina had needed such a confidant. And for John Wesley himself, though her relationship with him had been stressful at times, yet she had respected and trusted him. He was unafraid to tell her when he felt she was in the wrong, and she

[1] Walter Shirley, *Narrative of Principal Circumstances etc.*
[2] *Selected Trevecka Letters*, vol. 2, p. 133.

had normally accepted his advice. The withdrawal of John Fletcher from Trevecca would inevitably impoverish the college. From this time onwards the Countess, now sixty-four years of age, hurt and troubled by some in whom she had placed her confidence, largely swung clear of seeking comment or guidance from her fellow workers on her decisions. Inclined on occasion to over-react to situations, Selina now had no one apart from John Berridge who might suggest that she could be in the wrong.

The controversy also led to a hardening of the rift between the Arminian and Calvinistic wings of the revival. While Whitefield was alive, Wesley and the Countess had generally worked together. A partnership, though strained at times, had been maintained. Selina had never intended that Trevecca should accept only Calvinistic students. The assistance of Fletcher and Benson and the Wesley brothers demonstrated the inclusive nature of her wishes for the college. Now Trevecca had necessarily become partisan in its choice of students.

Much more could be said on the literary wrangling that went on between erstwhile friends until 1776, but we must instead follow the Countess in the work to which she turned her hand in the remaining years of her life.

# 23

## 'SHE IS A MOTHER TO US ALL'

'I WISH', SAID KING GEORGE III, 'there was a Lady Huntingdon in every diocese in my kingdom.' This comment was made to Lord Dartmouth[1] after Selina had audaciously approached the King over the unacceptable frivolities and conviviality taking place at Lambeth Palace, which had been condoned by Archbishop Cornwallis and his wife. So impressed were the King and Queen Charlotte by the Countess, whom they had been anxious to meet, that they had detained her for over an hour, offering her refreshments and plying her with questions about her work and the college she had recently opened. The King remembered her from his childhood days when she and the Earl had attended the court of his father, Frederick, Prince of Wales. George III continued:

> There is something so noble, so commanding, and withal so engaging about her, that I am quite captivated with her Ladyship. She appears to possess talents of a very superior order – is clever, well-informed and has all the ease and politeness belonging to her rank ... she is an honour to her sex and the nation.[2]

While the king might wish he had a Lady Huntingdon in every diocese of his kingdom, he could never have conceived of the way in which her influence was about to spread throughout the land during the next ten years of his reign as the students of Trevecca College travelled tirelessly preaching wherever they went. A

[1] Dartmouth was President of the Board of Trade at this time.
[2] Seymour, *Countess*, vol. 2, pp. 283–4.

unique enterprise in the life of the church, Trevecca's influence was to be even more widespread as it set a pattern for the training of preachers which would be followed by other institutions.[1]

Deprived now of the friendship of John and Charles Wesley and feeling the loss of George Whitefield, Selina devoted herself to the college with all its needs, its opportunities and its incessant calls on her time and purse. In an elegy on the death of Whitefield, dedicated to the Countess, William Williams of Pantecelyn had addressed some of his verses directly to her, recalling that Whitefield had preached at the opening of Trevecca only two years earlier:

> Let patience reign; run thy allotted race,
> Choose out such youths as may the temple grace;
> And let your college gracious striplings train,
> To preach the Victim for transgressors slain.[2]

This was indeed the Countess's aim. Among the first of the 'gracious striplings' was a young man by the name of John Clayton, who would eventually join the ranks of Dissent and become pastor of King's Weigh House Chapel, London. His biographer has included valuable material that throws light on aspects of daily life at Trevecca.

We are given an interesting description of how Selina chose her students. Most candidates for Trevecca came with the recommendation of one of the better-known preachers of the revival. In

---

[1] Dr G.F. Nuttall, in his booklet, *The Significance of Trevecca College* (London, 1968), listed a number of centres for the training of preachers set up on similar lines to Trevecca. These included: Lady Glenorchy's establishment at Oswestry under Edward Williams; another enterprise started in 1778 by three well-to-do business men in Hoxton, London, that resulted in a residential academy in Mile End, London under a Congregational minister as tutor. The Newport Evangelical Institution opened in 1783, established at Newton Pagnell and financed by John Thornton, was also founded on similar lines to Trevecca.

[2] William Williams, *An Elegy on the Rev. Mr George Whitefield* (Carmarthen, 1771).

Clayton's case it was George Whitefield himself who had drawn her attention to this promising young man. Having heard of his conversion and his earnest desire to serve God, she asked to see him. Clayton's obvious intelligence, natural bearing and general conduct of himself impressed her but also 'the brokenness of spirit and self-renouncing humility' she saw in him, coupled with 'his evangelical sentiments and his earnest but chastened zeal'. Nor was the young man over-confident. Instead he showed a 'diffidence in his own competence for so great a work as the ministry'. The Countess saw these qualities as 'signs of a gracious spirit taught and led by God,' and invited John Clayton to come to Trevecca to study.

A student named Thomas Cannon recollected the Countess asking him if he could give up all and put up with the many trials that accompanied the life of an itinerant preacher. His reply, 'Anything for Christ, my Lady', satisfied Selina and assured him of his place at Trevecca.[1] In some cases she asked prospective students to write a dissertation entitled 'What is Faith' without reference to any book other than the Scriptures.[2] Men were first admitted to the college as probationers and when they had proved their worth and suitability for such a calling were confirmed as *bona fide* students.[3]

The Countess was right in her evaluation of John Clayton. He would indeed become a preacher of marked usefulness in the church of Christ. But all was not plain sailing at the outset. For many students their removal to Trevecca would be the first time they had left their homes. College life in those days was regimented and demanding. They soon discovered that 'her Ladyship was a stern disciplinarian in the government of her students, in the domestic as well as the scholastic arrangements of

[1] *An Authentic Narrative of the Primary Ordination* (London, 1784), p. 38.
[2] Joseph Shipman's essay can still be seen among the Cheshunt Foundation Archives.
[3] C.F. Archives.

the college'.[1] The routine was always the same. Each day the students rose at five o'clock, and at 6 o'clock, when a prayer bell rang, they were expected to arrive punctually in the main hall for a service of worship. Nor did Selina insist on standards for her students which she herself did not follow. Whenever she was in residence she would appear immaculately dressed and sitting waiting in the hall at six in the morning as the students filed in. Clayton himself describes the scene: 'She cast a searching glance around her, to satisfy herself that none appeared in negligent attire, or betrayed an inattention to the requirements of cleanliness and neatness, on which she was wont to lay great stress.'[2]

Every weekend the college emptied. On a Friday afternoon, or on Saturday, depending on the length of their journey, the students would saddle their horses and set off for various locations to which the Countess had appointed them. Some would serve nearby causes, but others had long distances to ride and would need to have hospitality arranged for them. All these arrangements Selina undertook. A letter to James Newben, who had been preaching in the Wiltshire town of Devizes, has survived among the Countess's papers. It serves as an example of the detailed arrangements she made for the student preachers:

Dear Newben,

I must request you to go to London as a student is there immediately wanted and as your horse will be of no use, so for you to go up by the coach or returning chaise on the road will be best. Should you want money to carry you, let me know; when in London Mr Keen will let you have any you want. Call upon him and he will order your places for preaching.

In great haste begging the Lord's blessing evermore to in any case rest upon your own soul and all your labours of love for his namesake. I am, dear Newben, your ever affectionate friend, S. H.[3]

[1] T. W. Aveling, *Memorials of the Clayton Family* (London, 1867) p. 17.
[2] *Ibid.*
[3] Rylands MSS., Letter 145, January 1772.

We may note from the above letter that although the Countess assumed overall responsibility for the students, she now had considerable back-up help from others.[1] Sometimes she wished a student to remain in a town for several weeks or even months, but generally the young men were expected to be back at their studies by Monday morning. A daunting assignment, it proved too much for some, especially those unused to study or handling horses and trekking across barren country tracks.

Although John Clayton was a competent horseman, he still found the weekly discipline arduous and after a short period he became depressed and overcome with a sense of failure. On more than one occasion his biographer tells us that he stopped abruptly in the middle of his discourse, burst into tears and had to leave the service he was supposed to be conducting. But Selina was no heartless taskmaster. Combining in her personality both strength and sympathy, she consoled Clayton, assuring him that he could and, with God's help, would achieve his goal.[2]

The Countess nurtured the students as a mother would her own family. One young man told his friend:

Her Ladyship is such a woman that nobody can refuse anything that she asks. She is a mother to us all and indeed she calls us her children. She takes so many of us into her room every night and makes us read a chapter [of Scripture] to her, and she explains it to us and there is few ministers could do it better and she prays with us.[3]

William Aldridge, preaching many years later, recollected this aspect of the Countess's relationship with her students:

She regarded her young men as her sons, as her family. With what affection and tenderness, wisdom and prudence have I heard her address the young men in the study around her. How has she

---

[1] In this case it was Robert Keen who was supplying the students with finances. Later it would be John Lloyd of Bath who paid many of the petty expenses on behalf of the Countess.

[2] Aveling, *Memorials*, p. 17.     [3] C.F.Archives.

warned, cautioned, reproved, comforted and encouraged us as she
saw cause like a true mother in Israel. With what earnest, feeling,
melting prayers has she poured out her soul to God among us. The
simplicity with which she would express herself, the variety of her
petitions, accompanied with many tears running down her aged
cheeks had dissolved all about her into a flood of weeping.[1]

The health of the students was a matter of constant concern,
particularly in view of Selina's longstanding interest in medicine.
Within a year of the opening of Trevecca one of the young men
fell ill and died. William Gibbons, conscientious and earnest, was
among the first batch of students to enter the college in 1768. But
after only a few weeks he was taken ill, possibly with tuberculosis
for his doctor ordered him to stop studying and take exercise
whenever possible. In addition to his physical disorder, Gibbons
experienced a measure of spiritual distress. Writing to the Countess he complained, 'The enemy of souls and my own wicked
heart made a very strong attack upon me by bringing all manner
of blasphemous thoughts into my mind.' She wrote back to the
troubled young man assuring him of her prayers for him. The
letter cheered him: 'When I heard the Lord had met your Ladyship in prayer for me, my heart seemed to revive within me', he
wrote. But the end was hard, and Gibbons complained that God
seemed to have deserted him in his acute need. Not until the last
moments of life did he gain any relief. His last words were, 'I had
been damned if Jesus had not died for me.'

Joseph Shipman too was taken ill during his third year at
Trevecca. As we saw, Shipman, once awkward and demanding,
had been remarkably blessed by God and changed at the time
when Fletcher had visited the college in November 1768. It was
a preparation for coming days of trial, for early in 1771 he
collapsed while preaching and his health declined sharply. Learning of his condition, the Countess paid for him to go to Bristol to

[1] William Aldridge, *A Funeral Sermon, preached in Jewry Street Chapel,*
*3 July 1791*, pp.16–17.

try the waters of the Hot Wells. When this failed to arrest the deterioration, she wrote kindly: 'Hearing you returned from Bristol hopeless of any good from those waters, I wish to follow you with every expression of tender concern.' But her concern was far greater than for his physical condition alone. Knowing from experience how easily illness leads to spiritual doubts and depression, she continued:

> I am not surprised at the different dispensations your heart seems under by your letter . . . O dear Shipman! Keep this point in the darkest hour, He died . . . This truth the great enemy of our souls can never attack. . . . Rest then your poor weary heart in safety upon his faithfulness . . . The various frames our oppressed and mortal body feels through infirmity make us what he knows will most effectually prepare us to enjoy, and that forever, those various bounties his precious blood has paid for. How shall I be able to express that tender regard which can alone supply all my prayers for you.[1]

In gratitude for all that the Countess had done for him, Shipman wrote back:

> I thank you for receiving me in my distress and educating me at your college, but above all in thrusting me out of doors when I first preached. It was the beginning of my usefulness.[2]

Three further months of weakness followed for Joseph Shipman before he died on 31 October 1771, exclaiming to his grieving friends, 'Don't weep; God is with me. I am happy; I am happy. I am upon a sure foundation. I am going to heaven.'[3]

Benjamin Wase was another student who felt indebted to the Countess for the kindness she had shown him at a time of particular need:

> I have not forgot before God my Lady's going on her knees to dress my legs. O! it often melts my soul. Please do pardon me, my Lady,

[1] Seymour, *Countess*, vol. 2, pp. 391–2.
[2] *Evangelical Register 1824*, pp. 35–6.     [3] *Ibid.*

though I am continually transgressing, I am, under the Lord, your Ladyship's humble servant to do what ever and forever what lies in my power for you.[1]

The love Selina bore for her students and the deep personal interest she took in each one gave them an unusual degree of spiritual trust in her wisdom and judgment. Thomas Jones, one of the earliest students could describe her as 'my best earthly friend'.[2] Frequent letters followed them when they set out to begin a month or two of preaching at the various chapels to which she appointed them. In return they wrote to her, reporting on the progress of their work. They would also ask advice and confide their anxieties of conscience and as they battled against indwelling sin, a sense of failure in the ministry, together with Satan's wiles and God's ways towards them that they sometimes found inexplicable.

George Goodrich, one of the initial batch of students admitted to Trevecca in 1768, wrote to the Countess expressing his gratitude and sharing such problems:

> I think I am more convinced than ever that it is the Lord Jesus Christ and he only that hath opened your Ladyship's heart to receive my brethren and me . . . For some time past I've been under great desertions, and at times found many sore and reverse temptations, but blessed be God he has delivered me in great measure.[3]

James Renfrew, who entered college in 1773, had a similar complaint:

> Many are the trials and conflicts of soul I underwent since I saw your Ladyship. I have been tempted to give up preaching and praying and everything that tended to godliness. I desire and long and sigh to experience more and more what it is to be a living sacrifice to God.[4]

[1] C.F. Archives.     [2] *Authentic Narrative of the Primary Ordination*, p. 28.
[3] C.F. Archives, 7 April 1770.          [4] *Ibid.*

John Clayton, whose nervousness when he first started preaching led to him breaking down on several occasions, imagined he would soon conquer this problem, but had to confess three years later:

> The road is still thorny and rugged. I formerly thought when I first began to speak that the great fear and distress with which I was continually exercised would wear off, but I find it otherwise, and fear I shall while unbelief and Satan live. These two potent enemies had nearly conquered me in a late conflict in which I was brought to envy the happiness of my horse. But all praise to a precious Christ for when I had no might Jesus became my whole strength and revisited my soul with the light of his countenance.[1]

John Meyer, looking back many years, recalled one scene clearly. He and another student, Jesse Seymour, were apprehensive as they faced an early preaching engagement. 'Methinks I see dear Lady Huntingdon now sitting in her parlour at the college saying (for these were her very words), "Come, come Meyer; come Seymour, you are only going to a few simple souls; tell them concerning Jesus Christ and they will be satisfied."'[2] Anthony Crole, recommended for training at Trevecca by Martin Madan and who became one of the most able of the Trevecca preachers, would later recall his student days with deep affection. 'Can I forget, can I ever forget', he cried rhetorically, 'the distinguishing mercies of the Lord our God who rendered our situation a little paradise on earth?'[3]

Owing to the Countess's determination to send out her students on preaching tours, the tuition they received at Trevecca obviously lacked continuity. After the resignation of both Joseph Benson and John Fletcher, the Countess had no

---

[1] *Ibid.*, Clayton to Countess, 12 February 1774.

[2] J. F. Meyer, funeral sermon for the Countess, *The Saint's Triumph in the Approach of Death* (London, 1791), pp. 39–40.

[3] A. Crole and J. Eyre, *The Order Observed at the Opening of the Countess of Huntingdon's College at Cheshunt* (London, 1792), p. 15.

ready replacement for these two men. She wrote to Dr Henry Peckwell who was currently serving a London congregation to try to secure his services for Trevecca; but received a negative response from him. However, he remained a close friend both of the college and of Selina's until his premature death in 1787 at the age of forty-one.[1] Although it had never been her intention to preside over the college herself, after several failed attempts to fill Fletcher's place, Selina appeared to have decided that a president was not necessary. Instead she would spend more time in Wales herself. It is not easy to determine who was the resident tutor for the students during the next ten or more years. It appears that one of the senior students often undertook to instruct the other men,[2] while the various names that occur in the correspondence of the times suggest that other men helped out for short periods. Finally William Williams's son, John, took over the position on a more permanent basis in 1782.

In spite of these difficulties most of the students acquired a working knowledge of Latin and Greek, and some theology. But by far the best instruction both in the theology of the heart and in the art of preaching came from their opportunities to hear some of the most outstanding of the eighteenth century preachers. Men of the calibre of William Williams of Pantecelyn, Daniel Rowland, Peter Williams and John Berridge were frequent visitors to the college, sometimes preaching to the students and local people every day while in the area.

Some of the Welsh students faced added problems because of their limited knowledge of English. The Countess regarded it as imperative that these young men should be equally at ease preaching in either language. Writing to Thomas Jones in August 1772, she refers to the blessing that had accompanied his preaching in North Wales. She proposed to send him back there in

---

[1] Peckwell subsequently became Rector of Bloxham, Lincolnshire. A highly-gifted preacher and able academically, he would have been an excellent man for the position.          [2] C.F. Archives.

response to the request of the people, but added, 'I hope you will not lose your English too much by this means as I am not satisfied unless my Welsh students are English preachers. Our calls are so extensive that I think a greater blessing may arise to your own hearts by a more enlarged sphere of action.' To facilitate their mastery of English it appears that Selina arranged for those Welsh students who had already learnt the language to teach those who had not.

Although many of the students recalled their Trevecca days with gratitude, not all enjoyed equal measures of the Countess's favour. Some soon discovered that they could well incur their patroness's displeasure for a variety of offences. Henry Mead, a student recommended by Whitefield, had entered the college in 1769. Like Crole, Mead would become one of Trevecca's most capable preachers and was one of a limited number to gain ordination into the Church of England. His early days at college, however, could well have given the opposite impression. He was far from well at first and maintained he required 'a diet of water and gruel, currants and butter, instead of the beer and cheese with which the students were served.' More than this, the Countess found him not a little extravagant with her funds. In June 1771 he put in a bill of £15.15s to cover the costs of his shoes, candles, having his clothes mended, a woman to clean for him, a doctor's bill, a barber, a blacksmith for shoeing his horse, turnpikes on the roads and other incidentals. The Countess was not at all happy about this and wrote a strongly worded letter to her expensive student. Mead was at once most contrite:

> I confess that if the things alleged against me in your last letter are true that I have spent fifteen guineas when five or six would have done, I deserve hanging more than any highwayman that ever suffered at Tyburn.[1]

However he continued by pointing out that the situation was

[1] *Ibid.*

not as bad as it at first seemed as some of the expenses had been met from other funds.

Thomas Jones[1] also needed to be cured of an extravagant streak. He was working in Dublin during the early 1770s together with John Hawksworth, a student who held a unique place in Selina's affections. In a letter to Hawksworth she comments indignantly that Jones 'exceeds more in a quarter than you had in half a year. If this propensity of extravagance continues he cannot continue . . . Sedan chairs and barbers . . . I am quite amazed! I beg you will regulate matters with him. To spend and be spent in his [Christ's] service is my only honour.[2]

Generous to a fault, the Countess always kept a vigilant eye on the expenses that the students incurred and made economies wherever possible. A letter to John Clayton written in 1774 illustrates both the blessing of God that was attending the endeavours of the students at that time and the close watch Selina had to keep on the bills:

Dear Clayton,

I have your letter; it gave me much pleasure in finding your days are employed for so dear and faithful a Master as we serve upon earth . . . Great, very great, [is the] increase everywhere of the work! Such a gospel day have we not known. May our hearts live near the Lord, and in true poverty of spirit evermore be at his feet, waiting his gracious smiles and directions. All is well at college. The Lord Jesus is with them. Could your clothes do tolerably, till this very bad weather is a little over, it would be well. I know you are so clean and careful. I can never wish you to have less; but new clothes to ride in must so soon be spoiled at this season, that I will leave it with you to judge; and when you see fit, order them, and send me the bill. I hope to be at Bath next week. I am so hurried I have not a

[1] A number of men of this name trained at Trevecca. This student is not to be confused with Thomas Snell Jones who entered College in 1773.

[2] Hawksworth Correspondence, 12 April 1774, C.F. Archives.

moment to spare, but to assure you I ever am,
Your faithful and affectionate friend. S.H.[1]

Where a student was in real need the Countess did not hesitate
to arrange for him to have new clothes. William Dunn, pioneering
a new work in the Chichester area, told his patroness, 'the neces-
saries I had at Brighthelmstone last quarter were: a great coat,
four shirts, two handkerchiefs, a pair of trousers, two pairs of
stockings and one pair of shoes. What they come to I cannot tell
but think the bill could not come to £5.'[2]

Although most students expressed appreciation for their
privileges in studying at Trevecca, not all were satisfied with conditions at the college. William Tyler was a gifted young man, and
when he was introduced to the Countess in 1773 she conducted
the usual interviews with him to ascertain his spiritual standing.
'Perceiving that he possessed a good share of intellectual stamina
and a correct knowledge of the scheme of salvation' she proposed
that he came to Trevecca to study. Tyler made it clear that he was
anxious to give time to his academic work and particularly to his
Hebrew and Greek. To his dismay things turned out far differently from what he had supposed. No sooner had he arrived than
he found himself sent off to preach in some needy area of the
country. He complained ruefully that the Countess's passion to
reach the greatest number of people with the gospel in the shortest possible time meant that the would-be student was always on
the move and he was allowed little of the time he coveted for
language study. He only stayed a short time at Trevecca before
leaving to study at Magdalene College in Cambridge.

The more able the preacher, the more likely he was to be sent
out to preach rather than concentrating on his studies. But not all
students acquiesced in the arrangements that Selina made for
them. Thomas Suter put up a spirited defence:

[1] Aveling, *Memorials*, Letter to Clayton, 1 December 1774.
[2] C.F. Archives.

I beg your Ladyship not to be angry with me in reminding you of your past promises to me respecting my coming to college. Three years almost, I have been in your Ladyship's Connexion, and have not been in college three months, whilst others have been there the greater part of that time.

Remembering that the Countess was already seventy-five at the time he was writing, he added:

If God should be pleased to gather you home to himself, I must then despair of any opportunity to improve myself. Although learning does not make ministers, it is necessary for ministers to have it that they may be able to vindicate the truths of God.[1]

Anthony Crole, who, as we have seen, recalled his Trevecca days with gratitude, also had to make strong representations to the Countess that he needed more study time. He had 'resisted her Ladyship's importunity in the most respectful but decided manner', and insisted he could not continue at Trevecca unless he was 'permitted to enjoy those literary advantages that he had been encouraged to expect'.

The Countess did not minimize the importance of a well-educated ministry, nor depreciate learning,[2] but with vast tracts of the countryside still untouched by the Christian gospel, and congregations urging her to send a student to supply their churches, she felt she must balance one urgency against the other. For this reason too she felt obliged to ration the resources available and would not allow a student to remain more than a few months in any one place. On a number of occasions they wrote pleading to be allowed to stay with their congregations. Sometimes she would accommodate their wishes for a few more weeks, but her policy of moving the students on from place to place remained unchanged.

[1] *Ibid.*
[2] Her early support of Doddridge's Academy is evidence of this.

John Honeywill was one who found that if he did not comply with the Countess's wishes her anger could be aroused. After a period of ministry to a congregation in Melksham, Wiltshire, he had grown so fond of the people that he refused to return to college when asked. Without further ado, the Countess wrote expressing her extreme annoyance and ordered the young man to return both the pony he was using for his itineraries and his preaching gown which had been supplied to him by the Countess. To Honeywill's credit it must be said that he had a long and fruitful ministry in Melksham remaining there for the rest of his life.

It may well be that to our modern way of thinking Selina was arbitrary and dictatorial in the way she ordered the students from place to place. It must be remembered, however, that these young men were fed, clothed and taught at Lady Huntingdon's expense and she naturally felt she had a right to implicit obedience from them. These were the days when young people would be apprenticed to their masters to learn a trade. Not only would the better off be expected to contribute towards their training, but their masters had undisputed rights over them. Some would be 'bound apprentice' and legally obliged to remain with their masters a specified number of years. For the Countess to exercise such authority over her students, who contributed nothing towards their training and maintenance, would be the accepted norm for the times.

For many others, however, their period at the college was one of joy and satisfaction. Because of the Countess's generosity these young men were given a unique opportunity to receive an education they would never otherwise have had. Both Oxford and Cambridge had become averse to accepting students of known Methodist leanings. In any case many could neither have afforded to matriculate to university, nor were they academically qualified. More importantly Trevecca provided an entry to the work of the

Christian ministry that answered the spiritual desires of these earnest young men who wished to serve God and his people. We can catch the exuberance of one happy student as he writes to the Countess:

> I am so happy and blessed in my studying hours, I cannot fully describe. I eat my meat with gladness. It does me much good. I thank God for all things. My heart is much engaged night and day for your Ladyship and all your undertakings. O! I want to be God's praying servant . . . I did receive the bill your Ladyship sent for which my most ungrateful heart returns many thanks, but I trust my God will more and more abundantly reward my Lady for all her kindness to me.[1]

---

[1] C.F. Archives.

# 24

## Missionary Endeavour

'Give the Lord your youth and strength over the whole world. He is everywhere and that will make a happy earth as his presence will a happy heaven',[1] the Countess had urged the Trevecca students almost twenty years before William Carey sailed for India. Such was Selina's world vision in days when travel was limited to horse-drawn vehicles and a sea voyage was still a daunting and dangerous prospect. It can only be explained in terms of a love for the souls of men born of union with the Saviour who said, 'Other sheep I have that are not of this fold; them also I must bring.'

Trevecca College had been opened little more than a year when the Countess made her first attempt to send out two of the students as missionaries to the East Indies. Seven volunteered to go and all the names were written on pieces of paper and placed in a hat; two names were then selected by lot: William Hewer and George Pecore.[2] Asking the society meeting in Vineyards chapel in Bath to give a day to prayer and fasting for the success of the enterprise, the Countess equipped the young men with all they needed for the voyage and booked their passage on a vessel bound for the East Indies – an overall cost of £600. Formal ordination would be of benefit for the would-be missionaries and so

[1] Rylands MSS., Letter 139, 3 August 1772.
[2] In adopting this practice of casting lots, the Countess was following a biblical practice used extensively by the Moravians and also occasionally by Wesley, Grimshaw and the Inghamite societies.

she urged the Bishop of London to waive the normal rules and ordain her students at short notice. The Bishop obliged in Pecore's case, but with William Hewer, not yet eighteen years of age, he declined, as Hewer was too young for episcopal ordination in any case.

The enterprise, regrettably, was a failure. By the time the small vessel reached the Cape of Good Hope, battered by boisterous winds as it had plunged its way through high seas, Hewer was homesick and disillusioned. He wrote to the Countess saying that he wanted to return to England, adding that his spirits were so low that he felt he could never make progress in the Christian life until back on English soil.[1] Pecore meanwhile pressed on, but when he reached Sumatra he took paid employment as minister to the British garrison there, a far cry from Selina's intention. Writing to the Countess shortly after hearing of the failure of the mission, James Glazebrook was not dismayed: 'Shall we give up the cause we embarked upon and calmly submit to the old Serpent? God forbid! Rather let us rise up with holy revenge, being determined to sell our lives dear and to die in combat rather than to be found cowards.'[2]

As this first missionary endeavour was crumbling, Cornelius Winter, who had sailed for America with George Whitefield on his final trip, arrived home early in January 1771 bearing a copy of Whitefield's Will. And surprising reading it must have made for the Countess:

> In respect to my outward American concerns which I have engaged in simply and solely for his great namesake, I leave that building, commonly called the Orphan House at Bethesda in the province of Georgia, together with all the other buildings lately erected therein, likewise all other buildings, lands, negroes,[3] books, furniture and

[1] William Hewer died the following year while in a pulpit.
[2] C.F. Archives.
[3] In common with Whitefield and many others of her generation the Countess's attitude to slavery was ambivalent. Although she later modified her view

every other thing whatsoever which I now stand possessed of in the province of Georgia to that elect lady, that mother in Israel, that mirror of true and undefiled religion, the Right Honourable Selina, Countess Dowager of Huntingdon; desiring that as soon as maybe after my decease the plan of the intended orphan house, Bethesda College may be prosecuted, or if not practicable or eligible, to pursue the present plan of the Orphan House Academy on its old foundation and usual channel. But if her Ladyship should be called to enter into her glorious rest before my decease all is to be left to James Habersham.

Also £100 humbly beseeching her Ladyship's acceptance of so small a mite as a peppercorn acknowledgement of the undeserved, unsought honour her Ladyship conferred on me in appointing me, less than the least of all, to be one of her Ladyship's domestic chaplains.[1]

That Whitefield should leave all his American concerns to Selina in this way was a commentary on his assessment of her abilities. Although she had shown interest in the Orphan House that he had established on the banks of the Moon River, ten miles south of Savannah in 1739, and had contributed financially to it from time to time, her many other preoccupations had precluded any further commitment to his projects. To rest the entire responsibility for the buildings and the recently acquired estates[2] on the shoulders of a woman of sixty-five whose health was far from robust and who lived some three thousand miles distant, bears testimony to his confidence in his friend and patroness.

---

as the endeavours of men like Wilberforce heightened the issue in the national conscience, in the early 1770s she felt that if the slaves had Christian owners their lot would be improved and they would have opportunities to hear the gospel.

[1] Whitefield's Will, English MSS, Rylands.

[2] Known respectively as Bethesda, Nazareth, Ephraim and Huntingdon, these estates comprised almost 2000 acres of land.

At his death Whitefield was still negotiating permission to establish a college in Georgia and had already added two wings to the Bethesda Orphan House to accommodate the prospective students. He hoped the Countess would be able to bring this project to completion. James Habersham (once schoolmaster at Bethesda and now in overall charge of its affairs), was living in Savannah. He included an accompanying letter with the Will suggesting that there was indeed scope for an institution to be set up at Bethesda similar to Trevecca with ample employment for both a president and tutor. He had to admit, however, that Bethesda was in a state of some neglect and was at least £2000 in debt – a debt that the Countess would also inherit.

Far from being dismayed at the huge accession of responsibility so unexpectedly devolving upon her, Selina was elated at the prospect of these new opportunities. 'This opening in America', she wrote to John Hawksworth, 'is the astonishment of all that love and fear the Lord!' Cornelius Winter himself was clearly the right man to oversee the Bethesda complex. He had returned from America to seek ordination for that very purpose, and also to enable him to minister effectively both to the Indian and the slave population in Georgia. Carrying letters of recommendation, he arranged for an interview with the Bishop of London, but, try as he might, Winter could not persuade the Bishop to grant him ordination. His connections with Whitefield and his known evangelical position closed the door firmly on any such prospect. For many months he tried in vain to coax the Bishop to change his mind and all the time Bethesda was deteriorating through lack of supervision. The Countess, meanwhile, arranged for the few remaining orphans to be housed elsewhere. With Habersham living ten miles away and Winter still failing to gain ordination, she realized that she must make alternative provision for the oversight of Bethesda.

No more time could be lost. A circular letter was sent out requesting all her friends and the churches they served to set

aside 9 October 1772 as a day of solemn prayer and fasting for
the future of the Georgia enterprise. More than this, she asked as
many as were able to gather at Trevecca on 3 October. The letters
sent to students throughout the length and breadth of the
country carried an imperative that could not be denied: 'Don't
fail to be with us', she instructed Hawksworth in Dublin in a
manner that only a Countess could. 'I must insist, if able and
alive, come to Wales directly, to the college.'[1]

Many gathered in answer to her urgent appeal. She would need
an ordained man to lead the delegation to Georgia and act as
president for the new college; in addition, a qualified man was
needed as tutor to the students that she hoped to gather. Lastly
about seven volunteers from among the Trevecca students, would
be needed, men prepared to leave home and friends to sail to
Georgia. There they would oversee the orphanage, supervise the
slaves who worked the land, learn the Indian languages and begin
to evangelize the Indian peoples in the back settlements.

A week of special services of prayer, preaching and consultation
followed at Trevecca and soon all was settled. William Piercy,
who had been preaching at the Lock Hospital under Martin
Madan, following his dismissal from his previous church in West
Bromwich, was to head the party. A man of persuasive charisma
and some preaching ability, Piercy seemed a good choice and had
the confidence of the students. Another ordained and senior
man, Charles Eccles, together with his wife, was to accompany
the party and act as tutor at the new college. Seven students were
also chosen: John Cosson, described as 'the closest walker with
God', was to be superintendent; Joseph Cook, whose evangelistic zeal had already been demonstrated in earlier preaching
endeavours;[2] Daniel Roberts, William White, Lewis Richards,
Thomas Hill and Thomas Jones. Accompanying this student

[1] Hawksworth Collection, C.F. Archives.
[2] See below, pp. 336-7, 433-4.

contingent was Betty Hughes, the housemaid from Trevecca, who was to be housekeeper at Bethesda.[1]

After travelling to Abergavenny for the day of prayer and dedication on 9 October 1772, the party returned to Trevecca for a further weekend of special services. On 12 October they all set off for London. The enterprise required a further outlay of funds and Selina once again paid for all the clothes and other items needed by the students and booked their passage on the *Georgia Packet*. This vessel was bound directly for Savannah and her captain was prepared to give the students preferential treatment on the voyage. Farewell services of proportions never before experienced in English church life followed at the Tottenham Court Road Chapel. Then on 27 October 1772 six students[2] and Betty Hughes went on board. As the young missionaries walked up the gangplank the large crowd who had accompanied them to the ship's side waved their hats and handkerchiefs wildly. William Piercy, his brother Richard, together with Charles Eccles and his wife were to follow later.

The Countess lost no time in writing to her students to encourage them on their way. As the ship waited for a favourable wind, Betty Hughes replied to the letter she had received. 'I am greatly obliged for your sweet letter I received in the Downs. It comforted my heart to find the Lord so gracious as to give you the spirit of prayer for me.'[3] Not many days had elapsed, however, before troubles began to attend the embryo mission. While the ship was still waiting to set sail, William White became ill, apparently with smallpox and had to be put ashore at Dover. During the week of delay that followed the students took the opportunity to leave the ship at intervals, returning to check on the prospects

[1] It was Betty Hughes who had crept into the room unnoticed when Fletcher had been exhorting the students in November 1768, and had also been blessed by God together with them.

[2] Lack of any further mention of Thomas Jones suggests that he had decided against going.

[3] C.F. Archives.

for sailing. Joseph Cook with several others went to visit friends
he had made in Deal during evangelistic work in the area. When
Cosson received a message from White asking him to preach his
funeral sermon,[1] he too went ashore to visit the sick man taking
Betty Hughes with him. In the event the ship finally sailed with
only two of the students on board, Joseph Cook and John
Cosson, together with Betty Hughes.

Not surprisingly frictions between the two young men, both
inexperienced and far from home, developed during the long sea
voyage as they were cooped up together in cramped conditions.
A letter from Cosson to the Countess sent soon after the arrival
of the *Georgia Packet* in Savannah on 26 December 1772
complained of Joseph Cook's behaviour and also that of several of
the other students who had missed the ship. The voyage itself
had been without incident, however, and a short sentence in
Cosson's letter adds an interesting note: 'May the Lord give your
Ladyship as comfortable a voyage as he has given us.' Evidently
Selina herself was planning to visit Bethesda after her students
and Piercy had prepared the way – a hope to which she clung for
some years.

Meanwhile James Habersham greeted the three travellers on
their arrival and took them to his home. No sooner had they
arrived than John Cosson asked Habersham if he would conduct
a marriage service for himself and Betty – a request that surprised
Habersham, though he complied with it. From there Habersham
escorted this advance party to Bethesda. Perhaps Cosson's report
on the conduct of his fellow students – both Joseph Cook and
those left behind – was coloured by the depressing situation they
discovered on their arrival. The place appeared to be in a state of
neglect. The contents of the homes had been pillaged; with no
furniture, no sheets, nor any livestock. 'When I first saw this place
my heart sank greatly to see such a delightful place in such a
situation', he wrote dismally; while Betty added, 'We went

[1] White eventually recovered but died at the college six years later.

together to the bottom of the burying ground and there poured out our souls in prayer.' 'Don't send the other students,' urged Cosson, 'there is nothing here to support them.' A letter from Joseph Cook confirmed the sorry state of affairs.

It was too late. The second party including the three students who had been left behind had already embarked. Arriving off Charleston at the end of January 1773, they reported a voyage that had been far from easy. Even though Piercy had enjoyed privileged accommodation, with a cabin to sleep in, he had been prostrated throughout and feared that 'a further two days of sailing would have killed him'. Daniel Roberts complained of the bad weather and 'a cursing cruel captain and a set of ungodly companions', but he also recognized that he and his friends were to blame for their circumstances. As young believers they had been taken off their guard: 'Not expecting the enemy from the quarter he came . . . we left our watch tower.' He could add, however, that God had used his experiences for his good.[1] Roberts confirmed the sorry state of things at Bethesda. The house was about to fall down unless repaired, and there 'was not one individual thing about the house that moves except one cow, a calf, one lame horse and four oxen that draw the water.' Undaunted by these adverse circumstances, the Countess offered to send out further men and equipment to bolster the mission. Betty Cosson too took a positive view: 'At times when I feel my heart warm I long to fly to the old college and stand up and tell the young men to come out in the name of the Lord and to be courageous in his cause for indeed I am a living witness that the Lord does reward his people even in this life.'[2]

Not two months had passed since his arrival before Joseph Cook was bitterly regretting having come. His wish had been to evangelize the Indians, but William Piercy, who was already becoming autocratic in his dealings with the students, would not allow this. 'I am now, after being sorely tried and limited, unable

[1] C.F. Archives.                [2] *Ibid.*

to see my coming to America is of the Lord. Therefore I would not have come for a thousand worlds', he told the Countess. However, despite the adverse circumstances, in April 1773 an opening ceremony was conducted to launch the new college. Then a further blow struck the struggling cause. The tutor, Eccles, wrote to the Countess in dramatic, if not self-righteous, terms to inform her:

> You have been deceived, grossly deceived and by persons you could least have expected it from. Two days after the opening of the college publicly, Mrs Cosson was delivered of a boy and so privately that none of us had the least suspicion until the poor babe proclaimed his mother's shame by his loud cries.

John and Betty Cosson had been officially married just four months. Only now did it come to light that the young couple had been married secretly on a fair day at Trevecca the previous summer. When the premises were virtually deserted they had asked a layman, possibly a fellow student, to read the marriage ceremony for them in one of the college rooms. Not realizing she was pregnant, Betty had been too afraid to tell the Countess the truth of her clandestine marriage before she sailed. The punishment heaped on the erring couple by Piercy and Eccles was draconian. They were to be turned out of their accommodation, even though, as Betty told the Countess, 'I have not where to lay my head nor the poor infant except the ground.' They were to be expelled from Georgia forthwith and if Cosson attempted to stay Piercy would preach and write against him wherever he went.

Deeply penitent and fearing that the Countess too would cast him out, Cosson wrote expressing his sorrow and added that he had often prayed 'with tears trickling down to the ground that the Lord would take me out of the world rather than suffer me to be a scandal'. Selina, however, took a far different attitude to the situation. First she asked John Cosson to come home to explain himself and paid for his return fare. Betty was to stay at Bethesda with her child for the time being. As she found her student sincerely contrite, the Countess freely forgave him and instructed him to send for Betty. She suggested that for a period at least he should return to his former business. Overwhelmed with thankfulness, Betty wrote:

> When Mr Cosson wrote for me to come home and told me how kind and loving your Ladyship embraced him and forgave him all, it broke my heart to pieces. It was almost impossible for me to believe that she loves me.

'He has sealed a pardon on my heart many times,' Cosson told the Countess, as he was given an inner assurance of God's forgiveness. Expressing his deepest feelings in verse, he wrote:

> All thy backslidings I have healed, to me thou yet art dear
> My pardon on thy heart have sealed, trust me and do not fear.

Some months later the Countess paid for John and Betty Cosson to return to Georgia, though nothing was ever the same for them. Piercy refused to grant Cosson any opportunities to preach, leaving him feeling useless and distressed. Betty busied herself making garments for the slave labourers at Bethesda, though she too felt desolate and even more so when her infant died. 'Alone in a desert, my heart yearns for the living streams', she told the Countess.

William Piercy, whose position had given him an inflated view of himself, appears to have considered himself the natural successor to Whitefield in Georgia. He aimed to imitate him by spending much of his time travelling and preaching. Strictly adhering to Church of England protocol, Piercy also lost sight of the fact that many Dissenters had contributed to the expenses of Bethesda during Whitefield's lifetime – a key factor in Whitefield's own thinking.[1] So when a Dissenter asked Piercy

---

[1] This was why Whitefield himself had refused to comply with the demands of the Archbishop of Canterbury that he should bring his plans for an academy at Bethesda under the control of the Church, and appoint a Church of England man as its president.

whether she might be buried next to her husband at Bethesda when she came to die, he refused her request. This evoked local indignation and marked a nadir for Bethesda, not only for Piercy but for the Countess too, as it was assumed that Piercy was merely carrying out her policies.

These were the days immediately prior to the American War of Independence and feelings were running high amongst the colonists. On 26 May 1773 an article of complaint against Piercy's policy appeared in the *Georgia Gazette,* in which the Countess also came in for hostile criticism. Three days later Bethesda was burnt to the ground. This disaster, commonly attributed to lightning, could equally well or even more likely have been arson. Only Eccles and a few slaves were on the premises at the time; one of the slaves clambered onto the roof to try to extinguish the flames, but losing his grip fell and injured himself. While Eccles tried to treat him, the fire took hold and soon the whole Orphan House was destroyed, although the two new college wings were preserved. News of the fire stunned Selina. 'No trials through my life have been equal to these', she wrote to Piercy soon after she had heard. 'My heart has never fainted until now – indeed I am sinking.'[1] Not only were the buildings lost but also much of the personal property of the students with which the Countess had equipped them. Even though James Habersham wrote optimistically about rebuilding the orphan homes Selina knew that the cost would be enormous.

'I am very low in spirits ever since the house has been burnt', wrote Lewis Richards, one of the students. Prohibited by Piercy from preaching to the Indians in the back settlements as the Countess had intended, he felt he must be out of the will of God: 'It appears to me the Lord is against us in this place.' Worse than this, Piercy treated the young men as little more than servants. 'I am determined, I insist upon it. If you do not

[1] C.F. Archives.

comply you shall go from here. You are not noblemen's sons and you shall not be used as such in this house.'[1]

'We are kept in the greatest bondage', echoed Thomas Hill, confirming Richards' complaint, as he told the Countess of the man whom he had 'once loved and esteemed beyond any in this world. I never thought', he added, 'I should meet with such cruelty from him.' Even though her students were young and inexperienced, a fact that may have influenced Piercy in the way he treated them, the situation was far from satisfactory. Without doubt the Countess had chosen the wrong man to head up her American endeavour.[2] Perhaps she had consulted too little with those who knew Piercy's record better than she did. Deceived by his obvious preaching gift she had written euphorically before he sailed of 'his great abilities, his blessed disinterested zeal for the cause of Christ'. To her he was 'a great and eminent preacher of the glorious gospel . . . I have the highest opinion and greatest honour for him.'[3]

In contrast to the insensitive treatment meted out to the students by William Piercy was the consideration they received from the Countess. 'Your Ladyship's letters are more to me than gold', wrote Joseph Cook. Daniel Roberts felt the same: 'Your Ladyship's kind letter I received for which I can never sufficiently bless God and your Ladyship.' He was grateful for 'the spiritual admonition, the motherly and wholesome exhortations and the concern' she had shown for him. Eccles, the tutor had already returned to England and now all the four remaining students wished either to be given freedom to preach among the settlers and the Indians or to return home.

What could the Countess do at such a juncture? There seemed only one course open to her. She must give up the Georgia

[1] *Ibid.*   [2] In his *Church History*, Haweis comments: 'Her choice [of workers was] not always judicious, though seldom were there ever less offences in so extended a work.' p. 253.

[3] C.F. Archives. The Countess to William Tennent in Charleston, 17 November 1772.

enterprise, recall Piercy and bring the whole project to a close at least temporarily. Perhaps she would be able to release the Bethesda lands to the Georgia Assembly and thereby recoup some of her losses. As she was contemplating this step a letter arrived from Piercy, urging her to continue her endeavour, to honour Whitefield's memory and fulfil her own long held desire for the enlarged spread of the gospel. Taking an unfair advantage of her low spirits and her concern for the spread of the gospel, he persuaded her that all would be well, the local people would be willing to shoulder the expense of building as many chapels as she could send preachers to occupy. Opportunities for the gospel among the Indian peoples were numerous.

Still believing Piercy to be an honourable man, Selina trusted him and took heart once more. Writing to John Hawksworth in September 1773, she was again hopeful that there might be a future for the work:

> My last letter informs me how my way appears to be much to the Cherokee Indians and in all the back settlements. We are assured that people will joyfully build us churches at their own expense and present them to us to settle perpetually for our use. Some great – very great – work is intended by the Lord among the heathen. Should this appear I should be rejoiced to go myself to establish a college for the Indian nations. I can't help thinking but before I die the Lord will have me there, if only to make coats and garments for the poor Indians.[1]

Unable to go herself at present, the sixty-six year-old Countess decided to have a life-sized portrait painted of herself and sent out to Bethesda to bolster up the morale of her struggling students so far from home. The portrait, encased in a handsome gold leaf frame, was painted by John Russell, who intended it to be a symbolic representation.[2] Standing at the mouth of a yawning dark

---

[1] *Ibid.*   [2] Recently restored, this portrait is now in the possession of the Savannah Home for Boys.

cave, the artist depicted the figure of a woman simply dressed, with one foot trampling on her coronet. From her hand hung a laurel, an emblem of victory. According to Selina's daughter, Elizabeth, this particular portrait was a most accurate likeness to her mother at that particular time of her life.

Despite the portrait and the numerous letters written by the Countess, little could now be done to rescue her mission in Georgia. Following the outbreak of the American War of Independence her four students at Bethesda, Joseph Cook, Thomas Hill, Lewis Richards and Daniel Roberts, each scattered to various parts of the country and mainly became Dissenting ministers. Both Cook and Richards embraced Baptist principles, while Richards eventually became pastor of a church in Baltimore where he remained for thirty years until his death in 1832. Nothing further is known of John and Betty Cosson, apart from the fact of Betty's untimely death in 1776 after she and John had settled in the American backwoods.

With the war came a breakdown in communications and years passed without any word from William Piercy. News gradually filtered through of this unworthy man, that his use of the Countess's funds was dubious at best. He now 'travelled with a phaeton and four fine horses – caused himself to be drove by one of Lady Huntingdon's students – hired a servant at Philadelphia to whom he gave 25 guineas a year wages, beside having two stout negro boys to attend him.'[1] His brother Richard, who was still attempting to make the Bethesda estate profitable and self-supporting, was a better sort of man. Loyal to his elder brother, Richard initially kept silent but eventually added incriminating evidence of the way Piercy had played fast and loose with the Countess's assets. 'Not a single shilling for all the income of the estates of the orphan house or my own estate was accounted for', complained the Countess. To complete the sorry tale of his misconduct, when Piercy eventually arrived home in 1782 and was

[1] C.F. Archives, cited by Edwin Welch, *Spiritual Pilgrim*, p. 166.

given a cautious welcome by the Countess, he actually began to sue her through the courts for salary he said was owing to him for the years spent in America. Accusing her of the 'most unjust cruel and dishonourable conduct', he threatened a suit in Chancery unless she agreed to arbitration. Litigation proceeded along its wearisome course with Piercy making ever-increasing demands. The Countess handed over all correspondence to her legal advisers, but it does not appear from the extant letters that any satisfactory conclusion was ever reached.[1]

Unlike John Wesley, the Countess had supported the cause of the American colonists throughout the war. Although plundered by the British troops at one point, Bethesda escaped large-scale damage for this reason. When the war finally ended in 1782, the Countess engaged an American politician to oversee her affairs. He too failed her through preoccupation with his own concerns and the unsettled conditions in the country in the immediate aftermath of the war. Little more could be done, even though she sent out other students to represent her interests. Eventually one of the most capable and responsible of former Trevecca students, John Johnson, went to America in 1790 to take charge of Bethesda and the Countess's concerns. But even he failed. Though the property was left in trust to Lord Dartmouth in Selina's will, the Georgia legislature forcefully confiscated all the Bethesda lands soon after her death in 1791, placing Johnson under temporary arrest. The Bethesda complex was then administered under the direction of a board of thirteen trustees.[2]

---

[1] The correspondence relating to this unsavoury affair may be seen among the C.F. Archives.

[2] Ten years after the Countess's death, in 1801 Bethesda was established as the Savannah Home for Girls. A further fire devastated the building four years later. In 1845 125 acres of the original Bethesda tract of land was purchased and used as a home for boys. It remains so until the present time and still retains the original name of Bethesda Home for Boys. The home's museum displays memorabilia of both Whitefield and the Countess.

The Countess of Huntingdon's Georgia enterprise is a testimony to her tireless determination. Even though she had lost thousands of pounds of her personal funds as a result of the fire, had encountered grave problems due to the war and had been deceived by one in whom she had placed her confidence, she persisted in her endeavour. Her students, though young and inexperienced, had also persevered. None returned to Britain and, freed from Piercy's domination, conducted noteworthy ministries. Despite the problems they faced in the early months, we learn from Seymour:

> Their labours were crowned with singular success – many by their ministry received the light of the gospel and vast numbers of our sable coloured brethren were called by their preaching and conversation to the knowledge and love of our Lord Jesus Christ.[1]

Far from blunting the edge of her missionary zeal, these experiences, as we shall see, stimulated Selina's resolve to continue to use her means for the spread of the gospel world-wide. Her strong belief in the final triumph of the kingdom of God and her sense of her own part in such a conquest spurred her ever on to yet greater endeavour.

Perhaps it would be fitting to conclude this difficult period in the experience of the Countess of Huntingdon with a tribute from Cardinal John Henry Newman. Though no friend of evangelicalism, he yet had eyes to see in all these circumstances and in the whole course of Selina's life the selfless and sacrificial zeal of a noble woman:

> What pleases us is the sight of a person simply and unconditionally giving up this world for the next . . . Lady Huntingdon sets Christians of all time an example. She devoted herself, her name, her means, her time, her thoughts, to the cause of Christ. She did not spend her money on herself; she did not allow the homage paid

---

[1] Seymour, *Countess*, vol. 2, p. 262.

to her rank to remain with herself: she passed these on, and offered them up to him from whom her gifts came. She acted as one ought to act who considers this life a pilgrimage, not a home . . . She was a representative . . . of the rich becoming poor for Christ, of delicate women putting off their soft attire and wrapping themselves in sackcloth for the kingdom of heaven's sake.[1]

[2] Cardinal John Henry Newman, *Essays Critical and Historical* (London: Basil Pickering, 1871), vol. 1, pp. 387–8.

# 25

# 'THE SURPRISING SUCCESS OF
# OUR LABOURS EVERYWHERE'

THROUGHOUT THE 1770s the labours of Trevecca students were used by God to penetrate areas of the country where little gospel light had shone for many generations. A glance at many an old denominational record book covering the 1770s and 1780s repeats a pattern that soon becomes a norm for the period. 'The preachers of Lady Huntingdon's Connexion were at work all over the Black Country, preaching to large audiences in the open air', wrote a Staffordshire Congregational church historian, adding, 'the presence of Congregationalism in Staffordshire is due to the Countess of Huntingdon.'[1] Although it was a far cry from the Countess's intention to swell the ranks of Dissent, this was in fact the tendency of the many societies that came into being over this period as a direct result of the labours of Trevecca students.

The rapid expansion of the work astonished even the Countess herself: 'O! It is great indeed and is extending far and wide', she exclaimed in a letter to John Hawksworth. 'From the number of young men I have received into the college . . . it looks as if the Lord seems resolved to cover the earth with a knowledge of his truth by their means!'[2] Writing to the same student in September 1772 she expresses her delight at 'the surprising success of our labours everywhere – many times ten thousand hear each day.'

[1] A. G. Matthews, *The Congregational Churches of Staffordshire* (London: Congregational Union of England and Wales, 1924), pp. 100 and 265.
[2] Hawksworth Correspondence, 13 October 1773, C.F. Archives.

Hawksworth had been sent to Dublin in December 1771 to consolidate a work that Methodist preachers had already pioneered there. Unlike most other students the Countess kept him there for several years. An able preacher, he soon found the people flocking to hear him. A correspondent of Wesley's reports:

> Mr Hawksworth, a Calvinistic minister under Lady Huntingdon, has come here and preaches regularly at Methodist hours in a large room and to great congregations. He is to stay here for some time and when he goes another is to be sent in his room . . . I have heard his discourses so praised that I did wish to hear him.[1]

Over the years Selina wrote a number of letters to Hawksworth. These he valued and preserved. They may still be read today, and form a commentary on the progress of the Trevecca students. By 1773 Hawksworth had begun to travel from Dublin into the outlying areas of rural Ireland. Henry Mead, now beginning to show his worth, was sent, together with others, to help in the increasing opportunities in Ireland. But Hawksworth was feeling the need of formal ordination, so that he could administer the sacraments to the many converts of his ministry. Writing to the Countess he laid before her the situation and the need of another to fill his place during his absence. She replied affectionately:

> I shall write tonight to the college and lay before them the call for Ireland and your removal from thence. Indeed, dear Hawksworth, my heart is much with you, and ever since I have known you, you have been as a dearly beloved son to me in the gospel. Your faithfulness and great disinterestedness in the Lord's labours have so much united my heart to you.

In this letter of October 1773 Selina also gives one of the few references to the exact number of students in the college at any one time:

[1] Seymour, *Countess*, vol. 2, p. 166.

I have as clearly and exactly informed you of the state of the work as possible and the college has much of the power of God and over-flows at present with numbers. Twenty-four are there at present and lively honest souls, with the greatest harmony and love that ever subsisted in such a place.[1]

Probably this figure represents the highest number of students during any given year; more normally there would be between ten and fifteen young men living and working at Trevecca.[2] Requests for help and for the services of the students were now pouring in from all sides, and so Selina continues:

Dear and precious souls are walking miles to London hearing I'm there to beg our help in different parts where the gospel has never yet been preached. Wales is blossoming like a rose – in all the English parts as well ... I keep to my old rule of going nowhere but from the call of the people first.

Here the Countess states a policy that she had long established for deciding where to concentrate her endeavours. Her 'old rule' stipulated that she would not start a work without 'the call of the people first'. A letter from a William Small in Stamford, Lincoln-shire, indicates the type of appeal she so often received:

We were given to understand that applications to your Ladyship were so numerous that it was impossible to answer them all, that the more important stands of the ministry must be first attended to.

[1] Hawksworth correspondence, 13 October 1773. C.F. Archives.

[2] According to Dr Geoffrey Nuttall's study of the number of students at Trevecca, about 230 studied there during the twenty-three years of the Coun-tess's life. This would give an average yearly intake of ten men. However, since Dr Nuttall completed his study, between two and three thousand letters from different students kept in the Cheshunt Foundation Archives have been analysed and categorized by the late Dr Edwin Welch. A considerable number of additional names of students to whom reference is made in these letters or who wrote to the Countess must be added to that number. See G. F. Nuttall, 'The Students of Trevecca College', Reprinted from the *Transactions of the Honourable Society of Cymmrodorion*, Session 1967, Part 2.

Here let me stop and weep over my hopeless fate. Oh Stamford! Indeed, I tell your Ladyship the truth when I say that my eyes do so run down with tears that I could write with them instead of ink if that would move you to pity and compassion. Here is a large town filled with immortals. No gospel ministers in the place, nor have been for a great number of years.[1]

When unable to meet such urgent requests it grieved her deeply. 'My heart is broke', she told Hawksworth, 'not to be able to supply all.'

However, the strategy of going only where they were invited did not mean that Trevecca students remained in those centres of population where Christians were already to be found. Far from it. Having established a bridgehead and built up local support for their endeavour, they then ventured out into the unevangelized areas of the country. Here they would take up their stand by some market cross, or thoroughfare where people could gather and then preach boldly. Some students were received gladly, others suffered physical and verbal abuse.

A letter from Henry Mead, written in November 1770 from Bridgewater in Somerset, gives a typical instance of the way Trevecca students continued their work after first having consolidated a local base:

I preached standing upon a cross which was erected in the middle of some crossroads to a great concourse of people who in general gave the greatest attention. One poor man was greatly alarmed declaring he could not sleep since he heard me preach lest he should open his eyes in torments. I pointed him to Jesus the only sacrifice for sin.[2]

Anthony Crole had a similar experience:

While in the Isle of Purbeck I preached every night to hundreds of the most simple seeking souls I have ever seen . . . and although

[1] C.F. Archives.   [2] *Ibid.*

there they have not heard anything of the gospel until within these
last three weeks, not one single scoffer was there amongst the whole
. . . It would have rejoiced your Ladyship's heart to have seen them
coming out; the aged and infirm upon chairs and stools to hear the
word of God.[1]

An example of the Countess's policy in action can be seen in
the progress of the students' work on the Kent coast. When some
Christians from Dover applied to Selina early in 1771 for the help
of a student, she sent William Aldridge and Joseph Cook[2] to the
area. Aldridge,[3] himself a fearless character, began by borrowing
a chair from a nearby barber's shop. Stationing himself in the
market place he started to preach to the people streaming out of
the local parish church. Missiles of many descriptions were flung
at the young man by the dispersing congregation until he could
continue no longer. But the desired effect had been achieved and
dismounting from his chair Aldridge announced that he would be
preaching in a disused meeting house that evening for any who
cared to attend. In the following days he reported that some who
had earlier hurled abuse or worse now wept openly for their sins.

From Dover the two preachers ventured into Margate and then
further afield to Folkestone. Reaching Deal they encountered yet
more opposition, this time in the person of the curate, Dr
Nicholas Carter, who sent an angry letter to the Countess whom
he addressed as 'old Mother Huntingdon':

Madam, I am surprised at your intruding yourself upon me and my
parishioners. A woman of your rank and education I should have
thought would have known better than to be guilty of such rude-
ness. Pray who gave you leave to send your preaching fellows into
my parish? I desire you will command them to withdraw from Deal

[1] *Ibid.*   [2] As we have seen, Joseph Cook was one the students who sailed to
Georgia in 1772.
[3] Aldridge later recorded the Countess's delight in such preaching, where
the preachers had 'no pulpit but a table or a stool and no sounding board but
the canopy of heaven'.

forthwith, or I shall take steps to compel them to make a hasty
retreat . . . .I had enough of this business when your favourite
Whitefield preached here many years ago, and I will not suffer a
repetition of the same.[1]

Unable to make headway at Deal, Cook and Aldridge took their
message of hope and salvation to Canterbury where the reception
was more favourable. In later years chapels were built in several of
these places to accommodate the worshippers converted initially
by the endeavours of these two young men. Aldridge was later to
say of the Countess:

> She was most refreshed if some sinner had been cut down under
> the word and sent away weeping and seeking redemption in the
> blood of Jesus. I believe the news of £10,000 a year having been left
> her would not have been so pleasing to her as to have heard of the
> conversion of one soul to God.[2]

James Glazebrook, the student recommended by Fletcher from
Madeley, had been sent to Ashby, a difficult assignment, as Selina
well knew from her own experience. In May 1772 he could report
news that must have surprised the Countess: 'Crowds of serious
hearers attend [the services] and the Lord enlarges my heart to
speak to them . . . The great difficulty is the want of room. The
chapel is so thronged that people cannot get in.'[3] Not surprisingly
it was becoming unbearably hot, but the Countess had a suggestion to make. The wall between the chapel and the laundry room
could be knocked down, so giving extra space. A further letter
from Glazebrook makes an intriguing reference to a 'Nicodemus
apartment' in the enlarged chapel. According to tradition the
Vineyards chapel in Bath had such a curtained off corner where
the clergy and nobility might attend without being seen, but this
reference would indicate that such a procedure was also practised
elsewhere.

[1] Seymour, *Countess*, vol. 2, p. 133.
[2] W. Aldridge, *Funeral sermon*, p. 18.   [3] C.F. Archives.

A visit to the north-eastern port of Hull by Trevecca students in 1770 had an important consequence for the gospel in that city. Dr Joseph Milner, diligent, popular and highly capable, combined the offices of headmaster of the Grammar School and lecturer at one of Hull's most influential churches. Though far inferior intellectually to the erudite Milner, these students spoke of a wisdom through faith in the Son of God to which he was a stranger. Their preaching affected him profoundly and before long he became a new man in Christ. Reporting to Romaine on a letter she had received from Milner, the Countess told him that Milner had said that he thanked God that she had sent her students to Hull, for through them he had been convinced 'of the great necessity he was under of securing an interest in Christ.'[1] Joseph Milner's conversion was one of the most important factors that led to a widespread work of God in that city. So great was the transformation in subsequent years that Rowland Hill could refer to Hull as 'the garden of the Lord'.

Up until 1770 the chapels established by the Countess had not amounted to many more than half a dozen places of worship built largely at her personal expense. These were to be found in locations such as Bath and Tunbridge Wells where the aristocracy flocked for health and leisure. But now as her students took their lonely stand at market crosses and open-air thoroughfares in towns and villages, preaching boldly to people largely ignorant of gospel truth, societies sprang into being as converts gathered together for mutual encouragement and fellowship. Soon these groups of new believers began to express a wish for a place to worship other than the local parish churches, so often inimical to their vibrant faith.

Not far from the Countess's London home in Park Street was an old Quaker chapel situated in Ewer Street in the present day borough of Southwark. In addition to her regular invitations to the titled classes to hear preachers in her drawing room, she had

[1] Seymour, *Countess*, vol. 1, p. 305.

opened her kitchens during the weekdays for the relief and instruction of the less privileged. Now she determined to establish a chapel where these people could gather for worship. Ewer Street, tucked in between Blackfriars Bridge and Southwark Bridge on the south bank of the Thames was ideally situated and for some time the Countess sent her students to preach there. In 1770 she purchased the lease on the property and then opened it as a place of worship.[1]

Amongst the earliest chapels to be opened was one in Brecon, some eight miles from Trevecca. Here the visits of the students had quickly yielded a harvest of men and women whose lives had been transformed by the gospel preaching they had heard. Hay-on-Wye, another town not far from the college, also became a centre for the activities of these young preachers. Initially thwarted in their endeavours by the local clergyman, the students persevered steadily until in 1771 the prospects for erecting a chapel were bright. If students were preaching in locations within easy reach of Trevecca, Selina would often accompany them, halt her carriage nearby and support their endeavours by her presence and her prayers. Not infrequently she too would find herself sharing in the abuse suffered by the preachers at the hands of a hostile mob.

Meanwhile reports were coming in from far different parts of the country. Devizes in Wiltshire was responding to the preaching of Trevecca students, while in Dover, where William Aldridge and Joseph Cook had pioneered a work, a disused and crumbling Presbyterian chapel was leased to the Countess. In a letter to John Hawksworth in February 1773 she wrote of the rapidly expanding work: 'I have no fewer than four new establishments within

[1] It is interesting to note that the Countess owned some consols (government securities) which she sold at this time, possibly to fund the expenses of her rapidly expanding work. A letter from her broker is extant which reads, 'We have this day sold £1000 of consols at £1.0175: £1017.10s. Paid brokerage, £1.5s. £1016.5s has been placed to your Ladyship's credit in account. Signed: Boldero, Carter Bramston and Snaith. 3 January 1770.' C.F. Archives.

these few weeks: Hull, Woolwich, Gravesend and Lincolnshire.
O how I want your prayers and those of all who love or pray for
the prosperity of our Zion!'[1] Perhaps the encouragements at this
time heralded a better period of health. Certainly she was able to
add in a further letter to Hawksworth, 'I was ill two months but
am now better and able to ride on horseback – mighty like one of
the poor Welsh women – O that I had the grace many of them
have!'

Later in 1773 came another important new development, this
time in Worcester. Writing again to Hawksworth the Countess
reported that she had two new students working in Lincoln and 'a
chapel at Worcester which is an exceedingly handsome one is to be
opened by Mr Shirley on the 31 of this month [October 1773].'
Walter Shirley and Rowland Hill had often preached at Worcester and now the fruits of that ministry were being gathered in:

> It will afford you unspeakable pleasure to hear of the amazing
> success that has attended our labours in Worcester. The chapel was
> crowded and multitudes went away unable to gain admittance ... I
> know not which way to turn, I have so many applications from the
> people in various parts of the kingdom for more labourers ... I feel
> that if I had a thousand worlds and a thousand lives, through grace
> assisting, that dear Lamb of God, my best, my eternal, my only
> friend should have all devoted to his service and glory.[2]

Meanwhile John Hawksworth's own labours in Dublin made
the purchase of a building to accommodate his hearers of prime
importance. An early plan to buy land and build was abandoned
when a chapel in Plunkett Street became available. Formerly a
Presbyterian church, it was no longer needed when the work of
that denomination sank to a low ebb. The old chapel was quickly
altered and repaired, and soon became a centre for preaching not
only for Hawksworth but for many others who travelled and

[1] C.F. Archives, Letter to Hawksworth.
[2] Seymour, *Countess*, vol. 1, p. 442.

preached in connection with the Countess. In October of that same year she gave her student a thumbnail sketch of recent developments:

> The present state of the work is as follows: two new students are in the west; Nuben and Aldridge in the Wiltshire work, the latter just removed to Dover. White is in London serving a very large congregation I have been called to supply with college services. Smith I have taken into Connexion . . . He and another student supply Woolwich, Dartford and another place we are called to serve. Kent promises great things.

As if all this was not enough, at the same time as the Worcester chapel was being built two yet more ambitious plans were forming in Selina's mind. The first was for a chapel in Princess Street in the heart of Westminster. Here a famous and long established Presbyterian church had fallen into serious decline. Served in the past by men of the calibre of Dr Edmund Calamy, the church had drifted towards Unitarianism and the congregation had dwindled.[1] At the same time a circumstance had occurred that planted the thought of purchasing this commodious building, seating more than three thousand people, into the Countess's mind. When the fire at Bethesda had destroyed much of her Georgia property in May 1773 her long standing friend Dr Henry Peckwell[2] hastened to her London home to offer his condolences. But instead of spending three or four days with Selina as he had planned, Peckwell stretched his stay to nine weeks during which time 'he has preached in the fields, and Tower Hill . . . so that ten thousand people have heard the gospel at least that never heard it before.'[3] So many were gathered into the kingdom through the

---

[1] Dr Andrew Kippis, ardent protagonist for Dissenting liberties and better known as a writer than a preacher, had been the previous pastor.

[2] Peckwell, who had declined the Countess's invitation to be President of Trevecca after Fletcher's resignation, was currently rector of Bloxholm and Digby in Lincolnshire.

[3] Hawksworth Correspondence, C.F. Archives.

earnest preaching of this gifted man that a chapel was urgently required to house such a congregation. What better could she do than purchase the Princess Street chapel? Helped by the generous gifts of some of her well-placed friends, the building soon passed to the Countess and was renamed Westminster Chapel.[1] Writing to John Hawksworth on 2 April 1774, Selina could scarcely conceal her delight:

> A large chapel of mine, holding more than three thousand is to be opened next week; this being in the heart of Westminster requires our most eminent ministers to follow up that preparation of heart the Lord has wrought.

As the congregation had been gathered as the result of Peckwell's preaching, he served it regularly until his death in 1787. When he was fulfilling other commitments the Countess arranged for preachers such as Thomas Haweis, Thomas Pentycross, William Jesse and Augustus Toplady to preach there.

No sooner was Westminster Chapel established than Selina was planning further projects for the advance of the kingdom of God. Her next thought was to buy the lease on land in Wapping, in east London. It was known as the 'Mulberry Gardens' because its location was marked by little else than a few mulberry trees. Here she would build a 'very, very large chapel' to provide another place of worship for a London congregation – a congregation far different from the well-to-do one she might expect at Westminster Chapel. Standing under the mulberry trees John Clayton, who had not long finished his Trevecca course, preached to all who would listen. With the help of men such as Henry Peckwell and a Lawrence Loughlan, recently returned from Newfoundland, a potential congregation was soon gathered. Purchasing the lease, though it had only twenty-one years to run, the Countess soon

---

[1] Whether the present day Westminster Chapel, erected in 1865 to replace an earlier chapel erected in 1841, was built to accommodate the successors of this same congregation is unclear but certainly possible.

engaged builders. Problems arose, however, and the Mulberry Gardens chapel was not opened for several years to come.

'Our work is spreading beyond the bounds of all our hopes', reported Selina in 1775. Chapels wishing to come under her auspices multiplied up and down the country. For the most part these consisted of meeting places built or bought to accommodate the congregations that came into being as the result of the preaching of Trevecca students. Whenever possible the Countess insisted that the local people who felt the need of a place of worship should fund it themselves, but in almost every instance she would add a generous contribution to the mounting expenses. Sometimes small groups of people took on projects that were far beyond their means and then turned to the Countess to bail them out. There were others who wished for the benefit of a place of worship but were little prepared to make any sacrifice to obtain it. Thomas Suter, another student, described the attitude of the people of a town where he had been preaching: 'I have endeavoured to try the disposition of the people with respect to the erecting or purchasing of a house for the worship of the Almighty but with little effect', he told the Countess. 'With many, as much religion as you please but keep out of my pocket. Touch my pocket – farewell religion, gospel, Christ's ministers and all.'[1]

In Bristol itself, scene of some of the earliest preaching of the revival, the Countess had erected a large place of worship twenty-two years previously to accommodate Whitefield's burgeoning congregations. Now, in 1775, as eager congregations continued to throng the Tabernacle, she decided the time had come to seek further premises nearer to the Hot Wells, a popular resort for the aristocracy, and also closer to her Clifton home. With an eye for seeing potential in existing buildings, Selina noticed a large Assembly Room sometimes used as a theatre in the area that she had in mind. A lease on the building of £40 a year was soon

[1] C.F. Archives, 28 February 1784.

negotiated and all that remained to be done was to transform it into a place of worship.

During this same year, 1775, a year in which the Countess herself was far from well, chapels were opened in numerous other places. In Maidstone, where William Aldridge and Joseph Cook had pioneered a new work, capacity congregations attended the opening services of a place of worship in November. In Norwich, the well-frequented Tabernacle that had passed from Wesley's preacher, James Wheatley, to the Countess and back again to Wheatley, finally came into the possession of the Countess as she negotiated a lease of £40 a year from Wheatley who now had only months to live. At Dorchester where Thomas Molland, another Trevecca student, had noted that 'the work here has suffered for a long time for want of room' a similar provision met the need. In the meantime reports were coming in of new buildings erected, leased or taken over in Gainsborough, Guildford and Petworth in Sussex.

It cannot be imagined, however, that any work of God could increase at so remarkable a speed without setbacks and opposition both from friends and enemies. Only a strong belief in the ultimate purposes of God for the success of the gospel nerved Selina to discount trials, opposition and criticism and to hold on with steadfast faith. An anecdote, recounted by Thomas Haweis, relates to this time. Evidently one of the bishops had complained to Francis Hastings about his mother's chapel building programme: 'I wish, my Lord, you would speak to Lady Huntingdon. She has just erected a preaching place close to my palace wall.' 'Gladly,' said his Lordship, 'but will you do me the favour to inform me what to urge, for my mother really believes the Bible.'[1]

Internal strife, strong differences of opinion, place-seeking and jealousy could also be found among the Countess's own supporters. Never a one to handle or defuse disagreements with any ease,

---

[1] Haweis, *Church History,* vol. 3, p. 254.

the Countess missed her friend George Whitefield most acutely at this point. To Augustus Toplady, therefore, she turned for advice when serious problems broke out while the Mulberry Gardens chapel was being erected. There appear to have been two main areas of contention, the first being over the choice of a resident minister. A strong opponent of settled ministries, the Countess was not happy when Lawrence Loughan from Newfoundland, whose preaching had helped to raise the congregation for whom the chapel was being built, wished to take over the pastorate. Only when he withdrew, urgently denying that he had ever entertained such a thought could the project proceed.

The second problem to beset the endeavour concerned the trustees of Whitefield's chapel at Tottenham Court Road, whom the Countess had appointed as trustees for the new work. Perhaps they were taking more upon themselves than Selina thought appropriate, for it seems they were hinting that they wished the new chapel to be registered as a Dissenting meeting house like Tottenham Court Road Chapel. She also suspected them of dealing less than honourably with her funds earmarked for the new chapel. Acting swiftly and ruthlessly the Countess immediately relieved them of their responsibilities. It took all of Toplady's wisdom to sort out the disputes. More than this, Selina received a strongly worded letter from her old friend John Berridge, reprimanding her fearlessly for her precipitate action in dismissing good and upright men in this way. In typical Berridge style he wrote:

Indeed, my Lady, I have seen and heard some things to please and some things to grieve me . . . I was told the trustees were suspected of a design on your Mulberry Gardens. What has occasioned the suspicion I know not, but I well know they had no more desire to steal your mulberries than to steal my teeth; I believe the profit of the mulberries (if that base thing had been in view) would no more enable them to buy a crust than my old teeth would enable them to bite it . . . Indeed my Lady, I am well satisfied that the trustees have been your hearty friends and faithful servants; and am sorry to find they are much offended at your suspicions. Could I discern lucrative views in them, as much as I love the Tabernacle (that old bee-hive which has filled many hives with her swarms), I would visit her no more, but the more I know of the trustees the more I am confirmed of their integrity.[1]

It need only be said that his letter seems to have been well-received by the Countess and soon the problems were resolved.[2] The builders resumed their work on the Mulberry Gardens chapel, which was at length opened for public worship in 1777.

When the cynic, Horace Walpole, had visited the chapel in Bath in 1765 he had been impressed with the quality of the singing he heard there. These musical compositions were the work of Benjamin Milgrove, a skilled musician who kept a fancy goods and toy shop in Bond Street, Bath. He was precentor and organist at the chapel and composed a number of hymn tunes, many set in parts with detailed instructions in the music for men and women to sing alternately. Some of Milgrove's work has proved of lasting excellence, with tunes still in use in the churches of today.[3] 'The singing here', reported a student in 1771 'exceeds anything in London. I suppose on Sunday evening we have a hundred hearers extra.'

Yet it was the singing that caused some of the most intransigent problems in Bath. Milgrove soon became upset because the singers were not performing his compositions according to his liking.

[1] Berridge, *Works*, p. 514.

[2] Whether the Countess reinstated the trustees is not mentioned in the correspondence of the times, but the fact that there were no further problems suggests that she did.

[3] The tune 'Harts' commonly set to John Cennick's words, *Brethren, let us join to bless,* and Charles Wesley's *Light of life, seraphic fire*; 'Mount Ephraim,' later adapted and called 'St Helena', commonly sung to Isaac Watts's hymn, *Come we that love the Lord;* and the tune 'Harwich', sung to Wesley's hymn, *All ye that pass by* (numbers 115, 369, 641 and 647 respectively in *Christian Hymns*) were all composed by Milgrove.

In 1772 he complained to the Countess that 'there is a division among the singers and my music is sadly mangled for want of proper attendance to learn'.[1] Although the situation was eventually sorted out, Milgrove was never again quite at ease with the way his compositions were used.[2]

Music and singing continued to play an important part in all the Countess's chapels. The fervour of a true and lively faith seemed to find its natural expression in song throughout the Methodist revival. The Countess's hymn book, a book that formed a unifying factor and a badge of identification in all her churches, both then and far beyond her own life span, went through numerous editions. The first, as we have seen, was printed in 1765 and contained 231 hymns. In 1770 a further edition was published with the addition of a few extra hymns, making 243 in all. By 1780 a hymnbook with 304 hymns had become the standard for the rest of the Countess's life and until 1854. These dumpy little books, measuring about three or four inches square, were bound in red morocco leather with gold tooling.[3]

The choice of hymns was largely her own, and each edition carried the words, 'Collected by her Ladyship' on the title page. In all probability, however, she was helped in the endeavour by her cousin Walter Shirley. Comprehensive in her choice, the Countess incorporated into her selection hymns by all the important eighteenth-century writers across a wide spectrum of doctrinal emphases. The work of Isaac Watts, Charles Wesley, Philip Doddridge, John Newton, William Cowper, Augustus Toplady, John Cennick, Walter Shirley, William Williams, Count

[1] C.F. Archives.

[2] Milgrove subsequently published his hymn tunes in instalments with Book 3 appearing in 1781 under the title, *Twelve Hymns, Set to Music for Four and Five Voices, with Organ Accompaniments*. These he dedicated to the Countess.

[3] I am indebted to Mrs Margaret Staplehurst, archivist of the Countess of Huntingdon's Connexion, who has made a particular study of these hymn books and owns several early copies.

SELINA COUNTESS OF HUNTINGDON

Zinzendorf, Joseph Hart, Gerhard Tersteegen and Anne Steele
was well represented.[1]

Without doubt, the quality of the singing at the Countess's
chapels proved an attraction to the outsider, though in at least one
other instance it was a cause of complaint. The Mulberry
Gardens chapel had been built so close to an existing Independent church in the adjacent Nightingale Lane that its pastor, Henry
Mayo, lodged a complaint with the Protestant Dissenting
Deputies saying that the singing at the chapel next door was so
loud that he could not be heard when he was preaching.

'Each week, each day brings new cries of "Come over and help
us"', wrote the Countess of Huntingdon to John Hawksworth
towards the close of 1778. Such words sum up this seventh
decade of her life: 'The burden and heat of the day must still continue my lot and while I am able to sustain it I am willing, living
or dying, to yield myself a poor unprofitable servant into his
hands.'[2] Seventy-one years of age, frail and tired, this dedicated
servant of Jesus Christ knew that she must carry on her labours
while life and strength remained. The 1770s had proved to be
years of rapid and unprecedented expansion in the work to which
the Countess had dedicated her time, strength and means. Often
she had looked with longing to a better country where she could
rest from the multitude of her exertions. But again and again the
pressing needs of her generation renewed her desire to serve her
God yet a little longer. To John Hawksworth she wrote:

Come life, come death, come devils, men or all their hosts of
infernal legions, yet the last moments will be so sweet as to make
good amends for all my sorrows.[3]

[1] John Julian includes an interesting article on the Countess's hymn books in
his *Dictionary of Hymnology* (London, 1892), p. 543, although Dr Edwin
Welch regards his list of editions as incomplete.
[2] C.F. Archives, Hawksworth Correspondence, 5 December 1778.
[3] Seymour, *Countess*, vol. 2, p. 188 (21 October 1781).

# 26

## OLD FRIENDS AND NEW

'I LIVE WITH MY PEN IN MY HAND', wrote the Countess to a friend in October 1776. One of her students has left it on record that sometimes she would sit six or seven hours a day, corresponding with Trevecca students on both sides of the Atlantic. Answering the incessant stream of letters would be time-consuming enough for someone in the best of health, but in addition to Selina's continued periods of illness, she was also experiencing increasing trouble with her eyesight – a factor that may well explain her often large and at times almost illegible handwriting. A number of letters written to her during the 1770s make reference to this problem. But pain in her eyes and physical weakness, arising from a recurring constriction of the throat that often reduced her to a liquid diet, did not deter the Countess from her ceaseless attempts to encourage her students and maintain contact with a growing circle of correspondents.

Nor did she forget old friends. Some she had lost in death. Her brother-in-law, early guide and friend, Benjamin Ingham, had never recovered from the ruin of his life's work in 1762 and when his wife Lady Margaret died in 1767 he appears to have found the loss insupportable. Little is known of his last days and in 1772 at only sixty years of age he too passed beyond his sorrows and disappointments.

Howell Harris died the following year, in July 1773. Thirty years had passed since Selina and he had first met. The friendship had been stormy at times, like many of Harris's relationships, and particularly towards the end of his life. In 1772 he had supported a student whom the Countess expelled from the college, and had complained to John Wesley who visited him that August, 'I have borne with these pert ignorant young men vulgarly called students, till I cannot in conscience bear any longer'. Harris's sentiment was in keeping with Wesley's own at the time, and recording it in his journal, Wesley added, 'What better can be expected of raw lads of little understanding, little learning and no experience?'[1] Selina's tribute when Howell Harris died was genuine and heartfelt. To William Romaine she wrote on 29 July 1773: 'It is impossible to describe the grief that is manifested everywhere . . . he was so beloved and so esteemed as the spiritual father of multitudes . . . Truly his loss is felt at the college where many were awakened by his lively ministry.' Describing his funeral she wrote:

> It was a day never to be forgotten . . . Not fewer than 20,000 people were assembled on this solemn occasion . . . to pay their last tribute to the remains of a great man. We had three stages erected and nine sermons addressed to the vast multitudes, hundreds of whom were dissolved in tears . . . . God poured out his Spirit in a wonderful manner. Many old Christians told me they had never seen so much of the glory of the Lord and the riches of his grace, nor felt so much of the power of the gospel before.[2]

Far different had been the death four months earlier of Lord Chesterfield. Despite having a godly wife and a sister like Lady

[1] Wesley, *Journal*, vol. 5, p. 482. Some Trevecca students may indeed have been 'pert and ignorant' but the attitude of these two pioneer preachers was also coloured by the fact that the Countess had achieved what they had both wished to do but had not accomplished for different reasons. The only way into the recognized ministry of the Church of England up until this point had been through a classical education at Oxford or Cambridge. These men, on the other hand, chosen for their preaching gifts and spiritual zeal but often with limited educational advantage, were now being offered the same privileges as better-placed young men.

[2] Seymour, *Countess*, vol. 2, pp. 291–2.

Gertrude Hotham and also the privilege of having heard Whitefield preach, Chesterfield had remained a hardened unbeliever. Even though he had affected Francis so adversely, the Countess, surprisingly, still spoke of him as her friend, but wrote, 'The blackness of darkness, accompanied by every gloomy horror, thickened most awfully around his dying moments.'[1]

The death of Lady Gertrude Hotham two years after her brother was a severe loss to Selina. Lady Gertrude's daughter, an early convert of Selina's Chelsea Farm gatherings, had died in 1750; but her son, Sir Charles, who had also listened to Whitefield's preaching, had made no profession of faith. In 1759, however, the death of his young wife to whom he had been married only two years, caused Sir Charles to turn at last to the enduring joys to be found in God. He was a capable young nobleman, whose conversion strengthened the cause of the gospel among the aristocracy and he became his mother's brightest hope and encouragement. Together with John Thornton and Lord Dartmouth he used his substantial means in support of evangelical testimony.

The premature death of this influential young man in 1767 was a heavy burden for his mother.[2] Her own course had only eight more years to run. In the spring of 1775 as Lady Gertrude sat reading a letter by an open fire she leant too close to it. The flames caught the ruffles on her clothes and quickly spread to the shawl around her neck and over her head. For a fortnight she suffered the effects of extensive burns with patient submission. As the doctor dressed her wounds she would speak to him of the tender kindness of her God to a poor sinner. Despite her pain Lady Gertrude yet maintained a thankful spirit to the end, and her last words, reminiscent of Lord Buchan's spoken just before he died, were 'Enough! . . . happy . . . happy.'[3]

[1] *Ibid.*, vol. 1, p. 464.
[2] When Sir Charles died he left the reversion of his Suffolk, Kent and Middlesex estates to the Countess. Documents in Huntington Library, California.
[3] Henry Venn writes of this to Mrs Riland in June 1775. *Letters of Henry Venn*, p. 225.

That same year it seemed that the life and service of John Wesley himself was drawing to a close. Notwithstanding all that had happened in recent years to mar their long-standing friendship, when news filtered through of his serious illness in June 1775, Selina was deeply concerned. While on a tour of Ireland Wesley had been drenched as the rain came pouring through the thatched roof of his lodging house not far from Londonderry. Regardless of the chill he had received, the seventy-two-year-old preacher travelled on fulfilling all his engagements. Even when seized with a fever three days later, he continued to travel and preach until he finally collapsed and for some days lay almost unconscious, hovering between life and death. The Countess, who was in Bath at the time and far from well herself, hastened to write to Charles Wesley to enquire after John:

> Christian affection engage[s] me to enquire after my old friend, your brother, who, I have heard this day (and not before) is so ill. Not being well myself, the hearing of his danger has affected me very much . . . and I do grieve to think his faithful labours are to cease yet on earth. How does an hour of loving sorrow swallow up the just differences our various judgments make . . . I have loved him this five and thirty years and it is with pleasure I find he remains in my heart as a friend and a laborious beloved servant of Jesus Christ. I will hope yet the Lord may spare him . . . May the Lord bless you and yours and cause the inseparable bond of his Spirit so to unite all our hearts to himself as to make us one in him and one with each other and that even when the rugged and crooked paths of mortality may separate for his wise and best purposes. I beg all that's kind to dear Mrs Wesley and I must ever alike remain your obliged friend. Bath, June 28 1775. Forgive the hurried scrap wrote with bad eyes, pain of body and of mind.

When Charles Wesley replied to Selina's letter a week later his answer was brief but depressing, as far as his brother's condition was concerned:

I deferred acknowledging your Ladyship's enquiry in hopes of sending you better news; but every letter from Ireland calls us to give up our friend. We expect to hear by the next that he has finished his course.

The work of all three is nearly finished; we shall be in our death not divided.

My partner presents her duty and thanks you for your kind remembrances of her, wishing you all the blessings purchased for you. I remain, your Ladyship's ever obliged servant.[1]

In the event, John Wesley gradually pulled back from the brink of the grave. As soon as he was able to move, 'trusting in God, to the astonishment of my friends, I set out for Dublin.' Within a week he was preaching once more. Charles Wesley's wistful comment that in death they would be no longer divided, was his last known communication with Selina.

With the after-effects of the 1770 controversy still rumbling on, it is not surprising that the Countess's student preachers should find themselves embroiled in a measure of conflict with Wesley's preachers, each accusing the other of doctrinal aberrations. A final letter from John Wesley written on 15 September 1776, in reply to one from Selina, addressed this issue:

I am so entirely satisfied with your Ladyship's favour of 8th instant that I cannot refrain from writing a line by a first opportunity to return my sincerest thanks. Your Ladyship observes extremely well that as all human creatures have a right to think for themselves, I have no right to blame another for not being of the same judgment with me . . . I also am persuaded that your Ladyship is not sensible of the manner wherein a number of the students have treated me. But let that pass. If your Ladyship will be so good as to give them a caution on that head I know it will not be in vain.

When Wesley laid the foundation stone of the City Road Chapel in London the following year, 1777, he allowed himself a

[1] Rylands MSS. Letter 81.

comment on Trevecca which, though partially true, would not have pleased Selina. It was, he said, in reality 'a school for training Dissenting ministers'. Rowland Hill immediately sprang to the defence of the Countess and published a provocative pamphlet in which he accused Wesley himself of 'building Dissenting meeting houses the kingdom over'.[1]

The Countess had more to do with John Fletcher than with the Wesley brothers during the 1770s. The breach with the Vicar of Madeley had been most painful. Writing many years after the controversy, Joseph Benson said of Fletcher, 'He was loved, he was obeyed, nay and almost adored, and that as well by her Ladyship as by every student.'[2] After Selina had complained to Fletcher that he had quoted in print the comment she had made in a private conversation,[3] he had made her a fulsome apology. Her letter of forgiveness was as sincere as the apology, and Fletcher was grateful. He wrote in September 1773: 'My dear Lady, How kind to your old servant in writing to me such cordial forgiveness for all my past transgressions . . . Receive my warmest thanks for such unexpected and undeserved tokens of Christ's love.' In February 1774, however, the Countess still remained anxious to repair the breach between herself and the man in whom she had placed utmost confidence in respect to her students at Trevecca. A face-to-face meeting would be far more likely to resolve any differences and so while she was in Bath, she approached a mutual friend, John Ireland, asking him to contact Fletcher and invite him to Bath.

In his reply to Ireland, Fletcher was again most grateful for the Countess's initiative. His first instinct was to go immediately. 'It is well for her that spirits are imprisoned in flesh and blood or I might by this time (and it is but an hour since I received your letter) have troubled her ten times with my apparition.' His comments on Selina in this letter were typically large-hearted as he

[1] Tyerman, *Wesley*, vol. 3, p. 256.　　[2] Rylands MSS.
[3] See above p. 284.

described her 'generosity,' her 'courage and a mind so much superior to the narrowness that clogs the charity of most'. However, Fletcher declined the invitation. He was still fully occupied in writing further polemics in defence of Wesley's position and was well aware that any renewed friendship between them would compromise both. 'I must follow my light', he reasoned, and 'I cannot do this without advancing some truths which I know her Ladyship receives as well as myself, but which, by my manner of unfolding them, will appear dreadful touches to the gospel of the day.'[1] Although cordial relations had been restored, there is no further reference to any future contacts between Fletcher and the Countess.

Even though some old friends had died and some had distanced themselves from Selina, others were still warm and friendly. John Berridge, as quaint and pithy in his expressions as ever, remained unchanged. 'Your letter just suited my case', he wrote, 'It was a plaster for a bleeding heart.' As he thought back on days he had known of God's evident power, he commented wistfully, 'I cannot wish for transports such as we once had, and which almost turned our heads; but I do long to see a spirit poured forth of triumphant faith, heavenly love and steadfast cleaving to the Lord.'[2]

John Berridge remained the one man who could speak frankly to the Countess and know he would not cause offence. In 1777 she had become troubled because of an increasing tendency among her students, and the churches which had sprung up as a result of their ministry, to join the Dissenters. Berridge had some wise words of caution for her:

Well, now I am prattling, I must even prattle on; an old man's tongue is like an alarm, when it sets off . . . I regard neither high-church nor low-church nor any church, but the Church of Christ,

[1] Tyerman, *Wesley's Designated Successor,* p. 300.
[2] Berridge, *Works,* p. 507.

which is not built with hands, nor confined to a singular denomination . . . What will become of your students at your removal?
They are virtual Dissenters now and will be settled Dissenters then.
And the same will happen to many, perhaps most, of Mr Wesley's
preachers at his death . . . Some years ago two of my lay preachers
deserted their ranks and joined the Dissenters. This threw me into
a violent fit of the spleen, and set me a-coughing and barking
exceedingly; but when the phlegm was come up and leisure
allowed for calm thought I did humbly conceive the Lord Jesus
might be wiser than the old vicar and I did well in sending some
preachers from the Methodist mint among the Dissenters to revive
a drooping cause . . . Dissenters may appear wrong to you, God hath
his remnant among them, therefore lift not up your hand against
them for the Lord's sake; nor yet for consistency sake, because your
students are as real dissenting preachers as any in the land.[1]

This was a timely warning for the Countess and a predictive one
too. Finding themselves increasingly unable to gain ordination into
the Church of England, her students were swelling the ranks of
Dissent in considerable numbers. According to her own principles,
the Countess should have been glad. Trevecca had been established in the first place to serve the whole Church of Christ, but
clearly she now had a problem when faced with the practical implications of those principles. Dissenters were still regarded with
suspicion and denied educational and social advantages.[2] Selina's
loyalty to the Established Church was deep-rooted.

Another friend whose care was becoming increasingly important to the ageing Countess was Lady Anne Erskine.[3] She,
together with Jenetta Orton, had been a constant companion and
personal assistant since she first accompanied the Countess on her

[1] *Ibid.*, pp. 515-6.
[2] In 1789 William Wilberforce could speak of 'the general evils of Dissent'
and say, 'The increase of Dissenters is highly injurious to the interests of
religion in the long run.' Cited by L. E. Elliot-Binns, *The Early Evangelicals*
(London: Lutterworth Press, 1955), p. 211.
[3] Lady Anne lived from 1740 till 1805.

travels in the late 1760s. As Selina grew frailer Lady Anne took on more and more responsibilities, answering letters and overseeing arrangements, but always deferring to the Countess for any final decision. A close bond of affection and unity of purpose sprang up between the two. Although more than thirty years separated them in age, Anne Erskine's letters to the Countess, written whenever they had to be apart, reveal the depth of her devotion. More than this, she understood her older friend and the Countess often felt able to confide her feelings in her letters to Lady Anne. Hannah Scutt, daughter of a member of the church in Brighton, was another younger woman on whom Selina now increasingly relied for help with the growing burden of administration.

Willielma Campbell, better known as Lady Glenorchy,[1] also remained in touch with Selina. Converted through the influence of Rowland and Richard Hill's sister, Jane, she had spent time at Bath in 1765 during which she had grown fond of the Countess and had been influenced by her example of dedication of all she possessed to the service of Christ. Willielma had followed this example to a marked degree and had also used her means to set up chapels both in Scotland and in England for the preaching of the gospel. From the beginning she had taken an active interest in Trevecca and had sent several large gifts of money to Selina to help in this costly commitment. One in endeavour and vision, Lady Glenorchy linked her work with the Countess's at a number of points. Her own concern for theological education led her to leave £5000 in her will to Jonathan Scott, the soldier converted at Ote Hall in 1759,[2] to set up an institution similar to Trevecca for training young men for the ministry.

Richard de Courcy, one of the Countess's travelling preachers, became Willielma's personal chaplain early in 1771, while the

---

[1] Lady Glenorchy lived from 1741 till 1786.
[2] See references to Scott above, p. 196–8. A close friend of Richard and Rowland Hill, Scott had established many chapels in the Midlands and the North of England.

chapels she established in England were regularly supplied with preachers from Trevecca. When she was most in need of a preacher for her chapel in Edinburgh it was to one of the Countess's former students that her attention was directed. John Clayton, the young man who had suffered much with nerves when he first began to preach, was Lady Glenorchy's choice. But Clayton was just about to be ordained as the minister of the Weigh Bridge Presbyterian Church, London,[1] when she wrote. Unable to accept her invitation, Clayton recommended his friend, another Trevecca student, Thomas Snell Jones, for the position.[2] An invitation from Lady Glenorchy followed, asking this inexperienced young man to preach for a few weeks in her influential Edinburgh pulpit – a pulpit that attracted as many as 2000 worshippers. This trial period soon turned to a permanent appointment. The people appreciated Thomas Jones's ministry, which was to last for the next fifty-eight years until his death in 1837.

When Lady Glenorchy had visited Bath in October 1776, together with her friend Jane Hill, she may well have been disappointed to discover that Selina was at Trevecca at the time. However, she attended worship at the Bath chapel, and met one of the Countess's newer friends. For there in the pulpit was a distinguished, intense but delicate looking man: none other than Augustus Toplady. He and the Countess had met initially in 1763 during his first curacy in Blagdon, Somerset. Not until 1768, however, would Selina have become aware of the acuteness of his intellectual abilities when he entered the 'pamphlet war' over the issue of the expelled students of St Edmund Hall. The forceful

---

[1] Clayton's decision to become a Dissenter, probably one of those to whom Berridge referred in his letter, was a cause of acute disappointment to the Countess. However, she retained her warm regard for him, and continued to correspond with him.

[2] Thomas Snell Jones was arguably among the brightest products of Trevecca College. He became Lady Glenorchy's biographer and in 1810 the University of Aberdeen conferred an honorary doctorate on him.

but sometimes vitriolic pen of this poet, preacher and staunch Calvinist, then vicar of Broadhembury, Devon, would have brought Toplady to the attention of the Countess once again in 1772 when he became embroiled in the *Minutes* Controversy and attempted to dismiss the arguments of John Fletcher and others who were defending Wesley. In 1774 Selina wrote to Toplady to ask if he would consider joining her itinerant preachers, but he declined her request. God had called him to labour within his own parish, he replied, 'and ought I not to see the pillar of divine direction moving before me very visibly and quite incontestably ere I venture to deviate into a more excursive path?'[1]

However, on 24 July 1775 the two met in Bath, the first time for twelve years, when Toplady had been invited to join the Countess to drink tea – a luxury still enjoyed mainly by the upper classes. This meeting with the Countess appears to have altered Toplady's mind on the issue of itinerant preaching. 'I drank tea yesterday with Lady Huntingdon,' he wrote to a friend, 'her conversation was very polite, very friendly and very spiritual.'[2] Captivated by her charm and persuasive zeal, Toplady agreed to preach for her. She had assured him that he would not be contravening any ecclesiastical protocol because the Church of England liturgy was used in all her chapels. For nine months Toplady travelled and preached in the Countess's chapels before he began a new ministry at Orange Street Chapel in London. His impressions of the Brighton congregation, which he visited on several occasions, were of the highest. 'I know of no congregation anywhere who seem to be more entirely after my own heart', he told a friend. 'Their union and fellowship with each other are uncommon considering their number.'[3]

---

[1] Toplady, *Works*, p. 862.
[2] Cited by T. Wright, *The Life of Augustus M. Toplady* (London, 1911), p. 168.
[3] Toplady, *Works*, p. 874.

In 1776 Augustus Toplady attended the eighth anniversary service at Trevecca. His description of the event gives us another glimpse of the magnitude of these occasions:

On the Anniversary Day in Wales the congregation was so large that the chapel would not have contained a fourth part of the people who were supposed to amount to 3000. No fewer than 1300 horses were turned into one large field adjoining the college; besides what was stationed in the neighbouring villages. The carriages also were unusually numerous. A scaffold was erected at one end of the college court on which a bookstand was placed by way of pulpit: and thence six or seven of us preached successively to one of the most attentive and most lively congregations I ever beheld. When it came to my turn to preach I advanced to the front and had not gone more than half through my prayer before sermon when the scaffold suddenly fell in. As I stood very near the highermost step (and the steps did not fall with the rest), providence enabled me to keep my feet . . . About forty ministers were on the scaffold and steps when the former broke down . . . The congregation though greatly alarmed had the prudence not to throw themselves into outward disorder: which, I believe, was chiefly owing to the powerful sense of God's presence, which was eminently felt by most of the assembly.[1]

Among those on the platform at the time, only Sir Walter Shirley was slightly hurt.

Toplady and the Countess met frequently during the last two years of the preacher's life as his ill-health brought him back to Bath and Bristol on a number of occasions. In his commonplace book he preserved some anecdotes from Selina's earlier years, scribbling them down soon after she had related them to him.[2] To Toplady she was 'the most precious saint of God I ever knew'.[3]

[1] *Ibid.*, pp. 875–6.
[2] For example, the incident recorded above p. 175.
[3] Letter to William Hussey, 6 Sept. 1776, Toplady, *Works*, p. 876.

---

Long and newsy letters passed between them when they could not meet. One of these tells of the new hymnbook he had compiled for Orange Street Chapel.[1]

Thomas Wills, also to become one of Selina's closest friends and fellow workers, was serving as the curate in charge in St Agnes, Cornwall, when he came to Bath in 1772 for the sake of his health. Born in 1740, Wills was early orphaned, and he and his brother were cared for by an aunt who lived in Truro. Hard though these circumstances were, they put young Thomas under the tuition of George Conan at Truro Grammar School. Conan, a Scotsman from Aberdeen and described as 'a scholar and a saint', had been instrumental in the conversion of Samuel Walker, now curate to an absentee vicar of St Mary's Church in Truro. Under George Conan's tuition the boy not only received a sound classical education, but more importantly was also introduced to Samuel Walker, under whose evangelical ministry he heard a clear gospel message. When Wills entered Magdalen Hall in Oxford in 1757 he quickly met up with Thomas Haweis, also from Truro, whose career had been similar to his own. Also educated under Conan and converted through the ministry of Samuel Walker, Haweis was then at Christ Church College. He took the younger man under his wing and God used the influence of a small group of praying Christians in the university to bring Thomas Wills into an assurance of salvation. After he had completed his degree, Wills was ordained into the Church of England ministry in 1764. Then he returned to Cornwall and took up the curacy at St Agnes under the watchful eye of Samuel Walker.

---

[1] Entitled *Psalms and Hymns for Public and Private Worship* (E. & C. Dilly, 1776). Having selected them from forty or fifty other collections of hymns, he was confident of the merits of this book, but adds, 'I was prevailed with at last to insert six of my own humble efforts which after all I do but fear stop out six better ones. May the whole publication be so owned by the Holy Spirit as to prove a blessing to Sion's travellers on their way to the Mount of God!' MS. in Robert Woodruff Library, Emory University, Atlanta, Georgia.

For ten years Wills conducted an increasingly useful ministry in this distant outpost of the land. So enthusiastic were his congregations to hear him preach that he had difficulty in reaching his own pulpit each Sunday, struggling to make his way through the throng of worshippers. Worn down with the constant demands of the ministry, Wills had travelled to Bath to try the waters, and it was not long before he met one of the Countess's nieces, Selina Wheler, who was there visiting her aunt. Two years later, in 1774, they were married.

The many letters from the Countess written to the young couple have been preserved for us, forming a commentary on her personal experiences during the hectic years of the 1770s. Soon after leaving Bath with his bride, Wills found time to send a note to the Countess who was then in London: 'Nothing was ever so kind as dear Mr Wills's five lines on the road', she wrote to her niece. 'It quite revived me. You are both near my heart.' Referring to the young couple, she had nothing but praise, as she told a friend: 'He is a most blessed and gracious man and married to a niece of mine, a heavenly and blessed soul also.'[1]

Pressures seemed to crowd in upon Selina on all sides. To her niece she wrote, 'One continued succession of hurry has met me in every place and I have but a few moments late at night to write a few lines.' The demands were to prove too much for her uncertain health and during the following year, 1775, the Countess faced another period of prolonged illness. A rest was imperative and she knew she would be sure of a welcome in St Agnes with Thomas and Selina Wills.

'God go with your Ladyship into Cornwall', Toplady wrote, 'and shine on all your efforts for the glory of his name . . . Open your trenches and ply the gospel artillery', he urged the sick woman.[2] Such an admonition was hardly necessary, for whether in good health or poor, Selina retained her overwhelming desire

[1] C.F. Archives, Hawksworth Correspondence.
[2] Toplady, *Works*, p. 873.

for the salvation of men and women. The plight of miners had always moved her profoundly, so now when she was in St Agnes the sight of the many tin miners bereft of the means of grace both disturbed her and immediately stirred her to action. In a letter of 25 September 1775 to John Hawksworth, we may catch the depth of her concern and the measures she had already taken:

> Their outward poverty, their sorrowful darkness is such that I cannot even think on without prayers and tears to the Lord that there his light may arise. If the Lord permit I wish to make three or four establishments in the heart of the tin mines for their consolation and salvation. Many extraordinary circumstances have united to call me here as soon as my work was done in Bristol. I have purchased a place that holds about 1000 people that is ready for you where thousands of tinners will attend.

Soon a string of churches sprang up as the Countess pursued her resolution. In West Looe, St Columb and Mevagissey chapels were built and a work was begun at St. Ives.

The following year found the Countess, now nearly seventy years of age, still far from well but struggling on bravely with the punishing round of activity. To her niece she says: 'I have longed to write to you myself but my head aches and business . . . and other letters oblige my attention . . . which indeed I find almost too much for me. Was [sic] you to see the loads of papers, I cannot do anything but look at them.' On a brighter note, however, she continues: 'Wonderful is the work all over this kingdom and new students offering convince me much more is to be done. But, my dear Linny, heaven seems open and I will repose my poor worn out body. I dare write no more. My eyes and my head say, "Forbear"'.[1]

A heavy fall for a woman of the Countess's age could have had serious consequences, and in April 1777 she told her niece of such an accident at Trevecca:

[1] Rylands, English MSS.

A fall in coming out of the chapel has made me appear like one who has been fighting with an earthly foe. My eye is so black, but the mercy [is] that I was not killed or my bones broken . . . The devil seemed to have a hard stroke at me, but the hand that held [me] proved his loving power to save.[1]

Continued ill-health dogged the Countess at this time. At last, in 1778, the only answer seemed to be respite by the sea and Teignmouth was the place recommended. Writing to Selina Wills she told of the kindness of her doctor:

Dr Ludlow's concern for me made him forget . . . everything but my safety and attend me to this place without fee or reward. Fearing the consequence might be fatal if not suddenly attended to, he argued for rest and ease with a kind of importunity . . . My fever was abated before he left me and my sleep now greatly restored.

From her bed the Countess could lie and watch the ships sailing past in the bay and discovered 'a sweetness in the air most uncommon'. But whether watching ships pass or sampling the refreshing air, the motivating force of Lady Huntingdon's life remained unchanged. She discovered a small group of Christians in Teignmouth despairing of ever attracting a gospel preacher to the area, and immediately sent for 'little Davis the student' who began to preach 'with much approbation'. In keeping with her policy of first establishing a bridgehead for the gospel in any place and then moving out to the surrounding towns and villages, she told her niece: 'As soon as I have strength I hope to spy out Torbay. I long for a standard to be set up there. Several towns lie around it and thousands of souls, (if it is the Lord's time) will hear. Thus I am comforted in hope my miserable dregs of time may yet praise thus him.'[2]

In 1778 the Countess asked Thomas Wills to become one of her personal chaplains, and for many years the energies of this

[1] *Ibid.*
[2] Letter to Selina Wills, 20 August 1778, Rylands, English MSS.

young man, whose preaching gifts were of the highest order, were expended on behalf of Selina's work. During each summer he would travel ceaselessly around the country, preaching in the chapels that were coming into being as a result of the labours of the Trevecca students. More importantly, by his challenging messages new congregations of converted men and women were gathered together, so providing additional opportunities for the Trevecca students.

# 27

# 'I AM TO BE CAST OUT'

LADY ANNE ERSKINE, companion to the Countess of Huntingdon
for the last five years or more, was travelling in her carriage on a
February day in 1772. Her journey took her through an area
known as Clerkenwell, then on the northern outskirts of London.
A dismal thief-ridden district, it had open fields on one side and
the grey crowded housing of a rapidly expanding metropolis on
the other. Suddenly she caught sight of the gleaming dome of a
massive circular building erected on the edge of the open fields.
A spectacular sight, this huge pleasure stadium, topped with an
elegant statue of the goddess of Fame, was known as the
Pantheon and had been built only two years earlier. With its
central arena, tiered galleries, boxed seats and gardens replete
with many a statue, the Pantheon was a deliberate imitation of the
Roman temple of the same name, rebuilt by Hadrian in AD 120.

As Lady Anne sat down that night to write to Selina she began
to describe in detail what she had seen:

> I suppose you have seen in the newspapers a great deal about
> what they call the Pantheon, a prodigious large fine building in
> Oxford Road intended as a place of public amusement, to outdo
> all things of the kind before exhibited. It is elegant and fine be-
> yond anything I ever saw in England – very like the finest chapels
> abroad.

Knowing her friend's propensity for seeing potential for the
gospel in unexpected places, Lady Anne could easily imagine

what she would think about such a building. So she added, 'I quite coveted it for you as I went past'.[1]

She was not the only one to have such a thought. When the wife of the wealthy business man, William Craven, who had invested all his capital, some £6000, to build this eighteenth century amusement arcade, viewed the vast structure against the London skyline, her prognosis for its future was as gloomy as the Clerkenwell district itself. The project would send them bankrupt, of that she was sure. More than that, she said she could even envisage a day when the despised Methodists might buy it up for a chapel.

The Pantheon was indeed a commercial disaster. Its location was poor and its reputation for bawdy amusement none of the best. Even the civil magistrate felt obliged to interpose his authority to check the unseemly 'public diversions'. Two years after Lady Anne had noticed the building, the proprietor became insolvent and the nearby Sadlers Wells company leased the property for the sale of carriages. This too proved an abortive enterprise and in 1776 the Pantheon again fell into disuse. The Countess of Huntingdon now became interested in it, but took a step unusual for her since the unhappiness of the 1770 controversy: she asked advice from her friends.

Walter Shirley, together with Augustus Toplady, Anthony Crole,[2] and one or two others met in Toplady's study to discuss the situation. Toplady was then deputed to write a tactful letter to Selina on the subject. Two other parties, he told her, were interested in the Pantheon – one wished to turn it into a tavern and the other wanted it for exactly the same purpose as she did: as a place of worship. After considering the matter from all points of view her friends were opposed to the idea that she should proceed. The expense involved in making the necessary changes would be

[1] C.F. Archives.
[2] A Trevecca student until his recent appointment as minister of Pinner's Hall in London.

immense; her funds were already fully committed; it was too big, the district was poor and access in winter impracticable. The possibility of the Countess being able to obtain men of sufficient ability to preach in so vast a building would be an added problem. 'On the whole,' Toplady concluded, 'dear Mr Shirley gave me as his private opinion that your Ladyship had better forego the Pantheon entirely.'

Selina was not at all happy about this advice:

> My heart seems strongly set upon having this temple of folly dedicated to Jehovah Jesus . . . I feel so deeply for the perishing thousands in that part of London, that I am almost tempted to run every risk; and though at this moment I have not a penny to command, yet I am so firmly persuaded of the goodness of the Master . . . whom I serve that I shall not want silver or gold for the work . . . Nevertheless with some regret I give up the matter at this time . . . but faith tells me to go forward, nothing fearing, nothing doubting.[1]

However, having asked advice, Selina agreed to abide by it and withdrew her name from the interested parties. In the event, the building was rented by a group of business men of Calvinistic persuasion and registered as a Dissenting meeting house under the protection of the Toleration Act. Alterations were quickly set in place changing the building from its appearance as a heathen temple to a place of worship for the living God. The opening services were conducted by John Ryland of Northampton on 5 July 1777.[2] Despite its being registered as a Dissenting chapel, two evangelical churchmen, William Taylor and Herbert Jones, agreed to be responsible for the conduct of worship. Renamed

---

[1] Seymour, *Countess*, vol. 2, p. 305. Quoted from *Evangelical Register*, 1837, p. 3.

[2] This would be John Collett Ryland (1723–92) father of Carey's friend, who was also called John Ryland, but was only twenty-four at the time. Ryland senior was known for his catholicity of outlook and friendship with men such as Rowland Hill.

Northampton Chapel, the former precincts of vice soon attracted
a far different clientèle.

One man, however, was highly displeased to see the Pantheon
turned into a place of worship. William Sellon, the son of Walter
Sellon, the Countess's old friend who had owed much to her in
the past, was the curate of St James Church, Clerkenwell.
Described as 'an avaricious pluralist', Sellon had built up a handsome stipend for himself out of a string of benefices. In addition
to St James, he was vicar of Portman Chapel in Marylebone and
he also derived income from a number of lectureships for which
he was responsible. In days when a country clergyman could
consider himself moderately well placed on £40 a year, Sellon
pocketed an estimated £1,300 annually.[1] Most of this income
was raised by voluntary contributions from his parishioners –
a method rare for the times. Therefore, when the people of
Clerkenwell began to attend Northampton Chapel in large numbers, his income fell correspondingly.

Two ordained clergymen of the Church of England preaching
in a Dissenting meeting house gave William Sellon the excuse he
was looking for to proceed against the unwelcome intruders.
First, he circulated in the parish a paper that maintained his right
as the incumbent of Clerkenwell to preach in the new chapel
whenever he pleased, and he asserted that income raised from the
letting of seats and other incidentals was rightfully his. When
Taylor and Jones refused to comply with such claims, he decided
to press charges against them through the Bishop of London's
Consistory Court. Sellon, who was influential and demanding,
won the case, and in February 1779 only nineteen months after it
was opened, Northampton Chapel was closed. These two
preachers were effectively silenced, their indictment being two-
fold: not only had they been preaching in a Dissenting chapel,

---

[1] Welch, *Spiritual Pilgrim*, p.153, cited from W. J. Pinks, *The History of
Clerkenwell* (London: 1880), p. 69.

but as Anglicans they had been conducting services in another cleric's parish without a licence from the bishop.

The Countess was watching these developments carefully. By October 1778 she realized that the outcome was likely to be unfavourable to the two preachers and began to lay interim plans to rescue Northampton Chapel and with it the cause of the gospel in that area. A meeting was arranged between her chaplains Thomas Wills and Cradock Glascott and William Taylor, one of the preachers facing court proceedings. As we have seen, the Countess had always maintained her right to appoint personal chaplains who would preach in her private chapels and not be under the jurisdiction of the bishops. Although she had already had a warning of the limits of this privilege when Whitefield had tried to register Tottenham Court Road Chapel under her name, she had not only disregarded it, but had stretched the point to cover many a chapel up and down the country where her students were preaching – places where she had no private accommodation.

As the results of the court case became definite the Countess, who was staying in Bath, was ready to act. A letter to Thomas Wills and his wife, written on 16 February 1779, explains her strategy:

> I set off tomorrow for London in order to finalise all things for the possession of Northampton Chapel, and to have it opened. I shall depend upon you being there and meet Mr Haweis and Mr Glascott, as Mr Taylor must not appear there just at first. One may go to Bath, the other [Herbert Jones] to Brighton for a time.[1]

She braced herself for opposition. Assuring her niece of the strength of her position, she added, 'It is not within their power to affect my privileges . . . and thus I shall tread upon the serpent and the scorpion and all the powers of darkness.' And on the same day she wrote courageously to John Hawksworth:

[1] Rylands, English MSS.

I think I see my way clear. I leave this place tomorrow to take possession of Northampton Chapel – a congregation of near 5000[1] souls in London. It is a great undertaking for such a poor worm but the things that are despised God chooses or he never would allow a poor unprofitable widow to serve in his church . . . Jesus and glory is enough for me in time and to all eternity, and I will be the plague of all those who want to sleep in a whole skin . . . Many great and effectual doors are opened just now and the more they afflict the more we multiply.[2]

The Countess communicated both with the Bishop of London and with William Sellon on 25 February 1779 explaining her action in taking over Northampton Chapel. To the bishop she emphasized that she intended to cancel the status of the chapel as a Dissenting meeting house and it would henceforth be under her personal protection as a peeress of the realm. The bishop was guarded in his reply: 'How far your Ladyship's protection will avail . . . I cannot pretend to say.'

The letter to William Sellon was more formal and written in the third person:

The Countess of Huntingdon's kind compliments to Mr Sellon. She is extremely sorry to find such unhappy differences have prevailed in his parish . . . . She takes this method of assuring him of her best wishes and hopes he will be satisfied that every mark of Christian respect will be shown him as minister of that parish and as nothing has ever caused any unhappy or unchristian differences wherever she has been, so she wishes peace and the best understanding may ever subsist on her coming into his parish.[3]

[1] Numbers attending the chapel were variously estimated. One who attended regularly put it as high as 7000 but the more conservative estimate of about 3000 was probably more correct.
[2] Rylands, English MSS.
[3] C. F. Archives, Countess to Sellon. I am indebted to Dorothy Eugenia Sherman Brown for some of the details in this chapter, taken from her unpublished doctoral thesis, 'Selina, The Countess of Huntingdon: Leader of the First Dissenting Methodists', Southern Methodist University, Dallas, 1986.

After signing a contract for a seventy-three year lease on the building, the Countess gave notice that the premises would be closed for a fortnight while certain alterations were made. The work she had in mind was the construction of a passageway linking the chapel to a large house immediately adjacent. This was the attractive jasmine-covered Pantheon tea gardens which would now become the Countess's own property, so complying with the regulation that a peeress's chapel must be part of her personal residence. In this case the chapel dwarfed her home by many times over. To mark its new ownership the Countess also announced a further change of name, reopening it for public worship on 28 March 1779 as Spa Fields Chapel. Thomas Wills and Cradock Glascott, together with Thomas Haweis, would officiate in turns. On the day of opening Thomas Haweis, her chaplain since 1774, set the tone for the future ministry at Spa Fields in an address on 'We preach Christ crucified'.

The preaching of Haweis, Wills and Glascott soon filled the vast domed building to capacity with serious-minded men and women who made their way in escorted groups along the dark burglar-ridden streets of Clerkenwell and across muddy fields to listen to preaching they would never hear from such men as William Sellon. Sellon himself received a personal invitation from the Countess to attend the opening services, an invitation he declined, threatening darkly that he was 'under the necessity of defending the church establishment and vindicating his own rights as minister of the parish'.[1]

From the standpoint of Sellon and the Establishment, the Countess's action contravened the parish system and was certainly 'irregular'. Little more than two weeks had elapsed before Sellon began to fulfil his veiled threat, Thomas Haweis himself being his first victim. Haweis, a loyal churchman who disapproved so entirely of Dissenters that he was unhappy that

---

[1] *Ibid.*, Sellon to Countess, 25 March 1779.

Selina allowed Trevecca students to become pastors of Dissenting causes, seemed an unwise first choice, particularly as he had the backing of a peeress of the realm. Undaunted, however, Sellon inaugurated legal proceedings and on 12 June the case came before the Bishop of London's Consistory Court. Sellon presented his indictment, demanding that Haweis should not preach or conduct other services at Spa Fields without his permission. Though the court adjourned for a period of five months and services continued to be held at Spa Fields, it was only a lull in the storm.

The Countess had appointed a committee of fifteen men to order the day-to-day running of the chapel and during this period these men had been preparing a legal defence for Haweis based on the rights of the Countess – rights she had been exercising for thirty years or more. Rationalizing her position, Selina explained that these privileges had in the past been 'supported by the judgment of an archbishop and bishops and also by the most eminent men, though no friends to religion'. But now she had a genuine fear of how far the determination and jealousy of a man like Sellon might extend. Nor did the opinion of one of London's leading barristers, John Glynn, which she had sought, ease her misgivings. 'Ecclesiastical law, *such as it now stands,* is against you at some points, points which would not be insurmountable were our bishops differently minded',[1] was his assessment of the situation. Although Selina disputed the right of an ecclesiastical court to overrule her rights as a peeress, there appeared to be few means of redress. She drafted a letter to the Archbishop and considered appealing to the King's Bench and though these letters are extant there is no evidence that they were actually sent.

When the Consistory Court met once more on 9 November 1779 it had two matters before it. One was the defence submitted by the committee on behalf of Thomas Haweis and the other was

[1] Seymour, *Countess*, vol. 2, p. 310.

William Sellon's next action, this time challenging Cradock Glascott's right to preach at Spa Fields. Thomas Wills had also been indicted but he had left London on that same day, so escaping for the present. The case rumbled on for many weeks, but Haweis' defence carried little weight with the judge. A peeress's chaplain was supposed to conduct worship for the family and invited guests, but, the prosecution argued, several thousand worshippers could scarcely be called personal guests even though the majority were admitted by the purchase of tickets. If the Countess had not had a reserved seat, she herself would hardly have been able to gain entrance to her own chapel. Although a petition signed by many Clerkenwell residents was presented to the Bishop, the case went against Haweis and on 26 May 1780 he was forbidden to preach any more in Spa Fields and ordered to pay costs himself. Glascott's indictment moved on slowly, but the outcome needed little guesswork. More seriously the verdict against Haweis also set a precedent and so became a ruling against the Countess and the whole of her work. It could now only be a matter of time before all her preachers were silenced, given the general antagonism of Church of England incumbents to a Countess who patronized or built chapels in their parishes.

Selina's predicament seemed to have no solution. Francis, for once sympathetic to his mother's dilemma, had tried to intervene on her behalf, but without success. The options seemed bleak. To her son she expressed her quandary in August 1780:

> The alternative for me plainly appears this at present, viz – either to shut up all my chapels in England and Wales which are numerous, with a still greater number of places not under that character, or to submit to a demission from the church by a law now existing against me.[1]

Realizing the loneliness to which such an action would inevitably lead, Selina concluded a letter to Francis with these words:

[1] C. F. Archives.

'My dear son, I have a faithful friend who said, "I will never leave you nor forsake you. No, that I never, never will." I have tried his promise often and he has never failed me yet. You must believe I extremely love you. S. H.'

Now forced to think the unthinkable, Selina, whose loyalty to the Church of England had been so marked a feature of her position despite her underlying desire for union with all true believers, had to face the possibility of severing those lifelong bonds. She would then have to protect all her chapels under the Toleration Act of 1689. To use that expedient could invite serious misunderstanding from her most faithful friends and fellow workers, even though many of the students were already serving Dissenting causes. As the pain of such a possibility began to crystallize in her thinking, Selina wrote to her former student John Hawksworth:

> I am to be cast out of the Church for what I have been doing these forty years – speaking and living for Jesus Christ . . . Blessed be God, I have not one care relative to this event but to be found faithful to God and man through all. You will smile and rejoice with me in all I may suffer for our dear Immanuel's sake. I have asked none to go with me and none that does not come to the help of the Lord by faith in the Son of God and lay all at his feet. Any other would do me no good.[1]

Throughout 1781 Selina hesitated before taking further action, although now she had reached the decision that a separation from the Church was the only answer. In April 1781 the committee at Spa Fields had come to a similar decision as they waited for their popular and well-loved preacher Cradock Glascott to be sent into ecclesiastical exile along the same route that Haweis had trodden the previous year. An urgent letter from the committee alerted the Countess to this further impending trouble:

[1] Seymour, *Countess*, vol. 2, p. 315.

We have the greatest reason to believe that Mr Glascott will be silenced . . . An immediate secession appears to us the only resort from those severities of ecclesiastical law which deprive us of one valuable and esteemed minister after another and will incessantly be employed against everyone who shall venture to come amongst us under the Establishment.[1]

But the Countess could not secede alone. Unless some of her preachers would come with her it would be of no avail. To one whom she hoped might take a similar stand, she wrote:

This cruel and bitter enemy of mine is suffered to go great lengths of repression; but herein also I must see life arise through death . . . In this case, I am reduced to turn the finest congregation, not only in England, but in any part of the world, into a dissenting meeting.[2]

Matters reached a climax in January 1782. It now became clear that, having silenced Haweis and Glascott, Sellon was still determined to inflict yet more damage on the Countess's cause. But only one man, her chaplain Thomas Wills, was prepared to cut his ties with the Established Church and come with her. The church itself was encouraged by Wills's brave stand and the secretary quickly conveyed his decision to the Countess: 'He is quite willing to stand forth alone, to give up reputation and every other consideration whatever since it appears that the glory of God and the support of his work in this place requires such a sacrifice at his hands.'[3]

One preacher was enough to serve Spa Fields and on 12 January the chapel was officially registered as a Dissenting meeting house once more. Two months later William Taylor, one of the original two men ousted by Sellon,[4] joined Wills in exchange for

[1] *Spa Fields Chapel Minutes,* para. 144, cited by Edwin Welch, *Two Calvinistic Methodist Chapels* (London Record Society, 1975), p. 54.

[2] *Ibid.*, pp. 311–2.

[3] *Spa Fields Chapel Minutes,* p. 63.

[4] Two years after these events Sellon suffered a stroke, with 'his mouth so distorted as to be unable to speak for two days'. Wills regarded this as divine retribution. Letter to Countess in C. F. Archives.

certain securities for his family promised by the Countess. Thomas Haweis and Cradock Glascott declined to do so. Apart from Wills and Taylor, Selina stood alone in this the severest crisis of her life. Virtually all her preacher friends either felt unable to preach for her any longer or expressed grave reservations at her action. Most remained friendly, but a short note written on a torn scrap of paper from William Romaine – one who owed much to the Countess – must have cut her to the quick. The exact context is unclear, but his attitude is not:

> Madam, I am an entire stranger to the report you mention and do not know nor desire to know one single step you are taking in this matter. I wish to mind my own business and not to interfere in the least with yours. It would be better for you if you heard more truths and fewer lies. I still pray for you and am your obedient servant, William Romaine.[1]

Henry Venn, John Berridge, William Jesse, her cousin Walter Shirley, Henry Peckwell and, of course, Thomas Haweis and Cradock Glascott, among others – all men who had delighted to work with the Countess – now believed that they would compromise their churchmanship if they preached in any of her chapels. To become a Dissenter was to enter a political and educational wilderness, whereas the Church, by virtue of her Articles and Homilies, her Prayer Book and liturgy was to them the haven of true religion.

The Countess had hoped for support from her Welsh friends, but even here she was disappointed. Rowland Hill, whom Selina had encouraged since his college days, had aided financially, and 'as my own son received into my house', acted in a far from helpful manner. First he intensified the misgivings among the Welsh Calvinistic Methodist churches about the Countess's decision, making it far less likely that any of their preachers would support her or preach among the Connexion chapels. To make matters

[1] C. F. Archives.

worse, Hill had allowed his strong sense of humour to run away with him and had taken 'us all up at times as his merry Andrews into the pulpit . . . leaving a bitter sting as far as he could through his evil jokes'.[1]

To make public jokes about one who had helped him was indeed inexcusable, but the offence that appears to have caused the ultimate breakdown in their relationship was Hill's intervention in the affairs of two congregations brought into being by Trevecca students and financed by the Countess. Selina accused him of 'trying to divide my friends from me', and of influencing them in such a way that would 'bring disgrace upon us all'. The situation has 'half broke my heart' she confessed to the Committee at Spa Fields when they wanted Hill to preach for them. As long as she lived, he must never preach there again, she stipulated.[2] Although Hill had defended Selina's work in 1777,[3] his biographer, Edwin Sidney, suggests that he was 'not one of her ladyship's most cordial admirers'. Nor did he find her authoritarian manner 'suited to a mind impatient of restraint'.[4] Despite all this, when plans for Rowland Hill's London church, Surrey Chapel, were being laid that year (1782), the Countess wrote to a friend commending Hill's abilities and evangelistic zeal. More than this, she sent a contribution for the proposed chapel.

Disillusioned and isolated, the Countess, who sometimes allowed her strong emotions to overcome her judgment, said some hard things at this time about the friends whom she thought had failed in an hour of opportunity. To understand the reluctance of these dedicated men to secede from the Church, we must remember not only the commonly-held suspicion of Dissent, but also the belief shared by many that a new day was dawning for evangelicalism within the Established Church. Thomas Wills's

[1] Seymour, *Countess*, vol. 1, p. 437.
[2] Letter to Spa Fields committee, March 1782, in C. F. Archives.
[3] See above p.354.
[4] Edwin Sidney, *Life of the Rev. Rowland Hill* (London, 1835), p. 437.

kindly biographer, when dealing with this act of secession on the part of his subject, expresses the attitude common to them all:

In my judgment it is an example by no MEANS to be followed. Some of my readers may say, I am surely a bigoted churchmen: this weighs very little with me. That I am a churchmen, [I am] so far from denying it, that I glory in it; and if any person is pleased to attach the epithet, 'bigoted' they are very welcome: we are all at liberty to enjoy our own opinion; and therefore I repeat that this conduct of Mr Wills (though circumstances might justify him) should by no means be an example: for considering the great majority of the clergy, who preach not the doctrines of our Church to those who do, I consider every desertion, or defection of her ministers, as so many stabs to her happiness, if not to her existence.[1]

The position the Countess's chapels now embraced was a half-way stance between the Church and Dissent; they became 'partial conformists'. Selina was never a Dissenter at heart. She had indeed been 'cast out', or perhaps we should say, forced out. Her decision to withdraw was taken as the only way to save her life work from certain demise. She still insisted that in all their services of worship the chapels in the Connexion should retain the Church liturgy. Her spirit was 'not that of theoretical dissent', maintained two contemporary writers in their *History of the Dissenters*.[2] The only difference would be that from this time her chapels would no longer be subject to the discipline of the Church hierarchy, and her preachers could occupy pulpits in any diocese in the land without fear of recriminations.

However, in cutting the knot that bound her churches to the ecclesiastical protocol of the Establishment, the Countess of Huntingdon had set a bold, even radical, precedent. Built into

[1] *Memoirs of Thomas Wills, by a Friend* (London, 1804 ), p. 88.
[2] David Bogue and James Bennett, *History of the Dissenters from the Revolution to the Year 1838* (London, 1812; reprinted Stoke-on-Trent: Tentmaker Publications, 2000), vol. 3, p. 101.

the basic structure of Methodism was an intractable tension between Church and Dissent. As we have already seen, the Wesley brothers had wrestled with the selfsame issues and temporarily shelved them. But now the new wine could no longer be contained in the old bottles. Arminian Methodism would soon follow, but early in 1782 Selina and her bold chaplain stood alone. Without a doubt Selina's work had brought a new breath of life to Dissent. It has been calculated that in the years that followed her withdrawal the number of churches applying for Dissenting status rose from 251 in 1782 to 832 by the 1790s. Many of these churches had Trevecca students as their pastors.[1]

Another persistent problem that had dogged the Countess's work was solved by her decision to register her chapels under the Toleration Act. Now the Connexion could ordain suitable young men without seeking permission from the bishops. Accordingly, the following year, on Sunday, 9 March 1783, an ordination service was held at Spa Fields Chapel. Six young men were ordained on this historic occasion in a service that lasted for five hours, starting at 9 o'clock in the morning. William Taylor and Thomas Wills shared the conduct of this service, which was attended by a congregation reported to be 'remarkably great', even by Spa Fields standards. Interspersing the service with appropriate hymns and prayer, Taylor first addressed the young men on the seriousness of the Christian ministry, and then solemnly read out the *Fifteen Articles of Faith* drawn up as a standard of belief for the Connexion.[2]

Each candidate was then required to sign the *Fifteen Articles of Faith*. With this accomplished, Thomas Wills called upon each

[1] John Wesley followed the Countess's example and began to ordain his own preachers without the sanction of the Church in 1784. This, too, added to the increasing number of Dissenting chapels.

[2] These Articles, to be found in Appendix 3, are a composite statement of Christian doctrine, drawn mainly from the *Thirty-Nine Articles* of the Church of England and the *Westminster Confession of Faith*. They were probably drawn up by the Countess herself in conjunction with Wills and Taylor.

in turn, starting with the most senior, to give an account of his conversion and call to the ministry. Wills then preached, including in his remarks a biblical justification for ordination at the hands of elders or presbyters in the New Testament sense of the word. The young men then approached the communion table in pairs and knelt down as Wills and Taylor laid hands on them, commissioning them to become preachers of the gospel of Christ. A further sermon by Wills followed, directed more to those attending who were already in the ministry. At last, as it was already 2 o'clock, proceedings ended with the celebration of the Lord's Supper. Taylor postponed his final sermon until the evening.

Only one seat in that great auditorium was empty. The Countess of Huntingdon was absent on this auspicious occasion. We may only conjecture on the reason for this. Perhaps she was ill, as was often the case. Perhaps at the age of seventy-six she felt unable to sit through the lengthy proceedings. But it may be that the emotional strain of being forced out of the Church she had loved all her long life made the poignancy of such an occasion too great for her to bear. Although the term 'the Countess of Huntingdon's connexion' was in regular use some years before these events, we may more accurately say that the Connexion itself was born on 12 January 1782, when Spa Fields seceded, and came of age on 9 March 1783 as a fully-fledged entity. An irrevocable step had been taken.

# 28

# Encouragements and Setbacks
# of Declining Years

THROUGHOUT THE 1780s the expansion of the Countess of
Huntingdon's Connexion continued apace. Bereft of many of her
former friends and preachers, the Countess still had many an
eager young man behind her, ready to traverse the length and
breadth of the country, preaching to gatherings vast and small. In
a letter dated 2 November 1785 to one who had pastoral oversight of the chapel at Bath, the Countess describes a service
conducted at the laying of the foundation stone of a new chapel.
Those present had 'universally cried out with their Amens and
instantly such a power of God filled the place that one and all fell
prostrate . . . the effects of this lasts upon the hearts of many and
one very poor old man said, "O Sir, my little cup runs over."
[Many] said they would gladly die on the spot so sensible were
they of the extraordinary power of God being over them'.[1]

Such scenes gave Selina confidence that, despite the fears and
disapproval that had been expressed concerning her course of
action, God was still pleased to bless her endeavours. Continuing
in this letter, she spoke of her encouragement at hearing that
numbers attending Bath chapel were increasing to such an extent
that additional space was becoming imperative. This would
involve more financial outlay but Selina could comment optimistically, 'Let us trust the Lord but fully and we shall have a dozen

[1] Rylands MS., to 'Carpenter', Letter 133. In addition chapels were also
opened in Bootle, Whitehaven, Weymouth, Newark and Berkhamsted at this
period.

more [chapels]. I have reason to believe this when nine chapels in five months are erecting or erected and Wigan makes ten, now just completing.'[1]

The opening of nine chapels in five months during 1785 confirms the picture of rapid advance.[2] It would seem that a number of these nine were in Birmingham and the surrounding district where Trevecca students had been active for some ten years. In Birmingham itself the Countess was offered the lease on the old King Street theatre. Here the people, accustomed to applauding performances by clapping, continued to express their approbation of any particular remark made by the preacher in the same way until the searching power of the message subdued them. Chapels were also being erected in nearby Stourbridge, Wednesbury, Wolverhampton and Walsall, while far to the east of the country another was opened in the cathedral city of Ely. Other cathedral cities such as York, Lincoln and Hereford also discovered a chapel audaciously rising within sound of their cathedral bells.

The Countess, soon to be eighty, was feeling her age to an increasing extent. In 1786 she wrote:

My long declining state of health occasioned the necessity of changing the air and a little relief from business which has been exceedingly heavy upon me from the daily great increase in the work. But here,[she was writing from Malvern in Worcestershire] it follows me [with] doors opening wide . . . indeed it is quite wonderful. I am yet weak but the air has revived me. Yet I must remove

---

[1] *Ibid.*

[2] In the village of Keld, in the Yorkshire Dales, stood an old chapel, in ruins for more than half a century. In 1789 Edward Stillman, a Trevecca student, was shown the chapel by local people. Walking to the centre of the ruins he stabbed his walking stick deep into the ground. 'Here will I have my chapel built and here will I preach the gospel', he stated. And he did. For almost fifty years he remained in the area and saw widespread progress amongst the villages in the Yorkshire Dales. See Thomas Whitehead, *History of the Dales Congregational Churches* (Keighley: Feather Bros., 1930), pp. 305–7.

soon to college again. Many sore trials in this great work the devil gives, but the Lord turns the bitter into sweet by making them trials of my faith and patience.[1]

As early as 1781 the Countess had felt the need to correlate the many diverse areas of her work and drew up a plan by which four of her most trusted and senior preachers should tour the country every summer. Each was assigned to a different area so that 'once at least every year the voice of mercy through the Saviour's inexhaustible merits should be sounded in the ears of millions, by gospel ministers sent into every city, town and larger village throughout the kingdom'. In 1781 Thomas Pentycross collected together the letters they had written to the Countess relating their experiences, printing them the following year,[2] but by then three of the four men had left the Connexion because of its new Dissenting status. Thomas Wills alone carried on the annual tours, leaving Spa Fields each May or June, and returning in September.

Fearless and eloquent, Wills was one of the most outstanding of the eighteenth century preachers. Ranking second only to Whitefield himself in the opinion of his biographer, Wills was 'lively, energetic and zealous in his Master's service, proclaiming to surrounding thousands the grand important and essential truths of the gospel'. He possessed 'a grand majestic voice that commanded attention',[3] his biographer added, and was an invaluable asset to Selina. Together with William Taylor he undertook much of the ministry at Spa Fields. When neither Wills nor Taylor was available to preach the Countess herself 'booked up' the pulpit with a succession of preachers. The ageing Daniel Rowland's son, Nathaniel, was a regular choice, as was David Jones of Llangan; some former Trevecca students also assisted

[1] To Carpenter, Rylands MS., Letter 129.
[2] Thomas Pentycross, ed. *Extracts of the Journals of Several Ministers of the Gospel . . . in a Series of Letters to the Countess of Huntingdon* (London, 1782).
[3] *Memoirs of Thomas Wills, by a Friend* (1804), p. 280.

and towards the end of the 1780s the Spa Fields pulpit would occasionally be filled by Thomas Charles of Bala.

Despite her advancing years Selina still kept a tight hand on the reins, controlling the movements of the students, directing them to different towns as she thought necessary or granting their urgent pleas to be allowed to stay longer in places where they were seeing progress from their labours. Robert Satchell was distressed when he heard that she had received adverse reports of his ministry at Chatteris in Cambridgeshire. To defend himself he gave a brief résumé of his ministry:

> You hear my labours have not been owned and blest . . . I am sorry your Ladyship should be so misinformed. It is true it is not so much as I could wish, for I could wish all the world to be converted. When I was at Frome hundreds and hundreds used to attend. When I was at Mulberry Gardens the chapel was as full as it could hold. When I was at Oundle the people seemed to have a great affection for me . . .[1]

This suggests that Selina was actually less in touch with the progress of the students than formerly. She still attempted, however, to keep a watchful eye on all their activities. Not all were as anxious to please as Robert Satchell. As she grew frailer and her grasp on the day-to-day running of affairs was impaired by recurring illness, some became less deferential, particularly if they were expected to leave a town where their ministry had culminated in a call from the local people to be their pastor. Each student who had passed through Trevecca undertook to serve the Connexion for four years, accepting appointments wherever the Countess thought fit to send him. But Thomas Green was not happy with this arrangement:

> I think it is very hard that a person who has a providential call from a church which is destitute of a pastor must be obliged to refuse it

[1] C. F. Archives, Satchell had fallen from his horse at the time and had broken one leg and dislocated the other.

merely because he has taken a rash step at his entrance into the Connexion and has entered into an engagement for four years merely to range up and down the country and have no settled place.'[1]

Despite all the multitude of affairs that necessarily filled Selina's days, there were two avenues of service and compassion that she could never forget. The first was education. No sooner had she professed faith in 1739 than she opened schools in Markfield, then in Ashby and Shepshed, all in Leicestershire. Now she attached schools to her larger chapels. The Spa Fields school, with sixty children attending, was funded entirely from voluntary donations and supplemented by chapel funds while the resident minister was supposed to oversee proceedings. Bath, a much smaller chapel than Spa Fields, also had a flourishing school connected with it. When Selina suspected, however, that too large a proportion of chapel funds – resources that should be used for the furtherance of gospel preaching – was being absorbed by school affairs, she insisted that this school should also be funded by donations; a decision that led to significant problems at the chapel.

The other sphere of service never far from Selina's mind was the prospect of a worldwide spread of the gospel. Wherever spiritual ignorance darkened the minds of the people, she longed for opportunities to send out preachers or even to go herself to spread the light of truth. Her efforts in America had been sadly thwarted both by events beyond her control and the failure of the one whom she had appointed leader in the work. Now, as Selina approached eighty, there came a new opportunity and she grasped it eagerly.

On a summer's day in 1786 she received a surprising letter from an old acquaintance, a certain Lord Douglas, then living in Brussels. A Roman Catholic by upbringing, Douglas had come to England ten years earlier and professed conversion to the

[1] *Ibid.*

Protestant Faith. He met the Countess when he attended the Lock Hospital Chapel where Martin Madan was then ministering. Douglas now wrote inviting her to come to Brussels together with Thomas Wills. Six hundred Protestant families were eagerly awaiting her arrival, he assured her, and she would have unbounded opportunities for establishing a gospel witness in the area.

Lady Huntingdon's response was enthusiastic though she was naturally fearful because of her advanced years: 'Flesh and blood at fourscore with painful infirmity would not make this its choice, but a little spark of that love that brought the Friend of sinners from heaven will make us not count our lives dear so we may finish our poor testimony of love for him with joy and peace', was her comment. Leasing a large chapel as a base for operations, the Countess decided to concentrate the majority of her financial support on this challenging new enterprise. After all, she reasoned, her funding for the chapels could only last a few more years in any case and would cease with her death, so why should they not face that situation now? More than this she anticipated ending her days in Brussels. To her friends in Norwich, Selina wrote, 'And now, farewell – farewell, my dear faithful friends; and if we never meet more to see each other below, we shall sing Worthy the Lamb with heart and voice to all eternity.'

Understandably there was considerable consternation among her friends at this sudden change of strategy. As we have seen, for some years Selina had not been in the habit of listening to the advice of others and few, apart from Wills, were in a position to point out defects in her policies. However, even he seemed initially satisfied with the Brussels plan and agreed to accompany her. The Countess began her journey from Trevecca to London to meet up with Wills but on her way stopped at numerous towns where chapels had been opened, doubtless to say her farewells. The journey took longer than anticipated and by the time she arrived in London, she discovered that the ship had sailed without them. Before new plans could be put in place, letters arrived to say that the whole exercise was part of a devious plot to allure her to Brussels where certain fanatics planned to assassinate the courageous old lady.

As might be expected, her fellow workers felt relieved at this overruling of the plans. From this distance in time we are not in a position to verify the facts of the case. Suffice it to say that the Countess herself was much disappointed and found it hard to credit that she might have been the subject of such a plot. She still hoped to go to Brussels. On 30 April 1787 Thomas Wills, who was now convinced that the whole enterprise was flawed, felt obliged to write a strongly worded letter:

> Through the interposition of divine providence this scheme has proved abortive, but the devil and the papists will be contriving some other plan to get us into their trap . . . I suspect the inform-ation of hundreds of Protestants longing for your coming. As few of them understand English it is evident the Lord has not given you a special call. How can you expect a blessing to run on this errand through the specious insinuations of others without a divine warrant or commission? . . . It is against light, against conscience, against the voice of God's people, the voice of providence and the entire will of God. I trust your Ladyship will excuse me speaking the sentiments of my whole heart.[1]

It is doubtful whether 'her Ladyship' did entirely excuse Wills for his outspoken comments. Even though she had been disci-plined throughout life by many severe trials, she was still unused to having her plans countermanded in so plain a fashion.

Until 1787 the Countess had still spent a considerable portion of her year at Trevecca. Now her increasing infirmity meant that she generally remained at her Spa Fields home in London and so could not oversee Trevecca affairs as closely or as adequately as formerly. Samuel Phillips, resident tutor at the college from 1784

[1] *Ibid.*

to 1787, wrote wondering whether she had forgotten her 'little poor afflicted family at the college'. The distance of Trevecca from London added to the problems of communication between the students and their patroness.

When John Williams, son of William Williams, became resident tutor in 1787 he was alarmed to discover how low standards at the college had fallen. Perhaps Selina had been taking less care over the young men whom she was admitting as students. Williams complained that some were 'little better versed in the history of the Old Testament than they are in Mahomet's Koran. They have heard something of the names of Abraham, Isaac, Jacob, David and Isaiah and this is almost all.' A student by the name of Simmonds, continued the frustrated tutor, 'cannot read any three verses of a chapter without committing a capital blunder, nay, he and another did not know their alphabet correctly when they came here. I have informed some of them about their faults about four, five or six hundred times, I mean of the same faults.'[1]

Although the Countess had intended that Trevecca should be primarily an agent for the speedy evangelization of the peoples, and not merely a school of theology, it would have to be said that the education at Trevecca had become woefully deficient by any standards. In its earliest days, and for many years after, the college had produced some able preachers, men of the calibre of John Hawksworth, John Clayton, James Glazebrook, Thomas Snell Jones, Anthony Crole and many others.[2] The guidelines set by Fletcher were of a high order, with most students mastering Latin and Greek. Williams felt embarrassed and ashamed that young men whom he was supposed to be training should be sent out to preach with an inadequate grasp of biblical teaching.

[1] *Ibid.*
[2] Many Trevecca men conducted ministries significant enough to merit long obituaries in different numbers of *The Evangelical Magazine*. See notes in Appendix 4.

Writing to George Best, who had himself been both a Trevecca student, then a tutor and was now serving in the capacity of personal secretary to Selina, Williams again complained that 'what knowledge and instruction any of them acquire in three or four months [they] immediately forget it almost entire.'[1]

Even more troubling than ignorant students was the number of unpaid bills that were accumulating. The cost of running Trevecca was estimated at between £500–600 annually, or half the Countess's total income. Her liquid resources were fast running out. 'I believe she often possessed no more than the gown she wore', wrote Thomas Haweis.[2] All her life she had enjoyed a pinch of snuff from time to time.[3] Now she deprived herself of this small pleasure in order to save a little money. More than this, she ordered the ploughing up of much of the Donington estate in order to grow corn for the supply of the college And still the bills mounted. John Williams wrote in desperation:

> There are a few workmen . . . unpaid and they keep continually a most dreadful noise about payment. I hope your Ladyship will be soon enabled to satisfy their impatient demands for they are extremely and unreasonably clamorous.

Averina Powell, now the housekeeper at Trevecca, and a most efficient one too, wrote on a similar line. The butcher would no longer supply the college with meat, while the grocer, who said he had been almost bankrupted by college debts, also refused to supply wheat and other provisions for the students. He had brought with him a bill for £81. Meanwhile, the tailoress, Joan Jones wrote indignantly to the Countess: 'I have supplied the college with several materials upwards of a twelvemonth. I have not received one single farthing. It is impossible for me to go on.'[4]

---

[1] *Ibid.*, 12 January 1788.
[2] Haweis, *Church History*, p. 252.
[3] An inhalant powder manufactured from the midrib of tobacco leaves, snuff had become widely used in Britain at this time, particularly in fashionable circles.
[4] C. F. Archives.

Clearly Selina was committed beyond her means – nor was she unaware of the problems. She complained that she was bearing an unequal burden of expense. To one who was demanding money, she wrote that she had to finance 'all this great work in England and Wales without one soul to help me with one shilling . . . Faith only sustains my burdens and keeps me free.' Had she done more to encourage the churches to be self-supporting, the situation might well have been different. The need for someone to assist at a practical level was becoming increasingly obvious, and it was at this time that George Best undertook the duties of a personal secretary – a position he held until the end of the Countess's life.

In view of all these problems relating to the college, it is not surprising that those closest to Selina were concerned about its future. An option towards which she was well-disposed was to move it to another vicinity. Hereford was one suggestion,[1] another, and one which was more acceptable to the Countess, was Swansea in South Wales where a further chapel was currently being built. These concerns, however, prompted the Spa Fields committee to take action to provide for the college, in view of the Countess's advanced age and the fact that her death would leave it without any means of support. A society was formed in October 1787 known as the Apostolic Society. Subscribers were invited to make donations to this Society specifically for the future of the college which was to be transferred to Swansea and placed under a board of seven governors, all laymen. Details of staff and even their pay were laid out together with the daily routine for the running of the college. The particulars specified for the future of Trevecca reflect the way it had already been functioning for almost twenty years and were largely the work of Selina herself. The only major difference, and one that suggests that Selina was concerned about the current low standards, was

---

[1] The Countess had actually purchased a building there in 1787 and was then financing the alterations to turn it into a place of worship.

that the students were to preach in the vicinity of the college for at least two years so that they could concentrate on their studies more effectively. The Apostolic Society was not a success, however, with few subscribers showing any interest, largely because its terms were not to be implemented until after the death of the Countess.

Thomas Wills was not happy about any of these plans. He had another idea which he had pressed on the Countess some years earlier. Trevecca should be closed down altogether, the students dispersed and placed under the personal tuition of more experienced men, preferably in rural Wales where costs would be less. We have seen how much the college had meant to Selina in its inception, maintenance and the undeniable benefits for the church of Jesus Christ that had sprung from the labours of its students. With Trevecca holding so high a place in her affections, we can scarcely be surprised to learn that she firmly rejected this option.

A glance at the Spa Fields minute book quickly reveals one thing: Thomas Wills was much loved by most of the church. 'Dear Mr Wills preaches sweetly and evangelically with much life and power and his divine Master owns and blesses his ministry', we read in a letter written to the Countess on behalf of the Committee on 21 January 1785. When William Taylor preached during the annual absences when Wills was touring the country, there is little more than a brief acknowledgement of the fact. As he was married to the Countess's niece and was popular in the Connexion, it is not surprising that Wills felt in a position to make strong representations to the Countess on issues where he thought she was mistaken. Twenty years earlier Howell Harris had noted of the Countess that she 'cannot bear contradiction'. Now she found it yet harder and this sometimes led to a degree of confrontation between Thomas Wills and herself. Several issues had arisen in the mid-1780s where they had disagreed. As we have seen, Wills had felt obliged to point out that to proceed with the Brussels plan was to disregard the clear will of God. His suggestions regarding the future of the college cannot have improved their relationship.

On a Sunday evening in August 1787 Wills announced to the congregation at Spa Fields that he was about to leave them for a six-week tour of the country as had become his custom for some years. William Taylor, together with a preacher by the name of John Bradford,[1] would be largely responsible for the ministry during his absence. While Wills was away he wrote a series of letters to Taylor and, as one pastor to another, felt free to share his aggrievement at some of the things the Countess was saying and doing. Little did he suspect that Taylor, who had carefully concealed his jealousy of the man whose ministry was clearly preferred to his own, might betray his confidence. Taylor promptly took all the correspondence and spread it before the Countess herself. She was indignant, largely because Wills had insinuated that on account of her advanced age, her decisions were becoming unreliable. Writing to Nathaniel Rowland, who often ministered at Spa Fields, she complained that Wills had written of her 'as if my intellect was gone'.[2] Seeing that Wills was

---

[1] John Bradford, an ordained clergyman of the Church of England, was antinomian in his theology. Following the 1770 debacle, an over-reaction among Calvinists to any emphasis on works had led to an increase in antinomianism among them. Some have even accused the Countess herself of it. But a careful reading of her letters, expressing a deep sense of personal sin and shortcoming, must quickly dispel such an assertion.

[2] Edwin Welch interprets these words as meaning that Wills had suggested that the Countess had become senile. This is too strong an interpretation, for she herself only complained that he had said she was acting 'as if my intellect was gone'. There is no evidence at all that she became senile in old age. Hinting, perhaps, at what Wills might have said in his letter, one of her former students in a funeral address for the Countess, said, 'It grieved her much to hear that she was represented in a state of superannuation, and that her sun would go down under a cloud. Blessed be God it has proved false.' A week before she died, the same preacher added, 'the vigour of her mind was unabated and her intellect as clear as in any period of her life.' William F. Platt, *The Waiting Christian* (Bristol,1791), p. 13.

in serious trouble, others who had also resented his unrivalled position with the Countess, added fuel to the fire by suggestions that Wills had been less than honest with the Countess's money. Deceived by such insinuations and hurt by Wills's own comments – comments for which he expressed deep remorse – Selina informed her chaplain that his services were no longer required at Spa Fields.

This was a regrettable episode in the life of so remarkable a person. Such peremptory dismissals of those who had previously served her well led even one of her most sincere admirers to say in the convoluted style of the day, 'Lady Huntingdon was in her temper warm and sanguine – her predilections for some and her prejudice against others were sometimes too hastily adopted – and by these she was led to form conclusions not always correspondent with truth and wisdom.'[1] Needless to say the Spa Fields church was shaken to the core by the sudden dismissal of their well-respected preacher. Writing of it, one in the congregation at the time said: 'This, as may be expected, spread a general alarm through the congregation, and his friends felt the most painful sensations imaginable; it was as unexpected as it was terrific. Some pacified themselves with hopes that these were merely reports without foundation, but in a very little time were convinced of the sad reality'.[2] There followed a popular outcry among Wills's friends and supporters. Reluctantly the Countess allowed him to preach at Spa Fields again, but on a temporary basis. In July 1788 his services were finally terminated.

This action on the part of the Countess had an unforeseen effect on all her churches. Wills was known and respected up and down the country where he had conducted preaching tours each summer since 1781. The churches in Bristol and Bath were profoundly disturbed, but such was the campaign now mounted against Wills, by those who had viewed his privileges with a

[1] Haweis, *Church History*, p. 253.
[2] *Memoir of Wills*, p. 211.

jaundiced eye, that the Countess became hardened in her attitude and more convinced of her chaplain's dishonourable conduct.

To exacerbate the situation the preacher currently ministering at Spa Fields, John Bradford, also took the opportunity to discredit Wills' ministry. He insinuated that Wills had been leading the people into error by introducing Wesley's perfectionist teaching. He had done this, so Bradford implied, by insisting that profession of faith must be matched by godly practice.[1] By this time, it is possible that the Countess had herself become so confused and prejudiced against her chaplain that she was actually willing to believe such libel, though she must have heard Wills preach enough times to give the lie to these remarks. When Wills asked permission to vindicate himself in the eyes of the congregation and say his farewells in one last sermon, his petition was rejected. Determined that he should not be silenced so unjustly, he printed his sermon and on 1 August 1788 his friends distributed it among the congregation as they came out of the service. Selina heard what was happening and she summarily forbade any further leaflets to be distributed. The words he had written were moving: 'I have not been speaking of an unknown God, for under my late heavy and unexpected trials his everlasting arms have been underneath me. He has been my refuge and succour, else I must have sunk under the burden.'

The damage resulting from the dispute was widespread throughout the Connexion. By retaining ultimate and personal responsibility for every decision in the Connexion, the Countess had placed herself in an invidious and unbiblical position. Had some form of church government been established to oversee the life of these churches, such a dispute would have been more

---

[1] A pamphlet entitled *The Arminian Skeleton*, written by William Huntington, the celebrated hyper-Calvinist preacher, was being circulated at the time. In it he charged Wills with being a legal preacher and an advocate of Arminian tenets. He had also accused Wills of not being converted. Many, believing these aspersions, forsook Spa Fields and became followers of Huntington.

easily contained. From a twenty-first century perspective it needs to be appreciated, however, that the men of the eighteenth century revival were above all evangelists, and few had a clearly defined doctrine of the church. Autocratic procedures were common and generally accepted in eighteenth century society and also, to an extent, in church life. This was particularly true in the Church of England where wealthy patrons often had undisputed authority.

Repercussions followed swiftly throughout the Connexion as a number of men resigned their positions or severed their links altogether. These included Joel Knight, an assistant minister at Spa Fields who had charge of the school. As a former Trevecca student, Knight had been ordained at Spa Fields and therefore knew the situation well. Griffith Williams, another well-respected former student who was currently ministering at the Countess's Mulberry Gardens chapel, also left the Connexion. So did William Green, in charge of the ministry at Bath, to mention but a few. Wills suffered severe ill-health as a direct result of the shock he had received. Not many months had passed, however, before it came to light that William Taylor, prime architect of the trouble, was not only guilty of an adulterous relationship but had been doing the very thing of which Wills had been falsely accused: defrauding the Countess of funds given for the support of the work at Spa Fields. As soon as these things came to light, she dismissed him but sadly did not re-instate Wills. For some time her former chaplain had no settled congregation but in 1790, two years after these events, he became the pastor of Silver Street Chapel, in Cheapside, London, and continued to experience blessing on his ministry.

With both her chaplains gone and the churches in a considerable measure of disarray, the Countess now stood in urgent need of a senior man to head up her work. Her eyes turned once again to Thomas Haweis. Although Haweis had not preached in any of her chapels for almost eight years since she had left the Church of

England, he had remained well-disposed towards the Countess. His wife, Judith, had died tragically in 1786 after she was thrown from a cart, and two years later he remarried. His choice was Jenetta Orton who, as we have noted, had been Selina's personal companion for many years, travelling with her and easing her burden of work. Jenetta owed her conversion to Haweis more than twenty years earlier, and had rescued him with financial help when he had been in deep trouble in the past. It was a fitting marriage and it opened the way for Haweis to respond to the Countess's invitation to join her again as her chaplain. A staunch churchman, Haweis retained his disapproval of the Dissenting status of the Connexion chapels, yet his return to the Countess's side was timely and restored much of the credibility she had lost in her handling of Thomas Wills.

Reflecting on the sad events of 1788, Haweis was later to comment:

> Was she a perfect character? No! This is not the lot of mortals on this side the grave. When the moon walketh in her brightness, her shadows are most visible.[1]

---

[1] Haweis, *Church History,* p. 253.

# 29

## 'MY TIME IS SHORT'

BENJAMIN TUCKER WAS IN DESPAIR. For some years he and a few others had rented a room in Castle Street in Swansea, South Wales, where they would meet to pray and worship together. Now the struggling cause faced hard times with internal divisions decimating their numbers. Although Trevecca students had preached in Swansea over the years, the differences of religious, cultural and national background among the Swansea converts had led to divisions in the society and now scarcely half a dozen still met. Then came the final blow for the beleaguered society: the landlady threatened to turn the key of the room in Castle Street the following week unless they could pay the annual rent of £3 for the continued use of the premises. Tucker and his friends were too poor to find such a sum. The troubled man paced towards the shore, reflecting on the situation; then he fell to his knees and implored the help of God. As he prayed the thought of the Countess of Huntingdon flashed into his mind. She was currently staying nearby, or so he had heard. Unable to write with any degree of accuracy, Tucker employed the help of a friend who set forth the predicament of the society in a letter to the Countess. On hearing of the need, Selina's first thought was to send the students once again to raise a congregation. Then they would be able to find enough money to pay the landlady.

A year later Benjamin Tucker was back with a further request. This time he wanted a chapel for Swansea. Although there were still a handful of society members Tucker's scriptural reasoning for his appeal pleased the Countess: 'There were but few in Cornelius's house, but at his invitation more came; and while Peter preached the Holy Ghost fell upon all them that heard the word.' Such faith demanded a response, and in 1786 Selina arranged to visit Swansea together with one of her students. Land in present-day Adelaide Street was soon leased from the Swansea corporation at an annual rent of £3.14s. The foundation stone of the new chapel was laid by a former student, William Aldridge, together with Benjamin Tucker.

Before long the walls and windows of a typical Countess of Huntingdon chapel in Gothic style began to take shape. One thing only delayed the building programme – Selina had taken a liking to Swansea and had insisted that a house should be purchased for her personal use within sight of the sea. With her home in Brighton now rented out she must have missed such views; but finding a suitable property was by no means easy. At last by 1787 all was nearing completion. An unusual degree of detail has survived on the Swansea chapel, detail that we repeat because it is likely to have formed a pattern for many of the smaller chapels. Walls were to be built to the height of nine feet above the foundations, gates were to be of iron work, with railings and lamps of decorative wrought iron. Soil removed from the site was to form part of a terraced walk leading to the chapel. An interior plan similar to that of the Bath Chapel was to be followed with the same positioning of the benches and music gallery. The eagle lecterns and pulpit, identical in style to those eagles with outspread wings that can still be seen in the former Vineyards chapel in Bath, were then put in place.[1] A further delay of more than a year followed, but at last on 5 August 1789 the Swansea chapel was officially opened by 'Mr Rowland', whether it was the honourable old Welsh preacher himself, or his son, Nathaniel, we do not know.

[1] C. F. Archives.

Bath chapel itself had been in a sorry state for a number of years. A split in 1782 had seriously reduced the numbers attending. This was brought about because, despite the new Dissenting status of the chapels, the Countess still insisted that only men ordained in the Church of England should occupy its pulpit.[1] And now the distress caused by the treatment of Thomas Wills, a well-loved figure at the church, had further weakened the cause. Thomas Haweis, whom the Countess appointed to minister there when he rejoined her Connexion, soon attracted the people back once more and we read that the 'house was crammed from door to door'. Self-confident and not a little loquacious, Haweis was nevertheless the right man for Bath at this time and the right man to help the Countess overcome the problems she had caused.[2]

Although he remained an Establishment man in his outlook and priorities, refusing even to attend any ordination services conducted within the Connexion, Haweis was an asset to the Countess in another sphere. His interest in foreign missions and his strong desire for the worldwide spread of the gospel matched her own deep longings. Despite her disappointment, first in America and then in the Brussels fiasco, Selina, now aged eighty-two, still dreamed and planned – for no less than a missionary scheme to cover the globe. In 1788 she had sent out two missionaries to New Brunswick and one to Nova Scotia.[3] As we noted earlier she had sent one of her most capable former students, John Johnson, to Georgia to try to recover some of her lost assets

---

[1] This illustrates the fact that the Countess was never a Dissenter at heart. Argyle Chapel where William Jay had his celebrated ministry was opened in 1789 as a result.

[2] See William Jay's comment on Haweis whom he knew well and whose deathbed he attended. *The Autobiography of William Jay* (Edinburgh: Banner of Truth, 1974), pp. 475–80.

[3] This was John Marrant, a black man converted under Whitefield's preaching in Charlestown, South Carolina, when he and a friend had intended to disrupt the meeting. After a period in England, working with the Connexion, Marrant was ordained by Thomas Wills at Vineyard Chapel in Bath in 1785 and was then sent back to Nova Scotia by the Countess.

at Bethesda. He also had a further agenda. The destitute plight of many of the native American Indians had long troubled the Countess, so now she planned to bequeath the estates she still possessed in Georgia to the founding of a university for these neglected peoples. The venture was to be financed from the sale of land which Johnson would salvage from the collapsed Bethesda project.[1]

During the autumn and winter months of 1789 Selina was seriously ill once more and little hope was held out for her recovery. But still she struggled on. 'I hope to see your Ladyship once again in your chair and be permitted to receive your commands,' wrote Haweis, somewhat obsequiously as she gradually regained strength. Still severely weakened, Selina was called to face a grief that affected her profoundly – the sudden and unexpected death of Francis, her eldest son. Despite his prodigal ways, she had loved him deeply and had always looked and prayed for a spiritual change. But it seems that it was not to be. Yet there was one straw of comfort to which the bereaved mother clung. As he lay dying Francis had asked to see James Matthews, the student expelled from St Edmund Hall in 1768, who had made a lasting impression upon him when he had spoken to the young nobleman of God's dealings with his own soul. Many letters of condolence, expressing sincere sympathy and understanding of the poignancy of her grief, arrived at the Countess's Spa Fields home.

Though often confined to a chair in her dining room, Selina still looked far beyond the four walls that imprisoned her ailing body. In her mind's eye she saw the triumphs of the gospel in far-flung places of the earth. But time was at a premium – the remaining days of her earthly life must now be few in number, this she knew for a certainty and so she planned ceaselessly for the advance of the kingdom of God. Far from settling down to a

[1] This plan too came to nothing. Johnson himself was even imprisoned for a period. See above p. 329.

pampered retirement, this brave old woman seemed to work yet harder as her days drew to a close. 'Let me die with my last breath labouring for him', was the aspiration she expressed in a letter to Haweis in the spring of 1790. Even though she had 'a fashionable cold' and had almost lost her voice, there was little relaxation, for 'all day long some new person wants to speak to me'.[1]

Two projects gripped Selina's imagination in particular. One was for a mission to Otaheite, a vision she had caught from Thomas Haweis himself. 'Your faithful zeal for the South Seas fills my many moments with joy and delight',[2] she wrote in April 1790. Her immediate plan, as she explained to her chaplain, was to request a certain Captain Roberts, due to sail to the South Seas shortly in his new vessel *Discovery*, to visit her and to ask him to examine the feasibility of establishing a Christian mission in the area, and report back to her on his return.

More than this, the Countess scanned her lists of students and former students to see if there were any suitable to become missionaries in so distant a location. Two names appealed to her, and when Haweis interviewed twenty-eight-year-old Michael Waugh and John Price, still only twenty-three, he found the young men well grounded in both Scripture and theology, but lacking in basic education. He undertook to instruct them personally and at his own expense during 1790 until he was confident that they were adequately prepared to face the challenges ahead. This was in marked contrast to the students who had sailed for America in 1772 whose youth and inexperience had been a clear disadvantage to them. Reflecting on all these developments brought much joy to Selina as her physical strength declined.

A second project also filled her mind with pleasure and anticipation in these final months of her life – a mission in Paris. Her

[1] MS. in the Leete Collection in the Centre for Methodist Studies at Bridwell Library, Perkins School of Theology, Southern Methodist University, Dallas, Texas. Hereafter Bridwell Library.      [2] *Ibid.*

writings are peppered with references to it. 'France has so possessed me after your letter', is a typical comment to be found in a letter to Haweis.[1] Her plan was to consult with the French ambassador who was currently in Bath and then negotiate to buy 'the finest church in Paris' for the base of her work. Expanding on the theme to Thomas Charles of Bala, then thirty-five years of age, Selina wrote, 'France is a beloved object for me; one thousand pounds I have offered for one of the finest churches in Paris.'[2] Her vision extended beyond Paris, as she continues to Charles, 'You will smile when I tell you Madrid may also stretch out her hands unto God', and her hopes were yet more inclusive as she concluded exultantly, 'I could drive the globe for our Immanuel's kingdom to come.'[3] All references to the Paris initiative suddenly disappear from her correspondence, however, and it is likely that the carnage of the French Revolution made the prospect of any further progress there impossible.

In 1784, six years before the date of the letter quoted above, Thomas Charles had reached an impasse in his life and all doors of spiritual usefulness had seemed shut against him. Unable to obtain a curacy, and rejected from other Church of England pulpits because of his forthright gospel preaching, Charles began to tour areas of North Wales on behalf of the Calvinistic Methodists. He now discovered that 'thousands flock to hear ... and [many], we have good reason to believe, are effectually called.' As a friend of William Williams, Daniel Rowland and David Jones of Llangan, Thomas Charles soon came to the attention of the Countess of Huntingdon.

When Selina first heard of the blessing attending his ministry, she lost no time in inviting Charles to take the pulpit at Spa Fields

[1] *Ibid.*, 24 March 1790.
[2] With her income of £1200 p.a. already insufficient for her many commitments, the Countess would have raised this money by the sale of some of her property.
[3] Cited by D. E. S. Brown, in MA thesis, Southern Methodist University, 1984, p. 82.

when he could be spared from his Welsh commitments. Eleven letters written by Charles to the Countess between July 1789 and February 1791 have survived. Although mainly concerned with practical arrangements for his visits, these letters reveal the warmth of the friendship that had sprung up between the Countess and the young Welsh preacher. Soon he would fill a great need in Wales as men of the calibre of Daniel Rowland and William Williams left their earthly labours.

Though the Countess longed for the worldwide progress of the gospel, she did not limit her schemes to far-off places. England and Wales still had many towns and villages untouched by the gospel. 'Six itinerant preachers I have ordered for all dark parts of Wales and eight I mean for the very darkest corners of England', she wrote to Haweis in 1790.[1] With Haweis, too, she shared another concern that moved her deeply: the plight of children and young people, destitute, streetwise and often ill. 'A great plan lies before me for saving the number of youth rotting alive by sad disease in hospitals at 12, 10, 9 years old and so ruined in the streets.'[2] Letters are extant that mention a further project the Countess envisaged at this time. She planned to purchase the Haymarket in Leicester[3] for a sum of £840. Here in the heart of her own home county a witness to the power of the gospel would be raised. Meanwhile she could report to Haweis that five new chapels were in the process of erection and five other towns were urgently asking for students to help them. 'Poor [George] Best and myself are day and night at work as faithful slaves.'[4]

Without detracting from the vision and zeal of the ageing Countess, it would seem that a number of her 'schemes' in these last years of life could be better described as aspirations. Not all were realistic. Her proposals for the triumphant advance of the gospel

[1] MS. in Bridwell Library.
[2] *Ibid.*, 25 February 1790.
[3] Now an extensive shopping precinct. Reference in C. F. Archives.
[4] MS. in Bridwell Library.

worldwide, though highly commendable, were frequently not viable. The progress she was witnessing in many avenues of her work throughout the country reminded her of the early days of the revival fifty years ago, she told Haweis. Perhaps this gave rise to these ever grander schemes. Few came to fruition, and if they had done she certainly would not have had the ready money to finance them all. This enthusiasm for noble ends, sometimes without sufficient evaluation of the means, was the same problem that Thomas Wills had faced over the proposed visit to Brussels, and similar attitudes were the subject of his complaints in his letters to Taylor. His reservations had not pleased the Countess, as we have seen. Even now when her friends initially tried to modify her plans for Paris, suggesting that she wait until the political situation in France and Spain was more stable, she had a ready answer, 'Oh for that faith that subdues kingdoms to Jesus Christ. For this my longing soul is athirst. My shame will be I have lived so little for him.'[1]

And still the chapel-building went on. In 1790 another owner of an amusement arcade, this time in the Whitechapel area of East London, found himself in difficulties. The large circular building was used for horse shows. Like Spa Fields, it was complete with siderooms, a stage, a wide central arena almost twenty-six metres in diameter where the horses performed, and tiered seats for spectators. It was easily convertible into a chapel, and the Countess found the owner's offer of the remainder of the lease, with seventy-eight years yet to run at a cost of £130 a year, an irresistible challenge.

But not everyone felt the same as the Countess about the project of a further chapel in London, and not far from the Mulberry Gardens chapel. James Oldham, chairman of the Spa Fields committee, had now become seriously concerned about the Countess's finances. With creditors already knocking at her door, he believed it was impracticable to take on further

[1] *Ibid.*

commitments. Arriving at her Spa Fields home to remonstrate with her about the issue, Oldham discovered that there was plenty of verve in Selina's spirit still to be reckoned with. She would need £500 to finance the new chapel and the coffers were empty, he told her. As the Countess listened to her senior committee member, probably with some degree of consternation, the post arrived. Opening one of her letters quickly, Selina's face visibly brightened and her eyes filled with tears as she drew out a draft for exactly £500. 'Take this and pay for the chapel', she said simply to the astonished Oldham, adding, doubtless with a touch of satisfaction, 'and be no longer faithless but believing.'[1]

Sion Chapel, as it became known, was opened on 28 November 1790 with services conducted by a John Ford, who was beginning to play an increasing part in Connexion affairs, and by David Jones of Llangan, the Welsh preacher whose friendship and assistance at Spa Fields had been of growing importance to the elderly Countess. The building could seat some two thousand worshippers, with six hundred free seats in the pit or Circle as it was still called.

By 1788 the Countess could compile a list of no fewer than a hundred and sixteen 'preaching places' for which she held ultimate responsibility. Some were chapels she had financed; some were existing chapels that she had supplied with preachers, mainly on a short term basis; to others she had sent students, and yet others had settled pastors who wished to be in association with her. In 1790 Selina realized that it had become imperative that some long term strategy should be devised to blend and hold together all these varied churches and situations. Her policy in the past had been to appoint a local committee to oversee all the financial and practical concerns of each chapel. This committee would be responsible to appointed trustees. But the Countess retained an overall right to appoint or dismiss committee members, trustees or even ministers if she felt it necessary or if her

[1] New, *Coronet and Cross*, p. 353.

wishes were crossed – a right she had exercised on a number of occasions.

Several abortive plans for the future were mooted only to be dismissed either by the Countess herself or by the Spa Fields committee, which, as the largest Connexion church, would have a major share of the responsibility in the event of the Countess's death. But in March 1790, in collaboration with a group of London ministers and laymen, giving themselves the name of the London Acting Association, Selina produced a *Plan of Association for Uniting and Perpetuating the Connexion*. This plan, bearing the signature of the Countess's secretary, George Best, was to be printed and circulated throughout the Connexion for the consideration and approval of all the churches. A covering letter from the Countess accompanied the *Plan*, warmly commending it to their acceptance.

The *Plan*, however, only mentioned sixty-four churches with two that included 'a horse ride', indicating that they covered a number of smaller chapels that were within riding distance. Even so the list contrasts strangely with the one hundred and sixteen preaching places listed by the Countess two years earlier. Probably the answer lies in the fact that the 'preaching places' in the 1788 list included hired halls, barns and disused chapels where students preached to regular congregations. Unfortunately no comprehensive list of all these places of worship now exists.[1]

Well thought-out and pragmatic, the *Plan* consisted of thirty-one separate clauses intended to ensure the continuance and smooth running of the Connexion. In brief, the churches were to be grouped into twenty-three different geographical districts. A committee was to be appointed for each district which comprised the ministers of the member churches, together with two laymen from each church. Each committee would be required to meet on a quarterly basis to discuss matters of concern in their separate churches. Ten days after it had met, the committee would

[1] For the text of the *Plan*, see Appendix 8.

forward details of all matters discussed to the London Acting Association. This Association, in turn, would report to the General Association which met annually. A tightly-knit system, it bore similarities to the basis on which John Wesley had organized his Methodist societies with their quarterly meetings and annual conference. Other clauses included procedures for dealing with matters in dispute, the position of students, the appointment of ministers, and the conduct of Association meetings. Also of importance, however, was a short clause that said, 'Each person to give not less than 1d a week'. This provision, one that had proved highly significant in Wesleyan Methodism when Wesley had introduced it in Bristol in 1739, would supply much needed extra finance once the Countess's generous contributions had ceased. Now, as she expressed it to Haweis, 'when the Lord calls for me, my absence will not make more than an old shoe cast aside.'[1]

Although men of the standing of Thomas Charles were happy with the *Plan of Association*, it was too late in Selina's life for an effective plan to be successfully initiated. And, regrettably for the future of the Connexion, it failed. This was because of the intransigence of two individuals, but individuals of key importance. The first was Thomas Haweis. He scribbled on the back of the envelope of the letter addressed to the church in Bath containing details of the *Plan*, 'If her Ladyship pleases to insist on the scheme being enforced at Bath, I shall be very sorry, as I am unable to concur in it, and it must separate me from you.' Haweis was first and foremost a churchman, and he had never approved of the Countess's action in accepting Dissenting status. He saw himself as the heir apparent of the Connexion, and could possibly envisage a day when he could bring it back to the Church of England fold. With the *Plan of Association* he would be stymied, and any move he might make would be submitted to the approval of a committee that gave even laymen a voice in decision-making.

[1] MS. in Bridwell Library.

For several months the Countess cajoled, pleaded, promised and suggested any number of options to Haweis to gain his support, at least tacitly, for the *Plan of Association*. She knew full well that without some structure her chapels would gradually secede from the Connexion and find refuge instead in the associations of the Congregational, Baptist and Presbyterian denominations. But her pleas and suggestions were in vain. Haweis' final answer came in June 1790. Two items he singled out as the basis of his objections: first, the introduction of laymen into positions of authority within the Connexion; 'Every minister and his labours are made wholly dependent upon them', he complained. The second objection was the raising of funds by the penny-a-week proposal. Here he was surprisingly scathing, revealing a degree of haughtiness of spirit. 'Overwhelmed with grief and shame', he had reflected on 'all the misery, mischief, disgust and division that must be the immediate result of such a penny collection. How your Ladyship's noble spirit can brook such an idea, I am totally at a loss to account.' Unless the *Plan of Association* were discarded, he continued, 'your Ladyship will love me, bless me and dismiss me.' He would submit to her decision in silence and 'cordially wish well to every person though my active services be no longer employed.'[1] The prospect of losing Haweis was one which Selina could not face. Suffering from 'spasms [of the throat], stone and unceasing thirst and the constant opposition to all nourishment', she was in no position to argue with him. Haweis, it seemed, would win the day.

There was another, however, who strongly opposed the Plan. Faithful, loving, loyal over many years, Lady Anne Erskine had become indispensable to Selina, who depended on her care day and night and loved her dearly in return. Lady Anne had helped the Countess for so long that their minds acted as one. She knew instinctively what the Countess would wish in any given situation, and if Haweis was the heir apparent of the Connexion,

[1] C. F. Archives.

Lady Anne was certainly the heiress to all the Countess's prestige and position. She would slip easily into the role of patroness of students and chapels alike when the Countess should be taken from all her labours. Perhaps the thought of such a position now appealed to her. Records of the times suggest that Lady Anne's opposition to the plan was intense. 'Your Ladyship has no truer friend than Lady Anne', wrote Haweis on 12 June 1790. 'Consider this subject again, my dear Madam, I entreat you.'

Weary and ill, the Countess capitulated. A letter quoted by one of her preachers, written at this time, reflects the sorrow she felt over the demise of her plans:

I have with many an aching heart felt the vast importance most faithfully to preserve the pure and blessed gospel of Jesus Christ among you when I am gone. A variety of ways, my many hours of sorrowful prayers and tears have suggested . . . but alas where my best confidence has from time to time been placed, the Lord has confounded it. I resolve therefore to make known my requests to him alone . . . Ever remember in your prayers your poor old door-keeper in the Lord's house, and your servant for his sake.[1]

Selina had already made her will in January 1790, and now she left it unaltered. In it she had said:

I give and devise all my freehold, copyhold and leasehold houses in London, Bath, Brighthelmstone, Tunbridge Wells and Hereford[2] and the furniture therein and also all my chapels there, together with all my other chapels and houses and furniture, with everything else belonging thereto, and used therewith respectively . . . unto the said Thomas Haweis and Jenetta, his wife; the said Lady Anne Agnes Erskine and John Lloyd,[3] now of Swansea.

[1] Cited in J. Wilson, *The Believer's Conflict*, a sermon preached at Barton-upon-Humber, 3 July, 1791 (Hull, 1791), p. 12.

[2] Surprisingly there is no mention of her Swansea property.

[3] John Lloyd, who had formerly lived in Bath, had been a friend over many years and had had responsibility for much of the Countess's finances, paying students and other expenses incurred in connection with their services for her.

These four were entrusted with all her property, to be regulated for the best advantage of the Connexion, with the added proviso that upon the death of any one of the original four, another be appointed to take the place of the deceased member of the quartet, always ensuring that four people had overall responsibility for all the assets of the Connexion. But there was something of far greater significance to the Countess of Huntingdon. Concluding her will, she wrote:

> As I have always lived a poor unworthy pensioner of the infinite bounty of my Lord God and Saviour Jesus Christ, so do I hereby declare that all my present peace and my future hope of glory, either in whole or in part, depend wholly, fully and finally upon his alone merits. Committing my soul into his arms unreservedly as a subject of his sole mercy to all eternity.[1]

[1] From a copy of the will, by courtesy of the Archives of the Countess of Huntingdon's Connexion.

## 30

# 'MY WORK IS DONE'

EVEN IN EXTREME OLD AGE the Countess of Huntingdon tried to keep a grip on the affairs of her students and chapels. Confined to a chair in her dining room at Spa Fields for most of the day, with failing eyesight, suffering pain and debilitating weakness, she still received applications for the college and letters from students. One example, typical of many such letters that she received, was from Lewis Jones who had been preaching for some time in Norwich. Now he felt he needed a move and in June 1790 wrote to the Countess:

> I do not, dear patroness, desire a change for my own ease, though I find the labour rather hard. Preaching three times every Lord's Day to so large a congregation has I fear impaired my constitution … but this moves me not. I care not how soon death comes to remove me hence. I only desire a change hoping it would be profitable for the congregation and for their furtherance in the gospel.[1]

Other former students would write asking for permission to relinquish their itinerant work that they might accept a call to a settled pastorate. William Melsham was one. He felt he could no longer support his family without a regular income, and so wrote in December 1790 explaining the situation. A Dissenting church in Lincoln had 'with one voice' invited him to become their pas-

[1] C. F. Archives.

tor, he told her, and his 'family called aloud for that relief which it is out of my power to give them'.

As so often happens in old age, Selina faced the death of a number of her friends and associates. For many years she had held Daniel Rowland of Llangeitho in high regard. Letters to his son, Nathaniel, often asked after his father. But in the summer of 1790, fearing that her old friend might not live much longer, she had an unusual request: 'My Christian love to your dear old father, and tell him that I have passed my word that in one thing he will oblige me.' She then explained that many would appreciate an engraving of Rowland, and, if he would be agreeable, she would send an artist – none other than the king's own artist – to paint his portrait and then the engraving would be taken from the painting. 'The engraving will be very fine and the picture, like, I am sure, and therefore, no unkind refusal to me', she concluded. Rowland did not refuse and the picture was completed just a week before his death.[1] Declaring himself 'a poor sinner depending fully and entirely on the merits of a crucified Saviour', he died on 16 October 1790. 'The old oxen are taken from the field, and the great work not yet accomplished', grieved David Jones of Llangan, who conducted the funeral service. When Selina heard of the death of her friend she had another special request to make – that all his papers and information concerning him should be gathered together and sent to her. Perhaps she intended to commission a biography. Sadly these papers have been lost to posterity, for by the time enquiry was made after them some years later, the Countess herself had died and no one knew of their whereabouts.

William Williams, affectionately known as Billy Williams to his close friends, was also failing. Confined to one room, he looked back on days when he had travelled nearly three thousand miles a year for over fifty years. And now, he could move no more than 'forty feet in a day, from the fireside to the bed'. Soon he too was

[1] The well-known engraving is now in the National Library of Wales.

released from all the restrictions of failing strength for in January 1791 the Welsh poet also died. 'Poor Wales,' wrote Thomas Charles, when the Countess told him of Williams's death, 'as it never was so highly honoured, so it also never had such heavy strokes. My heart bleeds with those thousands of my brethren.' As well as losing another friend, the Countess was immediately confronted with a pressing problem. John Williams, who had been the tutor at Trevecca for the last four years, decided he must relinquish the post to care for his widowed mother. Thomas Charles promised to do all in his power to try and find a satisfactory replacement tutor for Trevecca.

Old friends too had gone. John Fletcher had died in 1785; Charles Wesley had followed on 29 March 1788, whispering 'Lord . . . my heart . . . my God'. We cannot doubt that the Countess mourned deeply the loss of this friend whose prayers, she once declared she valued 'more than thousands of worlds'. Nor did she forget Sally Wesley in her widowhood, and even in her own weakness she asked her secretary, George Best, to send Sally a turkey. In a letter dated 20 January 1791, Best assured Sally that though the Countess was 'this day confined to her bed and still continues to suffer very much', yet she still remembered her 'very kind and old love for you'. Selina also did all in her power to help Sally's son, Charles, forward in his musical career and appears to have fostered a genuine affection for him.[1]

Only six weeks after that letter was written John Wesley too finished his earthly course. Just four days before his death, he had prayed:

> Till glad I lay this body down
> Thy servant Lord, attend!
> And Oh! my life of mercy crown
> With a triumphant end.

[1] Rylands MS.

It was a prayer God answered. 'There is no way into the holiest but by the blood of Jesus', he was heard to declare; and, 'The best of all is, God is with us', he assured his friends who waited anxiously around his bed. Throughout his last night on earth, when his speech had almost failed, Wesley struggled to repeat the first line of Isaac Watts's great hymn, 'I'll praise my Maker, while I've breath'. 'I'll praise . . . I'll praise . . . ', he began over and over again until on 2 March 1791 he left for ever the sphere of his vast labours, with both its controversies and its blessings, to praise God perfectly in a better world.

The Countess has occasionally been described as authoritarian, peremptory, sometimes petulant and even vindictive to a degree towards those who had offended her.[1] These things could be true in part. It would be anachronistic, however, to judge Selina by modern standards, forgetting the cultural distinctions that coloured the thinking not only of the aristocracy but of society as a whole. Her weaknesses, together with the traits of Shirley temperament that had marked the family for generations,[2] provide a foil against which we must measure her exceptional achievements and her unquenchable zeal for the spread of the gospel. Whatever her failures might have been, never can she be described as self-righteous. Even though she retained a sense of the position of the rank into which she was born, she was humble and self-effacing before God. In her correspondence with her students we often find her writing to them as fellow Christians, locked in the same endless battle with indwelling sin and the powers of darkness.

Not many months before her final illness she readily admitted to one who visited her that 'so much sin and self' mixes with our

[1] An example of this may be found in the fact that in her will she specified five men who were never to be allowed to preach in any of the pulpits of her churches. Amongst these were Rowland Hill, Thomas Wills and, with good reason, William Taylor and John Bradford.

[2] We are reminded of the bitter family infighting and of the way Washington Shirley seized the family fortunes, flouting his father's will.

best endeavours. 'I confess, my dear friend,' she continued, 'I have no hope but that which inspired the dying malefactor at the side of my Lord; and I must be saved in the same way, as freely, as fully, or not at all.' And again, 'I see myself a poor worm . . . what hope could I entertain if I did not know the efficacy of his blood and had turned as a prisoner of hope to this stronghold.'[1]

Selina's final illness had begun towards the end of 1790, and God had been preparing her to face it by giving her unusual disclosures of his love. Not many days before she was taken ill, as she came from her bedroom to sit in her accustomed chair, she had said to Lady Anne, 'The Lord has been present with my spirit in a remarkable manner: what he means to convey to my mind, I know not; it may be my approaching departure; my soul is filled with glory; I am as in the element of heaven itself!' And to David Jones, who was visiting her shortly afterwards, she repeated ecstatically, 'O Jones, my soul is filled with glory, my soul is filled with glory!' When Lady Anne asked her how she felt, she exclaimed, 'I am well; all is well – well forever. I see, wherever I turn my eyes, whether I live or die, nothing but victory.'

Selina's condition varied throughout these last months of her life. Though emaciated and often in pain, whenever she felt able she exchanged her bed for her customary chair. Her secretary called often to see her and wrote letters at her request, while Lady Anne and Hannah Scutt took it in turns to watch over her. The attempt to send missionaries to Otaheite in the South Seas occupied much of her thought, particularly as preparations seemed to be progressing well. When Thomas Haweis came to her bedside he had much difficulty in deflecting her mind from the subject. Problems arose, however, when the two missionary candidates refused to sail without episcopal ordination[2] – a

[1] These quotations relating to events during the last days of the Countess are taken from Thomas Haweis, *A Short Account of the Last Days of the Honourable and Most Respected Lady, Selina, Countess Dowager of Huntingdon* (London, 1791).

[2] William Jay adds 'ignobly and deceitfully'. *Autobiography*, p. 476.

condition that effectively ruled them out. 'We shall find others, I doubt not', declared the frail woman robustly.

Letters continued to arrive at her home asking for the services of students, reporting on the progress of the work, or even on the sorrows and hardships her men might be facing. She was still concerned about making arrangements for the Spa Fields pulpit. During May and June 1791 David Jones had been preaching, and often found a few moments to call at the home next door to the chapel and speak with the Countess. Then came a message from his bishop that his presence was urgently required at Llangan. The Countess realised that she would need to find a preacher to fill the unexpected vacancy. Who could come at such short notice? She thought of Thomas Charles at Bala. Surely her friend would oblige her in this emergency. With unsteady hand she wrote, dating her letter 12 June 1791. This was to be the last of the many thousands of letters that the Countess of Huntingdon wrote:

My days of suffering not being ended, I avoided (when tolerably able) to add any of those feelings to so kind a heart like yours. You have my faithful love and regard for you and yours. Since we parted I know not a day (but when the Lord smiled) but I was passing the great Tribulation and I think while this lasts you will not deny me the great pleasure and joy of seeing you here. I am sure dear Mrs Charles will yield her consent while so critical to the poor old widow's importunate request. Dear Mr Jones must indulge his bishop with his presence – could my dear friend be here by Sunday 19th instant or at the latest on Sunday to preach here the 26th? You would be a wonderful comfort to me . . .
My dear friend, let me have a line to assure me of your kindness. I am weak and low and immersed in the great business of preparing a mission for the South Seas and the Indian nations in America. I wish to die and would [do so] in my dear and blessed Master's business. I can say no more from weakness but it must

ever be to assure you and dear Mrs Charles how appreciative I am. SH[1]

That final week of the Countess's life was one that her friends would never forget. Thomas Haweis sat beside her much of the time and David Jones was another welcome visitor. Her words were few. Much of the time she seemed scarcely conscious and often appeared to be praying. 'I am encircled in the arms of love and mercy,' she whispered, and at another time, 'O! I long to be at home.' Never did she express satisfaction with anything she might have achieved during her long years of service for God: 'How little can anything of mine give a moment's rest to a departing soul?'

With all her immediate family already dead, apart from her daughter Elizabeth in Ireland, there was none of her own to watch with Selina during those last days and hours of life. But Lady Anne and Hannah Scutt took it in turns to sit with her when she had no visitor. Thoughtful for them, the Countess said kindly, 'I shall be the death of you both. It will be but a few days more.' Her doctor, John Lettsom, attended her faithfully. Although he did not share her beliefs, he came to appreciate the rugged faith of his grand old patient. He knew too how to deal with her. When she enquired anxiously whether David Jones had been given the *draft* due to him for his services at Spa Fields, he replied tersely that the only *draught* he wished her to be concerned with at that moment was the *draught* he prescribed for her.

To Dr Lettsom we owe an account of Selina's last day of life: 'My work is done', she had said simply, 'I have nothing to do but to go to my heavenly Father.' And that night as he sat beside her, he had heard her whispering over and over again, 'I shall go to my Father this night. Can he forget to be gracious? Is there any end to his loving kindness?' Even now in the final hours of life, the

[1] The original of this letter is kept in John Wesley's Chapel, Broadmead, Bristol.

concerns of her endeavour to send missionaries to Otaheite were still on her mind.[1] 'Indeed, her whole life seemed devoted to one great object, the glory of God and the salvation of his creatures,' Dr Lettsom wrote as he concluded a letter to Lady Anne.[2]

'Is Charles's letter come?' Selina enquired anxiously on that last morning of her life. Hearing that his reply had indeed arrived, she continued, 'It must be opened to see if he comes.' As Lady Anne was leaving the room to open the letter, the dying Countess added, 'To know if he comes – that is the point.' These were her last known words. Hearing that Thomas Charles could come, Selina was assured that the congregation at Spa Fields would now be provided for. She could be at rest. All was indeed well – well forever. On 17 June 1791, at the advanced age of eighty-three, her work, that grand gospel work that had spanned more than fifty years, was done.

Pulpits of the many chapels of the Connexion up and down the country were draped in black as the news quickly spread that God had taken his honoured servant away: away from the scenes of her toils, her sufferings, her mistakes and her incredible achievements to that home she had desired. Precise in her wishes, the Countess had left detailed instructions for her funeral. Dressed in a favourite white gown which she had worn for the opening of one of her chapels, she was to be buried in simplicity in an unmarked grave in the family vault in Ashby-de-la-Zouch beside her husband, Theophilus. No monument to her memory was to be raised.[3] Her coffin, in accordance with her directions,

[1] Five years later a mission to the South Seas finally came to fruition after the founding of the London Missionary Society on 20 August 1795. Thomas Haweis, David Bogue and John Eyre, a former Trevecca student, were largely instrumental in its formation and, following the purchase of a 300 ton vessel named the *Duff*, thirty young missionaries were commissioned at the Countess's Sion Chapel to sail for the South Seas – a sight that would surely have gladdened Selina.

[2] The whole of John Lettsom's letter is to be found in Appendix 1.

[3] In more recent times a commemorative slab has been added near the place where the Countess was buried.

was to be draped in black and must bear only a plate with her name and age.

On 27 June three coaches each drawn by six horses followed the hearse as it left her Spa Fields home. No funeral service, no crowds, no graveside orations marked the occasion. The coaches made their way through Islington, Highgate and on towards Barnet. Here all but three of the men accompanying the cortège left the procession and returned home, for she had asked that only one coach should proceed as far as Ashby. None but George Best (her secretary), Thomas Weatherill (a Spa Fields committee member), and Lemuel Kirkman (a former Trevecca student who had been ordained at Spa Fields), witnessed that lonely committal as the Countess's coffin was lowered into its final earthly resting place.

Most of her friends and contemporaries who might have left stirring accounts of the life and achievements of the Countess had predeceased her. But on 3 July 1791 sermons were preached from many pulpits by former Trevecca students and other close associates recording their sincere appreciation of her and their sense of loss. Some that were later printed give choice additional insights into the character and experiences of the Countess. David Jones remained in London and preached at Spa Fields, using for the title of his address Joseph's last words, 'I die, but God will surely visit you.' Having spent much time with Selina in the final weeks of her life he was particularly qualified to speak:

> We want no marble monument to perpetuate her memory. This will remain, indelibly remain, on those precious souls who through her instrumentality have been brought from darkness to light. God has honoured me with her acquaintance for nearly thirty years, and I have been with her in many of her public excursions for the spread of the gospel. We have often been met with the enmity and scorn of the world; yet Jesus, the leader of his despised host, has frequently

refreshed our souls. But now she has taken wing for a better world where the enemy's arrows cannot reach her.[1]

William Platt, another of her former students, preaching a sermon entitled *The Waiting Christian*, had good cause to remember from his college days that one could not easily argue with the Countess. 'She was a very strong reasoner and I believe any who have been in her company will allow that they have never met anyone to exceed her as to the force of argument.' Yet, he continued, 'where will God's Israel find another who spent her all for the good of their precious souls, even to denying herself those comforts that her enfeebled body needed?' Her hardest trials, and those that came closest to breaking her spirit, 'were those she received from many she loved as her own soul'.[2]

William Aldridge, whose sermon contained the most additional material on the life of his patroness, spoke of the 'noble elevation of her soul', adding that in his view it would be hard to find a woman her equal. He also included the fact that the immediate cause of the Countess's final illness was a chill she had caught two weeks before she died, and until that moment she had even been hoping to pay a final visit to her dearly loved Trevecca.[3] Timothy Priestley, echoed the sentiments of many when he said, 'What a rare example was the late Countess who laid aside her state, her carriage, her equipage to which she had been accustomed from her infancy, that she might be more able to help the needy and assist in carrying on the cause of her great Master.'[4]

Even Thomas Wills, a man of generous spirit, paid tribute to Selina's memory. For him, the veneration in which he had held her had once bordered on idolatry, he told his congregation at

[1] David Jones, *Funeral Sermon*, 3 July 1791, p. 17.

[2] William F. Platt, *The Waiting Christian*, pp. 12–13.

[3] William Aldridge, sermon preached at Jewry Street, London, 3 July 1791. Much of the material of his sermon has already been quoted, particularly in Chapters 23 & 24.

[4] Timothy Priestley, *A Crown of Eternal Glory* (London, 1791), p. 30.

Silver Street. He believed the Lord had permitted the sad events of 1788 to correct this imbalance. Alluding to the dependence of the Church on Christ himself for its glory, he added that in his view she remained:

> one of the brightest luminaries that had ever shone in the gospel hemisphere, though like other stars shining with borrowed or reflected light . . . Thousands, I may say tens of thousands, in various parts of the kingdom heard the gospel through her instrumentality that in all probability would never have heard it at all; and I believe through eternity will have cause to bless God that she ever existed. She was truly and emphatically a Mother in Israel, and though she was far from a perfect character, yet I hesitate not to say that among the illustrious and noble of the country she has not left her equal.[1]

Perhaps old John Berridge should have the last word. 'Ah,' he said when he heard that his long-standing friend had died, 'is she dead? Then another pillar is gone to glory. Mr Whitefield is gone, Mr Wesley and his brother are gone, and I shall go soon.'

'Yes, sir,' replied the one who brought him the news, 'it is not probable you will long survive them; and although some little differences of opinion existed between you here, I have no doubt you will unite in perfect harmony in heaven.'

'Ay, ay,' replied the frail old preacher, himself deaf and almost blind, 'that we shall; for the Lord washed our hearts here and he will wash our brains there.'[2]

---

[1] From the *Memoir of Thomas Wills*, pp.231-2.
[2] Berridge, *Works*, p. liii.

# APPENDIX 1

# LETTER ON THE DEATH OF THE COUNTESS OF HUNTINGDON

DEAR LADY ANNE ERSKINE,

I deeply sympathise with thee, and all the family in Christ in the removal of that evangelic woman, so lately among us, the Countess of Huntingdon. Your souls were so united, and your affections so endeared together, that I cannot but feel in a particular manner on thy account; lest the mournful state of thy mind may undermine thy constitution, and endanger a life spent in mitigating the painful sufferings of body of our deceased friend whilst living. Her advanced age, and debilitated frame, had long prepared my mind for an event which has at length deprived the world of its brightest ornament. How often have we, when sitting by her sick bed, witnessed the faithful composure with which she has viewed this awful change! Not with the fearful prospect of doubt – not with the dreadful apprehension of the judgment of an offended Creator – hers was all peace within; a tranquillity and cheerfulness which conscious acceptance alone could convey. How often have we seen her, elevated above the earth, and earthly things, uttering this language, 'My work is done; I have nothing to do, but to go to my heavenly Father'? Let us, therefore, under a firm conviction of her felicity, endeavour to follow her, as she followed her Redeemer. Let us be thankful that she was preserved to advanced age, with the perfect exercise of her mental faculties; and that, under long and painful days and nights of sickness, she *never* repined; but appeared constantly animated in prayer and thankfulness for unutterable mercies she experienced.

When I look back upon the past years of my attendance, and compare with it the multitudes of others whom my profession has introduced me to, I feel consolation in acknowledging, that of all the daughters of affliction, she exhibited the greatest degree of Christian composure that ever I witnessed; and that submission to divine allotment, however severe and painful, which nothing but divine aid could inspire.

It was on the 12th of this month, that our dear friend appeared more particularly indisposed, and afforded me those apprehensions of danger, which on the 17th finally terminated her bodily sufferings. I had, on former occasions of her illness, observed that when she expressed a hope and desire to go to her heavenly Father (for this was often her language); she usually added some solicitudes upon her mind respecting her *children*, as she spoke of her people in religious profession; adding, 'But I feel for the good of their souls.' When under the utmost debility of body, she has continued this subject in animated and pious conversation, extending her views to all mankind; she has expressed a firm persuasion in the gradual and universal extension of virtue and religion. Wherever a fellow creature existed, so far her prayers extended. In her last illness, I never heard her utter a desire to remain longer on earth. A little before she died, she repeatedly said, in a feeble voice, just to be heard, 'I shall go to my Father this night', adding, 'Has God forgot to be gracious? or is there any end of his loving kindness?'

It was on this day she conversed a little on the subject of sending missionaries to Otaheite, in the South Seas, in the pious hope of introducing Christianity among that mild but uninformed race of people: indeed her whole life seemed devoted to one great object: the glory of God, and the salvation of his creatures.

JOHN COAKLEY LETTSOM
18 JUNE 1791

# APPENDIX 2

# BIOGRAPHICAL WORKS ON THE COUNTESS OF HUNTINGDON.

THE TWO-VOLUME WORK of Aaron Crossley Hobart Seymour, *The Life and Times of Selina Countess of Huntingdon,* first published in 1839,[1] has provided the Christian church with an invaluable handbook, not only on the Countess of Huntingdon, but on the whole of the evangelical revival of the eighteenth century. It has, however, had many critics, some for understandable reasons, others for less worthy ones. Unfortunately Seymour tends to ramble from one subject to another and writes with an over-deferential regard for the aristocracy. The descriptions he gives of the Countess have created around her an atmosphere that sets her apart from the joys, sorrows and mistakes that are common to us all. 'The illustrious subject of the present memoir was an example of piety, benevolence and zeal', is a typical description. The major criticism levelled at the work, however, is that of inaccuracy. Certainly, where comparisons are possible, we do find a considerable level of discrepancy between letters printed by Seymour in his *Life and Times* and the manuscript letters. One letter we noted contains more than twenty such deviations from Selina's original.[2] Most of these variations are of little consequence, but here and there the sense of the letter is altered. More seriously there are times when letters of different dates are fused together and altered to make a coherent whole, without any indication in the text that this has been done.[3] The majority of the

---

[1] Reprinted by Tentmaker Publications, using clearer print and including an index (Stoke-on-Trent, 2000).

[2] Seymour, *Countess*, vol. 1, p. 41–2.

[3] An example of this is found in vol. 1, p. 46–7 where a letter of 9 January 1742 and one of 19 April 1742 are combined.

letters written by the Countess and cited by Seymour are no longer extant, making further detailed comparisons impossible. One explanation for these inaccuracies is that Seymour was not always in possession of the originals and was therefore dependent on the work of a hurried copyist employed by the Countess. Another, of course, is Selina's handwriting, which has baffled many would-be transcribers of her letters.

The writing of biography in the modern sense was still in its infancy when Seymour published his work and exactness in quotation was not considered as important as it is today. That there are also a few mistakes on matters of fact here and there in the book we would not deny; but this is not altogether surprising when one considers the quantity of material crammed into his fifty-five chapters. An example is his assertion that Selina and her husband were present at Fetter Lane Society meetings in 1738.[1] This was a year prior to her conversion in July 1739, and John Wesley himself gives no indication of having met her until his diary references during the spring of 1741. Another instance of an incorrect statement was noted by Luke Tyerman in his biography of John Fletcher of Madeley, *Wesley's Designated Successor*. He draws attention to the fact that Seymour names Joseph Easterbrook as the first tutor at Trevecca College.[2] This position was in fact filled by John Williams. These, and one or two other similar misinterpretations or mistakes, we have noted in passing and attempted to correct with documentary or circumstantial evidence wherever possible. However, such instances do not invalidate the bulk of Seymour's work, which remains an important source for the study of the eighteenth century evangelical revival. Those who completely by-pass his information necessarily impoverish their work. Seymour's indifference to chronological order and our lack of access to many of his sources may make the task of subsequent biographers of Selina more difficult, but they do not constitute an adequate explanation for the wholesale rejection of his *Life and Times* by some modern writers. We suspect that a dislike of his evangelical stance is more likely to be a major cause of offence. We have decided, therefore, while making full use of early manuscript material

[1] *Ibid.*, p. 19.
[2] *Ibid.*, vol. 2, p. 96; also see above p. 240 n.

wherever possible, also to follow Seymour's account of events and only query his version when there is clear reason to do so. We would reject the claim made by the late Dr Edwin Welch[1] that Seymour fraudulently manufactured material and inserted it into his narrative. This is a serious charge. For his main example of such unworthy conduct he points to the correspondence of Sarah Duchess of Marlborough.[2] According to Seymour's text, the elderly Duchess confessed to Selina her own sense of spiritual need and told her of her wish to hear Whitefield preach and to see the Countess more often. Welch regards these two letters quoted by Seymour as forgeries. To substantiate his assertion he quotes the Duchess of Marlborough's recent biographer, Dr Frances Harris,[3] who dismisses the same letters on the grounds that the wording in them does not sound like the Duchess. On this slender basis she suggests that the letters were fabricated by Seymour in order to add kudos to his subject. Harris also believes that the letters are not genuine because she maintains that the Duchess would never have referred to the poet, Alexander Pope, as 'that crooked perverse little wretch at Twickenham' – words attributed to her at the conclusion of one of the letters in question. However, an earlier and well-respected biographer of the Duke and Duchess of Marlborough, Stuart Reid, writing in 1914,[4] had no such problem with the letters, nor with the 'evidence' which Welch and Harris claim as proof of forgery. He knew what they evidently did not, namely that the Duchess of Marlborough had indeed had a sharp altercation with Pope before the date of the disputed letters. Pope had insulted Sarah by depicting her character under the guise of 'Atossa' in a 'brilliant but bitter' poem, of that name.[5] The Duchess, who had always been generous to the poet, gave him £1000, thought to be for the cost of suppressing the work. This he failed to do, hence her anger. Far from being evidence of forgery, the reference to Pope is a confirmation of their authenticity – information that neither

[1] *Spiritual Pilgrim*, p. 212.
[2] Seymour, *Countess*, vol. 1, p.25-6; see also above pp. 88-9.
[3] Frances Harris, *A Passion for Government – the Life of Sarah, Duchess of Marlborough* (Oxford: Clarendon Press, 1991).
[4] Stuart J. Reid, *John and Sarah Duke and Duchess of Marlborough* (London: John Murray, 1914).
[5] *Ibid.*, pp. 453-4.

Dr Harris nor Dr Welch has noted. Reid has no doubts about the friendship between the Countess of Huntingdon and the Duchess of Marlborough in the early 1740s, and writes:

> Selina, Countess of Huntingdon, crossed her path towards the end of her life. She was the patron of George Whitefield and a woman whom religion had made radiant. The Duchess had known many courtly and latitudinarian bishops, agreeable, accomplished men of the world, who were ready to talk about anything but religion. When she heard that Whitefield preached with impassioned ardour, she betrayed a sudden desire to hear him. But illness prevented her. So Lady Huntingdon came to see her and improved the occasion.[1]

In 1858 Alfred H. New published a more orderly account of the life of the Countess entitled *The Coronet and the Cross*. He was dependent almost entirely on Seymour for his material, as was Helen Knight, whose work, *Lady Huntingdon and Her Friends*,[2] was first published in 1853. In 1907 Sarah Tytler, also relying on Seymour, produced a substantial volume with a similar title, *The Countess of Huntingdon and Her Circle*.[3] This work is well-written and interesting, though Tytler tried to weave a fictional element into her account to give added appeal. A number of shorter works on Selina, to which reference has been made in the bibliography, have appeared during the course of the twentieth century. The fullest of these is *The Elect Lady*, by Gilbert Kirby.

In recent years two academic studies on the Countess have been published. In 1995 Edwin Welch's work, *Spiritual Pilgrim*, to which reference has already been made, drew attention to a quantity of little-known material relating to her. I am indebted to his careful classification and documentation of these manuscripts. They consist largely of family correspondence and of letters from Trevecca students and others written to the Countess, kept in archives not only in Britain but also in the United States. As an archivist, however, it was never Dr Welch's intention to write a biography of the Countess. Rather he

[1] *Ibid.*, p. 475.
[2] Republished, Grand Rapids: Baker Book House, 1979.
[3] London: Pitman, 1907.

aimed to clear away erroneous traditions, in order to prepare the way for others. Objective and well-disposed, he was not, on his own admission, in entire sympathy with the Countess's evangelical faith.

Two years later came Dr Boyd Schlenther's book, *Queen of the Methodists*.[1] Though painstaking in its detailed research, this treatise approaches the Countess from an unsympathetic perspective, and therefore fails to present an accurate evaluation of her life and work. Dr Schlenther's misinterpretation of her evangelical faith is apparent throughout. One or two quotations chosen at random demonstrate this. Referring to her refusal to regard 'good works' as a satisfactory means to secure her salvation, he writes: 'The main resulting problem was that her call for an experience of instant conversion at the sound of emotive preaching could prove seriously detrimental to a Christian life in progress . . . Stimulated by visions and extreme "highs" of intense faith, she never learnt to live without them . . .When they failed, as fail they did, she was brought to despair.'[2] And again, 'What led to Lady Huntingdon's "conversion" to Methodism was a combination of increasing anxieties – religious, emotional, health, family and financial.'[3] Later he adds, 'Whatever had constituted her conversion experience, Selina Hastings clearly had found no inner peace.'[4]

To write a new biography of Selina Countess of Huntingdon is no easy task. I have tried to give a fair and unbiased account of her life, and to interpret her actions in the light of her own deep and all-pervasive faith – a faith in the power and purposes of God that carried her through a long life of earnest endeavour, sorrows, misjudgments, but above all of magnificent achievement in the cause of the gospel.

---

[1] Subtitled, *The Countess of Huntingdon and the Eighteenth Century Crisis of Faith and Society* (Durham: Durham Academic Press, 1997).
[2] *Ibid.*, p. 2.
[3] *Ibid.*, p. 15.
[4] *Ibid.*, p. 38.

# APPENDIX 3
## SHIRLEY FAMILY TREE[1]

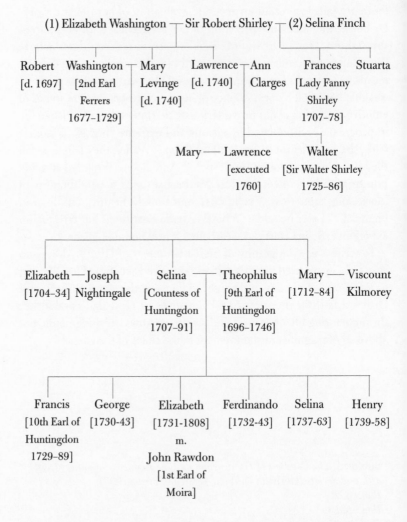

(1) Elizabeth Washington — Sir Robert Shirley — (2) Selina Finch

Robert [d. 1697]

Washington [2nd Earl Ferrers 1677–1729]

Mary Levinge [d. 1740]

Lawrence [d. 1740]

Ann Clarges

Frances [Lady Fanny Shirley 1707–78]

Stuarta

Mary — Lawrence [executed 1760]

Walter [Sir Walter Shirley 1725–86]

Elizabeth [1704–34]

Joseph Nightingale

Selina [Countess of Huntingdon 1707–91]

Theophilus [9th Earl of Huntingdon 1696–1746]

Mary [1712–84]

Viscount Kilmorey

Francis [10th Earl of Huntingdon 1729–89]

George [1730–43]

Elizabeth [1731–1808] m. John Rawdon [1st Earl of Moira]

Ferdinando [1732–43]

Selina [1737–63]

Henry [1739–58]

[1] Only names of those mentioned in the biography are included in the family trees.

# APPENDIX 4
# HASTINGS FAMILY TREE

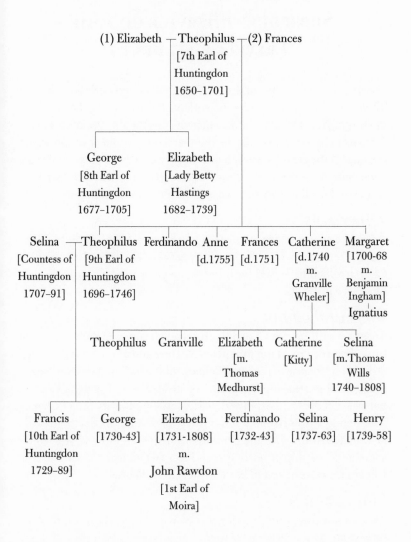

# Appendix 5

## Subsequent Service of Some Trevecca Students

In SPITE OF their limited and sometimes chequered period of study at Trevecca a significant number of students trained during the Countess of Huntingdon's lifetime became men of considerable usefulness in the Christian church. Some may be numbered among the most outstanding men of the early nineteenth century. We have been able to trace the contribution of some of these men, although others, who may well have conducted fruitful ministries, have unfortunately been forgotten.

*JOHN ADAMS*
Adams began preaching at nineteen years of age. After a period of training at Trevecca in 1772 he became pastor of Salisbury Independent Church which he served for thirty-seven years until his early death at fifty-three in 1805.

*WILLIAM ALDRIDGE*
Together with Joseph Cook this courageous young preacher was sent from Trevecca to Maidstone, Dover, Deal and Canterbury. Denied ordination because of the unwillingness of the bishop to ordain men of evangelical persuasion, he preached at Mulberry Gardens Chapel. Later he left the Connexion and became pastor of Jewry Street Chapel, conducting a twenty-one year ministry there until his death in 1797. His relationships with the Countess remained good and she would sometimes worship at Jewry Street. From his ministry at least sixteen young men were drawn to become preachers themselves.

*SAMUEL BEAUFOY*
After an ungodly youth Beaufoy was converted and became one of the early students at Trevecca. He was among the six to be ordained at Spa

Fields in 1783. From 1793 until his death thirty years later he conducted a long ministry at Town Sutton in Kent.

## JEHOIADA BREWER

When the young woman whom Jehoiada Brewer loved deeply died, he began to seek God and came to the Bath chapel where he heard Cradock Glascott preach. Brewer's conversion and his earnest zeal recommended him to the Countess and soon he was sent to Trevecca. Highly intelligent, he excelled at the classical languages but when he tried to obtain ordination into the Church of England, like other Trevecca students, he was refused by the bishops. After a period in Cheltenham, Brewer began a thirteen year ministry in Sheffield attracting a large congregation. His final church was in Birmingham where a chapel to accommodate the several thousand hearers that were regularly attending his ministry was being built at the time of his death in 1817.

## THOMAS BRYSON

Bryson was converted under William Aldridge at Jewry Street. The Countess heard of his zeal, but instead of sending him to college sent him to a needy area of Nottingham to preach. He finally entered Trevecca in 1780. Described as zealous and compassionate, he was pastor of an Independent church in Derby until his early death at the age of forty.

## JOHN CLAYTON

One of the earliest and most notable of the Trevecca students, after some years of itinerant preaching, Clayton became pastor of the influential Weigh Bridge Presbyterian Church, London in 1778. His son and grandson also became preachers.

## JOSEPH COOK

Joseph Cook was born in Bath in about 1750 and converted under Whitefield's preaching. Recommended for Trevecca, he entered the college at the age of nineteen. He quickly proved himself an able preacher when he was sent to Dover, Deal, Margate and Canterbury together with William Aldridge in 1771. He was one of the students sent by the Countess to Georgia in 1772 and remained in America for the rest of his life. Accepting Baptist principles, he was baptized by

SELINA COUNTESS OF HUNTINGDON

immersion in 1777 and became pastor of Euhaw Church, Upper Indian Land in South Carolina. He died there at the age of forty leaving a widow and fifteen year old son.

## ANTHONY CROLE

A Scotsman, Crole was a cabinet maker by trade. He came to London to set himself up in business but his conversion under Martin Madan changed the course of his life. Highly gifted academically, he was ordained in 1776 after three years of training at Trevecca. He became pastor of the influential Pinner's Hall Independent Church in London for twenty-six years until his death at the age of sixty-three. He preached at the opening of Cheshunt College in 1792.

## THOMAS ENGLISH

Born in 1751, Thomas English was converted under the ministry of William Romaine in 1766. After four years under Romaine's preaching he was accepted at Trevecca, studied well and was ordained in 1775. A three year ministry in Gosport, Hampshire, was followed by a long ministry in Woburn. From there he extended his ministry, establishing new churches in High Wycombe and other nearby places. A gifted poet, English also published a number of theological pieces and occasional sermons. He died in 1809.

## JOHN EYRE

Another of Trevecca's most outstanding students, Eyre, who was born in 1754, was turned out of his home at his conversion with only one guinea in his pocket. The Countess made provision for him and, recognizing his quality, sent him to Trevecca in 1778. He preached with considerable success in Cornwall, especially at Tregany. After his ordination he had ministries in Reading and Hackney, London. He was one of the founder members of the London Missionary Society. He died in 1803 at the age of thirty-nine.

## DANIEL GIBBONS

During Gibbons' period of training at Trevecca the Countess sent him to preach in Ulverstone, Cumberland. He grew to love the people of neighbouring Lancashire and would often preach in the major towns. He was ordained in a church in Lancaster, but refused a pressing invitation to become the pastor there. After a period of itinerant ministry he finally returned to Ulverstone where he was much loved by the people. His early death in 1785 cut short his useful life of Christian service.

## JAMES GLAZEBROOK
Among the earliest Trevecca students, Glazebrook came from Madeley, and was described as a man of 'uncommon zeal and unaffected piety'. After some years of itinerating, he wanted to be ordained, but not until 1777 could he secure this because of his connection with the Countess. His longest ministry was at Warrington in Lancashire. A sensitive man, he suffered much when his work there was eventually disrupted by problems in the church. After the death of the Countess, her daughter, Elizabeth, who had the patronage of the parish church in Belton, Leicestershire, offered this to Glazebrook. Here he finished his earthly course in 1803 at the age of fifty-nine.

## JOSEPH GRIFFITHS
Born in 1757, Griffiths was converted under the ministry of Thomas Maxfield. By an unusual combination of circumstances he decided to visit Trevecca and was so impressed by all he heard and saw that he remained as a student. After some years of itinerating at the request of the Countess, Griffiths had an extended ministry in Melbourne, Derbyshire, and evangelized in nearby Derby itself. His final and longest ministry was in Aston, Berkshire, where he preached for seventeen years. A diligent Bible student, upright and dependable in all his dealings with others, Joseph Griffiths was a preacher whose ministry must have given much satisfaction to the Countess. He died in 1818.

## JOHN HAWKSWORTH
An able preacher, friend and correspondent of the Countess, Hawksworth spent some years consolidating the work begun by Calvinistic Methodists in Dublin and the surrounding area. Ordained in 1773, Hawksworth returned to Ireland. In 1775 he married a young woman from the Moravian church established by the labours of John Cennick before his early death in 1755. In 1782 Hawksworth left the Connexion and joined the Moravians. The Countess was much grieved by his decision, feeling it would end his evangelistic endeavours. Hawksworth settled in Wem, Shropshire, for a short period and then

joined the Moravian community at Fulneck in Yorkshire. However, he withdrew from the Moravians some years before his death in 1810.

## JOHN JOHNSON

Johnson was converted under the preaching of John Clayton, also a former student who was then preaching at Norwich. He began his studies at Trevecca in 1780 and was one of the six first students to be ordained at Spa Fields in 1783. His first church was in Wigan, Lancashire and under his ministry William Roby, who also attended Trevecca for a short period, was converted. Johnson went to Georgia as a representative for the Countess to try and recover her Bethesda assets. He was unsuccessful and later returned to become minister of St George's, Manchester, in which city Roby also had an outstanding ministry. He has a place in the *National Dictionary of Biography*.

## THOMAS SNELL JONES

Born in 1754, Thomas Snell Jones was eighteen when he started at Trevecca college in 1773. While he was assisting the elderly minister at Plymouth Dock in 1775, Jones met Lady Glenorchy when she was visiting a friend of his in Exeter. This apparent chance meeting in 1779 led to Jones being invited on a temporary basis to supply ministry at her Edinburgh chapel, built to seat 2000. The congregation responded warmly to the twenty-six-year-old Jones and later that summer he was ordained into the Presbyterian ministry. For the next fifty-eight years Jones conducted a memorable ministry in Edinburgh, being awarded an honorary doctorate in 1810. The three Bonar brothers, John, Horatius and Andrew were all brought up under his ministry. He died in 1837.

## HENRY MEAD

Henry Mead, a profane and godless young man, came under great conviction of sin before his conversion at Tottenham Court Road under the preaching first of Howell Davies and then of Whitefield. Recommended by Whitefield, he was among the second batch of Trevecca students who started college in 1769. He volunteered to be among the students who went to Georgia in 1772, but instead was sent to Dublin to assist John Hawksworth. One of the few students to gain episcopal ordination, Mead became minister at Ram's Church in Hackney, London, and had a lectureship at St. John's, Wapping.

## GEORGE TOWNSEND

One of the founders of the London Missionary Society in 1795, George Townsend was born in 1755, and converted under the ministry of Whitefield. 'Had I a thousand lives, they should all be devoted to the cause of Jesus', declared the young man. When the Countess heard of his zeal she asked to meet Townsend and then offered him an opportunity to preach at the Mulberry Gardens Chapel. After this he was sent to Trevecca, but his ability and popularity meant that he did more itinerant preaching than studying. Like others at Trevecca, however, he was 'made a preacher by preaching', and, following two years at the Connexion chapel at Cheshunt, he had a long and fruitful ministry in Ramsgate, Kent.

## MATTHEW WILKS

Born in Gibraltar in 1746, Matthew Wilks was converted under the ministry of William Piercy before the latter went to Bethesda in 1772. Piercy recognised Wilks' abilities and insisted on his going to Trevecca. There he made good academic progress and happened to be the appointed preacher at the college chapel in 1775 when Robert Keen, one of the trustees of Moorfields and Tottenham Court Road, was visiting Trevecca. Much taken with Wilks, Keen invited him to preach at the Tabernacle which had been served by one or two men on a temporary basis since Whitefield's death in 1770. For more than fifty years Matthew Wilks preached in both the Moorfields and Tabernacle pulpits. Together with John Eyre he was behind the initiation of *The Evangelical Magazine* in 1793. Described as one of the 'Fathers' of the London Missionary Society, Wilks was instrumental in propagating its work, preaching in support of it with great effect.

## WILLIAM WINKWORTH

Winkworth was another of the Trevecca students to gain episcopal ordination. Several long letters addressed to him by the Countess have survived. He became chaplain at St Saviour's, Southwark, and also chaplain to Surrey Gaol. An ardent evangelist, we are told that in his preaching Winkworth 'did all that human efforts could to render his discourses effectual for the salvation of those to whom he proclaimed the unsearchable riches of Christ'.

# APPENDIX 6

## AND AFTERWARDS . . .

WRITING IN 1794, three years after the death of Selina, Countess of Huntingdon, the editor of Augustus Toplady's collected *Works* could describe her life as one of 'most extensive usefulness and . . . intrinsic excellence in the cause of Christ'.[1] Sadly, however, the work that she left behind has suffered seriously over the years. 'Had the Connexion been regularly organised and legally established during her lifetime, and had the Trustees and ministers been compelled to adhere to a constitutional order, the Countess of Huntingdon's Connexion would at this time have occupied one of the most conspicuous positions among the religious denominations in England', wrote Alfred New in 1858 as he concluded his biography of the Countess.[2]

Instead, as we have seen, the Countess was overruled in her plans for the future of the Connexion, and, although it came as a surprise to Haweis, he discovered that in her Will she had left the trusteeship of the Connexion entirely to him, together with Jenetta his wife, Lady Anne Erskine and John Lloyd. After her death Lady Anne perpetuated the Countess's role by superintending the affairs of the college and the financing of the chapels. Haweis, meanwhile, undertook to organise the regular supplies for the many pulpits of the Connexion, between them retaining the exclusive nature of the leadership that the Countess had exercised.

[1] Toplady, *Works*, p. 488.
[2] A. H. New, *The Coronet and the Cross*, p. 358.

Lady Anne died in 1804, but the Connexion continued to expand for some years with new chapels being built or acquired. In 1807 a Central Trust was formed but this included only seven of the churches in the Connexion – those where the property was freehold rather than leasehold. In 1820, following the death of Thomas Haweis, an attempt was made to implement the original Plan of Association as it was first drawn up before the death of the Countess, but the endeavour proved abortive for by this time the oversight of the Connexion by a board of trustees had become a fixture and although further churches were added to the Central Trust, the majority remained outside of it. Despite this, there were still some 35,000 people worshipping regularly in churches associated with the Connexion in 1828, nearly forty years after the death of the Countess.[1]

As originally conceived, the Connexion was essentially an evangelistic agency – even a missionary organization, dedicated to a policy of reaching optimum numbers with the gospel of Christ in the shortest possible time. Since the early 1760s the Countess had consistently discouraged any regular or settled pastorates among her churches. But as the eighteenth century drew to a close the desire for settled ministries and the need to build up converts in the faith became increasingly prevalent. As this was inimical to the policy begun by the Countess and perpetuated by Lady Anne, it is not surprising that many churches sought a haven in other settled denominational structures. Not until 1868 did regular pastorates become the official policy of the Connexion. The inclusion in the *Fifteen Articles of Faith* of a statement binding the Connexion to the practice of infant baptism also became an obstacle to those in the Connexion who became convinced of Baptist principles.

Gradually the majority of chapels brought into being by the labours of the Countess and her students began to drift away from the Connexion, most becoming Congregational churches. A decline was therefore inevitable and a Trustees report of 1842 lists just 34 chapels in the Central Trust, though others still retained their links with the Connexion. Disputes between the ministers and the Trustees through-

Gilbert W. Kirby, *The Elect Lady* (Trustees of the Countess of Huntingdon Connexion, 1990), p. 54.

out much of the nineteenth century further weakened the cause, relegating the Connexion to a minor player on the evangelical scene.

By the 1920s the Connexion was reduced still further, being affected, in common with other churches, by the decline in church attendance throughout the country. With a heritage of ageing buildings, big repair costs coupled with reduced congregations and income, many of the larger chapels of the Connexion had to accept inevitable closure. Today some twenty-four chapels remain, mainly in country areas, making up the Countess of Huntingdon's Connexion. These represent a wide spectrum of theological positions.

On the brighter side is the missionary wing of the Connexion. In 1788 the Countess had sent John Marrant as a missionary to Nova Scotia where he established a number of churches. When Sierra Leone was designated a haven for emancipated slaves in 1787, and the Sierra Leone Company formed in 1790, America was glad of a place to send some of its unwanted Nova Scotian citizens who had supported the British in the War of Independence. Converts from Marrant's churches were uprooted and moved to Africa in 1792 carrying with them their evangelical traditions and their Connexion hymnbooks. Though only 1031 survived the journey, these men and women established a number of Countess of Huntingdon churches both in Freetown and in the surrounding countryside.

Reports of such churches reached Britain as early as 1824, but only when two men from Sierra Leone attended worship at Sion Chapel in Whitechapel, London, in 1839, bringing with them hymnbooks identical to those used by the congregation, did the knowledge of these sister churches become widespread. Since then the Connexion has carefully fostered the Sierra Leone wing of its work, and even today, despite all the setbacks, there are perhaps a dozen 'Countess' churches dotted around the Sierra Leone countryside.

The subsequent history of Trevecca is one of change and amalgamation. The lease on the buildings ran out in 1792 and as the Countess had not left any funds to finance the college, the decision was made to move it to Cheshunt in Hertfordshire and rename it Cheshunt College. Strictly controlled by a board of trustees, the college initially maintained much of its original character. Although its doctrinal base was widened to take in students from churches of other denominations, most young preachers still found their service within the Connexion churches. As churches began to press for settled pastorates the emphasis on itinerant preaching gradually died out. Once this unique characteristic had been abandoned, there was no reason to retain the college's distinctive status, so in 1850 it opened its doors to the students of the Newport Pagnell Academy, a Congregational or Independent College begun in 1783, the two merging as one academy. With the universities opening their doors to Dissenters, the need for basic education became less important, and so, in 1904, Cheshunt moved once again, this time to Cambridge so that students might take advantage of university lectures. In 1967 the separate identity of the college came to an end when its own Cambridge premises were closed down. The Cheshunt students were then accommodated at Westminster College, Cambridge, where candidates for the English Presbyterian Church ministry received their training. For ten years the two colleges existed side by side, but in 1977 the institution begun by the Countess of Huntingdon in 1768 amalgamated completely with Westminster College.

Trevecca still lives on, however, in the Cheshunt Foundation Archives housed in Westminster College. Here thousands of letters and artifacts from the college's past are carefully preserved, and, by painstakingly piecing together the disparate strands of the story, recorded in letters from the students to their patroness, the Countess of Huntingdon, much has been and more may yet be gleaned concerning Trevecca's earliest colourful days.

# Appendix 7

# The Fifteen Articles of the Countess of Huntingdon's Connexion

The Fifteen Articles were drawn up in 1783 and read at the first ordination of the Connexion. In 1793 they were enrolled in Chancery as a schedule to Cheshunt College trust deed, from which this copy (Cheshunt MS. C 16/3) is taken.

I. Of God.
That there is but one living and true God, everlasting, without body, parts, or passions; of infinite power, wisdom, and goodness; the Maker and Preserver of all things, both visible and invisible. And in unity of the Godhead there are three persons, of one substance, power, and eternity, the Father, the Son, and the Holy Ghost.

II. Of the Scriptures.
That it pleased God, at sundry times and in divers manners, to declare His will, and that the same should be committed unto writing; which is therefore called the Holy Scripture, which containeth all things necessary to Salvation. The authority whereof doth not depend upon the testimony of man, but wholly upon God, its Author; and our assurance of the infallible truth thereof is from the inward work of the Holy Ghost, bearing witness, with the Word, in our hearts.

III. Of Creation.
It pleased God, for the manifestation of His glory, in the beginning, to create the world and all things therein; and having made man, male and

female, after his own image, endued with knowledge, righteousness, and true holiness; he gave them a command not to eat of the tree of knowledge of good and evil, with a power to fulfil it, yet under a possibility of transgressing, being left to the liberty of their own will, which was subject unto change.

IV. OF THE FALL OF MAN FROM ORIGINAL RIGHTEOUSNESS.

Our first parents sinned in eating the forbidden fruit; whereby they fell from their original righteousness, and became wholly defiled in all the faculties and parts of soul and body. And being the root of all mankind, the guilt of this sin was imputed, and the same corrupted nature conveyed to all their posterity descending from them by ordinary generation.

V. OF ORIGINAL SIN.

Original sin standeth not in the following of Adam, as the Pelagians do vainly talk; but it is the fault and corruption of the nature of every man, that naturally is engendered of the offspring of Adam; whereby man is, as far as possible gone from original righteousness, and is of his own nature inclined to evil, so that the flesh lusteth always contrary to the spirit; and, therefore, in every person born into this world, it deserveth God's wrath and damnation. And this infection of nature doth remain, yea in them that are regenerated, yet without dominion; and although there is no condemnation to them that are in Christ Jesus, yet sin in them is evil, as much as in others, and as such receives Divine, fatherly chastisement.

VI. OF PREDESTINATION AND ELECTION.

Although the whole world is thus become guilty before God, it hath pleased Him to predestinate some unto everlasting life. Predestination, therefore, to life, is the everlasting purpose of God whereby (before the foundations of the world were laid) He hath constantly decreed by His counsel, secret to us, to deliver from curse and damnation those whom He hath chosen in Christ out of mankind, and bring them by Christ to everlasting salvation, as vessels made to honour. Wherefore they which are endued with so excellent a benefit of God, are called according to God's purpose, by His Spirit working in due season; they, through grace, obey the call; they are justified freely; they are made sons of God by adoption; they bear the image of Christ; they walk religiously in good works, and at length, by God's mercy, they attain to everlasting felicity.

VII. OF CHRIST THE MEDIATOR.

It pleased God in His eternal purpose, to choose and ordain the Lord Jesus, His only begotten Son, to be Mediator between God and man, the Prophet, Priest, and King, the Head, and Saviour, of His church; unto whom he did, from all eternity, give a people to be His seed, and to be by Him in time redeemed, called, justified, sanctified, and glorified. He, therefore, being very and eternal God, of one substance and equal with the Father, did, when the fulness of time was come, take upon Him man's nature, yet without sin, being conceived by the power of the Holy Ghost in the womb of the Virgin Mary; so that two whole, perfect, and distinct natures, the Godhead, and the manhood, were inseparably joined together in one person, without conversion, or confusion; which person is very God and very man, yet one Christ, the only Mediator between God and man. This office of Mediator and Surety He did most willingly undertake; which, that he might discharge, He was made under the law, and did perfectly fulfil it by an obedience unto death; by which perfect obedience and sacrifice of Himself on the cross, which He, through the Eternal Spirit, once offered up unto God, He hath fully satisfied Divine Justice, and purchased not only reconciliation, but an everlasting inheritance in the kingdom of heaven for all those whom the Father hath given Him. To all of whom He doth, in His own time, and in His own way, certainly and effectually apply His purchased redemption; making intercession for them; and revealing unto them, through the Word and by His Spirit, the mysteries of Salvation; effectually enabling them to believe unto obedience; and governing their hearts by the same Word and Spirit; and overcoming all their enemies by His almighty power.

VIII. OF THE HOLY GHOST.

The Holy Ghost is the third person in the adorable Godhead, distinct from the Father and the Son; yet of one substance, glory, and majesty with them, very and eternal God; whose office in the church is manifold. It is He who illuminates the understanding to discern spiritual things, and guides us into all truths; so that without His teaching, we shall never be effectually convinced of sin, nor be brought to the saving knowledge of God in Christ. And His teaching, whether it be by certain means which He ordinarily makes use of, or without means, is attended with an evidence peculiar and proper to itself, therefore styled the demonstration of the Spirit and of power. By which divine power He not only enlightens the understanding, but gives a new turn or bias to the will and affections, moving and acting upon our hearts, and by His secret, energetic influence effecting those things, which we could never attain or accomplish by our own strength. Nor is His guidance less necessary in our lives and all our actions. Without His assistance we know not what to pray for, or how to pray aright. He confirms us in all grace; and He is the author of all holiness. It is He that assures us of our personal interest in Christ, and that sheds abroad the love of God in our hearts. He seals believers unto the day of redemption; and is Himself the earnest of their future inheritance. He administers comfort to us in our temporal and spiritual distresses, by applying to our minds season-able promises of God in Christ Jesus, which are yea and amen; and, by receiving the things of Christ, and shewing them unto us. Thus He encourageth and refresheth us with a sense of the favour of God; fills us with joy unspeakable and full of glory, and is to abide with the church for ever.

IX. OF FREE WILL.
The condition of man after the fall of Adam, is such, that he cannot turn and prepare himself by his own natural strength and good works to faith and calling upon God; wherefore we have no power to do good works pleasant and acceptable to God, without the grace of God by Christ preventing us, that we may have a good will, and working with us when we have that good will.

X. OF JUSTIFICATION.
We are accounted righteous before God, only for the merit of our Lord and Saviour Jesus Christ, by faith, and not for our own works or deservings. Wherefore that we are justified by faith alone, is a most wholesome doctrine, and very full of comfort. And this is done by pardoning our sins, and by accounting our persons as righteous by imputing the obedience and satisfaction of Christ unto us, which is received and rested upon by faith; which faith we have not of ourselves, but it is the gift of God.

## XI. OF SANCTIFICATION AND GOOD WORKS.

They who are effectually called and regenerated, having a new heart and a new spirit created in them, are further sanctified, really and personally, through the virtue of Christ's death and resurrection, by His Word and Spirit dwelling in them; the dominion of the whole body of sin is destroyed, and the several lusts thereof are more and more weakened and mortified, and they are more and more quickened and strengthened in all saving graces to the practice of true holiness; without which no man shall see the Lord.

Works, which are the fruits of faith, and follow after justification, though they cannot put away our sins nor endure the severity of God's judgment, yet are pleasing and acceptable to God in Christ, and spring out necessarily of a true and lively faith; insomuch that by them a lively faith may be as evidently known, as a tree discerned by the fruit.

## XII. OF WORKS BEFORE JUSTIFICATION.

Works done before the grace of Christ, and the inspiration of His Spirit, are not pleasant to God; for as much as they spring not of faith in the Lord Jesus Christ; neither do they make men meet to receive grace; yea, rather, for that they are not done as God hath willed and commanded them to be done, we doubt not but they have the nature of sin.

## XIII. OF THE CHURCH.

The Catholic or universal Church, which is invisible, consists of the whole number of the elect, that have been, are, or shall be gathered into one, under Christ the head thereof, and is the spouse, the body, the fulness of Him that filleth all in all. The visible church consists of all those throughout the world who profess the true religion, together with their children. To which visible church Christ hath given the ministry and ordinances of the Gospel, for the gathering and perfecting of the saints in this life, to the end of the world; and doth by His own presence and Spirit, according to His promise, make them effectual thereunto.

There is no other head of the church but the Lord Jesus Christ; nor can the Pope of Rome, in any sense, be head thereof, but is that Antichrist, the man of sin, and son of perdition, that exalteth himself in the church against Christ, and all that is called God.

## XIV. OF BAPTISM.

Baptism is a sacrament of the New Testament ordained by Jesus Christ, not only for the solemn admission of the party baptized into the visible church, but also to be unto him a sign and seal of the covenant of grace, to be continued in the church until the end of the world; which is rightly administered by pouring or sprinkling water upon the person, in the name of the Father, Son, and Holy Ghost. This sacrament ought to be administered but once to any person; and we also hold, that infants may, and ought to be baptized, in virtue of one or both believing parents; because the spiritual privilege of a right unto, and a participation of the initial seal of the covenant, was granted by God to the infant seed of Abraham; which grant must remain firm for ever, without the Lord's own express revoking or abrogation of it; which can never be proved from Scripture that He has done. Again, they that have the thing signified, have a right to the sign of it; but children are capable of the grace signified in Baptism. And some of them (we trust) are partakers of it; namely, such as die in their infancy; therefore they may and ought to be baptized. For these and other reasons, we believe and maintain the lawfulness and expediency of infant baptism.

XV. OF THE LORD'S SUPPER.
The supper of the Lord is not only a sign of the love that Christians ought to have among themselves one to another, but rather it is a sacrament of the body and blood of Christ, and of our redemption thereby, called the Lord's Supper, to be observed in His church to the end of the world, for the perpetual remembrance of the sacrifice of Himself in His death; the sealing of all benefits thereof to true believers; their spiritual nourishment and growth in Him; their further engagement in, and to all duties which they owe unto Him; and to be a bond and pledge of their communion with Him and with each other as members of His mystical body. Insomuch that, to such as rightly and with faith receive the same, the bread which we break is a partaking of the body of Christ, and likewise the cup of blessing is a partaking of the blood of Christ; though in substance and nature they still remain bread and wine as they were before. Those, therefore, that are void of faith, though they do carnally and visibly eat the bread and drink the wine of this sacrament of the body and blood of Christ, yet they are in no wise partakers of Christ; but rather to their condemnation do eat and drink the sign or sacrament of so great a blessing.

# APPENDIX 8

# THE PLAN OF ASSOCIATION, 1790

PLAN FOR AN ASSOCIATION FOR UNITING AND PERPETUATING
THE CONNECTION OF THE RIGHT HONOURABLE THE
COUNTESS DOWAGER OF HUNTINGDON, 1790

In consequence of an invitation from the Right Honourable *Selina Countess Dowager of Huntingdon,* several ministers and laymen, who wish well to the cause of Christ and her Ladyship's connection, have formed themselves into an Association, called 'THE LONDON ACTING ASSOCIATION'; for the purpose of assisting her Ladyship, during her life-time, as far as she shall be pleased to accept of their services, in carrying on the work of the Gospel of Christ in her connection; and, as far as they may be enabled, for perpetuating the same after her Ladyship's decease. Being desirous of using such means as appear to them (under God) most likely to carry the same into effect, they beg leave, with all deference, to submit the following Plan to her Ladyship's considera-tion; which, if approved, they further beg may be printed, and a copy thereof sent to every Congregation in her Ladyship's connection; not doubting but they will cheerfully unite and engage with them in their feeble attempts to carry on the great and important work.

PLAN

I. That a General Association be formed, entitled 'THE COUNTESS DOWAGER OF HUNTINGDON'S GENERAL ASSOCIATION.'

II. That the whole connection be divided into proper Districts

[448]

III. That the Districts be as follows, viz.[1]

1. LONDON DISTRICT:
   Spa Fields Chapel, Mulberry Gardens, Sion Chapel, Holywell Mount Chapel.[2]

2. READING DISTRICT:
   Reading, Wallingford, Goring, Rickmansworth, Basingstoke.

3. FEVERSHAM DISTRICT:
   Feversham, Dover, Milton, Tunbridge Wells.

4. BRIGHTHELMSTONE DISTRICT:
   Brighthelmstone, Lewes, Chichester, Oat Hall.

5. ELY DISTRICT:
   Ely, Chatteris, Ramsey (Huntingdonshire), Peterborough.

6. SUDBURY DISTRICT:
   Sudbury, Fordham, Woodbridge.

7. BATH DISTRICT:
   Bath.

8. BRISTOL DISTRICT:
   Bristol, Swansea.

9. WINCANTON DISTRICT:
   Wincanton, a horse ride,[3] Froome.

10. ST COLUMBE DISTRICT:
    St Columbe, a horse ride, Star Cross.

11. GLOUCESTER DISTRICT:
    Gloucester, Hereford, Coleford, Banbury.

[1] Original spellings of place names is retained throughout.

[2] Little is known about this chapel except that it was established late in the Countess's life, possibly in 1789, and that William Platt, who preached a funeral sermon there after the Countess's death, was the first minister. Nor can we account for the absence of such chapels as Westminster Chapel from the list. Ewer Street Chapel had become a Baptist Church and the Countess had relinquished responsibility for it.

[3] A horse ride consisted of a series of preaching places which a student might visit in succession on horseback. The Countess usually provided the horse.

12. WORCESTER DISTRICT:
Worcester, Evesham, Kidderminster.

13. MONMOUTH DISTRICT:
Monmouth, Broad-oak, Langadock.

14. BIRMINGHAM DISTRICT:
Birmingham, West Bromwich, Handsworth, Edgebaston.

15. WOLVERHAMPTON DISTRICT:
Wolverhampton, Dudley, Bilston.

16. ASHBY DE LA ZOUCH DISTRICT:
Ashby de la Zouch, Ashbourne.

17. WIGAN DISTRICT:
Wigan.

18. ULVERSTONE DISTRICT:
Ulverstone, Whitehaven.

19. Norwich District:
Norwich.

20. LINCOLN DISTRICT:
Lincoln, Gainsborough, Newark.

21. HAXEY DISTRICT:
Haxey, Pinchbeck, Partney.

22. YORK DISTRICT:
York, Hull, Helmsley.

23. MORPETH DISTRICT:
Morpeth.

IV. That a committee be formed in each country district: consisting of the ministers for the time being, together with two laymen from each congregation; and that they be called 'THE COMMITTEE OF THE COUNTESS DOWAGER OF HUNTINGDON'S ASSOCIATION FOR THE DISTRICT OF'.

V. That the London Acting Association be considered the committee for the district of London.

VI. That each committee shall meet once a quarter, or oftener if necessary: the members thereof determining the time and place of their meetings.

VII. That they at such meetings take into consideration and deliberate upon all matters which concern the cause of Christ in her Ladyship's connection within their district.

VIII. That within ten days after every such meeting the committee shall transmit an account of their proceedings to the London Acting Association, who shall lay the same before the General Association at their annual meetings.

IX. That no Congregation nor District Committee contract any debt, but what they agree to discharge, without the consent of the General Association previously obtained.

X. That one or more of the ministers present do preach at each meeting of the committees.

XI. That all the ministers in her Ladyship's connection, together with the laymen who compose the District Committees, be considered as members of the General Association.

XII. That, in order to avoid unnecessary expense and trouble, and also to prevent the congregations being unsupplied if all the members were obliged to attend, it is proposed that a minister and two laymen from each District Committee be deputed to meet the London Acting Association in London once in every year; who, together with the Trustees of her Ladyship's College for the time being, shall compose the General Association.

XIII. That each district pay the expense of its deputation attending the General Association.

XV. That the state and concerns of the connection at large be laid before the General Association at their annual meetings.

XVI. That all disputed matters, which cannot be otherwise settled, shall be finally adjusted by the determination of the General Association.

XIV. That a minister be appointed to preach every day during the meeting of the General Association.

XVII. That a delegated power from the General Association shall constantly reside in the London Acting Association, to transact the concerns of the connection during the intervals of the annual meetings; and all their proceedings be laid before the General Association.

XVIII. That every minister, offering himself to join the connection, shall, if approved of, be received by the General Association.

XIX. The Lord having in the present age much blessed itinerant preaching, it is proposed that circuits be formed in different parts of the kingdom, for the further spread of the Gospel of Christ; and that preachers be sent out and supported by the connection, as collectively considered, so far as the Lord enables and their finances will allow.

XX. That every minister and student in the connection, who may be in town at the time of the meeting of the General Association, be at liberty to attend the same; but the latter not to have a voice in their deliberations and determinations.

XXI. That the minutes of the General Association be printed, and a copy of them sent to every District Committee.

XXII. That an account of the names and places of abode of all the ministers and students in the connection be entered in a book kept for that purpose.

*And, in order more effectually to carry this plan into execution, it is proposed:*

XXIII. That a fund be raised, separate and distinct from the supplies raised by congregations for the support of their respective places of worship, and also from the fund called the Travelling Fund and the Fund of the Apostolic Society.

XXIV. For this purpose, the members of the Societies in particular, and the friends of the connection in general, are invited to contribute an assistance of not less than a penny a week each person.

XXV. That this fund be called 'The General Association Fund.'

XXVI. That the money contributed be received by a treasurer, appointed by each district; who shall nominate and appoint such persons, at each chapel or place of public worship, as may be necessary to collect it. The money to be transmitted by the treasurer after each quarterly meeting of the district to the treasurer or treasurers of the London Acting Association.

XXVII. That books, agreeable to a plan now used by the London Acting Association, be recommended to the treasurers and collectors of the districts.

XXVIII. That collecting the subscriptions and contributions be ever considered as a labour of love and free service.

XXIX. That the disposal of the money be restricted solely to the determination and appointment of the General Association, for such purposes as they shall think proper, provided the same be for the benefit and sole use of the connection.

XXX. That no money for new buildings, or erection of galleries, be taken from this fund without the concurrence of at least seven-eighths of the General Association.

XXXI. Should a division of the connection at any future period be attempted, it is proposed that, so long as eleven members of the General Assembly continue united to carry on the cause of Christ in this connection, agreeable to the foregoing rules, they shall be considered not only competent, but fully empowered, to conduct the same.

It is requested, if any alterations in the districts be thought necessary, that the London Acting Association may be acquainted therewith.

*By order of the Countess of Huntingdon, and the Association,*
Spa Fields, March 3, 1790.<br>GEO. BEST, SEC.

# BIBLIOGRAPHY

## MANUSCRIPT MATERIAL

*Bridwell Library, Southern Methodist University, Dallas, Texas:*
Leete Collection: correspondence with Judith Wordsworth, Joseph
Townsend, Thomas Haweis and his wife.

*Bristol, Methodist New Room:* Two letters of Countess of Huntingdon.

*Cambridge, Cottenham, Countess of Huntingdon Connexion Archives:*
Original letters from Countess, 1783–90; Copies of letters to
Countess, 1760–84; Trevecca College title deed.

*Cambridge, Westminster College, Cheshunt Foundation Archives:*
Hawksworth Collection; Letters from Trevecca students; William
Piercy; James Habersham; William Williams, etc.; Murray papers.

*'Church History, Collected from the Memoirs and Journals of the Revd.
Mr Ingham and the labourers in connection with him',* 1779. By William
Batty (transcribed by M. Ratttenbury).

*Drew University, Madison, New Jersey:* Family correspondence of
Countess of Huntingdon.

*Emory University Library, Atlanta, Georgia:* Several letters; Augustus
Toplady Papers.

*Hull University Library:* Hotham correspondence.

*Huntington Library, San Marino, California:* Hastings family
correspondence; Countess's Commonplace Book.

*Leicester, Leicestershire and Rutland Record Office:* Hastings family
letters; Early letters to and from family friends.

*London, Dr Williams's Library:* Poem on death of Countess, 1791.

*Manchester, John Rylands University Library:* Black Folio, Countess's correspondence with Charles Wesley and others; Letters to Thomas Wills and Selina Wills; Letter to John Hawksworth; George Whitefield's Will.

*Manuscripts in private hands*
Four letters of Lady Huntingdon, 1769–84 (Peter Conlan, Kent).

## PRIMARY PRINTED SOURCES

Berridge, John. *Whole Works*. ed. R. Whittingham, 2nd ed. London, 1864.

Beynon, Tom, ed. *Howell Harris, Reformer and Soldier.* Caernarvon: The Calvinistic Bookroom, 1958.

Beynon, Tom, ed. *Howell Harris's Visits to London.* Aberystwyth: The Cambrian News Press, 1960.

Beynon, Tom, ed. *Howell Harris's Visits to Pembrokeshire.* Aberystwyth: The Cambrian News Press, 1966.

Chesterfield, Lord. *Letters to Lord Huntingdon.* ed. A. F. Steuart. London: Medici Society Ltd., 1923.

Cottingham, John. *The Righteous Shall Be in Everlasting Remembrance, Funeral Sermon for the Countess of Huntingdon at Mile-End Chapel, July 10, 1791.* London, 1791.

Haweis, Thomas. *The Life of William Romaine.* London, 1797.

Haweis, Thomas. *An Impartial and Succinct History of the Rise, Declension and Revival of the Church of Christ. Vol. 3.* London, 1800.

Jones, David, of Llan-gan. *A Funeral Sermon Preached at Spa Fields Chapel . . . on the Death of the Countess of Huntingdon.* London, 1791.

Nuttall, Geoffrey F. ed. *Calendar of the Correspondence of Philip Doddridge DD (1702–51).* Northants. Record Society, vol. 29, 1978.

Pentycross, Thomas. ed. *Extracts from the Journals of Several*

*Ministers of the Gospel in Letters to the Countess of Huntingdon.* London: Hughes and Walsh, 1782.

Platt, William Francis. *The Waiting Christian, being the substance of a discourse occasioned by the death of the Countess Dowager of Huntingdon, 3 July 1791.* Bristol, 1791.

Priestley, T. *A Crown of Eternal Glory, a Funeral sermon occasioned by the Death of . . . Selina Countess of Huntingdon.* London, 1791.

*Selected Trevecka Letters.* transcribed and annotated by G. M. Roberts. 2 vols. Caernarvon: Calvinistic Methodist Bookroom, 1956.

Shirley, Walter. *A Narrative of the Principal Circumstances relative to the Rev. Mr Wesley's Late Conference, held in Bristol, August the 6th 1771.* Bath, 1771.

Walpole, Horace. *Private Correspondence. Vol. 3.* London, 1820.

Waring, George. *A Sermon Occasioned by the Death of the Countess of Huntingdon.* Birmingham, 1791.

Welch, Edwin. ed. *Two Calvinistic Methodist Chapels.* London: Record Society, 1975.

Wesley, Charles. *Journal.* 2 vols. Grand Rapids: Baker Book House, 1980.

Wesley, John. *Journal.* Standard edition, ed. Nehemiah Curnock, vols. 1-8. London: Kelly, 1909–16.

Wesley, John. *The Letters of the Rev. John Wesley.* ed. John Telford, 8 vols. London: Epworth Press, 1931.

Wesley, John. *Works.* Vols. 25 & 26. ed. Frank Baker. Oxford: O.U.P., 1982.

Whitefield, George. *Letters,* ed. J. Gillies; *Works.* Vols. 2 & 3. London, 1771.

William, Williams. *An Elegy on the Reverend Mr G. Whitefield . . . Presented to her Ladyship.* Carmarthen: 1771.

Wills, Thomas. *Memoirs of the Rev. Thomas Wills, by a friend.* London: 1804.

## WORKS ON THE COUNTESS OF HUNTINGDON

Knight, Helen C. *Lady Huntingdon and Her Friends*. Grand Rapids: Baker Book House, 1979.

New, A. H. *The Coronet and the Cross*. London: Partridge & Co., 1858.

Schlenther, Dr Boyd Stanley. *Queen of the Methodists, the Countess of Huntingdon and the Eighteenth Century Crisis of Faith and Society*. Durham: Durham Academic Press, 1997.

Seymour, A. C. H. *The Life and Times of the Countess of Huntingdon*. 2 vols. London, 1840.

Tytler, Sarah. *The Countess of Huntingdon and Her Circle*. London: Pitman, 1907.

Welch, Edwin. *Spiritual Pilgrim, A Reassessment of the Life of the Countess of Huntingdon*. Cardiff: University of Wales Press, 1995.


## SHORTER WORKS

Lady Catherwood. *Selina Hastings, Countess of Huntingdon – an English Deborah*. Evangelical Library Annual Lecture, London, 1991.

Figgis, J. B. *The Countess of Huntingdon and her Connexion*. London: Partridge, 1891.

Gentry, Peter. *The Countess of Huntingdon*. Peterborough: Foundery Press, 1994.

Kirby, Gilbert. *The Elect Lady*. Trustees of the Countess of Huntingdon's Connexion, 1990.

Little, Bryan. *Selina Countess of Huntingdon*. Bath: Huntingdon Centre, 1989.

Smith, Wanda Willard. *Selina Hastings, The Countess of Huntingdon*. Southern Methodist University, Texas, 1997.

Tyson, John R. 'Lady Huntingdon and the Church of England.' *Evangelical Quarterly*, Spring 2000, pp. 23–34.

## Background Material

Abbey, C. & Overton, J. *The English Church in the Eighteenth Century.* 2 vols. London, 1878.

Aveling, T. W. *Memorials of the Clayton Family.* London, 1867.

Baker, Frank. *Charles Wesley as Revealed by His Letters.* London: Epworth Press, 1948.

Baker, Frank. *John Wesley and the Church of England.* London: Epworth Press, 1970.

Barbeau, A. *Life and Letters at Bath in the Eighteenth Century.* Heinemann: London, 1904.

Bayne-Powell, Rosamund. *Eighteenth Century London Life.* London: Murray, 1937.

Bayne-Powell, Rosamund. *Travellers in Eighteenth Century England.* London: Murray, 1961.

Benham, Daniel. *Memoirs of James Hutton.* London, 1856.

Bennett, Richard. *The Early Life of Howell Harris.* London: Banner of Truth, 1962.

Bogue, David & Bennett, James. *History of the Dissenters from the Revolution to the Year 1808.* Vol. 3. London, 1812.

Bready, J. Wesley. *England: Before and After Wesley.* London: Hodder & Stoughton, 1938.

Burder, S. ed. *Memoirs of Eminently Pious Women.* London, 1815.

Crookshank, C. H. *Days of Revival, History of Methodism in Ireland.* Vols. 1 & 2. Clonmel: Tentmaker Publications, 1994.

Dallimore, Arnold. *George Whitefield, Life and Times of the Great Evangelist of the 18th Century.* Vols. 1 & 2. London & Edinburgh: Banner of Truth, 1970 & 1980.

D'Auvergne, M. N. *Tarnished Coronets.* London: Werner, 1937.

Ella, George M. *James Hervey, Preacher of Righteousness.* Co. Durham: Go Publications, 1997.

Elliot-Binns, L. E. *The Early Evangelicals, a Religious and Social Study.* London: Lutterworth Press, 1955.

Evans, Eifion. *Howell Harris – Evangelist.* Cardiff: University of Wales Press, 1974.

Evans, Eifion. *Daniel Rowland and the Great Evangelical Awakening in Wales.* Edinburgh: Banner of Truth, 1985.

Gill, F. C. *Charles Wesley, The First Methodist.* London: Lutterworth Press, 1964.

Harris, Frances. *A Passion for Government – The Life of Sarah, Duchess of Marlborough.* Oxford: Clarendon Press, 1991.

Hietzenrater R. P. ed. *Diary of an Oxford Methodist.* Durham, N.C.: Duke University Press, 1985.

Hughes, Hugh G. *Life of Howell Harris, the Welsh Reformer.* London, 1892.

Hutton, J. E. *History of the Moravian Church.* London: Moravian Publication Office, 1909.

Jones, David. *Life and Times of Griffith Jones of Llanddowror.* London: S.P.C.K., 1902.

Jones, M. H. *The Trevecka Letters.* Caernarvon: The Calvinistic Methodist Bookroom, 1932.

Jones, T. Snell, *Life of Willielma, Lady Glenorchy.* Edinburgh, 1824

Kielmansegge, Count Frederick. *Diary of a Journey to England, 1761-1762.* London: Longmans, 1902.

Knox, Ronald. *Enthusiasm.* Oxford: The Clarendon Press, 1950.

Lawton, G. *Within the Rock of Ages, Life of Augustus M. Toplady.* Cambridge: James Clarke, 1983.

Light, Alfred W. *Bunhill Fields.* London: Farncombe and Sons, 1914.

Lyles, Albert M. *Methodism Mocked, the Satiric Reaction to Methodism in the Eighteenth Century.* London: Epworth Press, 1960.

Marshall, Dorothy. *English People in the Eighteenth Century.* London: 1956.

Marshall, Dorothy. *Eighteenth Century England.* London: Longmans, Green and Co., 1962.

Matthews, A. G. *The Congregational Churches of Staffordshire.* London: Congregational Union of England and Wales, 1924.

Medley, A. W. *The Life of Willielma, Viscountess of Glenorchy.* Bible League Quarterly, March 1999, and following.

Morgan, Edward. *The Life and Times of Howell Harris.* London, 1852.

Nightingale, B. *Lancashire Nonconformity.* Manchester, 1892.

Nuttall, Geoffrey F. *Howell Harris 1714–1771, The Last Enthusiast.* Cardiff: University of Wales Press, 1965.

Nuttall, Geoffrey F. 'Howell Harris and the "Grand Table".' *The Journal of Ecclesiastical History,* vol. 39, no. 4.

Nuttall, Geoffrey F. *The Significance of Trevecca College.* London: Epworth Press, 1968.

Nuttall, Geoffrey F. 'The Students of Trevecca College, 1768–1791.' *Transactions of the Honourable Society of Cymmrodorion,* 1967.

Oliver, Robert. *The Arminian Controversy of the Eighteenth Century. Division and Dissensions,* Westminster Conference Papers, 1987.

Ollard, S.L. *The Six Students of St Edmund Hall.* London, 1911.

Outler, Albert. ed. *John Wesley.* New York: Oxford University Press, 1980.

Overton, J. H. *The Evangelical Revival of the Eighteenth Century.* London: Longmans & Green, 1891.

Pibworth, Nigel. *The Gospel Pedlar, The Story of John Berridge and the Eighteenth Century Revival.* Welwyn: Evangelical Press, 1987.

Pickles, H. M. *Benjamin Ingham, Preacher amongst the Dales, Forests and Fells.* 1995.

Rack, Henry D. *Reasonable Enthusiast, Life of John Wesley.* London: Epworth Press, 1989.

Sidney, Edwin. *Life of Sir Richard Hill.* London, 1839.

Sidney, Edwin. *Life of Rev. Rowland Hill.* London: 1835.

Squires, Anthony. *Donington Park and the Hastings Connection.* Newtown Linford: Kairos Press, 1996.

Stout, H.S. *The Divine Dramatist, George Whitefield and the Rise of Modern Evangelicalism.* Grand Rapids: Eerdmans, 1991.

Teffry, Richard. *Memoirs of the Rev. Joseph Benson.* London, 1840.

Thomson, D. P. *Lady Glenorchy and Her Churches.* Crieff, Perthshire: The Research Unit, 1967.

Todd, John R. *By the Foolishness of Preaching.* Barton-in-the-Beans Baptist Church Publication, 1989.

Torbet, Robert. *A History of the Baptists.* London: Carey Kingsgate Press, 1966.

Tyerman, Luke. *The Oxford Methodists.* London: Hodder & Stoughton, 1873.

Tyerman, Luke. *Life of George Whitefield.* 2 vols. London: Hodder & Stoughton, 1877.

Tyerman, Luke, *Wesley's Designated Successor.* London: Hodder & Stoughton, 1882.

Tyerman, Luke, *The Life and Times of John Wesley.* 3 vols. London: Hodder & Stoughton, 1886.

Wakeley, J. B. *Anecdotes of George Whitefield.* London: Hodder & Stoughton, 1879.

Welch, Edwin. 'Lady Huntingdon's Chapel at Ashby.' *Transactions of the Leicestershire Archaeological and Historical Society*, 66, 1992.

Wheelan, W. *History, Gazetteer and Directory of Northamptonshire.* London: Whittaker & Co., 1849.

Williams, E. N. *Life in Georgian England.* London: Batsford, 1962.

Wood, A. Skevington. *Thomas Haweis.* London: S.P.C.K., 1957.

Wright, T. *Augustus M. Toplady.* London: Farncombe & Son, 1911.

## MANUSCRIPT THESES

Brown, Dorothy Eugenia Sherman. 'Selina, Countess of Huntingdon:

Selina, Countess of Huntingdon

Leader of the First Dissenting Methodists', M.A. Thesis, Southern
Methodist University, Dallas, 1986.

Brown, Dorothy Eugenia Sherman. 'Evangelicals and Education in
Eighteenth Century Britain: a Study of Trevecca College, 1768–1791.'
Ph.D. Dissertation, University of Winconsin-Madison, 1992.

Dowling, Frank. 'The Countess of Huntingdon's Chapels'. M.Sc.
Thesis, Oxford Polytechnic, October: 1992.

Francis, Matthew. 'Selina, Countess of Huntingdon (1707–1791)'.
B.Litt. Thesis, University of Oxford, 1957.

Harding, Alan. 'The Countess of Huntingdon and Her Connexion in
the Eighteenth Century'. Ph.D. Thesis, University of Oxford, 1992.

Hull, James E. 'The Controversy between John Wesley and the
Countess of Huntingdon'. Ph.D. Thesis, University of Edinburgh,
1959.

Morey, Kenneth. 'The Theological Position of the Countess of
Huntingdon's Connexion.' B.A. Dissertation, C.N.A.A., 1990.


## MAGAZINES

*The Evangelical Magazine.* 1793–1845.

*The Evangelical Register for the Connexion of the Late Countess of
Huntingdon.* 1824, 1827.

*The Gospel Magazine.* 1767,1768, 1769, 1771, 1772, 1773.

# INDEX

Hastings, Lady Anne, 12–4, 34–7,
65, 98, 102, 123, 132, 166–7
Hastings, Lady Betty, 12–14, 15,
18–19, 27, 30–1, 34–5, 38–9,
46–8, 98, 178 n
Hastings, Lady Catherine, *see*
Wheler, Lady Catherine
Hastings, Lady Elizabeth (daughter),
20, 29, 50, 66, 79, 82, 107, 113,
166, 170, 178, 213, 328, 391, 399
her marriage, 167
letter from Wesley, 189–90
Hastings, Ferdinando (son), 20–1,
29, 49, 66, 83–4, 87, 148
Hastings, Lady Frances (Selina's
sister-in-law), 12–14, 29, 34, 38,
67, 88, 102, 107, 129, 138
Hastings, Francis (eldest son),
childhood, 19–20, 29–30, 35, 46,
49, 66, 79, 87, 94–5, 102, 123,
142
goes on Grand Tour, 113, 167,
170–1, 177
later life, 344, 374–5, 401
unbelieving attitudes, 99, 168–9,
192–3, 213, 248–9, 351
Hastings, George (son), 20, 29, 38,
48–9, 66, 86–7, 148
Hastings, Henry (son), 45, 50, 66,
79, 82, 84–5, 150, 166, 170, 174,
177–9, 213
Hastings, Lady Margaret, 12, 34–8,
47–8, 54, 67, 70 n, 95
Hastings, Lady Selina (daughter),
29, 50, 66, 82, 84, 107, 137, 166,
169, 213–6
Hastings, Theophilus and Selina, *see*
*under* Huntingdon

Haweis, Thomas, 8, 14, 36, 39 n,
40, 163, 199, 243, 361, 347–50,
352–3
as a chaplain, 371, 374–9
at Spa Fields, 347–53
marries Jenetta Orton, 371
missionary endeavour, 375–8, 390
objects to *Plan of Association*,
375–8
preaches for Countess, 218–9, 224,
342
trustee of Connexion, 384, 412
Haweis, Judith 208, 371
Hawksworth, John, student, 310,
318–9, 327, 332–3, 339–42, 348,
363, 351, 364, 399, 435–6
Haworth, Yorkshire, 95–6, 192, 194,
211–2
Haymarket Theatre, London, 191
Hay-on-Wye, Powys, 287, 339
Heitzenrater, R. P., 26 n
Hemington, Robert, 83
Henderson, John, boy tutor at
Trevecca, 261, 287 n
Hereford chapel, 383, 391, 410
Hertford, Countess of, *see* Somerset,
Duchess of
Hervey, James, 118, 123, 133, 183–4
Hewer, William, student, 315–6
Higson, John, 244
Hill, Jane, 226, 357–6
Hill, Sir Richard, 226, 245–6
Hill, Rowland, 226, 246, 289, 338,
340, 354, 357, 335, 368 n, 377–8
Hill, Thomas, student, 319, 326,
328
Hogarth, William, 43
Holy Club, Oxford, 18, 26, 118,

# WILLIAM GRIMSHAW
## OF HAWORTH

### Faith Cook

'Faith Cook's biography of William Grimshaw is a "must" . . . We are indebted to her not only for giving us a well-researched book but also for the account of a life of extraordinary fruitfulness – literally thousands came to saving faith through Grimshaw's tireless labours . . . This is a book well worth reading by those who are pastors (or intending pastors) of any denomination . . . the Haworth story powerfully illustrates timeless principles which are indispensable in any fruitful ministry.'

THEMELIOS

'This is an absolutely superb treatment of a leading figure in the revival that swept British society on both sides of the Atlantic in the eighteenth century. It is, in short, a gem of a biography . . . May God use books like this one to challenge us to a fresh and radical commitment to Christ and his Kingdom.'

EVANGELICAL TIMES

'Meticulously researched and beautifully presented, it is the definitive modern biography of one of the greatest, yet least known, figures of the Methodist revival. Highly recommended!'

JOY (NEW LIFE PUBLISHING)

ISBN 0 85151 734 X, 358 pp, paperback
ISBN 0 85151 732 3, 358 pp, cloth-bound